KU-540-839

This book is for Aziz Yehia (1950-84).
His love of film, and my love of him
made the book possible

in memoriam A.

Animula vagula blandula,
Hospes comesque corporis,
Quae nunc abibis in loca,
Pallidula rigida nudula,
Nec ut soles dabis jocos?
　　Emperor Hadrian

Gentle little wandering breath,
Of the body friend and guest,
Where now must you look for rest,
Pale and naked, hard as death,
Lost without your power to jest?
　　tr. Stephen Oliver

New Preface, 2012

It is twenty-five years since I wrote this book. There have been no subsequent biographies of Laughton. Indeed, I'm sad to say that Laughton – as an actor, at any rate – has increasingly slipped out of public consciousness. And not only that: even within his own profession, he is virtually unknown to anyone under the age of forty. A few years ago while I was working at the Royal Shakespeare Company I took an informal straw poll of my fellow actors: mention of his name to anyone not yet middle-aged drew a complete blank. This is tragic, in my view. We actors need our heroes, our models; we need to know what has been achieved – what can be achieved. And Laughton was one of the handful of actors in the last century – among them Mikhail Chekov, Nikolai Cherkasov, Greta Garbo, Louis Jouvet, Marlon Brando – who extended the possibilities of acting, expanding its vocabulary and reaching new heights of expressiveness. He was a great original, but he was not a one-off, like Katharine Hepburn, or Michael Caine, whom it is possible to imitate, but from whom it is not possible to learn. His approach to acting, and his ambition for it, remain a constant inspiration. He was that rare thing, the actor as artist. This idea was the theme of my book.

It was my first biography. As the author of a biography of Orson Welles which is – I hope I may say without appearing to blow my own trumpet – a genuine work of scholarship, I would now prefer to describe *Charles Laughton: A Difficult Actor* as a biographical study, like my books about Oscar Wilde and Charles Dickens. It was Laughton's acting, as I explain in the Introduction, that I was interested in, and I concerned myself with the life only insofar as it illuminated the acting. I wrote it for the best of all possible motives for writing a book: because there was nothing in existence that could tell me what I wanted to know about Laughton's acting, how he worked, how he thought. Elsa Lanchester's early biography of him, while not without charm, was whimsical in tone and, because she could not be honest about the complexities of being married to a homosexual husband, inclined to glide over the surface. Her autobiography – *Elsa Lanchester Herself* – was written after Laughton's death and was essentially concerned with their personal relationship, enabling her to settle many scores and repay many ancient grudges. The next book about Laughton to appear was Charles Higham's biography, written at the prompting of Lanchester, who was intent on further revenging herself on her late husband; Higham later told me hair-raising stories about how she had set private detectives onto Laughton as he pursued his sex life, and expected the biographer to print the photographs they had taken of him with – often quite literally – his pants down. The only other biography, by Kurt Singer, a Hollywood press rep, was a wretched piece of hackwork, cobbled together from newspaper cuttings and, worse, press releases.

None of them had anything to say about his acting. This, of course, was and is generally true of actors' biographies. In a sense, in writing about Laughton, I was on a mission; it was part of an ongoing project to find a way of writing about acting. My first book, *Being an Actor,* was about the actor as Everyman, and attempted to delineate the common experience of actors by looking at the professional experience of one average young actor – me. In *Charles Laughton: A Difficult Actor*, by contrast, I set out to look at the work of a genius of acting, to see what heights might be scaled and what the conditions were for that sort of greatness. I took issue with actors' biographies that concerned themselves only with their subjects' careers or with the occupants of their beds. I read them, of course, and not necessarily without pleasure. My objection to them was simply that they contributed nothing to an

understanding of acting as either craft or art. The best book I know about any actor as an artist is Parker Tyler's *Chaplin: Last of the Clowns*, and I tried to model myself on him, hoping to emulate something of his searching analysis and his hyper-sensitive openness to the resonances in his subject's work. (I would like to have imitated his deliciously fancy-pants prose, too, but wisely refrained). Another influence was Robin Lane Fox's *Alexander the Great*, which eschews any attempt at novelish continuity or authorial omniscience, instead constantly stopping the flow to ask: what does such and such a bare fact mean? What is its context? In doing so, Fox opens doors on history which no seamless narrative could hope for.

Those were my models. Actually doing the work was something else. I had written *Being an Actor* at high speed, having brooded on the material for several years, and I cracked on with *Charles Laughton: A Difficult Actor* with similarly determined energy, while pursuing my various day jobs, acting and directing. I scarcely knew where to start; writing about oneself is easy, of course, requiring very little research. This was different. I knew nothing about where to go, what to look for, how to take notes. Admittedly, I had help: the publisher provided me with a hundred man-hours of research. The agreeable and very thorough Canadian who did the work found the cast list and credits of every picture and play Laughton had ever been involved in, marked those people who were still living in one colour ink, those who had written books in another. Then he located as many reviews as he could find; after that it was over to me. In fact, I quickly discovered that though my researcher's work was impeccable, I had to do it all over again, because it is what you see in the adjacent column to the one you're supposed to be looking at that offers the real illumination. So, under my own steam now, I read every word anybody had ever written about Laughton; I read every play he'd ever performed; I saw, as often as not on a Steenbeck editing console at the BFI, every film he'd ever made. I even tracked down every original source from which any of the films had been drawn.

I sought out and spoke to anyone I could locate in the British Isles who had known him. Then I went to America; Laughton had lived half of his adult life there. I had a clutch of introductions and – which I was sure would impress any potential interviewees – the imprimatur of the BBC, who had asked me to make a radio documentary for them. I went out and bought the most expensive state-of-the art recorder I could find, and sometimes it actually worked, though not too well, alas, when I spoke to Billy Wilder. I was so awed to find myself eating bagels with the director of *Sunset Boulevard* and *Some Like it Hot* that I never plucked up the courage to ask him to stop swivelling round in his chair like that and could he possibly close the window? But he had astonishing things to say, peppered with vintage wisecracks; his unreserved enthusiasm for Laughton was thrilling to hear, as was his certainty that not only was he a great actor but a great intellect, too: 'He was a Renaissance man,' Wilder told me, which was exactly what I wanted to hear.

I interviewed over fifty people on both sides of the Atlantic, and learned to develop photographic hearing for the times (one out of two) when the tape recorder failed me. If it wasn't batteries, it was the mike; if it wasn't the mike, it was the tape; and if it was neither of those, I'd just forget to switch the thing on. On one occasion everything was perfect, bar one tiny detail: I'd left the microphone at home. I pretended that there was a built-in microphone, and switched on regardless, even checking the batteries at periodic intervals. I spoke to a huge range of people, some famous, some not. I spoke to Stewart Granger ('To know Charles was NOT to love him'); to Belita, the ice-skater whom Laughton had taken under his wing when she tried to become an actress, and who said he was 'the sexiest man alive'; to Benita Armstrong, who had seen me on a television programme talking about writing the book, and who invited me to tea to talk about her late husband John who had designed Laughton's season at the Old Vic and his flat in Bloomsbury. I had a chimerical telephonic relationship with an infinitely gracious and amusing Deanna Durbin, in retirement in Neauphle-le-Château, who, over three long conversations touching on many subjects, absolutely and totally refused to say a word about Laughton. I discovered the value of recommendations: it was Vincent Price ('eating with Charles was a carnal experience') who had put me onto Deanna Durbin, and Clare Bloom gave me Christopher Isherwood's number, but he didn't want to talk to me about Laughton either. He died not long afterwards, and I realise now that he had no desire to talk about someone who had died of the same disease that was at that moment killing him. A year later I phoned Isherwood's partner, Don Bachardy, to see whether he might have something to tell me. He too declined, saying that 'Charles was an enthusiasm of Chris's that I didn't share'. Instead, he said, would I care to let him draw my portrait? When he'd finished, he showed me the drawing: it was an extraordinary thing, half me and half Laughton. Showing it to me somehow released him to talk about Laughton: and what he said provided me with some of the most acute insights into the man and his acting of anyone I spoke to.

I managed to unearth the last few survivors of Laughton's family. Two female cousins with whom he had been brought up in Scarborough now lived together in London. I had been warned in advance that one was manic-depressive and that the other had recently had an unreliable set of dentures installed. On cue, the younger of the two started out vivaciously but quickly slithered into gloom and finally deep silence, while the other talked wittily and sharply about Laughton as a boy, but to a castanet *obligato* from the new gnashers. The sisters put me onto his brother Tom's widow, who thrilled me by telling me that she had a tape of a family gathering at one of Charles's visits back home on which occasion not only Charles but both his brothers and his mother spoke. When we sat down to listen to it, nothing but a soft hiss came out of the speakers. She had played it that morning, she wailed, and it had been fine; she had presumably pressed the record button while playing it back. Meanwhile, her new husband, a Scottish doctor, helpfully informed me that Laughton was sexually insatiable: 'He was homosexual, you see, and your homosexual is invariably promiscuous: it's in his nature.'

Eventually, I had gathered sufficient material to begin writing, at which point Nick Gray from Yorkshire TV called and suggested that it might be interesting to do a TV documentary as well. This was a tremendous bonus because it meant that I could reach certain people that neither a book nor a radio documentary would entice; Robert Mitchum was one of them. In the event, he chose to answer me only in monosyllables, an experience like trying to make small talk with Mount Rushmore. I guessed that a big organisation could provide better facilities for research, particularly in the celluloid sphere, and so it proved. Helen McGee, a celluloid sleuth of genius, tracked down extraordinary things, like a 1930 Movietone News sequence of Laughton making up in his dressing room at Wyndham's as the Al Capone-like gangster Tony Perelli in his great stage hit *On the Spot*.

We filmed the documentary as I was writing the book, so new discoveries could be fed from one into the other. I wrote quickly, in Scarborough, where Laughton grew up, in a hotel once owned by his brother, Tom, and having triumphantly delivered the manuscript ahead of time, I went to Los Angeles on a jaunt, taking the proofs with me. One night I found myself at some do or another, dining next to a nice chatty fellow. When I told him about the book he said, 'Find anything interesting in the Archive at UCLA?' I looked at him aghast, my mouth working but no words coming out. Finally I croaked, with an insouciant little laugh: 'Archive?' 'You know,' he said, 'the Laughton archive.' I laughed my pearly laugh again and beat a rapid retreat. The next day, I got a cab to UCLA's leafy campus, ran into the library, and breathlessly requested the Laughton archive. As I sat in the clinical room waiting for it, cold sweat formed on my brow. The door opened and three trolleys were wheeled in containing the twenty-six boxes of the archive. A feverish and rather brutal search revealed to my almost tearful relief that twenty-five of the boxes contained screenplays that Laughton had rejected. The twenty-sixth box contained pure gold – letters from Brecht, Orson Welles, sketches for pieces he was writing, an annotated script for his stage production of *John Brown's Body*. I made my notes, asked for my photocopies, and ran for dear life. I had warned my publisher, Nick Hern, then at Methuen, to hold the press; I was able to rewrite sufficiently quickly to accommodate what I had just discovered. Saved by the bell.

The book was, for the most part, very well received. Even then, in 1987, Laughton – once a byword for great acting, universally imitated, and almost universally admired – was beginning to fade in fame, and much of what I had written came as something of a revelation to my readers; the simultaneously-released television documentary was able to show in the flesh what I had attempted to describe on the page.

Shortly after the book appeared, I began to receive the letters every biographer half dreads and half longs for, pointing out, gently or not, solecisms of one sort or another, most of which I was able to correct in subsequent editions. One of the most remarkable of my correspondents was a then very young woman from Barcelona, Gloria Porta Abad, who evinced an unlikely passion for Laughton, and an even unlikelier persistent scholarship in matters Laughtonian which rather put my whirlwind efforts to shame. She has spent the last twenty-five years slowly unearthing deeply fascinating information about Laughton's schooldays and his time in the trenches during the First World War, which she has written up in a fine series of articles in impeccable English; she's even created a website with the splendidly feisty name of rootingforlaughton. Her work, and that of other isolated researchers has greatly deepened our knowledge of Laughton, and should be the basis of a new biography. But there is no sign of that on the horizon, and none of it materially alters our understanding of his acting; the new research has augmented and supplemented my findings, not, I'm relieved to say, invalidated them.

Except in one area.

I said at the beginning of this introduction that Laughton had faded from public consciousness, 'as an actor, at any rate'. But that was not the end of Laughton. The most unexpected, the most improbable, thing has occurred: he has become more famous for the one film he directed than for all the once legendary performances he gave as an actor. The irony is all the richer since the failure of the film, both critically and commercially, broke his heart. The outcome of this wholly unexpected development has been a great growth of scholarship concerning *The Night of the Hunter*. When I was writing my book, I had access to the manuscript (now successfully published) of Preston Neal Jones's outstanding work of oral history, *Heaven and Hell to play With,* which records the memories of as many participants in the film as were alive at the time of writing. I had personally spoken to the Sanders Brothers, who had been Laughton's Second Unit directors on the film, and, however monosyllabically, to the film's superb star, Robert Mitchum. I had of course read all the memoirs of those involved, and other interviews conducted with members of the team. Most of my information on the film – how it came about and how filming had proceeded – came from various interviews, not conducted by myself, with the film's producer, Paul Gregory. And Gregory, a colourful character, told a vivid story, especially about James Agee's contribution to the film. Whatever his previous triumphs, both as screenwriter *(The African Queen)* and as elegiast of the South *(Let Us Now Praise Famous Men)*, Agee, Gregory reported – and is duly quoted by me as saying – was a hopeless drunk, who produced a grotesquely overlong screenplay that Laughton never so much as looked at, instead himself writing a version more or less overnight, which they then proceeded to shoot; Gregory added that Agee had been booted off the set by Laughton. His wholly undeserved credit nonetheless stood, because, Gregory said, they didn't like to kick a man when he was down. In my biography, I added to this sustained vilification of Agee by crying fraud over the fact that Laughton's screenplay was later, posthumously, 'good enough,' as I said, 'to have been passed off for years (in *Five Film Scripts* by James Agee) as the work of a seasoned genius.' The original screenplay had long ago disappeared.

Some years after *Charles Laughton: A Difficult Actor* came out, I was asked by the BFI to write a monograph on *The Night of the Hunter*, and in preparation, I took stock of the latest research, by Jones and others. Various perfectly lucid memos from Agee had come to light which suggested that whatever he might have done in his spare time, he was far from drunk on the job, that Laughton seemed to respect him at all times, that he himself sought to share his credit with Laughton for the latter's contribution to the screenplay, that he remained on the payroll for the full five weeks during which he undertook re-writes, and that he took a keen interest in the editing of the film. I assimilated all this material into a revised view of Agee's contribution, but in the absence of the original screenplay, I concluded that nonetheless Laughton was substantially responsible for the script as filmed. The book duly came out to appreciative murmurings in the world of Film Studies. Then, a couple of months after publication, I received two letters within a very short space of time. One was from Paul Gregory, who, to my embarrassment, I had thought had gone to the great cutting room in the sky. When I had been doing the research for *Charles Laughton: A Difficult Actor,* I was told that after the death of his wife, Janet Gaynor, he had withdrawn to Palm Springs to raise squabs, and was incommunicado. His letter thanked me for the book, for its balance and accuracy, and hoped that we might meet one day.

The other was from the James Agee estate asking me whether I'd like to read the original screenplay. A couple of months later, I was in Los Angeles, and visited Gregory, but not before I had received and read Agee's screenplay. I discovered that despite a great deal of elaboration of incidents and characters in the novel characteristic of most first drafts, the original screenplay, with its six-section structure, was quite clearly the basis of the film as it was shot, with certain curtailments and excisions, certain condensations and extrapolations, of a kind that every director makes, either during pre-production on the set, during filming, or afterwards during the editing process. Clearly Laughton was the governing spirit in the making of the film, but the nuts and bolts of the writing of the screenplay were put in place by James Agee. All of this is brilliantly described in Jeff Couchman's book *Credit Where Credits are Due*, which any *The Night of the Hunter* enthusiast should eagerly seek out. In my long and very frisky meeting with Gregory at Palm Springs, I gently suggested that all this new evidence pointed to a very different story to the one he had told; he brushed the idea aside. Short of bringing him the original screenplay and taking him through it page by page, it is hard to know what would have convinced him to change his story. Why it was so important to him to demonise Agee and exalt Laughton, with whom his relationship, always difficult, eventually foundered beyond the point of no return, is a matter for conjecture. It is equally baffling to know why he – and Robert Mitchum – always insisted that Laughton loathed the child actors in the film (particularly Billy Chapin, who so brilliantly plays John in the film) and preferred not to work with them, leaving it to Mitchum to direct them. Grave doubt was cast on this version of events by another remarkable development in *The Night of the Hunter* studies, Robert Gitt's discovery and restoration of the rushes of the film, including many sequences where the camera had been left running after Laughton had called 'Cut' and gone to work with the actors before the next take. Laughton is shown as charming, affectionate, and playful with the children, now and then becoming quite strict with them – just as he is, in fact, with all the actors. A selection of these fascinating and moving examples of his directorial approach can be seen on the newly-issued Criterion edition of *The Night of the Hunter*.

Apart from these two matters, the writing of the screenplay and Laughton's approach to the actors, especially the young ones, I am pleased and relieved to find on re-reading the book that it accurately tells the story of what I conceive to be Laughton's heroic life in acting. It seems to me to be a story worth telling, both in an exemplary sense and because he was an altogether uncommon human being. I was surprised, this time round, at how central Laughton's homosexuality was to his work. It is a highly debatable question as to whether the torture that he underwent as a gay man, terrified of exposure and filled with loathing for himself, was an essential component of his art, but on a simple human level, it is cheering to see him making peace with himself at last, able finally to share in the (relatively) uncomplicated experience of loving and being loved by another. Great creativity can spring from anywhere, it seems: from profound alienation, but equally from a deep sense of personal equilibrium. Whatever its source, Charles Laughton's creative imagination was of the order of the greatest painters, poets, playwrights, architects. Such individuals come rarely, and we should cherish and try to learn from them. Actors' work is to a large degree – especially that of stage actors, of course – written on sand. Laughton made over fifty films, each one of which contains a performance which to a greater or a lesser degree represents his extraordinary vision; scandalously, only a fraction of them is available on DVD, but they can and should be tracked down. There is nothing like them. My purpose in writing this biography was to try to discover the conditions that allowed him to create such work. I hope that it still serves that purpose.

Simon Callow
Mexico City 2012

Contents

List of Illustrations

Acknowledgements

More than most writers, biographers are dependent on the kindness of strangers. When I started writing this book I took every opportunity to mention in interviews on television and in the newspapers that I was doing so, and the result was far beyond my expectations. People wrote to me from all over the world with reminiscences of Laughton and suggesting places where I might find further information. Ken Barrow, the distinguished biographer of Flora Robson and Robert Donat, was extraordinarily kind in this regard, directing my attention to archives whose existence I hadn't suspected and sharing his own research with me as both Robson and Donat were friends of Laughton – this proved invaluable. Constance Cummings provided me with an absolute treasure trove of press cuttings of the production of *The Man with Red Hair* (adapted by her husband, Benn Levy). Philip Jenkinson enabled me to see a number of rare Laughton films and put me on to an aspect of Josef von Sternberg's state of mind while directing *I Claudius* that I had hitherto not suspected. Benita Armstrong, Elsa Lanchester's best friend in the thirties, gave me brilliant glimpses of the life of the young couple. Benita, Charles Laughton's friend, student and fellow actor, not to mention being one of the world's greatest ice-skating artists, offered me many remarkable insights into Laughton as teacher, director and friend. But equally forthcoming were people whom I could never have tracked down had they not come forward; ex-employees of the Pavilion Hotel in Scarborough, secretaries, understudies, stage managers; all with some revealing glimpse of the great man. Absolutely indispensable among these were the memories of Ann Rogers, his secretary in London in the late fifties and John Beary, Personal Assistant and friend. To all of these many thanks; and especially perhaps to the lady whose name I have tragically lost, who furnished me with the three letters that Charles Laughton wrote to her aunt, Hepsebiah Thompson, from the front in 1919.

Billy Wilder was the first person I interviewed for this book, and Albert Finney was the last; they must stand for the vast army of Laughtonians who generously contributed reminiscences, analyses and recollected affections. Everyone was kindly disposed, even when their experiences at Charles' hands had not been agreeable.

In addition, I would like to thank Marion Rosenberg, my friend and agent, for putting me in touch with Roddy MacDowell, and in so doing opening many doors on Laughtons's life; Edward Johnson, who helped me fill in some gaps in my knowledge of Laughton's films, and in addition compiled the discography at the back of the book; Graham Jackson, whose initial spadework was the foundation for everything; and Ann Jack, who typed most of the book. The librarians of the Special Collections Department of the Research Library at the University of California, Los Angeles were wonderfully kind and efficient. My old friend, Peter Whitman, put me right on a number of matters, particularly those relating to the Oscars, on which he is a world authority. Charles Nolte who suffered under and learned from Charles Laughton when he acted for him in THE CAINE MUTINY TRIAL, kept a fascinating diary of the period which he generously allowed me a glimpse of; Bruce Zortman, Laughton's amanuensis during his last years wrote down the actor's sketchily remembered early autobiography and gave me sight of that most stimulating if frustrating document.

Nick Gray, director of the parallel television documentary, was with me every step of the way, funny and shrewd; while Helen McGee, who researched the programme, is without peer in her trade, a genius of the quick follow-up and the persistent phone-call; without her this book would be much less useful.

My friend Angus Mackay put his huge library and wonderfully-stocked mind at my disposal from the very beginning, and then read the manuscript with an eagle eye for fact and form; Nick Hern onlie begot the whole project and then patiently waited and watched throughout its elephantine gestation; Peggy Ramsay provided the inspiration and the encouragement in ways too numerous and too subtle to detail; and Bruno never once complained.

S.C.

Sources

While I was writing this book, Elsa Lanchester was dying; just before I finished it, she was dead. I never spoke to her, but I did have access to the twenty-six boxes of material in the Charles Laughton Collection, donated to the University of California, Los Angeles in 1964. I have conducted over fifty personal interviews, and read (I believe) every extant published word written about Laughton, including biographies, scholarly studies, and movie magazines. John Beary and Oscar Lewenstein were kind enough to send me letters written by Laughton. But he was not a prolific letter-writer, and, for his own testimony about himself, I have had to rely largely on the two compilations that he published, *Tell Me A Story* and *The Fabulous Country*, which, both in their choice of material and in their linking commentaries, were held by Elsa Lanchester to give the best impression of what he was really like. I have quoted freely from them, and the one sustained piece of writing by him, from *The Fabulous Country*, is reprinted in the appendix to this book.

Otherwise my invaluable sources have been *Charles Laughton and I*, written by Elsa Lanchester in collaboration with Benita Armstrong, originally in serial form for the *Daily Express*, her second book, *Elsa Lanchester Herself*, and Charles Higham's *Charles Laughton*. Mr Higham's book was written, with full access to the papers, under Miss Lanchester's auspices. These three books thus all reflect her viewpoint, and have therefore been used with respectful caution.

S.C.

Introduction

The starting point of this book was my realisation that I was not, after all, Charles Laughton. This useful discovery was made during the extremely brief run of *On the Spot*, in which I was involved some summers ago in London, and it led me to ask who he was and what was the nature of his talent. Two years of research revealed to me much more than I had bargained for, a giant and a hero of acting, who had pushed it further and deeper than any actor of our century. His relation to acting was complex and led him to withdraw from it into other, less all-consuming means of expression. I tried to follow him there too.

Charles Laughton was a 'difficult' actor, not only because he was not easy to work with, but also in the sense that some books, some paintings, are said to be 'difficult': they require close attention, they are not what, at first sight, they may appear to be. This book is a sustained attempt to write about acting, as exemplified by one of its greatest practitioners. It is an enquiry into what he was trying to do and how far he succeeded in doing it. It tries to discover what kind of an artist he was. It considers the question of whether it is possible to talk about acting as an art at all. His life was in many ways extraordinary, but the body of the book is concerned with it only in relation to his acting. The central account of his output, his oeuvre, is flanked on either side by chapters which attempt respectively to show something of where he and his acting came from ('Origins') and to understand his emotional life ('Coda').

In between is a saga of the heroic struggle of a great artist to transcend the complexities of his temperament and accomplish the enormous tasks he set himself.

Life with a capital 'L'

When I was a child all the grown-ups around me had a joke, that is to say, all the women grown-ups. If we passed a pair of lovers spooning on a park bench my mother would look significantly at my Aunt Winnie – and Aunt Winnie would say, 'Life with a capital "L"', and they would both laugh secretly and I would feel uncomfortable.

If we passed a gaudy lady on the street my Aunt would look significantly at my mother and my mother would say, 'Life, etc.', and they would both laugh and I would look at the lady and my mother would say, 'Don't look, Charlie. She's a theatrical!'

I remember the incident because the gaudy lady was dressed in white, with a white parasol and pink roses on her hat, and my mother nearly yanked an arm out of its socket and I became an actor.

I suppose by now you've got the idea.

Charles Laughton *Tell Me a Story*

PART ONE

Origins

Charles Laughton was born on 1 July, 1899, in the Victoria Hotel, Scarborough, of which his parents, Robert and Elizabeth, were proprietors.

Thus he just managed to squeeze into the nineteenth century, in whose shadow he lived most of his life. Certain other facts contained in the bald sentence above determined his being in the world. He was a Yorkshireman – a breed whose characteristic behaviour can easily be misinterpreted; and he was of tradesman stock. He was, indeed, for the first 25 years of his life, a hotelier – which proved excellent preparation for some of his subsequent ventures.

The Victoria Hotel, small for a hotel, splendid for a bed and breakfast establishment, is smack opposite the station – an ideal location, perfectly convenient if not absolutely salubrious. The Laughtons were kept busy; so busy that Charles and his brothers Tom and Frank can have seen little of them, even before the children were sent away to their several strict Catholic schools (Mrs Laughton, of Irish farming stock, was fiercely Catholic). The boys were left in the charge of various members of staff. A snug little hotel like the Victoria (it's still thriving today, with an emblem of Henry VIII as Charles Laughton adorning the outside) offered a thousand crannies for a neglected child to play in; and Charles found them all. Characteristically, he found an audience too: a chambermaid discovered trapped in the linen cupboard, while Charles, swathed in sheets, declaimed. It is said that she was perfectly happy to be ensconced with the infant Roscius in this way, giving a preview of his performance in *Spartacus* some sixty years later.

Outside the hotel was a bustling and attractive world for the boys, but especially the boy with the passion for performance. Minutes away are the beach and the famous spa with all its attendant amusements. Both England and Scarborough were at their Edwardian apogee, supremely self-confident and prosperous and structured. The demotic explosion of the twenties and thirties had not yet occurred, and the pictures of the period reveal a Scarborough still a spa, not yet a resort. So Master Charles and Master Tom and Master Frank would be taken by someone (not Mother or Father, to be sure) to mingle with the other young ladies and gentlemen a way off from the urchins beloved of Whitby's photographer-laureate, Frank Sutcliffe. Any desire to join them, like them to roll one's trousers up, or indeed rip one's clothes off altogether, would have been diverted by the arrival of the Punch and Judy Man, or the Fol-de-Rols, or the Pierrots on their little rigged-up stage. Head swirling with any of these, he could have gone on to the Mirrorama; or the Spa's theatre; or the bioscope; or the pleasure garden. What ordinary children crammed into two weeks, was perennial for him.

'"Scarborough the Splendid" is the style that has lately been suggested for this Brighton of the North, in lieu of that title Queen of Watering-Places which it seems to usurp from its Sussex rival', claims A. & C. Black's *Guide* of 1899. Shamelessly it continues: 'The nearest summary of it that we can give is as a union of Dover and Folkestone, on an enlarged scale, with a dash of Ramsgate, a touch of Tenby, a soupçon of Trouville translated into Yorkshire, at times, to tell the whole truth, a whiff of the North Pole; and *then*,' it sums up, 'there remains something peculiarly its own.'

In this demi-paradise Charles remained until his thirteenth year, in and out of the linen cupboard, one can only presume. That linen cupboard had become much, much bigger when, in 1908, the Laughtons, having made a brilliant success of the Victoria, first as managers, then as tenants, took over the splendid Pavilion Hotel, only a stone's throw away from the Victoria on the other flank of the station, but another world from that cosy little commercial travellers' hostelry. Built, according to Osbert Sitwell, who watched the Diamond Jubilee shindigs from its balcony, in the 'Luxembourg late-Renaissance style', its brochure boasted of 130 rooms, electric light and bells throughout, and magnificent suites of private apartments and public rooms. 'The Entrance Hall, Corridors and Lounge are spacious, and all the rooms lofty and well-ventilated, with Ladies' and Gentlemen's Lavatories and Bathrooms on every floor. The sanitary arrangements are perfect.' They had acquired this palace only thanks to the unremitting drive of Mrs Laughton, tough, proud, determined. Her husband, Robert, was carried amiably along in her wake. His special sphere was the catering, and he was known as the shrewdest man in the county when it came to a leg of mutton or a pound of greens. Up at five every morning to scour the market, he then generally withdrew from the running of the hotel, to pursue the more congenial activities of fishing and shooting. Either way, the brothers Charles, Frank and Tom, had to make do with surrogate parents chosen from among the myriad downstairs employees of the great enterprise: the maids and the bell-boys and the receptionists and the bootblacks.

The absence of intimate relationship with parents is notorious for the encouragement of two species, actors and homosexuals. One of the sons – Charles – was both; another, Frank, was homosexual. Tom, by contrast, was much married, and never set foot on any stage.

Robert's widowed sister Mary fulfilled some parental functions, and she and Charles shared and indulged botanical passions which never left him all his life. They would roam the Moors together, naming the plants and trees and birds. He was lucky to find an ally in these passions. It was a morbid and unmanly occupation according to prevailing mores, and the sort of thing that led his mother, when she could spare the time from the accounts and dreams of expansion, to describe Charles severely as 'artistic'. Episodes in the linen cupboard and altogether too much time spent with his head in books (not ledgers) were further indications of this unnatural inclination.

It is hard to ascribe any emotion at all to the bonny inscrutability of the child Charles as seen in photographs. But he certainly sticks out. His eyes confront the lens with rare force, a tough little tot, no charmer, on this evidence, but determined.

In a striking section of her first book, *Charles Laughton and I*, Elsa Lanchester quotes, with breathtaking but, one comes to find, characteristic insensitivity (or is it?), a letter from a contemporary of Charles', in which he says: 'He was the kind of boy one longed to take a good kick at.' Nothing in Charles' young face explains such a reaction so, allowing for early undifferentiated teenage barbarism, it must or might have been something in Charles' *manner* which provoked the hearty young gentleman's aggression: he was not *sportif*, he read books, he was tubby (not exactly fat). Cause enough. But if, in addition, he lacked the gift of invisibility, then he would seem to be reproaching his fellow students. If, despite his panic and fear, he couldn't quite suppress his personality, as he certainly couldn't in the family photographs – well, then he was really for it.

Charles' first steps in education were at an unremarkable local preparatory school – Catholic, of course; then at a French convent in nearby Filey, where he learnt perfect French; finally at Stonyhurst, whose forbidding name was wholly borne out by its regime of chilly austerity and mechanical instruction, reinforced by the tawse and the threat of eternal damnation. In an image of refined horror entirely characteristic of the Jesuits, Charles and his fellow thirteen-year-olds were informed that eternity was 'as if this world were a steel globe and every thousand years a bird's wing brushed past that globe – and the time it would take for that globe to wear away is all eternity.'

Whatever effect it may have on the soul, Catholicism (and its English variant) is another great manufactory of actors (and homosexuals, up to a point: though more homosexuals seem to be drawn to the church than are created by it). Ritual is obviously a contributing factor – incense, vestments, chanting, processing, the division between the altar and the congregation – all these find their counterpart in the theatre; but the drama of its imaginative framework – the opposition of heaven and hell, the great figures of the Trinity and the omnipresence of Mary in her many guises, the vast supernumerary cast – archangels, angels, seraphim, cherubim and so on; all are the stuff of drama. More obscurely, but no less certainly dramatic, is the cycle of sin, retribution and redemption.

And the Jesuits are sure as hell your men for putting it over. For Charles, whatever the positive gains in feeding his imagination, it instilled a lifelong guilt deep in his breast – a guilt which easily attached itself to his desire to make love to men, but which was in fact a more general guilt: a sense of not being right in the world, of not deserving what the world has to offer. It was the bane of his life.

Or perhaps it was his making.

He showed no great scholastic gifts: he won a couple of class prizes; one for English, and another for Latin Verse. His strongest suit was maths, which might have pleased his mother. She paid the college anxious visits from time to time to determine the direction of her son's talents, but nothing insisted. The only occasion during his time at Stonyhurst that he stood out from the crowd was something she'd probably rather not have known about: the school play. When he was fourteen he made his only appearance, in a Charles Hawtrey vehicle, *The Private Secretary*. Was his casting a subtle form of the snobbery under which he smarted throughout his time at public school?: – he was playing Mr Stead, a lodging-house keeper. 'We were greatly taken by his acting . . . his part was far too short; we wanted more of him for it seemed to suit him excellently.' He sat and passed his School Certificate in July of 1915, and then left.

There had been talk of a naval career for him, but despite the influence of a certain Uncle Charles, he failed to qualify for a life at sea, and so, inevitably, if reluctantly, he began to assume the mantle of eldest son and heir to the business. Eliza Laughton's ambition had transformed the Pavilion's clientele; it began to be fashionable. The

Sitwells stayed there while waiting for their house to be decorated, and other county families soon followed their lead. Eliza herself had long left behind the actual physical running of the hotel (though Eric Fenby, a Scarborian and contemporary of Tom and Charles, notes that she was never above 'tweaking' the bills). She had made herself chief executive, and was the visible and formidable figurehead of the enterprise. Every year she would spend a month in London, assembling her wardrobe, in which she would then, night after night, appear on the stroke of seven, dazzling Scarborough from her commanding position at the top of the foyer stairs. The little Irish barmaid had developed into a matriarch, a grande dame, a queen, as Fenby puts it. She was a holy terror to her staff and her family, missing nothing with her all-seeing eyes, and quick to give expression to any fault she might find. She was also generous, and kindly, but human warmth was not her leading quality. As befits a holy terror, she spent every spare moment on her knees in prayer. The working day was punctuated with visits to church, tellings of the rosary, contemplation of the missal. Charles, who loved and feared her in equal measure, was always nervous in her presence.

Robert Laughton drifted further and further away from the centre of things, spending as much time as he possibly could at the little farmhouse they owned at Lockton, on the edge of the Yorkshire Moors. Mrs Laughton would repair there for afternoon prayers, but their paths rarely crossed.

It must have been a great joy to Charles to discover that Eliza's training programme for him involved working at the very bottom of the ladder in a London hotel – not only wonderful to be going to the big city, but wonderful not to be under so much unrelenting pressure. It was not comfortable, either, being a Laughton in Scarborough. 'They were loathed,' says Eric Fenby. The town resented Eliza's upward mobility, her piety and her grandeur. Both Tom and Charles, in order to escape the taint of her queenly ways, would try to slum it sartorially; at about this point, Charles seems to have lost interest in washing, a taste he never really recovered.

He was pleased, too, to escape some of the hotel's clientele: Tom Laughton wrote, 'Charles liked people generally, but he was allergic to the establishment. Charles had no use for the pretensions of the so-called county set. It was something that, as a family, we came across in the business of the hotel, and Charles always reacted against it.' This experience, and the experience of being patronised by schoolboy snobs at Stonyhurst, radicalised him. He never became a socialist, but he was vigorously anti-snob; he couldn't stand toffs, and he always longed to be one of 'the ordinary people'.

The London hotel was Claridge's; and there Charles spent a couple of happy years. He made friends with his fellow-employees; he had free rein to observe (which was the only thing he really enjoyed about hotelling); and above all there was the theatre.

The wartime metropolis offered an altogether superior class of fol-de-rols to any he'd encountered up North. *Chu-Chin-Chow* became his passion; that and the acting of Gerald du Maurier, who startled his contemporaries with his throwaway technique, his audacious silent scenes and his spell-binding relaxation of manner. His performances made other actors seem heavy-handed. He seems a surprising influence until one examines Laughton's work more closely. Time and again, one is taken aback by the delicacy and, yes, the under-played nature of what he's doing. That's du Maurier's legacy.

Claridge's was a hotel much frequented by the stars, and Laughton could observe them at close range. What would not have been lost on him was that he resembled none of them. He was reasonably tall – 5 feet 10½ inches according to his press handouts – though somewhat round-shouldered; plump going on tubby; and possessed of a face that he was wont to describe as like an elephant's behind, or 'just a pudding', a concatenation of striking features set somewhat randomly in an undifferentiated globe of a face, topped by not easily controlled light brown hair. The ever-mobile eyes tended towards cunning and/or concealment, the irregular nose, bulbous towards its end, and the full fleshy lips, are almost indecently powerful. There's something about the face, in its latent state, that makes you uneasy; and the owner of the face seems to be wearing it uneasily, too, as if it had been moulded on him. What perhaps neither he nor anyone else knew at the time was that it was a uniquely expressive mask, capable of re-arranging itself at will, of reflecting the tiniest shifts of thought, of appearing startlingly ugly or overwhelmingly radiant.

It was the face, neither of a character-man (quirky, rugged, or whatever other dominant quality), nor, patently, of a leading actor. It was the face of someone who simply shouldn't be an actor at all. And there was nothing that could be done about it. No plucking of eyebrows, no altering of hairline, no straightening of teeth, by means of all of which Laurence Olivier, at nearly the same period, trans-formed his unruly features into an acceptable beauty, would trans-form this indeterminately expressive mug. Only inner conviction could do this.

Between the glorious spectacles on the stage and the scarcely more real life of a luxury hotel, the war must have seemed very distant, a rumour. It had staggered bloodily on for the last four years. By 1918, any delusions of glory had long since evaporated. The war was simply an insatiable leviathan which must be fed with increasingly young flesh. Returning to Scarborough, the eighteen-year-old Laughton signed up, not with the commission to which his education and class entitled him, but as a private. He didn't feel up to commanding, he said. The Royal Huntingdonshire Rifles were posted to Vimy Ridge, and the fat, sensitive boy found himself translated to the trenches, there to freeze and to starve, and on occasion, to stab eighteen-year-old Germans to death with a bayonet. He endured a year of this till Armistice; in the very last week of the war he was gassed. This parting absurdity brought him out in severe rashes on his back, which recurred throughout his life, and damaged his larynx and trachea.

His letters from the front (the very few that have survived) are boyish and extravagant in tone and mostly concern food, ('I tell you what I would like in a small parcel by itself. 1lb. of Greenlay's sausages, a little greece [sic] to cook them in, also one of those Tommy's cookers to cook them on. But you know big parcels are worse than useless because if you get a sudden notice to move you have to leave stuff behind.') They are written to Hepsebiah Thompson, the receptionist at the Pavilion, for whom Laughton obviously had great fondness ('Well, Miss Thompson, I am getting bleary-eyed so I fain would bid thee au revoir. So I remain forever your little toddler of bygone days Charlie. P.S. "Do it again, Mith Thomthon."') There are sharp glimpses of conditions: 'Please excuse the grubbiness of this letter because just as I was writing that last bit we had an order to pack up and had to make another move. Oh my word the mosquitoes and the other animals nearly drive me crazy . . . owing to the lack of a better projectile, I hurled your pot egg at a rat which was in the act of making off with one of my pal's soaps. R.I.P. Those blighted rats will take anything from paper to oil bottles. What they do with them goodness only knows', and typical anxiety about pleasing his mother: 'What does mother think of my letters? Do you think I could say more of some things and less of others or in fact change them to the good in any way?'

'Well, Pompo old thing,' he writes, 'you know your letters are always like a sea-breeze I can tell you . . . you always tell me something I like e.g. theatres, a subject which seems to be studiously avoided by everyone else who writes to me.' There is one line in these letters which resounds deeply and darkly, though: 'My one fear as regards this do is that it might knock the fun out of me.'

The lad in uniform who returned to Scarborough in 1919 certainly had a grim set to his features, as revealed in his homecoming photograph. Nor could he particularly expect a hero's welcome; his situation was too common. What was expected was a brisk return to business as usual. For six months, though, the boy that was remembered by everyone at home as being lively and fun would lock himself in his room for hours on end. He said, 'I'm no use to anyone like this.' The worst passed, but he was never as long as he lived altogether to escape the darkness he brought back with him. Soon enough, however, he resumed his duties in the hotel – now more significant because his father was ill (diabetes) and he must take his place at the head of things.

He consoled himself for this unwanted succession by joining one of the many local amateur groups, the Scarborough Players, and with them he played all kinds of unsuitable but no doubt highly enjoyable parts: Sir William Gower, in *Trelawny of the 'Wells'* for example; the photograph shows a very striking transformation; it's definitely *someone* staring balefully at us; whether it is Sir William precisely is, in this context, neither here nor there. He had a great triumph in the last play he did for the amateurs, *Hobson's Choice*, in which he gave his Willie Mossop; the local press most interestingly described his performance as

> ranking with the best examples of character portrayal – it was this interesting nonentity that Mr Laughton presented in such a compelling way that the audience watched the poor creature – such easy prey to a woman grasping at a last chance, that they pitied him – which was really *the highest form of admiration*. Mr Laughton's study of the evolution of the dullard was a splendid effort of the actor's art.

The *Scarborough Mercury*'s reviewer had hit the nail on the head. By this time, he was actually running the Players; Mollie Decker, his cousin, who was living with the Laughtons, recalls that the set was entirely furnished from the hotel, which was quite denuded.

In addition, he threw himself into the management of the Pavilion. Not into the day-to-day business of it; nor into the catering, or the service aspects of it. What interested him was the appearance of it, the production of it, one might almost say. He completely redecorated the interior; he hung paintings throughout; he installed a new bar; he brought a band in; he commissioned leaflets from local artists. His stupendous energies, such as were left over from the Players, were engaged, and when that happened, Charles Laughton was always unstoppable.

In 1922, Osbert Sitwell would stroll over to the Pavilion for meals: 'one evening, a rather substantial young man, a son of the house, came up to me from behind the desk in his office, and enquired if I would like him to show me the improvements that had been recently effected in the hotel . . . As he took me round, I noticed how marked a personality he possessed; moreover, in spite of an appearance entirely opposed to a conception of him as a sleek young foreigner in a tail-coat, he was so much the sleek young hotel director that it scarcely rang true, and made it seem as though he were giving an interpretation of the part . . . this was Charles Laughton.'

There was a limit to the run of even such a good part as that, and Laughton, now twenty-four years old, an advanced age for a young man yearning for the stage, determined to get a training. The outrage in the family circle was immense, only softened by paternal blessing. Robert Laughton, that genial gent, who was soon to die, was of the opinion that nothing would deflect Charles. The next in line for the succession, Tom, was summoned from the farm where he was learning *his* trade, and agreed to hold the fort.

'I shall never come back home to the business, Tom; I would starve in the gutter first,' Charles told Tom. Just as well; any less passion, and he'd never make it. Fortunately, he had more than mere passion: he had practical passion.

He was no naïve stage-struck youth when he made his application to the Royal Academy of Dramatic Art. He'd run a medium large hotel for several years, had command and responsibility. He may not have enjoyed the business side of the operation, but he did it – balanced the books, hired people and fired them. A hotel, moreover, is in many respects like a theatre: there's a backstage and an auditorium, the mechanics of the thing are supposed to be invisible, there are costumes and performances. Charles had managed his hotel just as if it were a theatre, and he had done so with some flair. In many ways it was an ideal preparation.

He was nonetheless hysterically nervous before his audition with the Royal Academy. The panel consisted of Claude Rains (who regularly taught at the school), Dorothy Green (a leading Shakespearienne, later Cleopatra to John Gielgud's Antony), and Kenneth Barnes, the principal, who remained at his post till the early fifties. Charles gave his Shylock, and it must have been all right, because the audition was on May 6th, and he was enrolled on the 8th. The school was still labouring under the post-war surplus of women – there were only four men in Laughton's class of twenty.

Despite this disadvantage, and before it had deteriorated into a sort of alternative finishing school in the forties, it was a highly prestigious institution, one of only two major drama schools in London (the other was Elsie Fogerty's much more recent Central School). The curriculum was crowded and very straightforward: fencing, dancing, gesture, elocution. At all of these Charles competed in the Scholarship Competition and received a Special Honourable Mention.

For the rest, the training, not based on any theory or system, was in the hands of the tutors, who worked on scenes. Dorothy Green directed Shakespeare scenes; Claude Rains, who was such an influence on the young John Gielgud, worked on various one-act plays. But the teacher who transformed him, who saw what was extraordinary in him and drew it, sometimes painfully, out of him, was the formidable Frenchwoman, Alice Gachet. She remained close to Laughton for the rest of her life, and indeed, he supported her with a small allowance during her declining years. At the outset of their relationship she told him, 'I will break your heart, but I will make an artist of you.'

Her special approach to him was to refuse to confine him to character roles: she insisted that he must play his lovers and heroes. And he flowered, moved and challenged by her confidence in him ('Knows what he wants. Gives everything to it. Breaking bad habits'). His confidence as an actor always needed to be supplied from without. Their bond was made even stronger by his fluency (thanks to the nuns) in French, a subject in its own right on the timetable. She directed him in a scene from Molière's *L'Amour médecin*, in which he played Sganarelle at his graduation performance.

The whole course had lasted barely nine months, and was essentially a whistle-stop tour through over forty different characters. As often with 'mature' students, he hadn't wasted a second or a word. Nor did he mingle easily, set apart by age and self-consciousness and the sense of making up for time wasted. Kenneth Barnes wrote: 'Sometimes, unobserved, I would watch him as he moved round one of the Academy's rehearsal rooms. He could people the room with his impressions and many variations . . . it was magic. Other students would take time to drink coffee and chatter, but Laughton used the time alone, creating. He was a student of infinite curiosity, always searching for a new and meaningful approach to whatever character he was studying.' In his end-of-term report, Barnes wrote: 'You have a marked talent and your acting is always interesting, but you must not rely on personality – when you give real care to a part your performance improves a thousand-fold.'

Under *Acting* the report said, 'Laughton is sometimes almost brilliant. He is handicapped and he knows it. He'll persevere and prosper.' And George Bernard Shaw, trustee of the Academy, had come to Gower Street to see scenes from *Pygmalion*, and went backstage to see Laughton. 'You were perfectly dreadful as Higgins,' he said, 'but I predict a brilliant career for you within the year.'

After the graduation performance (apart from Sganarelle he played Falstaff, amongst others) he won the Bancroft gold medal, awarded to him by a distinguished panel of practising and renowned players: Irene Vanburgh, Henry Ainley and Allan Aynesworth. It was presented to him by Sybil Thorndike on June 6th; as he went to collect it, Sir Johnston Forbes Robertson, *acteur noble* supreme, was heard to murmur: 'It's unkind. He hasn't a hope in hell of ever working, looking the way he does.' In fact, he had taken the morning off from rehearsals of his second professional engagement in order to collect the prize; and within six months, he was playing a sizeable cameo opposite the most famous romantic actor of the day, in the West End, in a production by the most exciting director in England. After what must have seemed an interminable limbo of waiting for his life to begin, he was hurtling down the tracks.

First Work

Charles owed his first job to Theodore Komisarjevsky, who had worked with him on *commedia dell'arte* scenes at RADA, and who cast him as Osip in his production of Gogol's *The Government Inspector* at the Barnes Theatre (Manager Philip Ridgeway, Business Manager Binkie Beaumont). Claude Rains was Khlestakov and he and the production were acclaimed. Charles' debut was thus on 26 April, 1926. A few days later, he received his first review in a national newspaper: he was thought to be 'good', and he was spelt Loughton.

The Barnes Theatre, a converted cinema, had a high reputation and no money; one of the network of 'little theatres' that constituted

London's experimental theatres, a sort of Fringe *avant la lettre*, performing little known European plays in daring productions. West End actors like Claude Rains and Martita Hunt were quite willing to appear for next to nothing for a few weeks, particularly if the producer was 'Komis'. Norman Marshall wrote: 'I have seen nothing more lovely in the theatre than the stage pictures Komisarjevsky created on that cramped little stage at Barnes.'

It was extraordinarily lucky for Laughton that his first job should be with this brilliant, combative *homme du théâtre*, rather than some humdrum rep producer, or West End Stage Manager – a breed wittily despised by Komisarjevsky, inventor, or at any rate definer, of 'Synthetic Theatre': theatre in which all the elements of production merged, none dominating. His visual and stylistic audacity had startled the English public, and would do so even more in his Stratford Shakespeares; but he never forgot the significance of the actor: 'the "inside" of an actor, call it "soul" or "consciousness", or whatever you like, is a very complicated and delicate instrument. That instrument is what matters most on stage, and only an extremely sensitive and careful producer can play on it without hurting the freshness of the actor's conception of the part and his own creation of it. The furniture, every detail on the stage, serve the same purpose as the sets, i.e., to suit the acting, and not vice-versa.'

Komis' brilliance had been evident from the beginning when, in Russia, he had started his career in the theatre as a designer. When his sister Vera Komisarjevskaya parted ways with Meyerhold, she invited – commanded, more accurately – her young brother Fyodor to take his place, and he directed her and her company for some months with great success. He left Russia at the time of the Revolution, and then proceeded to dazzle Europe with his sometimes perverse audacity. The visual sophistication and sense of the expressive potential of theatre caused sensations wherever they were seen. His fellow-artists (and that is how he regarded them) were carried away, not only by the excitement of his ideas, but by his great personal charm – especially the ladies, many of whom he married (and many more of whom he didn't: 'Come-and-seduce-me' was his nickname, according to John Gielgud). Innovative in everything he touched – the cinema interiors he designed for Sidney Bernstein's Granada chain, and the auditorium of the Phoenix Theatre, are typically original fantasies – he was the last person in the world to be rigid in his notions of casting. Talent was talent. Laughton was clearly bursting with it, and he trusted him.

To encounter such a luxury in one's first job – to be playing moreover with gifted and creative actors wearing their stardom lightly, not pulling rank or flaunting their wealth – was an invaluable beginning. At Barnes, Komis cast him as Solyony in *Three Sisters* and as the 'twenty-thousand-disasters', Yepikhodov, in *The Cherry Orchard*. This performance was remembered by Alan Dent nearly forty years later: 'I went round Bloomsbury telling everyone I had got to know about an astonishing, new, young, plump comedian I had just happened to see . . . I have never since beheld a funnier or more melancholy performance of this peculiarly difficult because intensely Russian character.' And Ernest Short reported: 'He makes the moonstruck clerk an unforgettable mixture of pathos and fun.'

Komisarjevsky played fairy godfather to Laughton during these first formative months, and when he came to direct Molnar's *Liliom* with Ivor Novello, at the Duke of York's Theatre, he cast Laughton in a small part – his West End début. But even better was to follow. The substantial part of Ficsur the pickpocket, 'Liliom's evil genius', fell vacant during rehearsals. Komis promoted Laughton. For a while dissatisfaction was expressed by certain members of the cast. Komis indicated that if Laughton left, so would he. Both stayed, and Charles had a big success: 'a most excellent piece of rascality from that promising actor, Mr Charles Laughton', wrote the *Telegraph*. C. B. Cochran, the impresario, one of the biggest men in the theatre of his day, knew that the unknown lad playing the pickpocket was 'the real thing'. Novello, on the other hand, (and perhaps he'd intuitively sensed this when he tried to get rid of Laughton), was dismissed as stagey and self-conscious. It was a clash of worlds. At that time, then, Laughton was the coming man.

Ficsur in *Liliom* is the first Laughton creation of which we have any account. To get the part right, he went down to the docks and studied pickpockets, for hours on end. Since at least the time of Lope de Vega, actors have been immersing themselves in the reality to which their roles refer. It makes for more interesting acting. It has nothing necessarily to do with 'truth', authenticity, or sociology. Firstly, you work so much better if you have a clear idea in your mind of what you're playing; secondly, absorbing the sensations of a model for a character can release all kinds of things in you that can take you by surprise, and bear no resemblance to the original model. It's a way of breaking the patterns embedded in your muscles and brain-cells.

Laughton was more interested in increasing the expressive potential of what he did than in naturalism; but he was also very concerned to *show* something to the audience. Hence the somewhat 'demonstrated' nature of his acting. Hence also its brilliant clarity and economy.

The run of *Liliom* was short; but for Laughton it was straight on to the next one. At this crucial moment, he was given more or less continuous employment in a variety of parts, in a variety of theatres, with full metropolitan exposure. He could so easily have gone into rep, been typed, developed into a heavy, become conventional. Instead he was allowed to grow in ideal conditions. Edith Evans attributed her growth to not having followed the repertory route: 'I should have caught all the tricks – the bad tricks of the provincial theatre of those days. I'd have picked them up quicker than anybody. I was very imitative indeed. And the Almighty saw fit to start me off with some of the best actors in London.' So with Charles.

In his next role, his co-star (or rather star, because his part was not substantial) was the very Sybil Thorndike who, seven months before, had handed him his Gold Medal. The play was *The Greater Love*, by that distinguished proselyte of the new drama, J. B. Fagan. This play was not, however, of the new drama; it was the old drama, with a vengeance. 'A jolly good play as a straightforward piece of non-educative romance', as Sybil's biographer, her son, John Casson, calls it; 'a story of intrigue and "love will conquer all" set in pre-revolutionary Russia.' From James Agate, it provoked a cascade of praise for Charles that, to any lesser spirits than Sybil and Lewis, who was directing, might have provoked a certain sourness. 'And now,' he says, in the middle of describing the third act, 'I must pause to say something about that very remarkable young actor, Mr Charles Laughton. Mr Laughton has played, to my knowledge, only three parts in London – the clerk in *The Cherry Orchard*, the wastrel in *Liliom*, and now this Russian governor. To my knowledge, I say, but only because of the programme. In each part this actor has been at once superb and unrecognisable, achieving his differences not by inessential wiggery but by seizing the essence of the character and making his body conform. This is character-acting as the great and not the little masters of that art have always understood it. To watch this sleek, polite, overfed tyrant wake from eupeptic slumber to smile a possible assassin to exile in Siberia – that was to be told something authentic about Tsarist terror. Pleasures too refined and cruelties too barbarous were in the flutter of those sleepy eyelids, the modulations of the indolent, caressing voice, the slow-moving, velvet hands. Now I am not going to make a song about these three performances and proclaim Mr Laughton a great actor on the strength of them. But I will say this, that whenever he has been on the stage, my eyes have never left him, and that on Wednesday night his silent abstractions held more of Russia than all the other talkers put together. It was something of a disappointment,' he concludes this ecstatic cul-de-sac in the main body of his review, 'when one found the play's *scène à faire* had passed this actor by.' Not, perhaps, to the other actors.

They must have been very surprised indeed, because, John Casson reports, during rehearsals, Laughton had seemed so inept that the author begged Lewis to sack him. 'Dressed in revolting, untidy clothes, forestalling 'hippies' by some thirty years, he was, Lewis said, impossibly difficult to produce. He wouldn't take direction, hardly knew a line, and even when he did he mumbled them . . . at the dress rehearsal it seemed as if all hope could be abandoned. It was not only insignificant, which wouldn't have mattered; he was glaringly bad, which did. 'Well, that's it,' groaned Fagan, 'he'll spoil the show.' And in the event, he stole it.' This is the first intimation of the 'eccentricity' and 'self-indulgence' which were to be Laughton's hallmarks in rehearsal. He was certainly taking a big risk: for a young, only slightly known, actor to espouse unorthodox rehearsal procedures, and, perhaps even more damaging, unorthodox sartorial choices, was to defy the conventions of the entire theatrical establishment, which, in 1927, was to take on a mighty opponent indeed. As it happens, Sybil and Lewis, of all people, were the least hidebound; they probably felt sorry for him. But he obviously came very close to being sacked. Why did he do it, then? There's no question that he was incapable of learning his lines or speaking them intelligibly. He was very hard-working, very intelligent, and always had 'a voice' (his cousins remember its beauty back in Scarborough). It would appear that he was trying for something unusual, something not apparently in the part as written, some – as Agate said – essence; something to do with oppression and cruelty; something Slavonic, too. The review suggests that he brought a strange sensuality, perhaps even sexuality, to the performance. That's a very self-conscious-making thing to do. Perhaps he was trying to hide what was brewing inside, a little embarrassed by it. It's very tempting, surrounded by high-powered and skilful performers simply to produce an efficient result so as not to hold everyone up, so as not to draw attention to oneself. Charles appears here to have taken the alternative escape route from anxiety: to have become secret with his work. That's not very friendly or helpful to your fellow-players, but sometimes it's unavoidable.

What Agate, ahead as often of his colleagues, saw was that

Laughton was doing something new, or perhaps something very old. He was re-minting acting. Original in himself, his body and his voice, he had also spent long years observing and cogitating. He had a lot to say; his language was acting, and he spoke it like no one else.

West End Star

In 1927, the year after he left RADA, Charles Laughton played seven featured roles in seven new West End productions: is this a record? Clearly, he was being recognised as something special. But the significant aspect of this phenomenal year is that the work was neither routine nor rubbish. The plays, including *Naked* by Pirandello and Euripides' *Medea* (again with Sybil Thorndike), and others, by lesser hands, were all challenging and interesting. And they all had a respectable amount of rehearsal time. By the seventh play of that year, *Mr Prohack*, by one of England's most famous *hommes de lettres*, Arnold Bennett, Laughton, playing the title role, was fully established as exciting and individual, a hot tip.

He had thus escaped the English repertory system, the touring and fit-up companies, and a large part of what 'being in the theatre' meant to most actors. He had never had to get a play on in three days, never had to struggle to make sense of a walk-on part, never had to work in tenth-rate plays, playing cardboard characters. Nor would he ever.

It helps to explain some of his subsequent attitudes. His work had taken place among the aristocracy of theatre talent. He had had time and quality on his side. He had never had to submit to the harsh disciplines endured by most young actors. In a sense, he hadn't needed them. He was obsessively hard working and took the theatre very seriously indeed. Laurence Olivier has vividly described the practical-joking, let's-get-this-show-on-the-road feeling of his rep experience. This was quite alien to Laughton, by inclination or experience. But the positive side of it – the sheer stamina, quickness of decision, the ability to paper over the cracks – the theatrical equivalent of what makes English musicians the best sight-readers in the world – none of this was part of his equipment.

The lack of that experience was exactly mirrored by his temperament: slow to decide, physically energetic but lacking staying power, almost morbidly perfectionist. It is not the best state in which to approach the English theatre. He much more closely, in fact, resembled a continental actor: *Ensemble Man*. His experience with Komis, a 'continental' director, if ever there was one, a *régisseur*, maybe gave him excessive expectations, too.

Many people with whom he worked (Hitchcock, Guthrie) came to see him as an amateur; many more (Wilder, Siodmak, Preminger) felt him, on the contrary, to be fiercely professional in never settling for less than perfection. He himself rather defiantly embraced the word amateur: 'It means lover, doesn't it? I love my work.' What is certain is that, though an actor of the greatest technical refinement, he never approached anything as a technical question. He seemed to view his roles not as problems to be solved or hurdles to be cleared but as challenges to self-knowledge: could he unlock the part of himself that would give meaning and life to the character?

In this sense, he was either an amateur or an artist, according to definition. His every performance was an encounter with himself, a liberation of another subjugated part of his psyche. Only from that would the transformations occur – and they did, in astonishing profusion. Each one let another bit of Laughton out of the bottle.

Simple ease of standing on stage as his skilful self was an experience of which he was innocent for many years. Simple ease in life came slowly too; in the twenties, in London, it was quite unknown to him. His family circle and friends from Scarborough recall a genial funster telling dreadful shaggy dog stories or doing 'his voices'; but that was before the war. It's significant that Osbert Sitwell had, only a few years later, found him to be playing the role of hotel manager.

It was Komisarjevsky again who had cast Laughton as Arnold Bennett's Mr Prohack. Bennett had gone into management with his mistress, Dorothy Cheston, Sidney Bernstein, and Komis. Sloane Productions, their company, had already staged *Paul I*, with Charles as Count Pahlen; this was Bennett's first play for them, drawn from his novel of the same name, adapted in collaboration with Edward Knoblock. Not specially noted as a dramatist, Bennett, on the strength of his novels and, almost equally, his journalism, was one of the most famous figures of the contemporary literary scene. The novel had been a great success some years before; and the play skilfully presented its main plot, about an easy-going Treasury Official who inherits half a million pounds from an unexpected source, only to discover the disadvantages of great wealth, and the regrettable effects it has on his family. Faintly Shavian, slightly Wellsian, the fable is told with sprightly wit, inverting values and turning situations on their head to satirise any number of contemporary subjects. The play was bound to attract attention; Charles compounded this by playing Prohack, the whimsical middle-class Official, as, unmistakably, the author himself. The author was not amused, but London was. In fact, Bennett, though the decent box office receipts allowed him to put a brave face on things, never reconciled himself to the performance, thinking it, according to his diary, 'vulgar' and 'bad'. In a letter, Bennett wrote that 'Laughton as Prohack has been praised to the skies by the entire press, and in my opinion, over-praised considerably. I think his performance is rough, and it is certainly not a faithful representation of Prohack as we conceived of him for the purposes of the play.'

Perhaps the tendency of the reviews to praise the performance at the expense of the play may have had something to do with it. 'To him alone, I think,' said *Theatre World*, 'lies the success of the play . . . his performance is superb . . . a little podgy man, childishly simple, possessing that dry sense of humour peculiar to the English, and above all that quality of accepting the most impossible situation with a sangfroid which is both the envy and the despair of all other nationalities.' The little man was a Laughton speciality, here receiving its first outing. His choosing to do so via an impersonation of Arnold Bennett is truly surprising, even to the critic of *Theatre World*. 'That this is deliciously amusing is not to be denied, but I am inclined to think that it detracts a little from the character of Mr Prohack.'

It is a curious thing for Laughton to have done, but it worked. To what extent did he intend it as a send-up of the mildly pompous Bennett? If so, that was very bold – the twenty-seven-year-old tyro from Scarborough taking on the world-famous author. Again, he seems almost to have courted the sack. Did Komisarjevsky abet him in it? There was a streak of barefaced cheek in his character, but this was going to lengths. No, it seems more likely that this was the only way he could make the thing work. Bennett, in a letter to his co-author, says that Laughton was 'very bad and wrong at all the later rehearsals.' The play is a quirky fable of capitalism; the man who inherits a half a million dollars is a genial, wry, breakfast-table philosopher, humorously bland. It may have been elusive for Laughton: no murk, no depths, no pressure within. And then, puzzling away at how to find this man in himself, he may have looked up in rehearsal and seen him staring him in the face. Authors are often very useful at giving clues to their own plays: not by explaining them, but simply by being themselves. Obviously, everything fell into place the moment he hit on the notion. It released him. 'Any middling actor can be senile and grotesque; Mr Laughton, invited to parody one of his authors, presented a marvellously tempered portrait, which was truthful to look and twinkle, yet showed a good deal of the man behind these natural defences,' said Agate. If you imitate the outer life of someone with sufficient connexion, you sometimes get an inner life for nothing; it just pops up of its own accord. 'As a technical feat the performance was immense. Mr Laughton acted with his whole body, and when you thought that facial expression and vocal intonation were exhausted, eked out these means with legs analytical, elucidatory, rhapsodical. To see him lean back on a sofa and keep the wit going with fat calves and lean slippers as a juggler does a ball – this was acting. But I must be careful,' Agate wisely concludes, 'or I shall fall into a panegyric.'

Theatre World, in its staider way, summed up: 'It is a performance of exceptional artistry; one which at last lifts Mr Laughton to the front rank of actors.'

At last. After eighteen whole months.

Prohack brought Charles not merely fame (even notoriety): it gave him the central relationship of his life, with the pert, quirky young actress playing his secretary; Elsa Lanchester.

She was 25, with a reputation for outrageous cabaret at the club run by herself and two friends, the Cave of Harmony. There she had given performances of 'Please sell no more drink to my father' and 'I've just danced with a man who danced with a girl who danced with the Prince of Wales', which had brought her great celebrity. Agate had singled her out on several occasions. *Prohack*, in which she played Laughton's secretary, was part of a general move towards 'legitimate' theatre. Her interest in Charles Laughton was part of a move towards legitimacy of a deeper kind.

'Outrageous' is the inescapable word for Elsa Lanchester at this time: the consciously Bohemian, red-headed elfin child of almost comically radical Irish-Marxist-Suffragette parents, she had trained with Isadora Duncan (whom she loathed), taught dance at the age of 13, run a children's theatre, posed for 'artistic' nude photographs, been a hired 'co-respondent' in divorce cases, and done snake dancing with the portly Ida Barr ('Ida Barr? 'Ide a pub, more like.') 'I did not know for one moment that I had some sort of compulsion to be different,' she writes.

But she did know that the brittleness of her social and emotional life 'was beginning to add up to despair within myself.' So when she got to know Charles – slowly, shyly on both their parts – she saw that he might offer an escape route. The strongest intimation that this might be so came from the completely unstrained silence that fell between them at an early meeting. Her bright provocations and his self-conscious tortuousnesses fell away into speechless security. A symptom of deep friendship – but not necessarily of sexual and emotional relationship.

This nonetheless followed. The relief of the new arrangement must have been overwhelming for Charles. A friend; a companion; someone to confide in; someone to lavish his attentions on – all complete novelties for him. She writes of the hours in bed at night, talking, talking, till dawn. Of his interest in her appearance. He took an active hand in selecting her wardrobe. She submitted because his eye was so good, even though his taste was far from what she would, till meeting him, have chosen for herself.

She had to pass the test of meeting his mother (who had advised him never to marry an actress, or a red-head. Elsa of course was both). She did so by dint of making the old lady laugh.

They lived separately for some while. She had an abortion. They moved to a flat in Dean Street, in Karl Marx's old house (which must have pleased her parents, if not his).

In other words, Charles was now in life. He was doing the things other people did.

After *Prohack*, came his startling performance in *A Man with Red Hair*, the Hugh Walpole shocker, adapted by Benn Levy. Laughton's last collaboration with Komisarjevsky, it is the first of his monster-villains. 'His entrance is like the first whiff of poison-gas we were once familiar with. A thing so evil and malignant that it can paralyse one's power to combat it by its apparent harmlessness, and yet so deadly if not grappled with at once. By what witchcraft Mr Laughton produces the effect, I don't know.' The critic of *Theatre World*, February 1927, knew how to enthuse. But his account is precise in its description of Laughton's aims. To invoke that inner state – to bring that murk actually onto the stage – was his task. He was, then and later, uninterested in psychology. He was not interested (either for himself or his characters) in the *why* of human action; only the *what* concerned him. He wanted to show what human beings were, to offer the raw material: not to explain it. Twenty years later, this made him an ideal collaborator for Brecht. But it is dead against the drift of acting in the twentieth century, where 'interpretation', both in directing and acting, has been the watchword: what does this character's behaviour *mean*? – not what is it? What is the play about? – never what is it?.

It is of course a priceless gift to critics, whose analysis of ideas is so far in advance of their powers of description.

In a magnificent letter of rage at the inadequacy of her performance of Lady Macbeth (to Laughton's Thane) James Bridie offered the following opinion to Flora Robson, one of the most radical statements about acting ever made: 'You are to stop being psychological – you know nothing about it, and it is a very technical job – when you are acting, develop a reflex system that flashes out the effect without the process of thought coming into the business at all . . . your job is to flick Lady Macbeth through your soul *faster than thought* and explain what you did after, if you can be bothered.'

Laughton was concerned to 'flick his characters through his soul', very much so. This method has a disadvantage over the interpretative method, however: it is very costly in soul.

Hugh Walpole's novel, and the play that Benn Levy made out of it, are exercises in *Schadenfreude*, literary experiments, explorations of how far one can really go. The situation is preposterous, the characters paper-thin, and the central, the eponymous, figure, Mr Crispin, is a contrived monster of sadistic revenge, scourging the world for his lack of beauty. But if he were real? If such a person really existed . . .? These are the questions Laughton asked, and the resulting performance shook people to the marrow. 'His performance was a *danse macabre* rendered by a human invertebrate, whose sagging flesh would somehow shape itself into all manner of harsh angles and gibbet-like postures', wrote Ivor Brown in *The Saturday Review*. *The Times* said, 'Mr Laughton's acting we are bound to admire, but we owe an evening of something very near misery to its skill.' St John Irvine, in *The Observer*: 'a very gargoyle of obscene desires. The sheer ability of his acting cannot easily be estimated.'

In the climactic scene of the third act, when Crispin has bound and gagged his victims, he reveals his soul: 'You have laughed at me, mocked me, insulted me – you and all the world: but now you are mine, to do with as I will. An old, fat, ugly man, and two fine young ones. I prick you and you shall bleed. I spit on you and you shall bow your heads. I can say 'Crawl' and you will crawl, 'Dance' and you will dance. I, the ludicrous creature that I am, have absolute power over the three of you . . . I can do whatever I like with you . . . the last shame, the last indignity, the uttermost pain.' Grand Guignol? Evidently. London was not unfamiliar with the genre: Sybil Thorndike had led a season of macabre, violent, spooky plays under that title at the Little Theatre some years before – but (as Sybil's presence in the cast more or less guaranteed) they were supposed to be tremendous *fun*. This was something rather different. Earlier in the play, Crispin talks to his American visitor about his 'philosophy of life: a little theory that my father handed on to me . . . my father used constantly to wonder whether it would be an entertaining experiment to cut my heart out. I think he eventually decided against it, however, on the grounds that it would mean the end of other and still more entertaining experiments . . . he stripped me and beat me till I bled. He wanted, he said, for my own good, to acquaint me with the heart, the innermost heart of life; and to understand life one must learn to suffer pain. Then if one could suffer pain enough, one could be as God. I went to Westminster School and they all mocked me – my hair, my body, my difference – yes, my difference. I was different from them all, I was different from my father, different from all the world, and I was glad that I was different. I hugged my difference. Different . . . different . . . different.'

Here were obviously many points of contact for Laughton. Another was art: Crispin is an aesthete. As he talks, he picks up a Rembrandt engraving: 'This is one of the most beautiful things of its kind that man has ever made, and I – am I not one of the ugliest things that men have ever laughed at? But do you see my power over it? I have it in my hands. It is mine. It is mine. I can destroy it in one instant (*He tears it to shreds*.) You must forgive my – my lack of reticence. It is just my little theory, you understand – to be above these things. – What would happen to me if I surrendered to all that beauty?'

Laughton made all this that could so easily have been melodrama, real; so real, that there was a serious move by the London Public Morality Council to have the play stopped: 'We are in possession of a volume of medical evidence that supports our view that the play should not be performed in public.' Charles gave an interview saying that he couldn't understand how it had passed the censor: 'I can only conclude that he didn't realise its nature.' Nor, according to a piece he wrote in *The Weekend Review* a couple of years later, did the author. 'My hero (or villain as you prefer) had been intended originally as a puppet twopence-coloured. I never dreamed that anyone could take him seriously. Laughton took him very seriously indeed, not for my sake or the play's sake, but simply because he had the clay in his hands, and must add a pinch here, make a false eyebrow there, lengthen the nose, twist the mouth, knowing that as he did so, a created figure, waiting and long imprisoned, would be liberated and escape to the chimney pots like a ghost in Stravinsky's ballet. Had the rehearsals continued another month, heaven knows what my Crispin would have grown to. Laughton works on his part as a novelist does on a novel or a painter on a picture, and he is at his best, as I believe Henry Irving was, when he has almost nothing to work on.'

This magnificent account of the actor as creator only stops short of asking where the contents with which he endows the 'almost nothing' come from. ' "It certainly will be a relief not to have to turn myself into a kind of psychological compendium every night," said the man with red hair to the *Daily Sketch*. "No one has the stamina to go on playing such a part for long." Charles Laughton, who made such a terrible figure in the title role of the play at the Little, took off his red wig. "The part attracted me, but it has been a terrific strain. At first it used to upset me thoroughly and make me all jumpy and although I have become inured to that by now, the interpretation makes such heavy demands upon one's physical and nervous energies that I feel I must have a rest." '

The element that informed his Crispin in *A Man with Red Hair* was an element present in most of his performances: confessional. Laughton was always publicly owning up to something, usually something rather unpleasant. As he paraded his (to him) physically ugly body before the public, so he thrust his (to him) morally and emotionally ugly soul at them.

This may have had a purging effect for him. As important, however, was its acknowledgement of an inner self, summoning repressed and shapeless desires and instincts out of the shadows and onto the stage. 'They may not be very nice, but they're mine!'

The paradox is that by putting them on the stage, firstly, they become attractive, by the usual mechanism by which anything done with conviction on the stage becomes attractive, and secondly, they become less real.

Also, Laughton was a wonderfully gifted actor. There was nothing raw about his work. The unshapely physique proved to be capable of mercurial movements – always a bewitching sight, the swift fat man propelled across the stage by the slim legs and dainty, well-formed feet later revealed in *The Private Life of Henry VIII* – and complete transformations; the voice, impaired by poison gas and bedevilled by easily inflamed tonsils, was not reliable, not up to all that its owner demanded of it, but it was resonant, with a range from cellos to trombones (no trumpets, nor ever would be. Double basses and even Wagner tubas later joined the band); an ear that was good without being great (fortunately for him: perfect mimicry is a terrible curse for a creative actor: no great actor has ever possessed it); and an instinct for phrasing, for handling the span of a speech and directing its energy towards the crucial words.

Every review he received on the London stage singled him out for special mention, frequently describing him as the main and sometimes only reason for seeing the play. It's hard to judge at this distance, but there is a possibility that Laughton's performances were in the nature of solo efforts, devised during long and tortured hours of self-communion without the participation of his fellow-players, and delivered more to the audience than to them. It is possible that that is what the lonely, obsessed man did. The kind of relaxation that makes team-playing possible would have been hard for him to come by. There is a sense of this sometimes in the films. If so, it is a grave fault. Laurence Olivier's advice 'not to lose yourself in the other actors' is wise, and courteous to the audience, but not to give anything to the other actors defeats them, you, the audience and the play. Few critics complained that Laughton had done that; there is, however, a single odd press report, in the *Express*, April 1928, which says: 'The eulogy Charles Laughton has received has given great offence to the sacred ring into which talent finds it so hard to enter . . . most actors at rehearsals act for the producer, Mr Laughton waits.'

1928 was as full as its predecessor. Apart from the Walpole run, Charles appeared for two nights in *The Making of an Immortal*, in which he played Ben Jonson to Sybil Thorndike's Elizabeth I (we that are young shall not see such sights) and then, briefly, he incarnated, as the Americans say, Hercule Poirot (another delectable thought). 'Of course it is Mr Laughton's incomparably fine performance of M Poirot that will draw London to the Prince of Wales Theatre.' The play was *Alibi* (based on *The Murder of Roger Ackroyd*), and it was produced by Gerald du Maurier, who may have made some contribution to what 'CBH' in *Theatre World* described as 'a piece of acting perhaps more finely polished . . . (than his Crispin) . . . his portrait of M Poirot is still more finished.'

Hugh Walpole as it happens, describes his performance, in the

same article in which he defines him as 'not our finest actor, far from it
. . . there are many who are, I think, in the general round at present
finer actors. But he is our supreme creator': '*Alibi* had a dreadfully
bad first act, as clumsy and maladroit an affair as I can remember, but
Laughton was terrific from his first entrance, not only in make-up – of
which he is sometimes a master and sometimes not – but also in all the
hints he gave you of his strange off-adventures. The plot that the
detective had to unravel was less than nothing; he was never more
thrilling than in the last act, when, his problem solved, with no
beauty, no voice, no kind of charm, he made love to a pretty girl. The
scene should have been revolting. You should have pitied the girl and
agonised for her escape, but in truth you felt that she was fortunate to
have a chance to live with so adventurous a spirit. She would find, you
felt, everything bad and everything good in this man. She would have
her shocks, she would have enchanting hours.'

Nothing is recorded of Laughton's encounter with his idol, du
Maurier: except one fascinating anecdote retailed by Emlyn Williams.
At the outset of the production, du Maurier asked him: 'Laughton,
are you a bugger?' To which Laughton stammeringly replied: 'N – no,
Sir Gerald. Are you?'

Du Maurier's question was presumably a reference to the hysterical
and malicious qualities Charles had brought to Walpole's Crispin. But
it must have given him a nasty turn. Because of course he was. He had
not spoken of it to anyone, least of all to Elsa. If he had hoped that
marriage would divert his desires, he was disappointed. His need for
sex with men had not cleared up like acne, he was still impelled to find
young men and sometimes even to bring them clandestinely home.
Elsa Lanchester believes that these encounters were furtive and
inspired by self-lacerating guilt: that Charles needed to sin, like a
minor key version of that figure of whom he sometimes seems to be a
thwarted alter ego: Oscar Wilde.

She may be right. There may also have been great pleasure; though
certainly little happiness, in the long run. In either case, one thing is
sure: he was leading a double-life. This can be tormenting, or
exhilarating. To have a secret; to have a dark and unknown other self,
cavorting and exulting in strange, dark and forbidden places – can
give an excitement to one's life. And work.

Lanchester is certainly right when she says that Laughton was
essentially a moral man. He must have regarded this side of him as
excremental; but he may have enjoyed the smell of his own shit.

Was it Charles' sense of his own ugliness that led him to desire beautiful men? All this must be guesswork. Even when he was completely reconciled to his sexual inclinations, in the last few years of his life, and sought out the companionship of fellow homosexuals, he only spoke of such matters with the utmost *pudeur*, according to Christopher Isherwood. It is reasonable to assume that Laughton's sexual appetite was strong, in view of his vast appetite for everything else: food, beauty, work. Had he so desired, he could have indulged it quite easily in the *demi-monde* of London's homosexual society, with its access to the easily and quite cheaply purchasable bodies of members of His Majesty's Services: it was a question of knowing the right bars (the Long Bar at the Trocadero, the 'Troc', for example) or the right private addresses. But even that required a certain boldness, a certain bravado, a touch of 'Here I am!' But now that was impossible for the plump young star, wishing his too, too solid flesh would melt. So perhaps he sought out the shadows. Perhaps that seemed more appropriate for the dirty thing he was about to do. Best perhaps to pick up some whorish lad, one of the many idly standing around the 'Dilly, and quickly discharge the pressure that had built up inside him, paying a few shillings at the end.

The idea of being looked at by a man with desire, not to mention love, was of course absurd, and probably wrong. That was his conviction.

He was nothing if not complicated. In life, as in acting, there could be no 'just getting on with it'. He must arrive at everything by the most devious and the most painful route, feeling perhaps that what was easily won was not worth having. This temperamental inclination led to a wonderful complexity in his work, but also to great misery for himself and those who surrounded him, privately and professionally.

In his social life at this time, he might have been expected to be riding the crest of a wave. Fame in the West End Theatre between the wars was something very different to what it is today. West End actors were pop stars, mobbed at their stage doors; but they were also the toast of that now defunct institution, smart society. Success on Laughton's level would be immediately rewarded by a sheaf of invitations to be propped up on the mantelpiece: cocktails with the Cunards, soirées with the Astors. Gossip columnists would be dispatched at regular intervals to discover his opinions on marriage, fashion, jazz; to winkle out his hobbies, his favourite reading and his taste in neckwear.

They found him a tough nut to crack. Lacking the later audacity of the Hollywood rags, they confined themselves to describing his appearance as eccentric, and that went for his conversation, too. 'There is a touch of arrogance in Laughton's manner; he gives the impression of a person who would not like to be contradicted or corrected . . . Laughton is himself one of the oddities of human nature: that pale puffy face, curious manner of walking, his shoulders hunched up, one a little higher than the other, that jerky step.'

They were too polite to mention it, but he was somewhat unusually dressed: not to put too fine a point on it, he was scruffy. And had perhaps not had a bath recently? Ever? His finger nails were certainly innocent of manicure, and probably soap, too.

Laughton was always careless of his appearance, to the end of his life. Lack of vanity? More likely a hatred of 'dressing-up', of formality of any kind – a childish pleasure in being 'mooky', in revolting against Eliza Laughton's sartorial strait-jacket. There also seems, as with his fellow-Yorkshireman, W. H. Auden, equally unenthusiastic about personal hygiene or sartorial propriety, an element of aggression in it. Auden hated his own body, too, the way in which it failed to conform to the norms of desirability, and Laughton and he both seemed to be refusing to engage in the doomed task of improving their appearance – think I'm ugly, eh? Right. Well *look the other way*. The body might have been being punished as well, the betraying body, letting the whole side down.

A couple of years later, in Hollywood, Tallulah Bankhead would refuse to shake hands with him because of those dirty fingernails. But in London, in 1928, Laughton's toilette was no obstacle. He could have more or less what he wanted. On this occasion what he wanted proved to be a major misjudgement, his first.

He'd seen an adaptation of *The Pickwick Papers* made for Basil Dean, and begged to be allowed to play Pickwick. Somewhat reluctantly Dean agreed, feeling that 'there was always something vaguely sinister about Charles' personality that he was never able to suppress, even in the most desirable characters.' He was evidently right. Even *Theatre World* was moved to observe: 'Laughton did not shine quite as expected' – though 'he looked the part completely'. Dean comments on how hard Laughton as usual worked: 'He could be seen in and out of buses, tubes and restaurants poring over a large volume of *Pickwick Papers*' (The *large* volume is a characteristic touch. Laughton liked to feel he was really working). But: 'in spite of his devotion to the Immortal Memory it must be admitted that (he) failed as Pickwick. A fruity voice, a jocose manner and a wonderful make-up were no substitutes for the inner benevolence of the character.'

It's hard to imagine the schoolmasterish martinet Dean getting on very well with Laughton, but his blunt words seem to have the truth of it. Benevolence was not a quality Laughton could easily command at this time of his life. It came more easily later. It would have made him feel hopelessly vulnerable to have exposed his *goodness*. There was far more muck to be got out first before he dare stand up in public and lay claim to any virtue.

It is not difficult to see what drew him to his next play, a ludicrous farrago called *Beauty*. Now that word always sent a shiver through Laughton's heart. The central character, whatever the absurdities of the plot, must have struck home very hard, too: Jacques Blaise 'an ungainly and unprepossessing astronomer for whom fair ladies are as remote as the stars themselves' becomes nonetheless convinced that a beautiful young woman has fallen in love with him, and tries to improve his appearance (by weightlifting and manicure!). In the end she falls, absurdly and unmotivatedly, into his arms. It was not a success; nor was he, specially ('It was asking too much of Charles Laughton to transform this tedious affair into something credible or worthwhile'); but the review contains an interesting aside that suggests that the whole-heartedness of his commitment was almost a byword: 'Blaise weeps once in every act and, Mr Laughton being one of our finest actors, very possibly during the intervals as well.'

Emotional intensity was still an uncommon quality on the English stage – not the rhetorical, high-flown emotionalism of certain classical actors, but direct self-exposure of Laughton's kind. He was accused of self-indulgence and indiscipline, which charges Laughton expressly rebutted some years later in an article for *Film Weekly*. For the time being, there continued to be an unease in some quarters about certain aspects of his work.

1929 was not his best year for reviews: 'Charles Laughton gives a remarkable impression – obviously it can be no more – of the handsome, athletic, Harry Heegan.' Then, even more unkindly, in praising Ian Hunter's performance of another role in the same play, the reviewer comments: 'It is a pity *he* was not given the role of Heegan.'

The play was *The Silver Tassie*, O'Casey's anti-war masterpiece, with its famous expressionist second act, designed by Augustus John. C.B. Cochran, the Diaghilev of English revue, had bravely decided to produce the play rejected by Yeats, and equally bravely cast in the leading part of the sportsman crippled in the trenches the young actor he had admired as Ficsur the pickpocket. O'Casey was delighted: 'he is a genius' he wrote of Charles to his friend, Gabriel Fallon. The director was Raymond Massey, and among the cast young Emlyn Williams, hot from Oxford, not missing a trick. His picture of Laughton at the time is brilliantly vivid, from the first readthrough on.

While everyone else stood around in the awkward or hysterical way of these occasions, Laughton was already in the wheelchair he would have to use in the last act, furiously trying to manipulate it. This drew unfavourable comment from the other young actors. It seemed ostentatious. It was. But it was probably the only way Laughton could handle himself. Small talk was not his forte; he felt neither one of the stars nor one of the company. And he knew he was physically miscast. 'Footballer, my foot', said one of the dozen or so walk-ons to Emlyn, 'he looks more like the ball.'

His fellow actors never saw him offstage 'except as a brooding baby in a wheelchair, obsessed by the difficulties of his part' – although, very occasionally, 'something would bubble out' – something about the difficulty of the bloody Irish accent. He would laugh helplessly – then return abruptly to misery. It's very understandable behaviour, but not, probably, very endearing.

Of the performance (the final act entrance) Emlyn has this striking thing to say: 'The broken soldier whirled among the dancers like a maimed bull on wheels. With a dance tune, and an invalid chair and the mask of a great actor, the moment encompassed the tragedy of war.' J.C. Trewin writes of him: 'speaking each word in the last two acts as if they were stamped with a branding iron . . . this podgy young Yorkshireman had given promise of genius.' Whatever else you could say about a Laughton performance, it was clearly never dull, and always the result of monumental labour to unlock the thing in himself that he needed. He always must find the key.

It must be stressed that his 'keys', which were to become more and more important to him, were not intellectual solutions – his understanding was perfectly able to solve the more or less simple psychological problems of the characters he played. The 'key' was the thing that would enable him to flood himself with the character's emotional state. And until he had found that key, his work was without life for him.

Theatrically, Emlyn seemed to follow Laughton around for a while. After *The Silver Tassie* came a revival of Reginald Berkley's farce,

French Leave, in which Laughton was promoted ('you'll be pleased to hear, my dear chap') from Private to General – 'an easy light-hearted success' with Charles, more comfortable with a smaller cast and enjoying the mild satire of his part, transformed in rehearsal into 'a happy enfant terrible'.

'Frightful dissensions are rife about Mr Laughton's assumption of General Root . . . Mr Laughton has been blamed not because his performance fails to evoke salvoes of laughter – his success in this respect is freely admitted – but because it does not keep the received truth concerning Brigadiers. The point about Mr Laughton's performance is that it *is* a performance, meaning a piece of deliberate acting and not the normal, hand-in-glove, round-peg-in-round-hole miracle of coincidence. Felicities of this order have no more to do with acting than changing the labels on bottles has to do with wine' wrote Agate in his notice – and then he was off into panegyric, which is nonetheless worth quoting because it contains sharp analysis of Laughton's equipment: 'The actor is young. His figure is podgy and devoid of any approach to military bearing. His features are dumpling: you might liken them to a broad champaign of flat, moon-struck rather than moonlit country. All this makes an admirable actor's mask just because, like Coquelin's mask, in repose it means nothing . . . mark, too, one feature which every great comedian has had – the long upper lip. But good character acting must be more . . . [it requires] intense apprehension of, and joy in, the character to be presented. Then again, good character-acting, like good art-work of any kind, must not only carry the artist's signature, but must bear the impress of his mind. I understand that Mr Laughton, when he took up the present part, went to look again at the Orpen portraits in the Imperial War Museum, with the result that his Brigadier is a reproduction of all that Sir William Orpen made us see in the more serious medium.'

During the run, he took a few days off to have an operation on his throat which he'd resisted and feared. After it the residual huskiness in his voice which had dogged him in the last few years disappeared completely.

This was done in preparation for a part which would need plenty of voice – a part written for him: *On the Spot*, by Edgar Wallace. It was to be the greatest triumph of his stage career, a phenomenon, both as a performance and as a play; though the play depends entirely on the leading actor's performance. It has never been revived with success.

The sensational aspect of the play was not simply its action; though in 1930 its tally of seductions, suicides and brutal killings must have seemed lurid in the extreme. What gave the play its electric charge was the fact that events almost identical to the ones portrayed on stage were happening at that very moment on the other side of the Atlantic. To that extent, the play resembles the Jacobeans' depiction of supposed Italian iniquities of their day: a sort of living newspaper: shock, horror.

The language has no poetic resonance, but it has an arresting actuality and urgency, hot from Wallace's visit to Chicago. Wallace took all of ten days to write it: a record, for him – ten *minutes* was more usual.

The central character, Tony Perelli, is preposterous, until you think about Al Capone; then it seems quite naturalistic. Discovered at an organ fondling his Chinese mistress, Perelli swiftly moves through sexual assault, betrayal, murder, and pimping, to end sobbing in front of a statue of the Virgin Mary. If the actor playing Perelli can make you believe in all of this, then the effect is breathtaking. If not, it's ridiculous.

Wallace knew his man. He'd seen Laughton in *A Man with Red Hair* and the moment he'd finished dictating the play to his secretary, 36 hours after he'd stepped off the boat from America, he sent her, with the script, round to the Laughtons in Dean Street. Miss Reissar struggled up the stairs, past whores and small snivelling children to the top flat, whose door was opened by a sluttish figure saying, 'Charles is out.' This was Elsa Lanchester.

Wallace was not disappointed by Laughton's reaction. He directed the play himself, and Miss Reissar was present throughout. She reports a most curious incident on the first readthrough. The whole cast was gathered on the stage of Wyndham's Theatre, with Wallace at the head of the table. No Laughton. Calls were made. Still no Laughton. Miss Reissar was despatched to the stage door. Had the stage doorkeeper seen Mr Laughton? Certainly not, he replied, the only person he'd seen was a tramp that he'd had to eject several times. Miss Reissar opened the door. There, smirking, was Laughton, none too formally attired. He accepted her invitation to come in, and the readthrough began. He read brilliantly; then left.

Miss Reissar did not report this story to anyone at the time, but, though it was unheard of behaviour for an actor of his time, it would not have surprised many people. His reputation was increasingly that of a man apart, an eccentric.

Rehearsals proceeded conventionally. Emlyn Williams (thanks to

Laughton) was co-opted into the cast after two or three days of rehearsal. Charles had felt that his predecessor in the role was too much the conventional heavy. Such, now, was his prestige. At the age of 30, four years after leaving RADA, he now had casting approval for a major West End production.

Again, it is Emlyn's account which gives us the most striking picture of the young star. It demands to be quoted at length.

Only one figure was discernible picked out under the working light, centre stage: Laughton.

As when he had swung about in his wheelchair, he was feeling his way to something, alone and absorbed. But this was different: he was pacing to and fro like a caged hobbledehoy, glaring and growling.

First, he experimented with a clumsy waddle, from which emerged a walking gait, lithe, graceful, tigerish; then the hobbledehoy stood stock still and scowled into the dark, blubber-lips pursed. He might just have been told that for the school play he had been turned down for the part of Cupid and was settling for a sulky Bacchus . . . as before the actors in the shadows studied him with the amusement of bystanders at a fair: weird way to work, rum cove, make a good story in the Green Room Club.

Edgar Wallace was certainly pursuing no avant-garde methods. Arriving late at rehearsals, he breezed in saying 'Sorry Charlie, 'ad to go to see a bloke about a racehorse. 'Alf a mo' while I catch up on the serious side of life' – the *Evening Standard* racing page.

There was no end to Laughton's avidity for perfection. Emlyn spoke some Italian, so was set to teaching Charles the phrases he needed for Perelli. 'In corners, syllable by syllable, I coached an eager bumbling pupil who immediately bumbled ahead of teacher. To see Laughton catch fire, and set fire to me, was intoxicating.'

Years later, his friend and pupil Belita said: 'Charles was a learner, he was always learning. If you were a learner too, you would get on with him. If not, it could be difficult.'

Although Wallace had written the part for Charles, it was scarcely typecasting (in the light of his previous 15 roles, what would that have been, anyway?), but it was totally within his range. He could command from within himself danger, violence, passion, authority, caprice, sarcastic wit. The only dimension hitherto unknown in his work was the blood in the veins of the role: naked sensuality. To release this, he devised a make-up which transformed him out of all recognition. The cameras of Pathé News recorded the process by which, before our very eyes, Charles Laughton gives way to Tony Perelli, a Jekyll-and-Hyde act as fascinating, in its way, as anything he ever put on film. He strides, vigorously and directly, into his dressing-room. He looks straight into the camera and tells us, in an impeccable cut-glass accent, what he's going to do: wig, face-paint, boot-black to match his own hair up, finally – 'a real secret, this' – the false eyelashes, 'a tip from Greta Garbo'. Bit by bit 'this pudding', as he calls his face, assumes contour, line, definition. As it does so, his accent becomes more and more Yorkshire, until, climactically, he assumes Perelli's Sicilian-American tones. 'Nize fella, very nize fella,' he says, flashing a mean·look at us, which, through all the crackle of the poor copy of the crudely made film, tells with some of the force that so bowled his audiences over. It contains real sexual aggression, and is both sexy and alarming, a million miles away from the suavely masterful campness with which he introduces the film.

Backstage, at the dress rehearsal, he appeared in swarthy make-up, with his long false eyelashes, in his Act One dressing-gown. '(He) gave us all a triumphant leer, and said in his Al Capone voice [*that* came from an Italian waiter he'd roomed with at Claridge's]: 'Who said-a I couldn' be sexy?' He was, in a new way. It made him happy as an infant.' The photographs in *Play Pic* vividly chart the range of mood he established in *On the Spot*, menace and sweetness, violent rage, lust, cunning, all within a completely un-English timidity, an almost literally smellable oiliness. 'In this present play of Edgar Wallace's,' wrote Hugh Walpole, 'he is loathsome and lost. But he is much more than that. He is a poet and a creator of beauty. Every squirm, every husky whisper is a key to an important truth – and a truth we feel he is showing us for the first time. – Thus it is to be a real creator.'

Malcolm Muggeridge, lunching with him, asked how he got into the right state of mind to play Perelli. Laughton told him that 'he used to remember how as a schoolboy he had believed that his fingers were going to drop off as a result of masturbating.' The key. (Muggeridge adds: 'this was my only, brief and not very pleasing encounter with the theatre and actors.')

On the Spot was, as Elsa Lanchester says, 'a colossal success.' It is interesting to note, *autres temps, autres moeurs*, that as a result of the colossality of the success, Laughton was visited in his dressing-room, not merely by fellow stars, not only by royalty, but by no less a personage than Mr Rudyard Kipling. It was the unmissable show of 1930.

It exhausted him, as well it may. The brief span of the play – it runs no longer than two hours – contains an amazing range of peaks to be scaled by Perelli, and he must drive the play every moment that he's on stage. 'Every night before the performance, Charles would have to lie on his back, remaining perfectly quiet and breathing deeply for over an hour. The doctor told Charles to spend as much time in the country as possible in order to keep his health.'

Stamina was a problem he never solved. He never mastered the art of conserving energy, of pacing himself through a role. In later life, because he was tired or ill, he learnt certain dodges, or sometimes just coasted, but at this time he simply gave his all, all the time. It's a dangerous thing to do.

There are two 'stories' about the run of *On the Spot*: one showing Laughton's theatrical *savoir-faire*; the other his lack of it.

During the out-of-town tour (no previews: an opening night was an opening night, by God) the sound system failed, and Laughton's organ-playing at the beginning of the play was silent. He made a joke out of it; and at the curtain call, came to the foot of the stage and told the audience: 'Ladies and gentlemen, you are the only people in England who know that I cannot play the organ. I hope you can keep a secret.'

Curtain speeches of one sort or another were still traditional after every performance. This one seems not to have fazed Laughton in the least.

The other incident, which occurred during the London run, completely unnerved him, however – as well it might: it's an actor's nightmare.

The actress, Gladys Frazin, playing Maria Poluski, Con O'Hara's moll, was involved in a high-spirited off-stage relationship with the improbably named Anglo-Italian director, Monte Banks. One afternoon between matinee and evening performance, she returned to her nearby flat for a little refreshment. He, in a characteristic burst of impulsive rage, flung all her clothes out of the window. She, her better judgement perhaps slightly impaired by the beverages she'd been consuming, simply placed a mink coat over her nakedness, and returned to the theatre, just in time to make her Act One entrance, which she did. By now the alcohol had begun to impair her powers of speech, so she wisely said nothing.

Charles, glimpsing the flesh under the mink, knowing that the next line was 'May I take your coat?' and receiving no reply to his cues, started to sweat heavily. His improvisations were not especially successful. 'I heard him turn from bullying gangster to terrified

Italian waiter who had worked at the Pavilion Hotel, Scarborough.' Suddenly Miss Frazin spoke: 'Oh Charles,' she said. The audience gasped. 'I mean, Oh Tony.' She giggled. The audience roared.

'Somehow, seemingly hours, actually minutes, later, she left the stage. Suddenly she remembered something: "Julian, honey, I gotta get back to Charlie. I never said my *lines* to him."'

This proved to be Miss Frazin's last performance.

Charles had not handled the situation too brilliantly. Thinking on his feet was not his strong suit. 'In repertory,' observes Emlyn, 'actors are conditioned to emergencies; Charles had never been in repertory.' It is scarcely blameworthy not to have been able to handle the Frazin problem; merely interesting to note that, though he was by no means a 'fourth wall' actor, lost in the truth of his role, he was in fact now and at many points in the future, quite capable of stopping the show, stepping out of the play altogether, either to address the audience, or take a prompt; was in fact in quite conscious control of the play as a vehicle which he was driving, and never in any doubt that the play was – a play. What he lacked completely were gifts of spontaneous improvisation.

Whether this makes him more of an amateur or more of a *pro* is a tricky question.

Self-consciousness was still a problem. He took Emlyn Williams out between the shows one day. Emlyn was amazed that the man who brazenly stared him in the eye every performance, couldn't quite bring himself to make eye-contact over the supper-table. His conversation was full of bluster and pretensions to intellectuality. It was simply an awkward encounter.

His encounters with Elsa's friends had not been great successes, either. Neither in the Socialist aristocracy of H. G. Wells and his friends, where Charles sat silently absorbing what was said, biding his time till *he* became a great man to whom people would listen, (upon which occasions, Elsa unkindly observes, he often seemed to be re-hashing what Wells had once said); nor with her Bohemian chums, whose hi-jinks he couldn't emulate, and where he seemed 'like an old gentleman, though he was barely thirty.'

There is a subtext here, it seems, which is patronising to the slow-moving, somewhat ponderous tradesman from Scarborough. It offers a sad glimpse of an outsider – almost everywhere, it would seem: intellectually, socially, even in rehearsal. Only on stage did he belong.

Not even, apparently, within the profession was he considered one of them. In an article entitled 'Charlie *Not* Their Darling', Agate wrote:

> There are in the English theatre two subjects which are like a red rag to a bull. One is the prowess of Mr Laughton. Any praise of this actor infuriates all other actors. (The other red rag is any new production by Mr Cochran) . . . What other actors say about Mr Laughton is this: Yes, of course he's good. But look at the parts he has had! To which my answer invariably is: Yes, let us look at the parts Laughton has had, and let us ask what other actor there is on the English stage who, given those parts, could have made so many and such different successes . . . I freely admit that three out of these fourteen performances by Mr Laughton were not good. But in none of these three failures and in none of the eleven successes has Mr Laughton in any way resembled himself, nor has any one creation been remotely like another. This is a feat. It belongs to an art of acting which very few players in the country at the moment are practising.

The article did presumably not endear him any closer to his colleagues. He now crowned his sensation in *On the Spot* with a darker play yet.

Payment Deferred, which opened at the St James' Theatre in May 1931 is a major crux in Laughton's life and work.

It was the end and culmination of an astonishing five years of creativity; the crowning glory of a brilliant succession of triumphs; a performance which cost him dear, and which was unlike anything his contemporaries had ever seen. It was the occasion of his departure for America.

And just before rehearsals for it started, the timebomb at the heart of his relationship with Elsa Lanchester went off. The explosion was contained, but the fall-out continued for the rest of their lives together.

It happened during rehearsals of *Payment Deferred*. Elsa was playing Charles' fifteen-year-old daughter. The story concerns a man who murders a rich young relative and then tries to live with the guilty secret. He had been unusually hard to live with during the preparatory period, immersing himself in the character's psychopathia and guilt.

Late one night, he came home in the company of Jeffrey Dell, the play's adaptor, and a policeman. He told Elsa that he must speak to her privately. When they were alone he become overwrought, and told her that he had a homosexual streak in him which he occasionally indulged. A young man with whom he had had sex for money had harassed him for more. A policeman had intervened, and this was the outcome.

Elsa immediately reassured him that it was 'all right'. Her politically radical background, her Bohemian circle of acquaintance (including not a few homosexuals) and her own instinctive permissiveness, all, theoretically, disposed her to treat the news lightly. She simply asked whether he had had sex with a man in their house. He had. Where? On the couch. Very well. Get rid of the couch.

Nothing more was said. Ever.

The case shortly appeared before a magistrate who was either very naïve, very worldly-wise – or gay. He dismissed the case, cautioning Laughton against 'misguided generosity'. The case was reported, but Laughton's name was not mentioned.

All this a week before the play opened.

Elsa's immediate first response was to go deaf in both ears for a week. The shock was total. 'I can think of no indication whatsoever that Charles liked young men prior to that time.' The mad romp of their outrageous life together suddenly ceased – for a moment, but a fateful one. Her awkward, *joli laid*, madly-talented husband was *queer*. Well – so what! On with the party! But nothing, of course, was ever the same again.

'If I had known all this before we were married it might have been very different, one way or another. But the deception is what hurt so deeply.' Nothing was said. 'It was only afterward, in later years that the boy episode proved to grow into a great wall – never mentioned, but distinctly *there*.'

So here they were with this kooky marriage in whose foundations a large crack had suddenly appeared, and they decided, without saying a word, to ignore the crack, carry on as if nothing had happened.

There were rehearsals to be got on with. Charles could have no difficulty in informing the character with what he had just gone through: and indeed, when the play opened, his performance was thought to have a force, a frightening realism, which amazed its audience. Elsa Lanchester consciously quotes from the review in the *Star*: 'there was a moment when, thinking his wife had discovered his secret, he collapses into hysteria. The sight of the quivering, blubbering wretch aroused mingled feelings of disgust and pity.'

During the run of *Payment Deferred*, he began to endure acute anxieties in a form familiar to actors under stress: while he was on stage, he felt that his clothes were falling away from him, that he was standing in front of the audience stark naked. He was persuaded to consult the English high priest of psychoanalysis, Freud's hagiographer, Dr Ernest Jones. After a couple of visits, however, he simply failed to show up. 'Jones told me,' he said, 'that I know more about myself than he ever would, so there seems little point.' Whether his anxieties were resolved is unrecorded (though Singer hilariously suggests that Laughton turned the tables on Jones, and analysed him, for which, according to Singer, Jones was very grateful). Perhaps Charles found that it was impossible to deal with the immediate problem, the hallucinations on stage, without dealing with the entire question of his sexuality. Perhaps, too, he sensed the sources of his work in the unresolved elements of his temperament, that he needed his guilts and secret exultations, that, in the famous Maoist phrase, like strong cheese they stink, but they taste great.

In a rare account of his approach, Laughton himself wrote (to a young actor who was going to play his part of William Marble on tour): 'Poor rigid hidebound Mr Marble, the laugh is with him and on the audience. They crucified him, and by the end of the play they know they did it in secret fear of their own hidden loves under the mask of virtue.' '*Hypocrite spectateur, mon semblable, mon frère!*' is Laughton's accusation to the audience. He dredges the lees of his own existence surrogately. The Christ-imagery is striking. 'By the end of the play they naturally want to crucify me for telling them so.'

The Star said of his performance: 'The acting of Charles Laughton was astonishing. At times I found it almost unendurable to contemplate the agonies and fears of the murderer . . . here was an utter abandonment to funk and terror.' The audience, as Laughton implied, were not keen on paying him to turn their eyes into their very souls, and Gilbert Miller, who had produced the play (which had, interestingly, been Agate's idea in the first place, intended from the beginning as a vehicle for Laughton) decided to cut his losses after three months and try the play's luck on Broadway.

What a relief this must have been! Elsa and Charles' life – still living in their modest flat in Percy Street – continued apparently unruffled. They spent weekends in the cabin they had bought near Guildford, a place built as a private hideaway for himself by Clough Williams Ellis (the great and eccentric architect) and reluctantly sold to the Laughtons after much close questioning as to their suitability. There was no water, no electricity, little furniture. It was a real tree-house actually built on trees, and surrounded by untrammelled nature. To get to it, you had to walk half a mile across a field. It was an idyll, and Elsa and Charles were as happy here as they would ever be in their lives, picking flowers, playing games.

But it was an escape. It was not where the centre of their lives resided, and it ignored the violent explosion their relationship had undergone. Charles was rising as rapidly as an actor has ever done; he had probably risen as far as he could in England. There had been an awkwardness between himself and Edgar Wallace. He had not liked Wallace's play *The Mouthpiece*, in which the leading part had been written expressly for him; now Wallace wanted to know whether he would commit himself to another play which he was planning. If not, he wouldn't write it. Charles did not commit (wisely, no doubt: the author's description of the part suggests that it might have defied even Laughton's gifts for bringing conviction to the improbable: 'the part I have in mind is a sort of Chinese D'Artagnan, except that he is entirely and utterly unscrupulous, but very game and philosophical to the last. He is steeped in Western philosophies, is a great quoter of the sages and is picturesquely executed in the last scene, after raping, off-stage, the wife of his benefactor'). Disappointed, Wallace ended their professional association. 'I cannot enthuse myself to write plays on approval even for the most brilliant of artists . . you have no rival and no competitor in your particular expression of art. If I write a part which you in your judgement regard as a bad play, or an unsuitable one for you, there is no alternative choice for the principal part, and one's work would be wasted, and that would lead to all sorts of irritations and unhappiness, so, Charles, that is definitely the end of us as a combination.'

Everything private and everything professional pointed to a change. The transatlantic journey was one easily made by English-speaking actors of the thirties back and forth, uncomplicated by any Equity restrictions. It was a logical development, a change from which they and their marriage could only benefit.

Broadway and Hollywood

Charles and Elsa crossed the Atlantic on the SS *Olympic*. For fun, they took with them a pornographic novel. As they neared the New York harbour, their nerve failed them, and they attempted to throw the book overboard, page by page. The wind was blowing in the opposite direction, however, and the boat sailed majestically into the harbour with pages of *Cherry Blossoms in Beachtime* clinging to its side. This sweet little story, recounted by Lanchester fifty years later, is a comic reworking of the sexual concealment which was now established at the centre of their lives.

They sailed in to a warm welcome. Broadway had heard of them. Laughton's performance was acclaimed again, if anything more passionately. John Mason Brown, a tough nut to crack, wrote: 'Mr Laughton's face is one of the most expressive masks that I have ever seen in the theatre. His hands and feet and his whole body are ever the willing and expressive instruments of the things he has to say. He does not say the lines, he thinks them. They can be seen gathering like clouds in the eyes. He can be cross with peppery violence, carnal with a grossness that is repellent, merry with the expansiveness of Falstaff, cruel with a hideousness that is sickening and afraid with a whimpering terror that is almost unendurable. He is the most remarkable character actor New York has been privileged to see in years.'

But New York was even more resistant than London to the experience of having its eyes turned into its very soul. The play lasted three weeks at the Lyceum Theatre; after which the producer took it to Chicago, where Laughton could examine at first hand the place he had done so much to immortalise in the London theatre. (In fact, the city of Chicago had banned *On the Spot* as a scandalous calumny). Prohibition was at its last gasp, but both Chicago and New York remained awash with bath-tub gin. The Laughtons appear to have been somewhat alarmed by the scale and speed of things – America was still a mythic and improbable place for most English people, a kind of historical and anthropological no man's land, peopled by hillbillies, scalp-happy Sioux and Italian mobsters. Social graces as practised in Shaftesbury Avenue (or even the Pavilion Hotel in Scarborough) seemed unknown. Elsa and Charles both, she from her radical and Bohemian background, he from his tradesman and High Art perspective, hated cant and snobbery; but they didn't yet know how to handle the hail-fellow-well-met directness of the greatest democracy on Earth. Some years later, Laughton wrote, in his commentary to *The Fabulous Country*, the book he edited which is in effect a love letter to his adopted land, 'I asked a policeman the way to the Empire Theatre and he said, "Can't you read?" And I was humiliated. I only thought, years later, that I must have been using a "My good man" sort of voice, and he, as a proper American, was not having any of that, and he slapped me down. ' But he knew there was something about the place that answered a deep need in him: 'the driver asked us where we wanted to go. We told him "The Chatham Hotel". And the driver, who must have had a hell of a day, said: "There are too many different places." We laughed, because *we knew we were free to say the same kind of thing too.*'

Laughton belonged to that generation of Englishmen to whom the nature of English social existence in the twenties and thirties was essentially false – pompous and restrictive. Sex had something to do with it – but language, customs, rubric were even more oppressive. 'I was the guest of the Savage Club in London, and Sir Austin Chamberlain made a speech. I was sitting next to Nelson Doubleday the publisher. Sir Austin was polite and imperturbable. At the end of the speech Nelson Doubleday said to me, 'Charlie, however thin you cut it, it's still baloney,' and I suddenly wanted to get on a boat and get back to New York so bad I could taste it.'

Auden or Isherwood might have said the very same thing.

During this first American visit, Laughton discovered another New World speciality: hype. His notices ensured an ever-ringing phone, and queues of producers at his door. They blandished him extravagantly with promises of huge sums of money and starring roles. What they never did was specify *which* roles. The blind slavery of a studio contract was clearly not for Laughton, however well paid. So he kept refusing.

Meanwhile, he and Elsa had met Ruth Gordon, who remained a friend for the rest of Charles' life. She introduced them to her boyfriend, the vulpine Jed Harris, already – at thirty – a fully-fledged monster: 'The Wonder Boy,' 'The Meteor', 'the man who invented Broadway.' There was no doubting his technical skill as a director: it was his personal qualities that were in question. Enough, perhaps, to observe that Laurence Olivier's performance of Richard III was closely modelled on him. A little of the charm of that famous interpretation belonged to Harris as well, though, because he persuaded Charles to repeat his Hercule Poirot in *Alibi* under his direction. The understanding was that Charles would be left to get on with the acting, while Jed dealt with the physical production. But this was not Jed's way, and immediately rehearsals began, violent disagreements broke out. The play was brilliantly reviewed, and Charles again acclaimed, but it managed no more than forty performances. The American retitling of the play – *Fatal Alibi* – proved apt.

Jed Harris was Laughton's first brush with the director-bully. His subsequent career was characterised by increasingly bitter and bloody engagements with this type. For the present, he was young enough and perhaps uncertain enough merely to resist. In time, his response to bullying became ingenious, comprehensive, and in one famous case, conclusive.

Everything in his temperament and his understanding of the art of acting rebelled against dragooning. He approached each role that he played as part of the whole. He had certainly thought as much about the work in question as the director, and he was not prepared simply to slot into some master-plan. Moreover, he was engaged in a very demanding activity: trying to animate unused parts of himself, to give fresh and original life to something existing only in the author's imagination and on a piece of paper. The most distinguished and successful theatre practitioners in England – Edgar Wallace, Komisarjevsky, Gerald du Maurier – had given him the time, the space and the trust in which to exercise his art. It is extraordinary that a certain species of director – Jed Harris was just the first – having recognised his talent and sought to work with him, should then deny his need of the quite normal conditions he required in which to function. Laughton must have felt particularly depressed by contrast with his previous experience in the play, working with his idol, du Maurier.

His depression came out in the form of bearishness towards Elsa, now unemployed again. She took refuge in innocent friendship with the stage manager of *Payment Deferred*: Joe Losey. Together they visited exotic dives, searching out louche novelty. They roamed Harlem in the small hours, hearing jazz, dancing, giving in to it all. Charles was nervous, and preferred to stay at home, brooding and angry.

Elsa went back to England.

As soon as *Fatal Alibi* dribbled to an end, Charles followed. There's really nothing more displeasing than to have received remarkable notices and then fail to sell tickets. It's like throwing a wonderful party to which no one turns up. Better, far better, an out and out flop. Neither the notices nor the kind words of those who do struggle along can comfort you. At some deep level, there is terrible rejection. Even with *these* notices, people don't want to see you. If you were giving away money in the street, they probably wouldn't take it.

As it happens, many of the audience during those two short runs were actors, and Laughton's performances blazed themselves into their memories. It was a completely new kind of acting. The combination of intense physical projection and deep emotional realism was potent in itself; but when the medium for all this expressiveness was a plump, rubbery-faced character man of medium height, the impression was indelible. Vincent Price called it super-realism. Whatever it was, it made Laughton, as he had been in London, a hero to the younger generation. Already they were flattering him with proverbial sincerity: he was starting to become one of the most imitated actors of his time.

Literally as the boat pulled out of New York harbour, a telegram arrived from Jesse Lasky at Paramount, offering a new kind of contract: a three-year, two-film-a-year contract with the right to choose his roles. By the time he'd arrived in England, he'd found out that the first film being offered had been written by his old friend Benn Levy, adaptor of *A Man with Red Hair*, and now in Hollywood. An anxious telegram to Benn Levy elicited the assurance that even if he, Levy, were to play the role, he couldn't fail. Elsa and Charles, under a continuing bombardment of wires from Paramount, packed their bags and set sail for America. Their experience of New York and Chicago would scarcely have prepared them for Hollywood, which in almost every way, culturally, physically, socially, was (and is) another world from the East Coast.

Climatically, they can have had little to complain of, but the curious eccentricity of the architecture ('late marzipan' they dubbed it) and the diffuseness of the city's layout were daunting. The movie industry's indifference to newcomers was much in evidence. Out here among the palm trees, on the beaches, on the golf-courses and by the swimming-pools, what this plump young actor did in *New York* signified little. Photographers snapped them, journalists interviewed them (or rather *him*), but in a politely baffled way, as if they were visiting Albanian royalty. What are you doing here? is the subtext of many a polite Hollywood enquiry.

Because, of course, after the hysteria of the courtship, the insistent demands to *get over here!*, he wasn't needed immediately after all.

He used his time, not socialising, not seeking out the British community, the 'Hollywood Raj' of which Sheridan Morley writes so vividly, not lounging on the sand, but in learning.

Laughton's experience of the processes of film-making up to that time was slight, and not particularly instructive. He'd been involved in a couple of shorts written for Elsa by H. G. Wells – very quirky little films dominated by her droll-bizarre persona. Charles walks, or rather, runs on in one as a gangster; in another he impersonates a Rajah. In 1931, while appearing in *Payment Deferred*, he'd made three films – *Wolves, Comets* and *Down River*, 'quota quickies' (to make up the quota of British movies required by Act of Parliament) – which are generally described as best-forgotten. There is, anyway, no choice, as they have disappeared from the face of the earth. *Kine Weekly* of May 1931, dismissing *Down River* as 'school-boy stuff' tells us that Laughton, playing a half-Dutch, half-Oriental skipper of a tramp being watched for drug-trafficking, is, understandably, 'never too sure of his accent. He has an opportunity to display his genius for make-up but fails to draw a convincing character.' *Wolves* was devastatingly summed up by the *New York Times*: 'A pack of human wolves held at bay by one of their number in whom there still glows a faint spark of chivalry while a fear-maddened woman flees a lonely Labrador outdoor camp in an open boat through an icy-fingered blizzard – these are the elements of *Wanted Men* (re-titled for America), the searing, action-crammed thirty-seven minute all-talking melodrama.' It took seven years for it to reach America: 'its self-sacrificing hero is none other than Charles Laughton, and the performance will set you to contemplating the marvels that have been wrought in him in these seven years.' Its other star, Jack Osterman, according to the review, 'when he heard a print had been unearthed, started saving up with the idea of perhaps buying it and making a bonfire of it.' As for *Comets*, it too seems to have disappeared, which is a great shame, because it contained among various other variety acts strung together in revue format, a performance by Charles and Elsa of their 1928 hit from Riverside Nights, *Frankie and Johnny*. This is the only known instance on celluloid of them singing together, though there is a poignant pirate recording of him grunting and her trilling through *Baby It's Cold Outside* from the 40's. Shortly after its first release, *Comets* was re-released without *Frankie and Johnny* which did have a further lease of life as a short, only shown in America. There is no trace of this, either, however, so we must assume it well and truly lost.

His only other pre-Hollywood film is in a rather different category: *Piccadilly*, 1929, directed by Ewald A. Dupont, the fitfully brilliant

maker of the U.F.A. masterpiece, *Variété*. A silent film, written by
Arnold Bennett, its central characters are played by Anna May Wong
and Gilda Gray. Charles appears in only one scene, in which he plays a
tetchy diner, only pausing from cramming food into his mouth to
complain. It is the first of many magnificent eating scenes Laughton
was to commit to celluloid, and it bears comparison with any of them.
It is a most compelling vision of greed; gross, but also Grosz, a pig in a
starched collar. Whether the distinguished German director
influenced Laughton towards it is impossible to say, but the performance would not be out of place in a number of U.F.A. films of the
period.

Apart from these, Laughton was a stranger to the studio. His
enforced wait was spent exploring the possibilities. A studio, even
more than a theatre, is like a feudal village, a network of craftsmen,
labouring away for the great Lord, the director. Hollywood had
bought the best talent in every department, just as it had bought him.
As he passed through their various hands, the wigmakers, the
costumiers, the sound operators, preparing for his screen tests, he
started to make the mental adjustment necessary to the new medium.

It was a medium to appeal to him in many ways. Perfectionist that
he was, he was always doomed to frustration in the theatre. Physical
limitations, of space, facilities and himself, compromised his achievement. He was deeply interested in, and disappointed by, the realisation of detail in the theatre: the cut of a costume, the join of a wig.
Film offered completely new possibilities of physical freedom and
quality of craftsmanship. As far as he was concerned, it offered him
two golden advantages that he exploited to greater effect than any
actor in the history of the cinema: the close-up; and the re-take. The
close-up enabled him to explore even further the nature of his special
gift, perceptively identified by John Mason Brown: the art of making
thought flesh. 'Movie acting is simple,' Laughton later said to Marius
Goring (only a year later, in fact, flushed with his discovery of the new
medium). 'Feel it in your *guts*, and then let it dribble up through your
eyes'. That plump mask might have been expressly designed to be
framed by a cinema screen. 'I'm certainly lucky,' he told *Picturegoer* in
1935. 'Imagine a face like mine photographing so well. My features
cut through the screen like a knife through cheese. It's sheer good
luck – but who would have believed it?'

His shameless exploitation of the right to re-take became a joke in
the industry: a rather expensive joke in some cases. In the theatre
where time is limited by the need to get the whole play more or less

right by opening night, a compromised result has often to be accepted, often for the good of all. The chance to re-take offered by movies is a perfectionist's heaven – and hell: to an actor of Laughton's fertility, it is tantamount to a recipe for madness. His acting faculty was a thing constructed of a million nerves, a-quiver with impulses. Every impulse, as it passed through him, provoked an adjacent impulse: an entire new set of vibrations was sounded, each with implications. So easy to become lost in a baroque tissue of resonating tendrils. But it is exactly this ability to form a character out of a thousand living cells which together form a breathing, complex organism that fitted him so wonderfully for the screen with its microscopic sensitivity. Watching him can be like watching film of plant life: nature's kingdom in a man. The linearity which makes Laurence Olivier for the most part such a disappointing film actor, but so exhilarating to see on stage, is entirely absent from Charles Laughton, as an actor and as a man. There are no straight lines with him: everything is composed of a myriad of tiny arrows, each pointing in a different direction. Hence the illusion of life itself.

The Benn Levy script, *The Devil and the Deep*, was delayed, so Laughton was 'lent' by Paramount to another studio – Universal – for his first Hollywood movie, another Levy script, and barely American at all. The story was by J. B. Priestley, most of the cast were English, and when they weren't – like Raymond Massey and Melvyn Douglas – they spoke with English accents; the setting was as English as the fog in which the eponymous house is enveloped. The film was directed by James Whale, fresh from triumphs with *Journey's End* and *Franken-stein*, but before that an associate of the Laughtons in various capacities: stage manager of *Riverside Nights*, habitué of the Cave of Harmony, and portrayer of Crispin's epicene son Herrick in *A Man with Red Hair*. It was with him that they dined on their first night in Los Angeles. 'You'll love it here,' he told Charles. 'I'm pouring the gold through my hair and enjoying every moment of it!' With their not dissimilar Northern English backgrounds, Laughton and Whale had radically different tastes. Laughton embraced High Art, Whale High Camp, in which style *The Old Dark House* is the uncontested masterpiece. It is an uncharacterisic début for Laughton: usually florider by far than any of his fellow-actors, in this film, he is virtually the straight man – not by any restraint on his part; far from it – he is splendidly full-blooded as a class-conscious Yorkshire businessman. Simply that never before or since has a director assembled such a cast of living gargoyles: Ernest Thesiger, with his air of a scandalised vampire; Boris Karloff, monumentally inarticulate; Eva Moore as Thesiger's sister, deaf and scowling; Elspeth Dudgeon as Thesiger's 102-year-old *father*. That Laughton makes any impact at all in his straightforward role is a remarkable achievement. Priestley had written the piece as an experiment in endowing the horror-story with 'overtones of psychological symbolism'. Laughton humanizes the conventional character, refusing to allow either writer or director to manipulate him. His bluff gaucheness at what must certainly be the most awful dinner party in the history of movies (waited on by Karloff, presided over by Thesiger, offering potatoes as if they were lice, and dominated by Eva Moore, cramming food down her gullet in fistfuls) is properly funny; but what marks the performance as distinctively his is his pointing up of something he always went after in a part: the plight of the underdog – in this case, as again, so often, the social and the sexual underdog.

The speech in which he describes his loathing for the bosses whose sneering drove his wife to suicide, and him to becoming a capitalist himself in revenge, is full of real feeling, the more remarkable because he allows it to emerge from his bluffness, and then to disappear back into it. Another actor might have sought to explain the character in terms of his bitterness; not Laughton. He simply states it: there is this, and there is this. You add it up.

Another original colour that he contributes is in the scene where his mistress, the good-time girl Gladys duCane tells him – rather unexpectedly, it must be said, in the development of the narrative – that she's going to desert him for the Melvyn Douglas character. He receives the news firstly with anger, then resignation, then – the Laughton touch – an odd, bashful tenderness: an affectionate forgiveness, which, in the prevailing preposterous context, is touching.

Laughton had no very warm feelings for any of the cast (though of course he had previously been directed by, and was later himself to direct, Raymond Massey). He never cared for Karloff; as for Thesiger . . . Elsa Lanchester describes a dinner-party she gave in Hollywood which sounds not much less awkward than that in the film. Rogers, the chauffeur-cook, had made and served the meal. When he brought in the main course, lamb, Thesiger spotted the slightly green apples accompanying it, and pointed at them. 'Arsenic apples!' he cried.

For *The Old Dark House*, Laughton was on loan to Universal; in a sense, he was on loan to the world of James Whale, as well. Stylisation was never a mode he cultivated: excess, certainly, but always to expressive end. The excess in Whale's film is a *reductio ad absurdum* so complete that it transcends its self-parody to attain to an absurdist vision. Laughton's art was always essentially a humanist one: his monsters were never born that way: they are never arbitrarily so: they were once otherwise, they could be again. Whale's characters haven't got a chance in hell. Mordaunt Hall (critic of the *New York Times*, not another character in the film – nor indeed the title part) welcomed the film with reservations – 'one may wonder why the motorists who seek refuge in the old dark house did not continue on their way immediately after encountering two or three of its occupants' – but was unqualified in his acclaim for Laughton's performance. 'It is a splendid portrayal.'

Paramount finally got their own script into shape by the time *The Old Dark House* was finished, and Laughton started to shoot the film he came to Hollywood to make: *The Devil and the Deep*, a vehicle.

It was to be Charles' first appearance before the American public: he had been released to Universal on the understanding that *The Old Dark House* would not be shown until after *The Devil and the Deep*. Jesse Lasky, head of Paramount, had great faith in Laughton, and liked to say afterwards that he had discovered him. The film's credits, after star billing for Tallulah Bankhead and Gary Cooper, end with the phrase: And Introducing the Eminent English Character Actor, Charles Laughton.

And Eminent English Character Acting, is, on the whole, what we get. It's not Laughton's fault that Tallulah's performance, dismissed at the time by both critics and herself, now seems an extraordinarily original portrait of an unfulfilled and oppressed woman, bored and unhappy, oddly attached to the paranoiacally jealous husband that Laughton plays. No doubt the wheel of fashion has turned to Laughton's disadvantage in this film, but now it is the uptight naval commander teetering on the brink of insanity who seems banal and obvious, while Bankhead's doomed chain-smoking beauty, burnt out by the emotional violence which has been done her, snatching an anonymous night in the desert with Cooper ('What do you want?' he asks. 'Never to have been born,' she says) is startlingly real. Cooper, too, with his voluptuously gentle masculinity and *nearly* wooden delivery, is spellbinding in a way that Laughton, infinitely the superior technician, and in a sense the more commanding personality, cannot manage. It is impressive, in a stagey way, but in terms of his development as a film actor, it is prentice work.

He knew it, too. He immediately recognised in Gary Cooper

something that was essential to film acting. 'He gets at it from the inside, from his own clear way of looking at life,' he said in an interview. For the rest of his life he always cited Cooper as the paragon of film acting, just as he continued to idolise Gerald du Maurier as a stage actor. His was the burden of the character actor: to turn yourself into a different actor for every performance – not merely to re-make the boundaries of your personality, but to shift your centre to accommodate them. Only then will the performance live – without that shift, the character will simply be an identification, not a reality.

His great achievement as an actor was to journey to the farthest reaches of his temperament and somehow make of the section of himself he was exploring, a whole man.

Not, alas, in *The Devil and the Deep* – except in certain scenes. The character he plays, Sturm, is shown in various social situations telling the same unfunny funny story, the telling being accompanied by a braying mirthless laugh. The laugh, and its relentless repetition, are brilliantly observed and reveal more of the man's insensitivity and pain than the explicit scenes of confrontation. There's a mechanical vivacity about the story and the laughter which creates an unforgettable image of a personality under pressure. Later, in the submarine, Laughton confronts Bankhead and Cooper. He falls into a sort of trance as he says to Cooper: 'Must be a happy thing to look as you do. I suppose women love you. It must be a happy thing' (a speech it is reasonably surmised Benn Levy wrote specially for Charles). As he speaks, his plump fingers stray onto his face, which he kneads into strange distorted shapes to make himself uglier than he is – a brilliantly original touch, painful to watch.

Sturm ends drowning in the sinking submarine. The scene called for hours of immersion in water, which Charles endured, even embraced, as he would so many physical trials in the course of 30 years of movie-making, in order to attain the reality of the character. He had a wretched time with Tallulah Bankhead, who had introduced herself by saying: 'So you're Charles Laughton. I hear you're going to be in *my* picture.' She despised the film, appeared to despise acting, and made no secret of her contempt for him. At every break in filming she played a record of *Falling in Love Again*. It is cruelly unfair that her continuance of this behaviour in front of the cameras should be so compelling, but that's life – or rather, that's show business, a phenomenon with which Charles Laughton had little connection.

Her comeuppance was, that it has taken fifty years for the quality of her performance to be recognised. As for Laughton: '*Newcomer Steals*

Show', said the *Los Angeles Times*. 'His is the outstanding histrionic contribution,' said the *New York Times*. He was set.

Paramount's next project for him was *The Sign of the Cross*. Cecil B. de Mille had chosen Wilson Barrett's play to mark his return to the studio on a new footing, and in his autobiography claims that when he saw Laughton in *Payment Deferred* in London, he knew that only he could play Nero. 'He was a fat man in a heavy moustache dressed in drab business suits for his role as a Dulwich householder, as far removed as may be from the decadent splendours of Imperial Rome; but he was inevitably Nero to my eye, for I saw in Charles Laughton the incredibly wide range of talent which makes every role he plays seem as if it had been tailored just for him.'

These handsome praises are somewhat ironic in view of the fact that Laughton was now confident enough flatly to refuse to play the character the way C. B. wanted him to. One can again only marvel at the certainty of purpose and strength of will that enabled the thirty-three-year-old chubby Englishman (six years out of drama school) to take on the Tsar of All the Rushes, the prototypical Director as Field Marshall, complete with uniform, maker of some of the biggest – in every sense – films of all time. In fact, de Mille was not a bully, simply an organiser; and he was fighting a battle against the front office throughout shooting, so he acquiesced in Charles' conception of the Emperor as feckless, theatrical, effeminate – as, to put it bluntly, an outrageous queen, even to the extent of furnishing him, as requested, with a totally naked young athlete to sit by his side during every scene. (Laughton had suggested Elsa to play the catamite, but de Mille, getting into the swing of things, proposed the young man.)

As ever, Charles had done his research, read his Sinkiewicz, too; but his conception of Nero had probably less to do with history or Polish literature than with a desire to avoid another heavy villain – which was de Mille's notion of the character – a longing to be funny (which he always claimed to enjoy more than anything else) and finally a yearning to step out of the sexual closet, however briefly and however fictionally. Elsa Lanchester shrewdly observes that playing Nero probably did him more good than a year's psychiatry.

The autobiographical nature of his acting thus continued. There is a wonderful freedom about his performance, his puffy white flesh – of which a great deal is on display – quivering with delight. His physical conception of the role seems to be heavily indebted to Aubrey Beardsley's Salome illustrations – more particularly his cruel caricature of Oscar Wilde. Elsa calls the performance 'Charles' wild

Wilde Nero' and that's just what it is. Agate, in his review, wrote: 'As Nero, Mr Charles Laughton enjoys himself hugely, playing the Emperor as the flaunting extravagant queen he probably was.' His contemporaries knew exactly what he was up to.

De Mille was allegedly in despair when the audience laughed at the previews. Exactly what he'd intended, countered Charles. The brilliant notices and wonderful business (despite the crash of '33) mollified de Mille to the point where he was able to write his mellow memories twenty-five years later.

It must be conceded that Laughton's performance somewhat compromises de Mille's moralising scheme: to hell with the Christians, the person we want to see is Nero, drawling epigrams, licking grapes, madly laughing. Peter Ustinov's later performance of the same character (in Melvyn Leroy's *Quo Vadis*) though witty in its own right, quite lacks the anarchy and the danger of Laughton's monstrous perverse baby, strutting and fooling and (yes, of course) fiddling while Rome burns.

The babyishness of Nero is shared by many of his characters, especially – for satirical purposes – those in power or, more pathetically, the oppressed. It was as near as he came to depicting innocence. The actual vulnerability of childhood coupled with the fantasies of omnipotence which are its antidote were well understood by Laughton. In the case of Nero, he was also amused to allude to the Fascist dictators of the period: but his perception of all power was the same: a childish charade. He never allowed a ruler any dignity.

At the end of filming, de Mille asked him who he'd like to play next, and, with the cheek which had informed his portrayal of Arnold Bennett in *Mr Prohack*, he replied: 'You'.

He'd done his two films for Paramount; in theory he was free to return to England. He didn't. He signed for one more picture; and then another. He was beginning to get a sense of what he could do with the medium.

His next film, *Payment Deferred* (producer Irving Thalberg, director Lothar Mendes), did not greatly increase his knowledge in that regard, but it is an indispensable record of his stage work. It is quite startling, though not strictly a film performance (in Orson Welles' definition, it dictates to the camera rather than inviting). The essential grammar of all Laughton's subsequent performances is there: the heavy lids, the sense of barely contained energy, the sexual voluptuousness a millimetre below the surface, the sudden accelerandos and heart-stopping ritardandos. His mastery of the elusive territory between lower-middle and middle-middle class is as subtle and as striking as it would ever be. But it is the number of variations he manages to create in this stock character that is breathtaking. From testy paterfamilias, to downtrodden clerk, to homicide, to newly-awakened lover (in the scene with his vampish neighbour, 'Madam Collins') the range of his William Marble is extraordinary. If one of the essential attributes of great acting is to offer value for money, Laughton was already, at the age of 34, a great actor.

The film failed at the box office, but, according to *Kine Weekly*, 'he proves, if proof were necessary, that he is one of the screen's greatest actors.'

There were incidental consequences to the making of *Payment Deferred*: one was his association with Irving Thalberg, with whom he formed an immediate bond, and but for whose demise (three years later) his subsequent professional development might have been quite different.

The other was the departure of Elsa Lanchester. Her independent career and indeed existence had ground to a halt. She was 'the wife', both socially and in reality: at the rate Laughton was working she can have seen little of him: late at night or early morning. Visiting him at the studio would not be a good idea. Nothing is more distressing for an out-of-work actor than to visit a place of others' work. Elsa's bright acerbic self would not take well to sympathetic enquiries. They may not even have known that she *was* an actress.

An unemployed actor in Hollywood is a citizen without a state. When the part of Winnie Marble in *Payment Deferred* – her part in both London and New York – went, despite Laughton's championship of her, to Maureen O'Sullivan, she simply went back to England, to look for a new house for them, to pick up a little self-respect.

Charles plunged into the next massive role: Dr Moreau in the film of H. G. Wells' novella, now called – why? – *Island of Lost Souls*. The shoot was full of physical discomfort, the director Earle Kenton (despite the cinematographer, Karl Struss' description of him as 'the most intelligent man I ever worked with') was pompous and bullying, and the part of the obsessed and sinister scientist was disturbing.

In it, as it happens, Laughton gives one of his very best performances. Perhaps the discomfort of the location (Catalina Island), the fog in which Struss immersed everything, and above all the presence of the restless and cooped-up animals created a kind of world of the imagination in which his creativity throve. He creates a frightening picture of a gentleman-monster, dabbling with the genetic basis of life, somehow suggesting that he himself is one of his own half-animal/ half-humans. The impression, which Laughton was particularly skilled at suggesting, that his clothes and indeed his very body can barely contain overwhelming impulses and desires, creates a dimension in Moreau which is both frightening and sympathetic. He goes towards his ghoulish task with such relish. In a James Whale movie this would be funny or merely off-the-wall; *chez* Laughton it's a manifestation of the life-force, albeit a perverted one.

His last stand, whip in hand as the animals and mutants turn on him, is pitiful and terrible. It's hard to think of another actor who could bring it off.

The whole film is remarkably concentrated and powerful. Bela Lugosi is fine as Moreau's mutant servant who leads the revolt of the mutants. Despite the publicity campaign's Nationwide Search For The Panther Woman, the film was not a success. It was not released in England, where the censor banned it, claiming that its events were 'against nature.' 'So is Mickey Mouse,' Lanchester wittily observed.

As a kind of *bonne bouche* Laughton ended his first stint of film-making with one of his funniest and most economical performances: Phineas V. Lambert in *If I Had a Million*, Ernst Lubitsch's compendium movie tracing the effect of an unexpected windfall on eight different people. Laughton's sequence, directed by Lubitsch himself – each episode had its own director – immediately became a classic, and has remained so. It couldn't be simpler, but there is a kind of genius in Laughton's restraint.

He plays a clerk sitting at a desk, one of hundreds (in a shot anticipating Billy Wilder's similar one in *The Apartment*). The letter informing him that he's been given a million dollars arrives on his desk and is dealt with in due course. Nothing on the clerk's bespectacled, droopily moustached face betrays a flicker of reaction. He punctiliously lays the letter to one side, folds it, and places it in his pocket. He gets up, walks the length of the office to the corridor. He waits for the lift. He enters it. He ascends. He disembarks, walks down the corridor. He arrives at a door, he enters. Another door. He enters that. Again. Finally he arrives at the door of the President of the corporation. He knocks. He's told to enter. With exactly the same phlegmatic moon-face that he's borne all along, he blows a raspberry and departs. End of sequence.

Even now, when the film is shown, audiences generally cheer at this point. It is the perfect instance of the revenge of the underdog – in its comic mode. Laughton created many variations, tragic and comic, on that theme, but the pacing, the dead-pan, the even keel of the *If I Had a Million* sequence is a sort of perfection, in the league of the great silent comedians. Like many of them, he creates the laughter by his very expressionlessness: the audience supplies the thoughts. This power of suggestion, rather than statement, is not usually associated with Laughton (though certainly, of course, with Lubitsch). Laughton himself said that the whole journey to Hollywood had been justified by working with Lubitsch. Their styles and preoccupations blend so perfectly that it is impossible to separate their contributions.

À propos of *If I Had a Million* Elsa Lanchester regrets, in her book, that Charles didn't work with more great directors – or, she says, great men in any sphere. This seems a little harsh on someone who made films with Renoir, Hitchcock, Wilder, Preminger, and who was a close friend of Henry Moore, Albert Manessier, and Bertolt Brecht, but certainly it is sad that Laughton never worked again with Lubitsch.

(There is an amusing postscript to the making of Laughton's section of the film. The producers were informed that the English censors would not accept the final raspberry: it would be necessary to make an alternative ending. Laughton himself proposed the replacement gesture: an unequivocable Vs up sign. He must have been as surprised as anyone to hear that the censors accepted this and it was duly made, causing shocks of delight among English audiences who could scarcely believe their luck.)

It is worth recalling again that Laughton had by the end of 1932, his first year in Hollywood, completed six major films, playing opposite and alongside world-famous stars (*If I Had a Million* alone boasts Charles Ruggles, W. C. Fields, Gary Cooper, George Raft). He had been acclaimed every time, generally deemed to have 'stolen the film' on each occasion. He was unquestionably *A Star*, though he didn't yet realise the full significance of that, either in terms of the power it bought him, or the public acclaim he would begin to receive.

What is most remarkable is not his meteoric rise, astonishing though that is, but how well he handled it. The poise and the ease of his performance in the Lubitsch film is almost unbelievable from a young Englishman, just turned thirty-three years of age, with only six years professional experience behind him, gifted neither with great beauty or great social *savoir-faire*. Faced with overpowering personalities, men used to being obeyed and women used to being deferred to, a publicity machine unparalleled in world history, the promise of limitless wealth and unimaginable fame, his focus never veered from the work in hand. He concentrated on getting better and more truthful with every performance.

It was an unusual approach in Hollywood, in 1932.

London Again

Agate: 'It will be extremely interesting when Mr Charles Laughton returns to these shores to see whether the crowd queues up for him as it does for a new actor who threatens to become a rival of La Garbo or La Dietrich . . . the reception accorded Mr Laughton when and if he comes will tell us which way the battle swings as between theatre and cinema.'

In fact, Laughton stepped off the ship to be greeted by a horde of photographers and journalists, at whom he flourished, symbolically, a walking-stick he brought back as a present. 'Who is it for?' they cried. 'The greatest actor of us all,' he answered. 'Who? Who?' 'I should have thought you would have guessed: Sir Gerald du Maurier, of course.' No movie star: the doyen of the English profession.

Laughton had come back to London almost certainly intending to resume his brilliant stage career. Virtually everything he had done in the theatre had been hugely successful. The range of work had been remarkable too, though it had not encompassed the classics. He wanted to push himself in every way, emotionally, physically and technically, and that meant the classics, which are both a training and a test. In London in 1933, *that* meant the Old Vic, the only theatre regularly performing a classical repertory.

Laughton wasn't an especially firm admirer of the Vic, which he found both dingy and worthy. Design – always a preoccupation of his – was a low priority, perhaps even somewhat frowned upon by Lilian Baylis, the Vic's formidable manager. Laughton wasn't an especially firm admirer of hers, either. He found her penny-pinching, pious and Philistine. However, the stimulating young Tyrone Guthrie was about to take over the artistic directorship, determined to shake the place up, so when Flora Robson brought them together over dinner, and they sparked each other off, a deal was struck: Charles and Flora would head the company for Guthrie's first season.

Lilian Baylis was as wary of Laughton as he was of her. She disliked film stars, in fact any stars at all, claiming that they brought the wrong kind of audience to the Vic – the despised 'West Enders'. She was there to serve 'our people', that is, the local South East Londoners, the same audience for whom her Aunt Emma Cons had founded the Vic – principally to get them off the streets and out of the gin palaces and give them something uplifting to fill their minds with: opera for preference, but Shakespeare (*most* of Shakespeare) would do – cheaper, too.

This approach to running the national theatre, which was what, by default, the Vic had become, was ludicrous to Charles. As an ex-hotelier he abhorred the drabness with which the theatre was run; as an intellectual, he despised the lack of artistic vision behind Baylis' attitudes. As a downright Yorkshireman, he was moved to cussedness by her (Anglo-South African) cussedness.

She guessed that he would want more money than her regular actors, and she suspected that he was merely *using* the Vic to learn how to act; and she was right, on both counts. He asked for £15 a week, instead of £10; and he had no Shakespearean experience. On the other hand, his salary in Hollywood had been $2,500 a week; and he was one of the most brilliant and acclaimed actors in England. Their relationship was full of little balance sheets like that.

Something she never really forgave him was that he brought with him a grant of some £1,750. He had approached the Pilgrim Trust and secured the money on the understanding that it would only be spent on costumes for plays at the Old Vic – not opera or ballet. What enraged her about this was that she had herself unsuccessfully approached the Pilgrim Trust on many occasions. They had been flattered by Laughton's movie fame into parting with the money: and with conditions! It was insupportable. But she did of course support it, because she needed the money so desperately. It rankled deeply, however, and eventually had a somewhat ugly outcome.

The incident encapsulates their difference of attitude. He wanted, as anybody would, anybody, that is, except someone with 'a wilful desire to run the theatre like a parochial charity', to improve standards of design. He would therefore use his new-found fame to divert some money towards the Vic. Simple. She, on the other hand, saw his move as typically swanky and West Endy and patronising. Acting in her theatre was known as 'helping the Vic': this was not helping the Vic, this was trying to take it over.

And so they stuck. His frustration and desire to take short-cuts is understandable; but her back-against-the-wall attitude has a certain nobility. To her the theatre was neither a commercial nor a cultural activity: it was a welfare service, *ad majorem gloriam dei*, akin to the facilities offered by the soup kitchens on the Embankment. Luxury of any kind was irrelevant and possibly harmful. It was the actors' *duty* to act at the Vic (for as little as possible); it was the audiences' *duty* to attend performances. Pleasure and passion had little to do with it. Laughton's great expressive soul, throbbing with pain and the longing for beauty, baulked at this.

Nonetheless, the season was planned: 'The Laughton Invasion,' as a somewhat unfriendly chapter heading in *Old Vic Saga*, by Harcourt ('Billy') Williams, Guthrie's predecessor, has it. Laughton would play Lopakhin, Henry VIII, Angelo, Prospero, Chasuble, Tattle and finally Macbeth: the whole gamut.

The season would open in October: meanwhile, two films, one in Hollywood for Paramount, the other, in England. This latter was the last thing Laughton could have predicted when he came back from America. 'English motion picture production will not begin to rival those from the mills of Hollywood for more than ten years,' he told journalists. But he hadn't met Alexander Korda yet.

Né Sándor Kellner, Korda had adapted his name from his *nom de plume* as a young Budapest film critic: *Sursum Corda*: lift up your hearts. This slogan appropriately describes his effect on the British film industry of the early thirties. He had moved from film capital to film capital in the manner engagingly described in his nephew Michael's book *Charmed Lives*: taking the largest suite in the largest hotel, eating in the best and most expensive restaurants, taking a box at the opera and moving about in a Rolls Royce – all of this on credit, of course – until the people that matter are so intrigued that they invite you to dine with them and eventually they give you money and you make a film. This infallible routine had been practised in Berlin, perfected in Paris, and polished in Hollywood, leaving in its path a number of unremarkable films, and a couple of good ones: *Marius*, in Paris, and *The Private Life of Helen of Troy* in Hollywood. The English operation was just beginning.

Already there had been *Service for Ladies* (another thing Korda knew a lot about) and *Wedding Rehearsal* – 'that amusing satire on Mayfair marriages.' But Korda was looking for something more substantial to launch his new company with. He immediately saw the potential of Laughton, rapidly rising in Hollywood. Typically he launched his brilliant, charming offensive by *cherchant la femme*: Elsa. He intimated to her that he was looking for a vehicle for her and Charles: an adaptation from the French called *Gust of Wind*. It was witty and brilliant, with a wonderful part for her, and she never heard another word about it. The talk shifted to a historical subject: *Henry VIII's Fourth Wife*, she to play Anne of Cleves. Eventually it ended up where it was headed for all along, no doubt: the sequel to the Helen of Troy film, the predecessor of the Don Juan film: the middle film in the '*Private Life of . . .*' sequence, *The Private Life of Henry VIII*, with Charles as Henry and Elsa squeezing in as Anne.

There are many stories as to whose idea the subject was – Korda's preferred version that he'd overheard a cabbie singing Harry Champion's music hall hit 'I'm 'Enery the Eighth, I am' being as likely as any – but it hardly matters. It is a typical Korda notion: elegant, slightly risqué. Charles was an obvious choice for the part – or rather, vice versa. And it is true that the Holbein portrait *does* look like Laughton – or rather, vice versa.

The significance of it in Laughton's career is that for the first time he was in on a project from the beginning. He was all but co-producer of the film. It was he who instigated the passionate quest for authenticity; he who dragged Korda down to Hampton Court again and again. Such texture as the film possesses derives from his research and drive, and, of course, from his nonpareil performance as the king. There is a tension between the Viennese boudoir humour of Lajos Birò's script, cynical about politics and sex alike, and the authenticity and weight of both the settings and the central performance; but the tension adds a special flavour to the movie.

Korda was an unremarkable director, and the film has poor structure and little flair; it is well enough performed by Merle Oberon and Binnie Barnes and Robert Donat (and includes a creaky performance by Lady Tree which is a matter of some historical interest); there is the odd expressive shot by the cameraman, the lugubrious Georges Périnal, and Birò's dialogue has a knowing, if second-hand, wit ('Would your majesty consider re-marrying?' 'I would consider it . . . the triumph of optimism over experience!') But it is Laughton's film.

Although Elsa Lanchester is essentially of the James Whale school of acting – extraordinariness for extraordinariness' sake, of which her exceptional performance in *The Bride of Frankenstein* is the apotheosis – when working with Laughton, she often transcends her quirkiness. As Anne of Cleves she is at her very best, direct and sparkling and unexpected. Their bedroom scene together is the film's best. True, her German accent, despite intensive imitation of Elisabeth Bergner (*because* of intensive imitation?), is fairly ludicrous, betraying her background in revue; but they play together with perfect understanding (something Laughton may not always have received).

As for him: it remains one of the greatest things he did, and one of the most achieved performances of film history. Impossible though it now is to separate the actor from the image of the role – outside the hotel where he was born is a plaque with the silhouette of the king – and despite the facial resemblance, neither the casting nor the performance are at all obvious. Laughton had never played anything remotely like it before, and never played anything like it again (except of course, for the sequel, *Young Bess*). He had played perverted villains, haunted murderers, little men, a decadent emperor on the brink of madness – all complicated, troubled men, ill at ease with their bodies or put upon by their situation. Here he gives a performance of complete extroversion, direct, strong, forceful. He is capricious, but there isn't the slightest suggestion that Henry's beheadings were due to bloodthirstiness or cruelty. He is open of countenance, entirely masculine, and unhesitatingly self-confident. He is shown as susceptible to charms of music, and art, and female beauty. He himself is, in person, remarkably attractive. His plucked eyebrows open his eyes out even further, the eye-shadow gives him a certain sensuality, and he shows a fine calf and a dainty foot.

In fact, he becomes the very image of the Tudor age: vigorous, straightforward, on occasion melancholy. He had told Agate that he intended to play him 'not as a phallus with a crown, but as the morbid introspective fellow he actually was.' On the contrary, he shows him to be impulsive, tender, generous. He refrains from portraying this particular monarch as a baby, preferring to show him as a toddler; with all the velocity of a newly initiated walker, he hurls himself across rooms, snatching at people and things along his way. That characteristic Laughton device, the sudden spurt, is employed to brilliant effect, as is its vocal equivalent, the impatient bark.

It is not a portrait in depth; it is, rather, full-length: strong, clear, and solid. Its most remarkable quality is its is-ness. It has stopped being acting or writing or filming. It simply *is*, the phenomenon called Laughton's Henry. It rings true.

A clue to his achievement of this quality, and of his general approach, was given by Laughton in a *Sunday Express* interview: 'I cannot quite say how I got my conception of Henry VIII. I did not take any historical acceptance of the man. I suppose I must have read a good deal about him, but for the rest I spent a lot of my time walking around the old Tudor Palace at Hampton Court, getting my mind accustomed to the square, squat architecture of the rooms and the cloisters. I think it was from the architecture of the houses and the rooms that I got my idea of Henry.'

It is also, of course, a remarkable technical achievement: but we have had those from other actors and yet they have remained mere displays of skill. The ageing is superlatively done by Laughton, each phase marked by a thickening of the body and a slowing of gait, till the old king (who really *has* become a baby!) is sunk into infant cunning and greed. The thirty-four-year-old man has disappeared completely, but then few people would, on meeting, have thought the tubby diffident slightly obstinate young man they might have met at supper the same person as the massive, centred titan exploding in Jovian laughter that hits the screen.

The production was somewhat delayed, so all Laughton's scenes were shot together – which may have added to the sense of white hot work – to enable him to take up his next task: the fifth instalment of his contract for Paramount, *White Woman*. Back to Hollywood he went; back to $2,500 a week, instead of the £1,000 he took for the whole of *Henry VIII*.

The entire Korda film had cost £50,000, a pittance, with all the players on a percentage in lieu of larger salaries. Initially, it seemed that they might never see any percentage payments, because the film proved impossible to place. Finally, United Artists somewhat reluctantly agreed to distribute it, and Korda, as if to trumpet the internationalism of the British film industry, staggered the première over three countries: Paris, New York, then London, where it opened on 23 October 1933. Shrewdly handled by Korda, the film burst on the three cities in triumph. It was a milestone for Korda, who built his whole subsequent empire on the strength of it; for the British film industry, which for the first time was taken seriously in the international film world; and for Laughton, who was also established in a way that he had not yet been. It was a crucial breakthrough. Hitherto he had carried character acting to the threshold of stardom – always held back by the eccentricity (euphemism for unpleasantness) of the characters he played. Here he was without qualification *A Star*: thanks in large part to the normality of the man he played. It was the only part for which he won an Oscar – only the seventh to be awarded, and the second to an Englishman. He didn't collect it in Hollywood; he was playing at the Old Vic, and read about it in an announcement on the Stage Door noticeboard. (When he did collect it, at a dinner in London, he took his audience somewhat by surprise in his acceptance speech: 'It was a sporting gesture – but there's the man who should have won it' – and he pointed to Walt Disney. 'There's your great man. Great because he is simple and unaffected.')

Certainly, however, the triple premières established Laughton in a new way. He was no longer the eminent English character actor, but a fully-fledged world-famous personality. The success of the film owed much to the Korda elements – the sexual naughtiness (having six wives! The stamina!) also (for 1933) the historical and monarchical irreverence; and then the ultimate extension of every stand-up comedian's wife gags: Henry beheads his when they get out of hand (lucky old Henry!). But Laughton received two of the greatest accolades available to an actor: confusion of the character and the actor ('Laughton,' the ads said, 'never raised his hands to a woman – he just chopped off their heads.' 'How to eat à la Charles Laughton: 1: Tear birds to shreds with your own hands . . . 5: Finish meal with a few choice burps.'); and imitation. Every street-corner, saloon bar, drawing-room and green-room mimic was doing his Henry. It came three times to Laughton, this accolade: with Henry, with Bligh, and again with Quasimodo. It is a rare and extraordinary tribute. Critically the film was applauded to the echo – but it was Laughton that dominated every review.

While the fate of the movie was still unknown, Laughton was back at Paramount, turning his attention to the wretched hack-work of *White Woman*, a Malaysian farrago directed by Stuart Walker and co-starring Carole Lombard. Curiously, however, possibly still high from the work on *Henry*, perhaps out of desperate boredom, he endows the character of Horace Prin, 'King of the River', with a colourful life all of his own, starting with a great curving moustache, going on to a Cockney accent owing more to the music hall than the sound of Bow Bells, ending up in an odd, jaunty, rolling walk. The whole effect adds up to something that surely cannot have been envisaged by the screenplay writers. They seem to have written him as a conventionally cruel river trader. With his giggling and teasing and playacting, Laughton adds many layers of refinement to Prin's unpleasantness. Using a whole battery of tics – screwing up his eyes, scratching his head, pulling at his moustache – he creates an impression which is oddly satirical – not Laughton being satirical (though he may easily have been sending up the script) but of Prin mocking everything, even language itself. The character takes a turn

for the Conradian when the natives start revolting: his mockery turns
to existential recklessness, spitting in the face of a delegation from the
Chieftain. The last scene of the film shows him playing cards with his
mate, demonically disregarding the ravening hordes outside, until the
mate is speared through the heart, at which he crossly says: 'And
here's me with a royal flush on me.' He then creeps out of the window,
presumably to death.

It's an original piece of acting, its preposterousness suggesting a
real malevolence, a kind of absurd comic destructiveness which in a
more credible setting, and with better support from the other actors
(Lombard, with whom Laughton could establish no rapport
whatever, is really quite sensationally bad), might have been very
striking indeed. 'Mr Laughton' said the *New York Times*, 'has an
enormous variety of technical tricks of voice and expression, and he
can enliven a performance even when it does not seem worth the
trouble . . . he provides another of his mincing portraits of murderous
and pathological scoundrels, leavening the character with his own
brand of sardonic humour.'

Charles Bickford plays the mate, well, and though, apparently,
they didn't get on, they act together very successfully. In particular
Bickford's entrance brings forth a remarkable display of flirtatious-
ness from Laughton, an eyeing up and down and a batting of eyelids
that adds another dimension of ambivalent malevolence to the
character.

Laughton used to invite the juvenile lead, Kent Taylor, and
Bickford, to his dressing-room, where he would rehearse scenes with
them, often suggesting interpretations quite different to those of the
director, which were, apparently, adopted. It takes a peculiar force of
personality, or at least a peculiarly high professional status, for this to
be acceptable to other actors – not to mention the director. Usually it
is regarded as a breach of etiquette. Everything, of course, depends on
the manner of doing. Very probably, if later reports from other
Laughton films are to be believed, he would suggest a mutual
examination of the scene in question, but then quickly take the lead –
become a teacher. He had certain intentions for his character; he knew
it would be impossible for him to achieve them in isolation; so he
attempted to 'guide' the other actors towards complementing his
work. It has never been suggested that he ever imposed reactions,
inflexions or gestures on his colleagues.

He was already taking a close interest in the whole film, never
simply *turning in a performance*; and on a film like *White Woman*, the

prevailing cynicism and perfunctoriness of the approach would lead him to more frequent interventions.

It is not necessarily a recipe for becoming liked.

Old Vic

As Laughton returned from America to begin rehearsing at the Old Vic, he was wired by Korda not to disembark at Plymouth, to carry on to Cherbourg where Elsa would meet him and travel with him to Paris for one of the world premières of *The Private Life of Henry VIII*.

The morning after, they read the brilliant notices at Le Bourget airport, hopped on the plane, and returned to London to start rehearsing *The Cherry Orchard* in the Waterloo Road that afternoon.

This breathtaking and rather enviable itinerary – wrapping one movie, attending the glittering première of another, starting rehearsals for an eight-month season of leading classical roles – reveals a small fact of some academic interest; namely, that Laughton was not contracted to the Vic Season, as Guthrie misremembers and most other accounts repeat, because of his success in *Henry VIII* on account of its not yet having opened. He was none the less already known – and perceived – as a *Hollywood* actor. Harcourt Williams in *Old Vic Saga* refers to him as 'the man from Hollywood'; and on the last night of the Vic Season, the gallery-ites called out 'Good Old Nero!'

The Cherry Orchard was the second play in the season, which had somewhat unhappily begun with *Twelfth Night*, featuring the eccentric casting of Lydia Lopokova, Mrs Maynard Keynes, ex-prima ballerina in the Diaghilev Company. Not only her Russian accent but also her habit of illustrating her emotions with expressive hand gestures had proved baffling; nor had another of Guthrie's innovations, a permanent setting designed by the distinguished architect, Wells Coates, met with much enthusiasm. It gave the production, in Guthrie's words, 'a suggestion, not of Illyria, but a fancy mess ball on a battleship.' However, it was a strong company, which, minus Mme Lopokova, went on to the Chekhov play: Athene Seyler as Mme Ranyevskaya, Leon Quartermaine as Gayev, Ursula Jeans, Flora Robson, James Mason, Marius Goring in other parts. The translation was by Guthrie's brother-in-law, Hubert Butler –

light, clear, fast-moving; very different, like the production itself, from the twilight Chekhov favoured by the English stage of the period. 'There must be a translation in manners as well as in language,' Guthrie wrote in the programme note. 'I hope we have not so botched the attempt as to substantiate the conception that Chekhov is "morbid" or foster the idea of "Russian gloom." '

The Laughtons had arrived halfway through rehearsals, and critical comment noted a certain unease in Charles' first night performance as Lopakhin. Fleet Street, of course, had been baulked of its first night sensation. It wanted Charles to split a gut, raise the roof, whip up a storm or, just as acceptably, fall down a great hole. Agate (who had expected none of those things) observed: 'Mr Laughton as was to be expected, made more of Lopakhin than has ever been made in this country. But,' he continued, 'as was also to be expected, this great artist put no more into the character than Tchekhov intended, thus blasting the hopes of anybody looking to see him gaze out of the window solicitous for bodies interred in the cherry orchard!' The photographs of the performance suggest a completely real, socially awkward kind of business man (he played the part with a distinct Yorkshire burr) with some emotional depths. Alec Guinness remembers Laughton's work as deeply impressive: subtle and delicate. In an end-of-season retrospective, Agate writes: 'His Lopakhin in *The Cherry Orchard* was a superb study of character in the best sense of that word, and that it was not hailed as the finest piece of acting in town, which it demonstrably was, can only be attributed to the fact that the part is not a spectacular one.' Realism was at the heart of Laughton's approach: if his dramatist had written an extravagant character, to whom sensational events occurred, then Laughton sought the reality of situation and character, and it was that, as Marius Goring has pointed out, that so astonished contemporary audiences. Accustomed to *Grand Guignol* as they were, they were astounded to have it taken seriously. When melodrama is played like Tom and Jerry, that is, nobody's really hurt, then it's harmless. If the dreadful events of *Maria Marten* or *The Bells* become real, they are deeply distressing to behold. What made Irving great was what made Laughton great. In a sense, it requires greater reserves of passion and imagination to carry those plays off than when you're supported by a text of distinction with a mature world-view.

But the same realism that had animated those contrived vehicles, when brought to a play of Chekhov's resulted in the same truth-to-life; the life was simply a less sensational one.

It was the third production of the play in which he'd appeared. He'd done it at RADA (Yasha – the part played at the Vic by James Mason) and at Barnes. Later, in Los Angeles, he played Gayev in his own production. He would seem to have been supremely equipped to play in Chekhov, and any picture of Laughton which takes no account of this virtually unknown side of him is partial. The phrase most often used of Chekhov is also the one which perhaps best describes Laughton's work: poetic realism. Barnstorming, 'hamming', the things of which he's most often accused, were modes into which he fell at the end of his career when he had transferred his creative aspirations into other media.

His next part was Henry VIII. By this time the film had had its spectacular premiere which Charles had attended with all six wives. On stage it was bound to disappoint, and duly did. Elsa pertinently observes in *Charles Laughton and I*: 'after seeing a close-up of a character the 'flesh' is bound to be rather a comedown.' Shakespeare's character lacks the range even of the character in the film; and Guthrie's production (the first of several of a play which was to become his party-piece) was full of free-wheeling invention which only served to underline the weaknesses of the play and distract attention from the central figures. Flora Robson scored a success as Queen Katharine; Marius Goring was singled out for his Cardinal Campeius; Robert Farquharson, rumoured black magician and model for Dorian Gray, made a somewhat chilling impression as Wolsey; and the costumes, a mixture of John Armstrong's from the film for the king, and Charles Ricketts' from the Casson-Thorndike production of a few years before for everyone else, were acclaimed.

But Laughton disappointed. If Laughton *v* The Bard was the name of the game, then he still hadn't quite engaged. He was warming over something he'd done before. 'I am going to the Old Vic to learn how to speak,' the world famous film star had announced with touching humility. On the first day of rehearsals Lilian Baylis had said to him referring to an interview he'd given: 'We've all heard you sleep with Shakespeare under your pillow, dear. What we want to know is, can you speak his beautiful words?' (A successful plea of justifiable homicide could surely have been submitted on less provocation.) But it was what everybody wanted to know. And *Henry VIII* couldn't possibly tell them. So it was something of a non-event.

Agate had not liked the film, or Laughton's performance in it: 'a bundle of buffooneries,' he called it. 'His performance in the play has a distinction unattempted in the film . . . given Mr Laughton's interpretation, his performance must be hailed as virile and lusty and full of animal spirits' but 'one regrets Mr Laughton's choice of reading.' During the same week, Clifford Bax's modest play on the same subject, *A Rose without a Thorn* was revived, with Frank Vosper as Henry. ('Much the better play . . . the best Henry the modern stage has seen or is likely to see . . . if you met him in his nightshift, you would still know him to be King of England.') The comparison between the two actors ('I don't want anyone to run away with the notion that I hold Mr Vosper to be a better actor than Mr Laughton!') hinged on this question of kingliness. Agate the historicist and Agate the snob may have combined in disapproval of Laughton's revelation of the tribal chieftain underneath the velvet and gold thread; to us, it seems highly authentic, straight from the pages of Lacey Baldwin.

Agate's running commentary on Laughton's development is fascinating and enviable. He seemed passionately to care about the actor's growth, above all that he should know himself for what he was and cultivate himself within that knowledge. He freely used the word great in these public progress reports, and seemed to challenge Laughton to fulfil the claim. 'On the whole,' he says of the film performance, 'it is no more than what one expected of him, which in the case of a really great actor means that he has failed. For the really great actor always gives you something which you did not anticipate.'

Laughton's Angelo was something which no one anticipated. *Measure for Measure* was rarely revived, on the grounds of both structural weakness and scandalous morality. The board of the Old Vic needed some persuading to include it in the season. Baylis didn't much care for it, either; on the occasion of its last revival she had told the director, Harcourt Williams, 'if we were doing it to help a *clinic*, that would be all right, but . . .' It was not thought to be particularly rewarding for the actors, either: the Duke a windbag, Isabella a prig, Angelo a cold, unattractive figure, with few lines to boot. 'The trouble with yer Angelo,' said Donald Wolfit to Marius Goring, 'the trouble with yer Angelo . . . is yer *duke*.' All this was transformed after Guthrie's production.

For this, the dear old Permanent Setting finally came into its own, with its twin columns, its platform and tiring room, and the steps leading down from either side, while curtains billowed all around. It enabled Guthrie to move the action along at great speed, while concentrating the focus for the numerous duologues; its formality was well adapted to his satirical sense of the play's *deus-ex-machina* dénouement. 'Since what obviously sets out to be a tragedy peters out halfway through the evening, the resolution has been wisely taken to turn the rest of it into the best kind of Cochran revue.' (Agate, of course.) The costumes were largely responsible for the visual dimension of the production, and were universally admired ('unimaginably lovely'). Roger Livesey manfully tackled the part of the Duke; James Mason didn't think much of his own performance as Claudio when he wrote his memoirs, but was well enough liked at the time; Elsa Lanchester played Juliet and, as a singing page, sang 'Take, O take those lips away'. Flora Robson, who played Isabella, wrote Guthrie, 'suggested an uncompromising and splendid young Scotswoman in difficulties on the Continent.' But then he thought both Robson and Laughton 'were oddly and wrongly cast. Laughton,' he said, 'was not angelic but a cunning oleaginous monster, whose cruelty and lubricity could have surprised no one, least of all himself.' But Laughton, with perfect textual justification, chose to play Angelo the other way round, as it were. Instead of playing the traditional cold puritan who is overwhelmed by violent and unprecedented desires, he played a man who has long repressed nameless longings, which now demand expression. One need barely speculate on the source of this interpretation; to which he added contemporary overtones of the rising Fascist dictators. What was remarkable, though, was not the interpretation, but the realisation.

Even now, the photographs of the production have the power to disturb. John Armstrong's costume for him turns Laughton into a terrible black bird, or, as many observers felt, a bat, while his features are full of dark malignant horror: 'When the actor shows us Angelo in the scene where he bargains with Isabella, brooding over the girl like a lustful black bat, he gives a glimpse of such murky depths in the man's nature that we no longer despise him for his sins. Instead we admire him that he fought his temptations so long.' This acute account – by W.A. Darlington, in the Daily Telegraph – is a masterly description of the Laughton effect. He doesn't tell you what to think or feel – he neither manipulates nor editorialises – he brings you face to face with the thing itself. That scene, according to Fabia Drake, was so overwhelming 'that an inner, awful excitement generated itself throughout the audience. When . . . Isabella says, as she leaves him. 'Save your honour,' Angelo replies, in an aside to himself, 'From thee even from thy virtue.' All the horror of what we sense may come to pass was encapsulated in those hardly-breathed six words.' Fabia

Drake accounts the performance 'one of the four truly great performances in a long lifetime of theatre-going.'

Marius Goring watched every performance that Laughton gave
during that season: he attributed the overwhelming impact of Angelo
to Laughton's mastery of close-up technique, which he somehow
adapted to the theatre. This is what Agate was describing when he
wrote: 'whenever the actor comes to anchor to deliver his soliloquies
of torment the house falls into a hush the like of which is rarely heard
in our theatre.' Obviously this performance was, like his William
Marble in *Payment Deferred*, phenomenal. 'It is a terrifying piece of
work,' said Darlington. The greatest tribute came from Lilian Baylis.
She never missed a performance of the Isabella-Angelo scenes. Sitting
in her stage-box, frying her sausages, she whispered to Marius Goring
as he passed by for an entrance: 'There are lots of things I don't like
about that man – but I don't want to miss a minute of this.'

A number of factors were involved in the achievement of this tour-
de-force. Firstly, without doubt, he discovered a deep identification
with Angelo: repression, hidden desires, cruelty. 'In moiling and
toiling over the conflicting forces in Angelo, Charles actually seemed
to clear up a kind of hangover that he had within himself, probably
caused by religious upbringing and the war,' wrote Miss Lanchester
in 1938. (In 1982, in her autobiography, repeating the sentence, she
deleted the last clause.) Secondly, the part is a relatively short one. He
was able to concentrate his energies and sustain the massive emotional
intensity without having to drive the play. Agate wrote: 'Continuing
his backdoor attacks upon the Shakespearean drama, Mr Laughton
has now promoted himself to that side-entrance which is Angelo.'
Thirdly – and I am inclined to rate this very highly – he had time for
preparation. Elsa Lanchester notes that he and John Armstrong had
been talking about ideas for a production of the play for a long time,
even down to cuts in the text and design possibilities. It had been
germinating in his mind for nearly three years, in fact, and he had
filled out every corner of the role with intense feeling. The tasks he set
himself as an actor were enormous; he needed time for the imaginative
connection to possess him completely.

And how did he speak 'the beautiful words'? 'Mr Laughton's voice
has not yet acquired the full resonance for blank verse' said Agate; but
it's more than simple resonance that blank verse needs – it's a sense of
pulse, an ability to sustain line-endings, an awareness of alliteration
and assonance. As it happens, however, Angelo's utterances are so
tortured and tortuous, the line – and the syntax – is so broken up by

emotional and mental twistings and turnings, that it is sometimes hardly verse at all.

So the great Laughton v Bard match was still unfought.

Agate concluded his account of Charles' Angelo thus: 'This performance whets the appetite which, after once more tantalising it with that dreary codger, Prospero, Mr Laughton promises presently to satisfy with his first attack on the real stuff – Macbeth.'

The dreary old codger – 'that endless chunnerer' – Agate was a thesaurus of abuse when it came to Prospero – 'that enchanting bore' – his exasperated dismissal of *The Tempest* and its central character was more common then than now – was played by Laughton as 'deriving snowily from Blake, Devrient's Lear, Michelangelo's Noah, M. Boverio's Noe, possibly Noah himself, and certainly Father Christmas. But alas, he made the old boy perform his hocus-pocus with a naughty little twinkle in his eye . . .'

Quite clearly, Laughton, and Guthrie, and just about everyone connected with the production, were all at sea. The Permanent Setting was off into the dock again, being replaced by a decidedly arid landscape, devised, James Mason darkly suggests, by Laughton himself and John Armstrong, who had imposed his surrealist tendencies on the set, at the expense of either atmosphere or reality. (Agate: 'an almost bare stage sparsely furnished with logs constructed out of pink Edinburgh rock, an igloo or wigwam made out of raffia as used by Miss Cicely Courtneidge for her production numbers, and three screens similarly fringed.') The Ariel songs were 'steel-furniture ditties'. The costumes, also by John Armstrong, 'succeeded in making the handsome actors look ugly and the ugly actors look funny,' according to Guthrie: his own direction, he admitted, was 'at once feeble and confused'.

The only positive comments about the production from any quarter are for Roger Livesey's Caliban ('a delicious monster compounded of Frankenstein and Petroushka') and Elsa Lanchester's Ariel. 'May I be forgiven for saying that until Miss Elsa Lanchester the part of Ariel has never been acted? . . . So impalpable to sight is this Ariel that his body seems to offer nothing to human glances. You see through him . . . in short, it is a lovely performance of exquisite invention.' The flying rig by means of which she was to have entered and left the stage was cut, but the performance still survived. And yet, during rehearsal she had been completely mystified by the part: 'I sat with Guthrie for hours, trying to interpret one great long speech that was very confusing. It was a little like learning ten alphabets in Greek backwards. Guthrie simply said he didn't know what the speech meant either.' Guthrie wrote: 'The only good thing was Elsa Lanchester's Ariel, weird and lyrical in a balletic style which was at odds with everything else in the production and which better direction would never have allowed.'

It has been suggested that Laughton insisted on playing Prospero instead of the Caliban for which he was obviously intended (James Mason says this); Benita Armstrong reports that Charles wanted to play Caliban, but was prevailed upon as the leading man of the season to play 'the old gentleman' (Agate again). On balance, it seems likely that Charles might have wanted a rest from monsters, and wanted to tackle the extended and elaborate verse that Prospero speaks. But of all Shakespeare's great characters, the usurped Duke of Milan is the least flesh-and-blood, the most schematised. There is a way of approaching the play and the character which sees *The Tempest* as a revenge play; or a working out of Shakespeare's own bitterness. But Guthrie's and Laughton's conception – in so far as they had one – seems to have inclined towards a rather arid sort of pantomime, from which nothing fruitful could come for Laughton. Agate wickedly suggests that, having failed to achieve Pickwick's benignity, he sought to make up for it as Prospero. 'Mr Laughton's failure is, however, more respectworthy than Sarah's [Bernhardt in *Lucrèce Borgia*]. She was merely following her stock-line of fascination, while he purposely discards familiar face-pulling, mowing and gibbering in order to extend his range. This is extremely good for Mr Laughton.'

The Tempest was extremely good for Mrs Laughton, too. As well as her biggest part in the season, it was 'my most serious and important acting relationship with Charles to date . . . in *The Tempest* our performances were almost entirely interdependent.'

In *Love for Love*, Congreve's Restoration comedy, their marriage saved large sections of the play being cut altogether. Somehow their matrimonial condition rendered the scenes between Tattle and Miss Prue, with their shameless *double entendres*, acceptable. Really *double entendre* is the wrong phrase, because their scenes together can only mean one thing. Miss Baylis and the Governors simply had to bite their lips and sit tight, because the production was an enormous success, gleefully staged by Guthrie, with Athene Seyler and Flora Robson as Mrs Frail and Mrs Foresight; three Liveseys, *père* and *deux fils*, as Sir Sampson, Ben and Valentine; and 'a clever performance of the servant Jeremy by Mr James Mason.'

Laughton obviously had a little holiday with Tattle: 'a delicious figure of fun and under-breeding, a mixture of wiggery and waggery, at once coy and servile, male yet mincing. This Tattle is a *Roi Soleil* about whom still hangs the barber's shop of his probable upbringing.' The photographs show another proto-Wildean figure, bustling with malice, which may have been quite a useful safety valve for him.

His next role, another Laughton-Lanchester number, was genuine Wilde: Chasuble in *The Importance of Being Earnest*. John Gielgud, in *Distinguished Company*, retails a fifty-year-old piece of gossip, namely that Guthrie initially cast Laughton in the part of John Worthing, but found him so unpleasant, that he persuaded him to play the Canon. There is no corroborative evidence for this. If it *was* Guthrie's feeling, he might have been amused to read in the *Daily Telegraph* review that 'there is no crime in the calendar of which I would not believe [Laughton's Chasuble] capable.' Agate found him 'out of the right cruet.' The revival was well enough liked, until all memories of it were effaced by John Gielgud's later production with himself, Edith Evans, Peggy Ashcroft and Gwen Ffrangcon-Davies: 'in my opinion,' wrote Guthrie, characteristically generous, 'the highwater mark in the production of artificial comedy in our epoch,' the only novelty of his own production being that 'Canon Chasuble appeared to be the leading part: Charles Laughton in a devastating, brilliant and outrageous lampoon.' It is hard not to suspect a strong element of anticlericalism in the performance, perhaps directed towards the incumbent of the stage-box, surrounded as she was by confessors and clerics of every shade.

Elsa was sharply reprimanded by Agate, feeling that Laughton's 'sacerdotal oil could not be said to blend with the vinegar of Miss Elsa Lanchester's Miss Prism. This young actress was recently said by me to have given one of the most beautiful performances I had ever seen; she now gives very nearly, and I really think quite, the worst!' 'On the last night,' she quite understandably writes, 'I think I had a good cry when I got to bed.'

And so to the real stuff. With *Macbeth* Laughton was decisively stepping into the ring. The haunted history of the play still daunts would-be interpreters. As usual, the superstition is based on practical factors: the play was frequently revived because one of the shortest in the canon; haste leads to accidents. Moreover, the part of Macbeth, due perhaps to the loss of a rumoured missing act in which the actor might have had time to recover himself, is one of the most physically punishing of all the great Shakespearean roles. Exhaustion leads to accidents too. Interpretatively, too, the character's Patton-like combination of soldierliness and poetic reflectiveness generally leads to the favouring of one element to the detriment of the other.

On every level, Laughton was at a disadvantage. Stamina, both vocal and physical, was his worst problem as an actor. Soldierly decisiveness was not in his scope; and though there was in his temperament a strong streak, in John Gielgud's phrase, of poetic imagination, the lyric and meditative modes were alien to him. The vein in Macbeth that he might most easily have tapped, the supernatural horror, was denied him by Guthrie, who cut the witches' scene. His programme note explained: 'by making the three Weird Sisters open the play, one cannot avoid the implication that they are a governing influence of the tragedy. Surely the grandeur of the tragedy lies in the fact that Macbeth and Lady Macbeth are ruined by precisely those qualities which make them great. All this is undermined by any suggestion that the Weird Sisters are in control of events.' Clearly Guthrie, notoriously shy of emotion and sensuality in the theatre, was equally uncomfortable with the occult. His production was the very last thing that Laughton's Macbeth needed to be: rational – or rather, rationalised.

When the play opened Laughton was the victim of·one of those ritual outbursts of blood-lust which seems to seize the critical fraternity when, after months of balance and qualification and hesitation, they unanimously sense a sitting-duck, upon which they fall with naked fangs, licensed to kill. There is always something unedifying about the spectacle, even at fifty years' distance, however bad the performance might have been: the unspeakable in pursuit of the unsuccessful. 'Alas! he cannot, for the life of him, observe the niceties of the iambic convention. And alas! alas! he cannot, for the life of him, manipulate a trailing robe. *He trips*! There was an unfortunate moment in his Macbeth. The banquet scene – Banquo's ghost. Mr Laughton's squeak and scurry of fear, clutching his showy skirts, would have been more appropriate to the distraction of some Roman magnate of the decadence, a Trimalchi aghast at a rat or a mouse, rather than the superstitious terror of a murderer before the risen spectre of his victim. However, of all Mr Laughton's performances at the Old Vic this season, his Macbeth is certainly the most interesting . . . He is not consistently exciting, but neither is he consistently dull. He never bores, though he might irritate, exasperate. He tends to a monotony of gesture and tone (he would be a great actor past question if he could keep his mouth shut).'(*Sketch*). *Daily Telegraph*: 'I am left

in doubt whether Mr Laughton understands Macbeth at all.'
Harcourt Williams: 'more the Sassenach tradesman.' *Daily Mail*: 'I
do not believe that Shakespeare intended Macbeth to be a petulant,
sulky schoolboy . . . nor do I believe that he would have ranted and
stamped his foot like a child of ten: he need not, I suggest, always have
soliloquised on A flat and allegro vivace at that. I can find no textual
evidence to support the idea that he looked in person like the bearded
lady at Mitcham Fair.' Agate: 'Mr Laughton was never within
measurable distance of any kind of grandeur, and his performance
beginning on the ground knew no heights from which to topple.'

Agate at least concluded his notice of the performance: 'if this
means that Mr Laughton is not a tragedian, I cannot help it; he
remains a great actor.' To this balm, Laughton might have added:
'None of the other Shakespeare roles Mr Laughton has played this
season has seemed to stir his imaginative sympathy so deeply.' (*The
Times*). Little else.

After a performance, James Bridie wrote to his friend Flora
Robson: 'My dear Flora, I didn't come back-stage to see you on
Wednesday afternoon because I was genuinely heart-broken. It's no
use lying about it, I thought your Lady Macbeth wrong, wrong,
wrong; lifeless, inept, even stupid . . . you acted Lady Macbeth like a
schoolgirl in a Dalcroze school in love with her head-mistress. Do read
the lines again before you go on, and get the horror of them into your
soul . . . do you know that when you said the Raven itself was hoarse I
expected you to follow up by saying when you had got the spare
bedroom ready for Duncan you'd go up and rub the bird with Sloan's
liniment . . . you are an artist of the theatre and a clumsy amateur of
philosophy. So is Tony. He is not as clumsy as you but he has it all
wrong. He is one of the "planning," "hard-thinking" brigade . . .'

Bridie's extreme and passionate reaction to Robson's performance
was not shared by the critics, who ranged from mild lack of
enthusiasm, to outright acclaim: 'This was the right actress in the
right part'; '. . . she took her chance magnificently.'

The first night was a bitter disappointment for Charles himself.
According to Guthrie, he was longing to play the role, and full of
interesting ideas. 'At the dress rehearsal his performance was electrifying. His acting that night bore the unmistakable stamp of genius.'
These words – electrifying, genius – were not frequently in the mouth
of Guthrie. He did not use them lightly. Fabia Drake was at that dress
rehearsal, and confirms the impression. Dress rehearsals, of course,
can be emotional, tired, affairs, in which, in the empty theatre, or just

surrounded by a few friends, with the set, the lights and the costumes together probably for the first time, judgements can blur. And indeed, something wonderful can under all those special and peculiar circumstances, take possession; and then disappear the following morning. For whatever reason, 'alas, he never again, except fitfully, recovered his greatness.' (Guthrie)

In the unique case of *Macbeth*, we have a scrap of evidence with which to reconstruct the performance: Laughton and the company recorded for the BBC the end of the play (Act V, scenes 5—7) from 'The Queen my lord is dead.' Making allowance for whatever inhibitions the radio studio imposed, it is still a vivid document. The recording is in fact quite ambitious: as well as three or four principals, there's a substantial group of soldiers, battles are fought, fanfares are sounded. It is reasonable to suppose that what we hear is a fair impression of how it sounded.

The first thing to note is Laughton's first utterance: significantly, it is non-textual: a deep sigh on hearing of the death of the queen. It is strikingly expressive. 'She should have died hereafter' wearily spoken, with a heavy stress on *died*. 'Tomorrow and tomorrow . . .' is soporific, the darkish brown voice monotonous, the cadences almost ecclesiastical. The messenger tells him that Birnam Wood is on the move: and he springs to life again with 'Liar and slave!' overlapping the dialogue, raging wordlessly. The subsequent 'if thou speaks't false' is also lumpily measured. He exits with animation, however. Roger Livesey as Macduff enters, with a radically different manner of speech – the elongated vowels and deliberately struck consonants of an earlier epoch – but spirited. When Macduff and Macbeth meet, Laughton starts to laugh: a laugh which at first seems to be merely melodramatic, but becomes genuinely chilling when it suddenly stops at Macduff's revelation of his Caesarian birth. In his final speech of defiance, Laughton for the first time uses the upper register of his voice, at the same time, rather engagingly, slipping into broad Yorkshire. The extract concludes with the twenty-one-year-old Marius Goring's very clearly spoken Malcolm.

There is no question but that Laughton is not skilled at using verse expressively. He alternates between the monotonous and the untextual. On the whole, the performance *qua* verse-speaking is featureless and flat. He doesn't take advantage of the medium, doesn't draw energy or sense from it. For him it's obviously a strait-jacket, from which he occasionally breaks to connect powerfully with a word:

'nothing' in 'signifying nothing' is memorably black, for instance.

He simply wasn't at home in verse. Records from his later years suggest that he never really came to terms with it. Why? Hardly lack of intelligence. Certainly not lack of work; he was obsessed by work, never leaving a problem alone till he was finished with it. No: what he found difficult was adapting his responses to the beauty and power of words, which he so keenly felt, to even as easy and loose a shape as the more-or-less iambic more-or-less pentameter. He had an astonishing command of rhetoric, and, as Charles Higham usefully points out, the *tirade*: the art of building a speech from climax to climax. In film after film, he would fit a speech, whether it was the Gettysburg address or something from the Bible, into his performance, and it would be spellbinding. He was a master of phrasing, and colour – but he must bring these from within – every pause and hesitation, every change of gear, every new register, from within, in response to a sequence of impulses felt by him. He couldn't get on the rails, preferring to make his own way down the middle of the tracks. By historical accident, it denied him access to the greatest roles in the English language, which happen to be in verse.

Laughton in verse, as the recording proves, was Laughton muzzled.

So he hadn't learned to 'speak' – though his voice was immeasurably strengthened, and his range of expression enlarged, by the end of the season. In fact, he had done his 'rep': a large variety of parts, some within his scope, some not. There wasn't the remotest possibility of his Prospero being anything other than a sketch; his Henry was neither here nor there; Tattle and Chasuble were fun, both for him and the audience; his Angelo was wonderful; and Macbeth was a disaster. A typical rep season, in fact. Unhappily for him, however, he wasn't a young actor cutting his teeth in the provinces: he was a world-famous film star, and a phenomenon of the West End stage.

It was an extraordinary thing for him to have done, humble and naïve at once. If he wanted to do a classical play, he could so easily have approached a West End manager: any one of them would have leaped at the chance. He could have had a company of his own; could have gone into management himself. But no, he wanted to go to the Vic. Not for itself, as we have seen. Nor was it glory, in which he was already covered anyway, that motivated him; not for him the reasoning of the young Laurence Olivier, four years later, taking the same route: 'To me, the Old Vic was the equivalent of the Old Bailey. Here

I would be judged for my classical work. Here I would pitch my stand and stake my claim. Here I could ease my way into the skin of the theatrical serpent, the skin that had been worn by Burbage down to Irving and Barrymore. There it was, pressed between the leather binding with the name William Shakespeare on the spine. There it lay, waiting to be moulded, shaped, hurled in the air and back again.' (*On Acting*). Laughton wasn't in competition for 'the mantle'; he didn't compare himself with the great dead; his hero was Gerald du Maurier who would no more dream of playing Shakespeare than fly. What he wanted was to do the work, and to do it quickly. He was deeply conscious of his late start, and of his lack of serious background. The Old Vic was his crammer.

'It is a real pleasure,' wrote Guthrie in the middle of the season, 'to work with such a marvellous band of enthusiasts. Several of the company are playing Shakespeare for the first time, and we have to work like niggers rehearsing the next play at the same time as we are playing the current piece. Fourteen hours out of the twenty-four spent in the theatre is an everyday occurrence.' Rehearsals started at 9.30, they broke at 5 for supper, and the curtain went up at 8. After the show, according to Elsa Lanchester, many of the company would troop back to the Laughtons' temporary service flat in Jermyn Street, where they would sit and eat sandwiches and drink and discuss the work till two in the morning. (Pure rep, again.)

Laughton didn't lead the company, as it were, from the front. His attitude in rehearsal was entirely egalitarian. He was quite open about his problems with the work, and was, Marius Goring admiringly observed, willing to try anything, not caring a fig whether it made him seem foolish. – At a certain point in rehearsals of *Macbeth*, for example, he came in in a state of great excitement: 'I've got it! I'm so sorry, I see it now: it's a *Scottish* play: Macbeth must be played Scots.' Guthrie: 'Interesting idea, give it a try.' After three days: Guthrie: 'It's no good Charles, worse than it was without, worth trying out.' So Charles gave it up. (The problem, Goring added, was that Charles couldn't do a Scots accent, anyway, it kept coming out Scarborough.)

The young actors were very excited by what they felt to be 'the new acting' that Laughton was essaying. Charles mumbled through the read-throughs, which was utterly unheard of, and greatly admired; and he never turned up with a finished performance. He was constantly exploring. Coupled with Guthrie's approach, brisk and brilliant and irreverent both to the Board and the Bard, the company was heady with excitement. John Allen wrote that it was 'far and away the

PAVILION HOTEL
SCARBOROUGH

Pavilion Hotel, Scarborough, Ltd.
Directors:
E., C., T. & F. Laughton
Telephone - 1040-1

A.A. ✱✱✱✱   R.A.C.

An advertisement for the
Pavilion Hotel during
the Laughtons' tenure.

Laughton in November 1928 at the time of *Pickwick*.
Charles and Elsa in February 1929.

Laughton as Hercule Poirot in *Alibi*, 1931.

WYNDHAM'S
THEATRE
London THE WYNDHAM THEATRES, LTD.   Lessee LEON M. LION

By arrangement with LEON M. LION
Mrs. EDGAR WALLACE presents

CHARLES LAUGHTON

On the Spot
A Play by
Edgar Wallace

PROGRAMME

THE PLAY

PICTORIAL

"ON THE SPOT"

No.
340

VOL.
LVII

1 s.
.NET

MONTHLY

On the Spot,
by Edgar Wallace,
1931, with Laughton
and Gillian Lind.

THEATRE WORLD SOUVENIR

Charles Laughton

Old Vic and Sadler's Wells

6

The two faces of Henry VIII. *Left*: Old Vic souvenir programme showing stage version. *Below*: London Films publicity photo showing screen version.

Opposite, top: Charles, Elsa and Mr J. C. Graham, European head of Paramount at a luncheon to launch *The Sign of the Cross*, January 1933.
Opposite, bottom: Charles (and brand new Armstrong-Siddeley) outside the Old Vic in October 1933.

Early films: *Piccadilly*, 1929.
The Devil and the Deep, 1932.
If I Had a Million, 1932.
Island of Lost Souls, 1933.

most exciting time of my life. Every night we used to walk out of the theatre, and over the bridge, in a state of intense exhilaration. We felt we were making history.'

Flora Robson, as Laughton's co-star, had a less happy time. Her relationship with Guthrie, formerly so close, seemed to have cooled, and she found Laughton impossibly difficult to act with. According to Kenneth Barrow: 'Charles was a difficult fellow-player. He was a self-obsessed actor who could only relate to the audience. Flora was exasperated at the way he would always look slightly down stage of her, when the sense of the moment called upon them to be looking fully at each other.' And she felt that he stole her inventions. He certainly seems to have stolen her thunder, and that may have been at the back of her complaints. His unbuttoned realism must have ill-matched her more restrained, plaintive manner. It must be admitted that Laughton seems not to have been willing to lose himself in another actor. But then few great actors are.

In every other sense, he was a most generous and lively, if occasionally despairing, man to have around. He offered wise advice to the younger actors (told James Mason to wipe off the treacle of make-up which was hiding and disfiguring his face) and was instrumental, through the Korda connection, in getting some of them their first film parts (Mason, Livesey, Goring). Agate records that 'it was graceful of Mr Laughton to come forward and demand our applause for the three Liveseys,' at the curtain call for *Love for Love*.

Elsa Lanchester, in *Charles Laughton and I*, writes: 'During the season we said, "In years to come we shall look back on this as one of our happiest times." We can do that now. We were aware at the time that we were enjoying ourselves, which is unusual.'

This did not, alas, apply to Laughton's dealings with Lilian Baylis. Relations between them never much improved – at an early meeting in her office he chain-smoked and, she claimed, flicked the ash into her dog bowl. Then there was the matter of the *language*: my god this, my god that, he said. Are you praying or blaspheming, Mr Laughton? she asked, because we don't like blasphemers at the Vic. He refused to be charmed by her. Despite her unseductive exterior, she was rather flirtatious, susceptible to and even encouraging of flattery, but Laughton simply refused to play the game according to her rules.

Things soured permanently when, at the end of the season, she presented Laughton with a bill for the expenditure on costumes not covered by the grant from the Pilgrim Trust. In view of more or less sold-out houses, he demanded to see the books and discovered, as he had suspected, that she had diverted funds into the opera and ballet budgets. He refused point-blank to pay a penny. In a letter to Guthrie at the end of the season, she wrote: 'It would be good if Laughton realised how he went back on his promises, he must have each production new from beginning to end and he would get the money for this. Nothing was said about good or bad business, it was a different offer which we accepted and he had failed to carry out.' Laughton was deeply angered by her belief that because he had made large sums of money in Hollywood, it was his duty to bail the Vic out.

After the curtain had fallen on the first night of *Macbeth*, that night to make the angels weep, he had sat slumped in his dressing-room, sick with failure, and she, garbed in her M.A. (Hon.Caus.) gown, had come backstage, allegedly to console him. She let out what Guthrie – who was present – knew to be a laugh of embarrassment, but which Laughton experienced as 'a hyena-yelp of triumph', caught him a 'sharp crack across the shoulder-blades' and said: 'Never mind, dear, I'm sure you did your best. And I'm sure that one day you may be a quite good Macbeth.' Laughton was convinced that she was still exacting her revenge for the Pilgrim Trust business. Richard Findlater is surely right, however, to attribute the remark to her lack of tact: 'Lilian was a monumentally tactless woman whose olive branches often appeared like knobkerries.'

Laughton failed to find popularity with Miss Baylis' 'people'. They, like her, were not going to be impressed by stars, whether from the West End or from Hollywood. Their favourite was Roger Livesey, sweet, good-natured, unpretentious, and not within a mile of Laughton's talent. He was cheered, applauded, laughed at, while Charles played to silence. The Mme Defarge-like leader of the stalwarts, a certain Miss Pilgrim, particularly plagued him: on one occasion she apparently collected his autograph at the stage door: in fact, he found he had signed a petition demanding the removal of Guthrie. Later, in *Love for Love*, she worked out his comic timing, and fiendishly killed every laugh by guffawing mirthlessly just before the end of the line. Houses, largely thanks to Laughton, were full. They wanted to see him, but somehow they never loved him.

The last night of the season was traditionally jamboree night, at which the audience acclaimed their favourites. 'Good Old Nero!' someone called from the gallery. 'Why don't you bring your wife up,' another cried. 'My friend,' says Laughton, 'a great many people have tried to do that, but they have not succeeded.' The audience also showed their appreciation in kind, placing small gifts for each of the actors on the stage. Roger Livesey received eight, others five. Charles received two or three. Later that night, Elsa Lanchester informed him that he hadn't actually been given any presents – anticipating an embarrassing situation, *she'd* bought a couple of gifts for him, wrapped them and put his name on them. 'Well I'll be damned,' he allegedly remarked, on hearing of this ploy.

For someone to do what she did suggests a wifely devotion of the most touching variety. For her then to *tell* him, suggests the opposite.

In his article entitled 'The Case of Mr Laughton' (May 1933), Agate expressed concern: 'I write this article because I have heard a whisper that he intends to devote the next twenty years to proving he is a tragedian. That indeed will be a tragedy, because it will be a waste of both time and genius. Mr Laughton needs no increase of intelligence, conceptual or representative, and his Macbeth will not be better if he thinks about it till he is ninety. It all comes back to the old question of an actor's physical characteristics, which are beyond his or any actor's power to control.' Agate (and G. H. Lewes, whom he extensively quotes in the course of the article) believed that if you lack a noble bearing and a noble voice, you cannot play a noble character, and that, looking as he did, 'Mr Laughton's essential genius is concerned with the portrayal of the sinister, all the more horrific because of the fleshly suggestion . . . but Mr Laughton is also a magnificent actor on the mimetic plane alone, and is a master of that kind of character-acting which is as much a matter of mind as of make-up.'

There seems to be some confusion here: if he is magnificent on mimetic plane, then surely his physical appearance is not of central significance? But in his last phrase, Agate seems to hit the nail on the head: that character-acting is as much a matter of mind as of make-up. It is surely a factor of temperament rather than physical endowment which makes an actor able to encompass a role, and Laughton's work must always be grounded in realism: he must believe in it within himself, or he could not produce it. In James Mason's striking phrase, he was 'a method actor without the bullshit.' Guthrie wrote: 'I think Charles Laughton did lack technique; when inspiration failed, as fail it often must, he had very little resource either of voice or movement.'

The truth is, he had almost infinite resource of voice and movement: it was his very versatility which had created the acclaim. What he could not do was to produce them at will. They only obeyed his imagination. This it was that limited the range of parts he could perform, and which would inevitably stop him from becoming a classical actor (or tragedian, as Agate prefers to say).

He had never had, and would never have, a success in a play which required him to adapt himself beyond his imagination. In the non-literary theatre in which he had up till now worked, he had brought far more to the characters than was in the characters. The authors were constantly (and on the whole delightedly) amazed by what he produced for them.

It was inevitable that he would, sooner or later, move towards the movies, because that is where the non-literary theatre took up residence. In movies, as in those vehicular pieces in which he made his name, the part was a kind of peg on which you hung what you thought might be interesting, or what you could do. In a 'literary' or 'classical' play, the role makes demands of you.

Laughton was miserable playing Macbeth. What he could bring to the role was not useful (certainly not in Guthrie's production); what the role demanded of him he could not give: it wasn't in him.

So he left the Vic. There was talk of him returning (to play the great prose roles: Dogberry, Pandarus, Falstaff and Belch) but it cannot have been too serious. The working conditions were impossibly frustrating for the perfectionist in him: he wanted to get things right. In the movies there was a chance of that. And in the movies – if one had the power and position that he had – once one had understood the essentials of the character, one could introduce new scenes to show certain aspects of him, cut other scenes to suppress sides which were not useful or interesting or about which one had nothing to say.

Laughton was not concerned to find a hypothesis that would explain all of a character; he was only concerned to embody certain features, to fill an outline with his own flesh and blood and experience. If he couldn't fill the outline with that reality – simple! He'd change the outline.

Which he was not at liberty to do at the Old Vic. At the Old Vic he had for the first time reached that point where the creativity of the actor starts to interfere with the creativity of the writer. It had been a nasty shock, because, as a literate and artistically ambitious man of the theatre, Shakespeare was of course his idol. He withdrew hurt.

He didn't spend the next twenty years trying to become a classical actor. In fact, he spent the next twenty years avoiding it. He made public statements averring his disillusion with Shakespeare – insisting on the irrelevance of Shakespeare. But it was his Great White Whale. He never stopped thinking about how to play Shakespeare. When, a couple of years later, he visited Alec Guinness' dressing-room after a performance of the modern-dress *Hamlet*, he invited him back to his flat in Gordon Square for the sole purpose, it seemed, of reading, first of all some of *Hamlet*, then a great deal of *King Lear*. This last, says Guinness, was 'an illumination'. He became obsessed by the iambic pentameter: perhaps he'd gone wrong there? So he spent hours – years – reading Shakespeare out loud to the ticking of a metronome. Then it was punctuation. Capital letters in the Quarto were no typographer's error: they denoted operative words. He taught these dubious notions to his students.

When, old, fat and sick, he staggered into the ring again to lick the Bard, it was too late. But he never had a chance. His time at the Vic should have taught him that.

Hollywood Again

Amongst other considerations, the thought 'who needs it?' must háve crossed his mind. Treated as an enemy within the walls by Lilian Baylis, and a fumbling upstart by the English press, he may well have wondered why he was languishing obscurely in the Lower Cut, SE1, only six months after being the first English actor to be honoured by a Hollywood at its fabled height of glamour. He was world famous, England's celluloid ambassador.

Laughton was sufficiently complex, both intellectually and temperamentally, to transform these petty emotions into a philosophical position, but there is no doubt that he felt sniped at by cliques: by the establishment, theatrical and journalistic. At least Hollywood was free of these. It catered, moreover, to an infinitely larger and more genuinely important audience: the people. And it was of today, relevant to everyday life. Perhaps one could use this great new medium to spread ideas and stimulate deep emotions . . . it was characteristic of Laughton to rationalise emotional impulses: to justify his evolution. Whether the rationalisation preceded the impulse, or vice versa, is hard to determine. Certainly, his inclinations were populist; just as certainly, he had been deeply hurt by his London experience.

The result is that he returned to Hollywood with no heavy heart; determined, rather, to do something quite remarkable.

The Barretts of Wimpole Street, on the face of things, was not obviously the film in which to do it. The play had been a great success in both London and New York, but the role of Barrett *père* (Cedric Hardwicke on stage) was neither the largest part, nor the most interesting, being essentially a heavy father, with melodramatic overtones. The most original feature of the character was the incestuous element in his relationship to his daughter – but that element had, of course, been filletted from the script in anticipation of Hays Office objections. The director, Sidney Franklin was, moreover, wholly opposed to the casting of Laughton.

Irving Thalberg, who was producing, serenely prevailed. He persuaded Laughton that it was a clever move to follow Henry with a smaller part, and Laughton immediately saw the possibilities for continuing his assault on Victorian repressiveness. As for the incest theme: 'they can't censor the glint in the eye,' as he said at the time. His work on the role proceeded as usual: he found a model for the character to release his deeper, darker feelings. 'As a matter of fact,' he wrote in *Film Weekly*, 'I based Mr Barrett on an acquaintance of mine whose sadism, prudery and long-drawn-out prayers I had often suffered in my youth.' It's never the simple observation with Laughton, though; it's never impersonation. He embodies both what he saw and his attitude to it. *Pace* Laurence Olivier, *pace* Tyrone Guthrie, he doesn't love his character, he hates him. As an actor, his state of mind is that of a prisoner playing his warder, the victim playing his attacker. This is one of the many reasons Bertolt Brecht and he found such common ground. Laughton is always present, pointing and shouting, crying 'Look! This is what you're up against!' His unfolding of the character is designed to make the danger more real. 'During the filming of the early sequences, the director complained that I was exercising far too much restraint and that Frederic March and Norma Shearer were nosing me out of the picture. 'All right,' I said 'give me a chance!' Presently, when they were beginning to think Mr Barrett wasn't such a bad man after all, I let myself go and allowed the real, selfish, despicable Barrett to come to the fore.'

This use of contrast ('a black white, black white effect,' he calls it) is not to be confused with presenting 'a rounded portrait'. It's a technique of demonstration. The intention is neither sympathy nor balance but direct exposure to certain phenomena of the human character. It is designed to frighten and to appall and to distress: never to satisfy or to explain. It is meant to haunt and to brand itself on the brain.

Thus Barrett. Laughton shed 50 lbs to play the part, and sporting mutton-chop whiskers, dressed in the frock-coat of the 1830s, he presents a figure at once frightening and pitiful. There is something weird about his appearance, inhuman, bat-like. In fact, the performance has a not dissimilar quality to that of Max Schreck in Murnau's Dracula film, *Nosferatu*, a self-consuming intensity that is heart-stopping, and a million miles away either from what Rudolf Besier (the original author) can have intended, or what Mr Barrett can have resembled in life. It is also in an entirely different mode to the work of Norma Shearer and Frederic March. March plays competently and pleasantly *en jeune premier*, though, according to Agate, 'he is just a joke in so far as he must be supposed to resemble the poet . . . we feel the intricacies of "Mary had a little lamb" would be beyond him.' Norma Shearer, equally unconvincing as the author of the *Sonnets from the Portuguese*, nevertheless holds her own in terms of sheer radiance and self-management. The scenes between her and Laughton are remarkable precisely for the tension created between his anguished repression and yearning and her placidity: an ocelot ogled by a succubus.

Sidney Franklin, the director (who later won an Academy Award for 'consistent high achievement', and was responsible for *The Good Earth* and *Mrs Miniver*, amongst others), simply avoided Laughton – understandably. His nervous enquiry as to how Laughton saw his role being answered with the snapped reply: 'Like a monkey on a stick,' he wisely withdrew from further discussion. In fact, Laughton was describing his view of the part with some precision.

Franklin was that admirable figure, a thorough-going pro. Such people were Laughton's sworn foes, because he wanted to believe that he was an artist, and that he was engaged in an art. To be an artist was his aim and his justification. As the word 'artist', then and now, in London and in Hollywood, is regarded in the English-speaking world as hilariously pretentious for an actor to use of himself, Laughton took defensive refuge in the word 'amateur', pedantically insisting on its strict French meaning of 'lover'. To him, he said, acting was lovemaking, so he proudly proclaimed himself an amateur. Pros, he told Garson Kanin, were whores.

It takes two to make love, and in this relationship, the director was required to be the more or less reluctant other. Sidney Franklin was not prepared for any such intimacy. So Laughton went solo. There is a term for lovemaking for one, which has a generally derogatory implication, and this term must often have been used of Laughton, no doubt on the set of *The Barretts of Wimpole Street*, perhaps on the day Laughton was unable to continue with the Bible-reading scene, because he suddenly found the whole Judaeo-Christian tradition of morality so funny. He laughed and laughed, terrible mad laughter, it is said, wave upon wave of it, till everyone else was caught up in it, and the film had to stop for the day while he got over it.

This was no straightforward corpsing, such as had occurred a few days before, when Norma Shearer and Maureen O'Sullivan had collapsed at the first sight of his mutton-chop whiskers. He hadn't found that in the least bit funny, and had rather crossly left the set. No, what had happened to him in the Bible scene was that he'd been overrun by the anarchic and dangerous emotions he was dealing with – his own, particularly: his life – the whole mess of contradictory and sometimes paralysing impulses and repressions he was opening the lid on. He went a bit mad, in fact.

If acting is a creative art – *if* it is – then it is perfectly reasonable to demand for it conditions similar to those of the painter or the writer: the right, that is, to make a mess, to splash around, to make drafts and sketches, to have a wastepaper bin at your side. In any creative activity, art is madness, craft is sanity. The balance between them makes the work. But in movie-making, where rehearsal is rare, it is thought unprofessional for an actor not to have sorted out all his problems before the cameras roll.

The difficulty is, of course, the collaborative nature of the enterprise. The director of genius is the man who can provide the stability and the focus by which everyone can go fruitfully mad at once. Charles Laughton did not work with many directors of genius; Sidney Franklin was certainly not one of them, and his film would have melted into the great celluloid graveyard were it not for the performance of his moody and slightly mad star, which was universally acclaimed. 'Mr Laughton is, of course, superb.' (*New York Times*)

No doubt partly to escape from the dank and fetid climate of Wimpole Street, and partly for the sake of a return match with another doughty opponent, Dickens, Laughton next signed with Metro-Goldwyn-Mayer for *David Copperfield*, to play Micawber. David Selznick was the producer, and from the beginning had been undecided as to whether Laughton or W. C. Fields was the more right for the part; but Cukor was keen on Laughton, and he contributed more classical tone to what was planned as a very *distinguished* product indeed. Laughton immersed himself in the novel and the illustrations and devised a make-up for the screen-tests which was held to be quite brilliant. When filming started, however, Laughton lost his confidence completely, and begged to be released, which he accordingly was, to be replaced by Fields.

These are very unusual events. Lanchester recalls that Laughton always despaired after the first few days of filming, but that the producers always persuaded him to continue, which he did, *on condition* that the first few days would be re-shot, but they never were, because no one could ever find them (a likely story, but it might have persuaded a longing-to-be-persuaded Laughton). On this occasion, however, he was adamant, and everyone agreed with him – Selznick, Thalberg and Cukor. There had been no rows, no temperaments. He simply couldn't relax into the part. It wasn't working at all.

His feeling at the time was that he was mis-cast, that Micawber was always 'on', and that what was needed was someone naturally extrovert, someone with an act of his own, as it were, which he could simply graft onto the character: Fields, in fact. Cukor suggested to Gavin Lambert that Laughton didn't have the geniality for the part – the common criticism of his Pickwick, which had been an egregious failure of his London stage career; though it's hard to believe that he was completely lacking in that quality to those who have seen his gentle busker in *St Martin's Lane*.

No, the difficulty lay not in the content of the role – optimism, 'elasticity of emotions' and 'that inexpressible sense of doing something genteel', as Dickens describes it, all of which were well within Laughton's range – but rather the form. Acting Dickens is more problematic than would appear from the printed word, where one glorious speech seems to succeed another, where the characters are so vividly realised, and indeed visualised, and where the theatrical management of the individual scenes is so assured. All of that is exactly what makes the characters live so vividly *on the page*. Stood up and made to move around, as it were, they prove to be highly ingenious concoctions of effects – catch-phrases and catch-gestures serving the scenes to which they belong as so much colour and movement. The author, moreover, offers a wonderfully droll commentary on the characters which is difficult to incorporate. This makes the books ideal material for epic theatre presentations like *Nicholas Nickleby*, but makes performances of the kind that Charles Laughton was interested in giving – namely, explorations of the Unconscious – extremely difficult. Dickens characters are nothing if not Conscious. To make them succeed, an extrovert simplification, allied to a precise reproduction of the rhythms of what are, in effect, turns, is called for. There is no room for manoeuvre either down-wards, into the recesses of the character, or sideways, into subtext. Up, up and away with your Dickens character. So Charles left, quite rightly.

During his brief period on the film, he impressed Cukor particularly in two respects: anti-Semitism ('a terrific prejudice concerning Jews') and pioneer Method acting. The first, of which there is no evidence whatever from any other source, is most likely a feature of Laughton's anti-Capitalist Establishment feeling. Jews as big-wigs, fat cats, a common radical sentiment of the early thirties. The second is of course very familiar, by now, and no doubt entirely true: 'He was the first actor I encountered who prepared to make a laughing entrance by going around doing *ha-ha!* sounds for hours.' One thing Laughton clearly didn't in the least mind was being thought ridiculous.

Laughton's next film, his last on his original contract for Paramount, called on him to do *ha-ha!* sounds more than he'd ever done before, or ever would again. It is *Ruggles of Red Gap*, his comedy vehicle, a huge success in its time, and, according to many interviews, and Elsa Lanchester, Laughton's favourite among all his parts. Whether it is held to be funny or not is of course a matter of taste. Certainly it is enormously interesting in his oeuvre, a very personal film in many ways.

It was apparently his suggestion to remake the story, twice filmed before, by Essanay in 1918, and by Paramount in 1923, with Edward Everett Horton in the title role. Obviously the idea of the English butler lost at cards to an American nouveau riche family and translated into the Wild West had autobiographical associations for him, both personal, as an Englishman discovering America and hereditary, as the scion of generations of butlers and hoteliers. The final shape of the script owes a great deal to him, as most of it was written by his and Elsa's old friend from Cave of Harmony days, Arthur Macrae, brought out to Hollywood at his special behest. Most importantly, Leo McCarey, the director, was his suggestion. McCarey, responsible for many of the best-loved comedy films of the century, from *Duck Soup* to *The Bells of St Mary's*, is immortal as the man who paired Laurel with Hardy, and went on to direct many of their films. It was in this connection that Laughton was eager to work with him. He had a passion for slap-stick, reinforced by a conviction that it was a genuinely Popular Art; in which he craved to be involved.

The resulting performance – though it must be stressed that this was not so for its original audiences – all too clearly bears the marks of a highbrow on holiday, like a Lateran bishop in a party hat. There is no doubt that the performance is intended to be funny – Laughton all but flourishes *Laugh*! placards at the relevant moments – but the comedy is woefully heavy-handed, particularly by comparison with the gloriously funny actors surrounding him: Maude Eburne as a Tugboat Annie figure, Mary Boland and the adorable Charles Ruggles as the nouveaux riches, and above all, Roland Young (hot foot from the *David Copperfield* set, where he had just played his brilliant Uriah Heep) as Lord Bassingwell, a performance in which words proceed from his mouth with no movement of either jaw or lip. As befits a social comedy of this sort (wonderfully directed by McCarey) they – and all the other members of a flawless ensemble – portray types with such certainty, the nail, in every case, is so firmly hit on the head, that they become archetypes. Laughton, on the other hand, seems both comedically constricted and uncertain in character. The ingredients of his performance – stiff walk, bowler hat, off accent, pop eyes – have been carefully and intelligently assembled; but somebody forgot to put them in the oven. Even his appearance, in fact, jars. Somehow he fails to *look* like a butler. What does a butler look like? As many different things as there are butlers, of course; but in a film where the character's profession is the very essence of the story, it is incumbent on the actor to look like Butlers Everywhere. This Laughton signally fails to do. With his blond flaxen hair parted centrally and his sour, petulant features, he possesses none of the classic features of that great English invention, the gentleman's gentleman. He is neither all knowing, nor imperturbable, neither dictatorial nor fathomlessly discreet. He is instead rather emotional, uptight and, it must be said, ever so slightly camp, which could be appropriate (God knows, Edward Everett Horton was as mimsy as they come) but in this case, is not. (A famous story re-told by Garson Kanin bears on this. After a gruelling day, an exasperated Leo McCarey finally burst out: 'Jesus Christ, Charles, do you *have* to be so nancy?' Charles replied: 'But my dear fellow, after eight o'clock a bit of it is *bound* to show.' A graceful and self-knowing joke, if ever there was one.)

Why the miscalculation? In a sense it was the Micawber problem again (though this time it evidently didn't disturb Laughton): namely, the character doesn't call for re-creation of the actor; what it needs is for the actor to bring a ready-made persona. Otherwise the character intrudes, the audience's attention is drawn to complexities which are irrelevant, and the machinery of the plot gets clogged up.

Secondly, Laughton actually lacked the gift for the balletic, one might say the choreographic, side of comedy – the side in which Chaplin and Keaton, for example, excelled. Unfortunately, he seems to have been oblivious of this, and many of his films are marred by would-be comic sequences of dismaying ponderousness – the puddle-hopping sequence in *Hobson's Choice* is the supreme instance of this deadly lack of self-knowledge – but *Ruggles* contains quite horrible examples of abortive schtick, punctuated by many a roll and pop of the eyes. Laughton was very capable of being funny, but he was not at all comic. When he tried to be, all the spontaneity on which he prided himself, all his inspired 'amateurishness', was replaced by a paralysing use of so-called technique – a laboured calculation and striving for effect. Thirdly, the underlying themes of the film meant a great deal to Laughton, maybe too much, in this context. The depth of feeling that he brings to some scenes is quite out of place; though in some cases very fine in itself. When he speaks of his family never having failed his lordship's family, when he speaks of the joys of being his own master, when he ejects a disagreeable diner from his new restaurant, above all when he supervises the kitchen, the unforgettable depth of experience and feeling, and again, the sense of anger and outrage behind the observation, are quite something. They simply belong in another film, and contribute to the unsatisfactory feeling of what is in fact a very well-structured film.

A further reason for Laughton's disappointing performance was piles; or rather, something infinitely worse, a rectal fistula, which struck during rehearsals, and caused him to spend some weeks in hospital before filming started. He was not completely recovered by the time filming began, and was indeed in some pain during much of the shoot, which would certainly account for the generally subdued nature of his performance, as well, perhaps, as certain other physical features of it. He had told W. C. Fields about his embarrassing ailment, and all he had got from *him* had been a telegram – addressed to Charles Thesaurus Laughton – saying *Hope the Hole Thing is Better*.

His time in hospital was significant in a number of ways. It marked the beginning of his brief but momentous friendship with Joseph von Sternberg. In his autobiography *Fun in a Chinese Laundry*, which is every bit as entertaining as its title suggests, and which bears as much relation to real events as his film *Catherine the Great* does to history, von Sternberg claims that Laughton, whom he hardly knew, came to him sobbing and suicidal, believing that he was in the grip of terminal venereal disease – whereupon von Sternberg, an expert, presumably, in these matters, arranged doctors, hospital, and treatment. Laughton was eternally grateful, although it must be admitted he later showed it in some peculiar ways. Elsa Lanchester observes that, having brilliantly and efficiently arranged matters, von Sternberg only visited Laughton once, but that seems perfectly decent.

The second thing that happened to Laughton in hospital was a slight enough incident, but it affected him deeply, and crystallised a growing feeling about himself. What happened, simply, is that after the operation and while he was convalescing, pottering around the hospital corridors he ran into a man who had come to visit his wife. 'Won't you pop into her room,' the man said. 'It'd cheer her up such a lot to see you.' Laughton of course did, and the woman smiled when her husband introduced him as the man who had played Henry VIII. It was, said the husband to Laughton afterwards, the first time she'd smiled since she'd been in the hospital.

A simple incident, obviously, but it was the first time, he says, that he had had real contact with his audience, and understood the significance of stars in the lives of 'ordinary people' – though he never said anything as patronising as that. Neither on the stage in London, nor since his translation to Hollywood, had he had a direct sense of whom he was addressing. It had been the work, the part, the play, the film. It was here, in this hospital, that the evolution of his understanding of what it was to be an actor began. Elsa Lanchester says that he sorted a number of things out for himself while he was in hospital; this may have been among them.

He would do well to meditate on the meaning of fame at this moment of his life, because the release of *Ruggles of Red Gap* marked another high-water mark in his popularity and critical acclaim. None of the aforementioned cavills were shared by contemporary critics – except for one, that is: his old friend, James Agate, now more niggardly with praise, feeling that the stage had lost a great actor, and the screen gained only a moderate one. 'If this Ruggles with the expression of a Chadband at once oleaginous and hangdog were to apply to me for a situation, I should expect him to be the inside member of a gang of crooks arranging to steal my spoons.' His was a rare voice, however – and there is some trace of his well-known snobbery in the comment. For the rest: unqualified triumph. 'Is this the perfect cast?' asked Freda Bruce Lockhart, in banner headlines. 'Laughton's is a comedy performance of the most consummate virtuosity I have ever seen on the screen, proving him to be a film star of the first order, as none of his trick dramatic performances have done . . . he has, too, achieved an almost incredible reality . . . this reality is never lost sight of.' Within the profession, too, there was great acclaim. René Clair, greatly admired by Laughton, sent a telegram of congratulation – 'than which,' he wrote, 'there can be no higher praise.'

His performance transcended the film, too, in another, unexpected way, which added greatly to his popularity in America, and further served to establish him as a kind of folk hero, as opposed to a mere actor. In the film, Ruggles somewhat improbably recites the Gettysburg address (another cause for indignation by Agate: 'I am quite certain this sensitive artist would never have faced the London footlights as a shock-headed butler with a passion for reciting the speeches of Abraham Lincoln.') He does so very beautifully, too beautifully, in the circumstances, perhaps, but the point is, the American public, like the cowboys in the film, proved not really to know the most famous of American speeches. The irony that it was an Englishman who returned the speech to the national consciousness was not lost on anyone. It embodies everything for which Laughton was beginning to prefer America to England, and the passion with which he accordingly performs it, is in large measure what lends it its quality of discovery: both of the speech and the ideas it contains. It is a notable example of rhetorical speaking – something to which Laughton was increasingly drawn.

Clearly, despite any physical inconvenience, Laughton had enormously enjoyed *Ruggles*. It must, indeed, have been a great relief from the pulverising task of opening the sluice gates of his id, and flooding his system with the contents – even if it was only then that he really functioned as a creator. With what heavy heart then must he have approached *Les Misérables* to play Inspector Javert. But his creative juices could not fail to respond to the character, so close to Laughton as to be almost a self-portrait – obsessed, repressed, fanatical, conscience-ridden. It's one of his most overwhelming performances, now virtually lost to view due to the caprices of distribution.

The film as a whole is very successful. The script simplifies Hugo's novel into a duel between Valjean and Javert, a sensible approach to the vast sprawl of the book. Frederic March as Valjean gives a 'strong dramatic performance' – not interesting, but solid, and clear and sincere. Cedric Hardwicke is full of sombre compassion as the Bishop of Beauvais. The film is masterfully lit by the great Gregg Toland; and the direction, unexpectedly but completely satisfactorily, is decidedly Slavonic, with Alfred Newman's chanting monks on the soundtrack, and huge double profile close-ups alternating with swirling misty ensemble scenes. Captions dividing the film into Acts, almost stations of the cross, add a formal intensity which has nothing to do with Hugo's book but is very powerful. All this was the contribution of Richard Boleslavsky, the director, whose relationship to Laughton is unrecorded, but upon which a little profitable speculation might be ventured.

Boleslavsky was responsible for a number of vivid dramatic films – *The Painted Veil, Clive of India*, and *The Garden of Allah* among them. His background, like that of another Russian emigré, Rouben Mamoulian, was the Moscow Art Theatre; he had been Laertes in the legendary Gordon Craig-Stanislavsky *Hamlet* of 1911, and, despite his limited success in the part, had continued to progress through the company until finally he was made director of the First Studio. During the Revolution, he served with the Polish Lancers (his family was Polish) and recorded his experiences in two autobiographical books, *The Way of the Lancers* and *Lances Down*, which were acclaimed as some of the finest writing to come out of the revolution. He returned to the Moscow Art Theatre, came to America with the company, and stayed to found the American Laboratory Theatre, forerunner of Strasberg's Studio. Into its curriculum he introduced, for the first time, elements of the Stanislavsky System, and thus in the American theatre occupies the position of Moses: or perhaps John the Baptist.

In 1933, by which time he had directed many films in Hollywood, he published a short digest of his teaching in dialogue form. It's called *Acting: the First Six Lessons*, and it is an enchanting, shrewd and entirely jargon-free document, still one of the most useful and accessible things ever written about acting. Although elementary in its form, it represents the later development of Stanislavsky's teaching, in which the extreme concentration on emotion memory had evolved into a technique for working on the voice, the body, and – Stanislavsky's and Boleslavsky's favourite word, and we may assume, one of Laughton's – the soul. 'The soul of the artist, the source of all art,' says Boleslavsky; and, in a famous passage from the end of the book: 'Don't look at me now, dearest friend, look into space and listen with your inner ear. Music, and the other arts which follow naturally, will be only an open road to the whole of the universe. Don't miss anything in it. Listen to the waves of the sea . . . inhale their spirit and feel at one with them, even for an instant. It will make you, in the future, able to portray the eternal parts of universal literature . . .

above all, don't forget your fellow-men. Be sensitive to every change in the manifestation of their existence. Answer that change always with a new and higher level of your own Rhythm. This is the secret of existence, perseverance and activity. This is what the world really is – from the stone up to the human soul. The theatre and the actor enter this picture only as a part. But the actor cannot portray the whole if he does not become a part.'

If he read them, these words could hardly have failed to stir Laughton deeply, in their semi-pantheistic feeling, in their breadth of vision of the actor's work – and in their sense of the elemental. What after all, was Laughton trying to do, if not to release the souls of his characters?

Whether through Boleslavsky's direct influence, or the presence at close quarters of such a very large spirit (Boleslavsky is remembered even now by his old students at the Lab as an incandescent speaker, an inspirer), Laughton evokes Javert's soul in *Les Misérables* with unforgettable power. The very first glimpse of him in the film is remarkable. He stands at the desk of his superior in the police force, listening to his dossier. The costume (Laughton devised it himself) creates an immediate impression of intense containment, of pressure: a short cloak over a tight tunic, long boots giving the actor (still slim: 34/35 were the thin years for Laughton – physically, that is – certainly not financially or artistically) the impression of having long, stiff legs; on his head a little cap, seemingly rammed tight on his skull, and framing the unsmiling, almost contourless orb of his face, glowing coldly with frozen misery and single-minded sureness of purpose.

It is now more than an appearance: it is an apparition. As the recital of facts rolls on, he remains perfectly motionless. Then the fact is announced that his father had been imprisoned, and served in a galley. The orb cracks – only for a second, but it is unforgettable, because it seems as if the whole man might split straight down the middle, such is the force of the impulse. Then the structure reasserts itself and when he speaks, it is with an even voice, tense but steady. Laughton uses a kind of London lower-middle-class accent, which quite acceptably wanders, under extreme duress, into Scarborough. Why not? He's playing a Lyonnais who has moved to Marseilles: a newly-acquired accent does tend to slip away at moments of crisis.

Javert's sense of duty, which both shackles him and prevents him from falling apart, informs Laughton's playing of his scenes of confrontation with Valjean, above all the scene where he comes to him to offer his resignation because he has infringed regulations – he has lived by them, now he must go down by them. The curious feeling of someone about to burst apart is physically uncomfortable to watch. Never for a moment in Laughton's performance does the audience share Javert's lust for Valjean's blood; instead they are transfixed by the spectacle of a man who has filled the vacuum created by his fear with a monstrous, inhuman destructiveness of which he is ultimately the victim. He has become his quest. In a way hard to analyse, Laughton constantly suggests the pain which gave rise to this obsession. As he spies on Valjean, the moon face transfigured with destructive longings, as watchful as a cat waiting to pounce on a bird, as ardent as a voyeur hypnotised by the object of his infatuation, as hungry as a dog ogling a plate of meat, he cuts a figure that is both chilling and pitiful, and which is always preparing us for the climax of both film and performance: the moment when Valjean surrenders himself, and Javert, at the hour of what should be his triumph, simply melts away into pity. It is a devastating moment, as steel turns to honey. With impeccable taste, the director chooses not to show the drowning of Javert, elliptically implying it with empty boots and swirling Seine.

'This sequence was, in my opinion,' Laughton wrote, 'the finest thing I have ever been able to accomplish on the screen.' He continued making films for another 25 years, but it is hard to disagree with what he says. ' "What a tragedy!" I wanted the audience to exclaim, "to have one's whole life overshadowed by a fanatical sense of duty?" ' This is exactly what they do exclaim; but it is not the tragedy of one man, a fictional character, that they marvel at. It is the tragedy of us all, of life itself, of, yes, the human condition. The ability to shift the audience from thinking Poor him! to thinking Poor us! must surely be a mark of greatness in an actor.

It is noteworthy that, on this film, as with so many of his most remarkable achievements, the circumstances of filming caused him great physical discomfort. Wading through the sewers, day in and day out, imagining the smells and dankness, focused him more and more on the agonies with which he was filling his being. It is hard to avoid the feeling that there was an element of self-punishment in Laughton, possibly with sexual overtones. Who can say, for sure? In fact, Laughton was highly sensitive to pain, and disliked physical discomfort. Perhaps pain was the quickest route to feeling; and feeling was the basis of his art. Quite clearly, he was haunted by guilt. 'As far as we know,' says Charles Higham, 'Laughton had no sexual relations whatever in the years 1934–35,' so it wouldn't have been a simple guilt for actions. Perhaps for thoughts . . . no doubt a continuing legacy of Stoneyhurst, the triumph of a Catholic upbringing: perpetual unease, nameless doubt, existential anxiety. He had rejected confession, while retaining guilt; embraced the nettle, dismissed the dock-leaf.

And so it was left to his acting to cleanse his soul; and again, on *Les Misérables*, says Miss Lanchester, it worked: 'he gave one of those cleansing performances that gave him a little peace.'

The film was well enough received: 'Somehow the picture seems more vivid and important than the novel,' wrote James Shelley Hamilton, 'though Boleslavsky yields to his temptation to prettifying the scenes with unnecessary dabbling in mere effects of light and shadow.' He had no hesitation about Laughton, however: 'the astonishing revelation is that of Charles Laughton as Javert, a picture of a tortured spirit, fighting against something it cannot understand, for which one must go to the greatest works of art for a comparison. One wonders if Victor Hugo himself put into that character all that Laughton brings out of it.' Critics – those who sensed what Laughton was trying to do – were straining for superlatives. For others (Otis Ferguson, for example) 'he continues to be a baffling figure, impressive even in his inevitable overplaying.' There is something in this performance that touches nerves so deep, that the spectator either submits to it or refuses it altogether.

After it, he returned to England where Elsa already was. Korda was trying to lure him back into the fold, and they started work on what proved to be a time-consuming wild goose chase: *Cyrano de Bergerac*, a long-standing passion of Charles'. Laughton was only in England long enough to help set the project up with Korda: the problem, as always – until, at any rate, Anthony Burgess' miraculous version for the Royal Shakespeare Company in 1984 – was the translation. They lighted on an admired poet of the time, author of *The Uncelestial City, Signposts to Poetry*, and a striking memoir of his Jewish childhood, *Now a Stranger*, Humbert Wolfe (not, as improbably reported by both Lanchester and Higham, Virginia's husband, Leonard Woolf).

After setting the project up, Laughton returned to Hollywood at the behest of Irving Thalberg to play Captain Bligh in the film of *Mutiny on the Bounty*. Before he went he did his research. Lettie Greig, his cousin from Scarborough, visiting the Laughtons for supper, recalls his arrival, three hours late, in a state of uncontrollable excitement, having been to Gieves' in Bond Street and discovered the original records for Bligh's uniform – from 1789. The authenticity wasn't the point; it was what it did to his imagination. Costumes had a particularly powerful effect on Laughton, one of the most useful levers to his creativity. Edith Head, queen of Hollywood costume designers said: 'Put Charles Laughton in front of a three-way mirror and you were apt to get the whole play. Charles had the amazing ability to adjust his body to his clothes. You could put a suit on Charles and by his body control that suit could change amazingly before your eyes.' Lanchester writes: 'Charles could look at you from under a hat brim like nobody else . . . before any production, Charles would play with his new props – putting on a hat and taking it off, hanging it up and taking it down, at home, in his dressing room, or in the producer's office. This was a time of fun for Charles and any audience around him . . . he knew he could captivate and mesmerise.'

During the honeymoon period of preparation, he could fool around with the stupendous instrument that was his talent; like a hunter picking off plaster ducks with his gun to make children laugh. Alas, when the work started in earnest, the fun evaporated.

Mutiny on the Bounty was a novel by Nordhoff and Hall, the rights of which had been acquired by Frank Lloyd, actor, writer, winner of two Academy Awards, with a view to playing Bligh himself. He was dissuaded from this folly by the advance of large sums of money from MGM, for whom Thalberg now bought the project. It is alleged that Lloyd insisted that whoever play Bligh should do so in the bushy eyebrows for which he, Lloyd, was famous. This savage self-satire seems less likely than that Laughton was perpetrating another of those sly jokes which had served him so well as Mr Prohack and the Man with Red Hair. Certainly, Laughton had no time for Lloyd; but then, for once, nor did anyone else. Thalberg was involved in continuous fracas with him, mainly over his handling of the cast. 'He was always good on sea pictures,' said Geraldine Farrar. 'I liked him as a director, but he had better luck with ships than people.' Unfortunately, on *Mutiny* he had to handle two rather high-powered people with very little in common.

Clark Gable was unlikely casting for the eighteenth-century Englishman, Fletcher Christian, and felt so himself. He particularly dreaded wearing breeches. To the amazement of both himself and his studios, he had become the very image of American manhood, admired by guys and gals alike – ideal husband, lover, friend, boss, buddy. His acting was limited, but true; his powers of transformation negligible. Good looks and inimitable sexual charm were his strong suits; that, and the rare quality of relaxed masculinity. He was a heaven-sent partner to a succession of divas – Garbo, Crawford,

Constance Bennett – but he was less easily matched with men. Good-natured and generous though he was, he was nervous about competition in the area where he felt himself vulnerable: acting; and in 1935, Charles Laughton *was* acting.

Laughton's feelings about Gable, as may be imagined, hinged on appearance; though not, as is commonly assumed, a simple opposition of his ugliness with Gable's good looks. Gary Cooper's perhaps even greater beauty had not disturbed Laughton in the least: he had frankly admired him, both as an actor and in physical terms. Perhaps the key word, here, however, is 'beauty'. Cooper, with his ravishing androgyny, full of lip, luxuriant of eyelash, gentle of manner, had – at least in his performing personality – found a perfect balance between his masculine and his feminine elements, which was no threat to Laughton. It was exactly the balance that he longed to achieve himself but which for most of his life resolved itself into a battle, rather than a blend. Gable, on the other hand – 'certain as the sunrise,' as his *New York Times* obituary put it, 'consistently and stubbornly all man' – was the very thing Laughton could never be; and also the very thing to which he was always deeply drawn, sexually. In his oblique way, as so often, he expressed some of the complication of his feelings in a comment to a newspaper: 'Clark Gable dramatizes himself. He makes you feel full of pep. You see Clark Gable and you say, I'll go out and have half a dozen dates.'

It could well be that this underlying feeling was responsible for the thing that distressed Gable so much during filming: his only real complaint against Laughton, with whom he otherwise got on very well: namely, that he wouldn't look him in the eye. For Gable, to whom acting essentially meant re-acting, this was fatal. Having a clear and real relationship with his fellow actor was Gable's life-line. If Laughton delivered his speeches sideways, into the ocean, he was lost. Laughton undoubtedly had good reasons of character and situation for doing so, though Gable was not the first to complain of it: Flora Robson, likewise an essentially 'relating' performer, had found it intolerable, too. It is, in fact, rather in the nature of Laughton's view of his characters: each man a self-contained universe of pain. This was of no interest to Gable. Again and again he stormed off the set bitterly denouncing Laughton for trying to exclude him, cut him out of the scene. This was his technical naïveté, his innocence of the art of acting, his lack of inner resource.

As it happens, the conflict was very good for the movie. The relationship between Christian and Bligh is tense and competitive and full of underlying complexity; perhaps, in Gable's case, the most complex piece of work he did until the performances of his last years, when life and disappointment and illness had added a layer or two to his persona.

Laughton's performance is again remarkable for the vision he offers of a soul trapped by itself. His first appearance, replete with Frank Lloyd eyebrows, Gieves' uniform, and mouth downturned with self-disgust and rage, introduces us to the whole cancer of repression, inner and outer. Here is a man who is no vulgar sadist; he is someone in whom rigid application of rules has filled his brain and cast out any vestige of tender feeling. There is no flicker of enjoyment in his harshness; he is serving an exigent god, punishing himself as much as his victims. The clipped adenoidal voice, godsend to a million mimics thereafter, perfectly expresses the pressure inside the man. The sense of an impending explosion is hypnotic, and makes every scene in which he appears dangerous and disturbing; against one's instincts, one feels for him as much as for Christian – hating him and fearing for him simultaneously.

Almost the peak of the performance, because the most naked revelation of the cancered soul, is the scene in which the Tahitian chieftains step on board to greet the crew. Bligh attempts to be charming. It is an excruciating spectacle, brilliantly funny and painful, as he attempts to reverse the downward trend of his mouth, and somehow summon a smile. Again, there is the sense of the armour cracking, huge inner urges long since imprisoned surging towards the surface; but the lid is clamped firmly back on.

After the mutiny, aboard the little rowing boat in which he and the loyal rump of the crew have been set adrift, expecting to drown or die of dehydration, he hurls his famous defiance of Christian, and enters the music hall forever. It's such a famous moment that it risks seeming to be a parody of itself, but, no, it transcends its imitations and remains one of the most enduring images of a brave villain, a man true to his lights, prepared to go to hell in the name of a false code. It, and the journey, during which the sun slowly fries the passengers of the little boat, are magnificently real, all the more, perhaps, for having been shot (not on the ocean, as were the early scenes on board ship, but in the tank on the MGM lot) not merely once but *twice*, because of an error in continuity. 'We have conquered the sea!' cries Laughton at the end of the voyage, and the cast and crew are reputed to have cheered and wept. It's not hard to see why.

'When I have a part like Father Barrett or Bligh, I hate the man's guts so much that I always have to stop myself overacting and be real. Parts like that make me physically sick,' Laughton told a journalist. The problem was to strike a balance between the character and his attitude to him. With Bligh, as with his best performances, the balance, or perhaps one should say, the tension, is perfectly found, so that not merely do you see the man, see what he has become – you want to do something about it. The effect of Laughton's work at its best is to make the audience active instead of passive.

His relationship with Gable had warmed over the shoot. One day, according to Higham, Gable, as a supreme gesture of comradeship, had taken Laughton with him on his visit to a brothel. Laughton was apparently deeply touched (and presumably deeply anxious). On another day, Gable had found him gazing sadly at a fisherman, saying to himself, 'I wish I were that man.' They seemed by the end of the movie, at any rate, to have achieved a degree of understanding.

The shoot ended relatively happily. On the last day, Laughton assembled the crew and the cast and recited the Gettysburg address, to enormous applause. It increasingly became Laughton's habit, at home and at work, in the streets and over supper, to quote, at considerable length, great pages from world literature. He apparently did so with complete unselfconsciousness, and they were received with attention and admiration. He had a comprehensive memory of large sections of the Bible, the novels of Thomas Wolfe, the masterpieces of Jacobean prose, and so on. He had a wonderfully resonant, if not very strong, voice, and he phrased with fine timing and a unique ability to sound the vibrations of meaning and association in a word. None of this makes these impromptu performances any the less extraordinary. It is most unusual, it must be stressed, for an actor to act when not being paid for it. Unlike pianists or singers, we are not ready at the drop of a hat to perform for the delight of our fellow-guests. Indeed, most of us would rather die than do so. But Charles Laughton obviously found it easier than making small talk, which he anyway regarded as a waste of time. So, without preamble, and assuming everyone else to be equally keen to do something profitable rather than twitter away, he would recite. And his shyness would disappear.

It is here that one can see for the first time the drive towards story-telling, or rather, being a story-teller, which finally became his preferred self-image.

Laughton parted from Thalberg, looking forward, no doubt to a long and continuing partnership. Thalberg – 'the most brilliant producer in the world today,' Laughton had said – had collaborated most happily with Charles, advising him, being advised, sharing dreams and visions. He believed that Laughton, with his enquiring brain, good taste and inexhaustible energy, should produce as well as perform in his films. They planned to set up a company together. This company might have been a highly creative and productive harnessing of Laughton's talent. But Thalberg, alas, died; the heart disease which had haunted him for years finally turned fatal. Laughton never knew an anchor like him again.

Nick Schenk, a junior movie mogul, saw the preview of *Mutiny on the Bounty*, and cabled head office: 'TELL THALBERG IT IS THE WORST MOVIE EVER MADE.' Nick who? Otis Ferguson's review begins '*Mutiny on the Bounty* is one of the best pictures that have been made.' It is in fact a marvellously competent piece of work, exciting and economical in its story-telling, seductive and imaginative in its creation of the Tahitian paradise, and containing a good performance by Franchot Tone, as well as a fine performance by Gable, a great one by Laughton, and a tremendous partnership by them both. The film was nominated for an Academy Award, as were *Ruggles of Red Gap* and *Les Misérables*. Laughton himself was nominated for (but did not receive) an Oscar for Bligh, which was voted the best performance of the year by the New York Critics' Circle. Otis Ferguson wrote: 'He is genius itself and in an exacting role: he has never played a part of such devious subtleties and frank power and neither has anybody else in the movies. For his soundness of instinct, his range of talent and perception, it should be enough to say that no man can really wear the shoes of a great character without, in his own way, fitting them.' Mark van Doren, most distinguished literary critic of his day, wrote: 'Charles Laughton's performance fixes him in my mind at any rate as by far the best of living actors.'

A couple of years later the performance received an accolade which may have meant even more to him: in *Donald Duck goes to Hollywood* Walt Disney included Captain Bligh among those met by the eponymous fowl. Like many subsequent impersonations, the cartoon emphasises the stiff upper lip aspect of the performance, and misses the inner rage completely. But what can you expect from a duck?

Korda Again

Needless to say, Korda was very keen to acquire Laughton again. Nothing he had done since *Henry VIII* had had quite the éclat of that international blockbuster; while Laughton had gone from triumph to triumph. The project they lighted on, *Cyrano*, was an ambitious one, and they went a very long way towards making it happen; but ultimately, for reasons which are not entirely clear but can easily be guessed at, it was not to be.

In fact, after an almost unbroken arc of activity from the day he left RADA, Laughton now had a substantial pause: ten months, which is a long time in the career of the hottest film star in the world. Of course, he was under contract to Korda during all of that time – and longer; for two years, in the end – but his frustration must have been considerable as Korda thrashed about, looking for suitable vehicles. (This was a common experience of actors under contract to Korda, trapped in gilded cages.) But Laughton gave himself passionately to the work on *Cyrano*. The author of the translation, Humbert Wolfe, later published it, with an introduction which memorably conveys the madness of working for Korda – the sudden summons by telephone, the bouts of intense work, the subsequent silences, the financial generosity, the charm, the sheer Hungarian-ness of it all. He also gives an account of working with Laughton which leaves one very impressed.

He and Laughton were sent away together to work on his version, written in three weeks flat: the version, in fact, that he later published, and very decent it is, too. Korda and Lajos Biro, his literary advisor, felt that maybe it was a little too slavish to the French text. Laughton and he were to free it up.

'I am not likely to forget the evenings which I spent with Laughton in his upper-part in Gordon Square. The ritual was always the same. I arrived at eight to find in the austere room a new floral welcome . . . Laughton wore a bright dressing-gown over some form of black silk pyjamas, looking with his yellow hair like the raw material of all the actor that there is. We sat at a long bare table, where all that could be done with meat and vegetables was skilfully and quietly served. We spoke chiefly of Shakespeare and Chekhov. To Laughton a great play was a source of lovely terror. He knew exactly the effect of every line, but how, he would ask with blazing eyes, could any man have ever known enough to produce that effect? It wasn't human, he felt . . . This was, I have subsequently thought, a deliberate preparation for the work that was to follow. You could not, Laughton felt, move straight from dog-racing to the immense concentration which his conception of acting verse demanded.'

It is hard, in reading this, to resist a feeling of suspicion. Wolfe had never met an actor before he met Laughton, and he seems to have gone for the whole Great Actor package hook, line and sinker. *The Thinker, The Votary of Art, The Humble Servant of The Author*, not to mention the black silk pyjamas – Laughton seems to have acted out a whole sequence of *tableaux vivants* for the innocent poet.

But then he delivered the goods. 'He stood there, a little square man in an ordinary drawing-room. As his strangely thrilling voice began to bring the words to life, the room melted. A shadowy theatre took its place. Crowds of musketeers, citizens, fruit-sellers and gentlemen of the court suggested themselves in the middle-distance . . . a stage came into remote being with its scenery for 'Clorise'. And in the centre of it all, all magnificently insolent, arms akimbo, raking moustaches, insinuated, threatened, laughed, gesticulated and finally drew his sword with a great parade, Cyrano – all Gascony in a string of couplets.'

There are many accounts of Laughton's overbrimming histrionic appetite, particularly in impromptu situations, for an audience of one, or half a dozen. The anguish and doubt disappeared, and the sheer joy of self-expression overwhelmed his listeners. Spontaneity, his most elusive quality, was suddenly present: but it was a prepared spontaneity; Laughton was no inventor, no improviser; he had lingered long and lovingly over his texts, and they were ready to surge out of him on any wave of emotional freedom that might come by.

With *Cyrano*, he was really formidably thorough. It is unusual for an actor to be as well prepared for a part even when he's actually filming it; Laughton was still only at the preliminary stage.

First he acted the text in French. That is considerable testimony to his fluency. Rostand's text is one of continuous virtuosity, rhythmically difficult, a torrent of tongue-twisting quibbles and sallies. Laughton demonstrated to Wolfe how the *ballade* in Act One was constructed to the rhythm of fencing strokes. Immediately after performing in French, he performed Wolfe's version ('he was word-perfect'). 'Laughton stood before me smiling. "I see," he said, "that you agree. Your version may be a better *ballade*, but I can't fence it."'

They discussed the difference between the French and English approach to romantic themes, the possible translation of the word 'panache', they considered cuts, the re-shaping of passages.

'Laughton put the play in training, and was sweating off its redundant fat in order to get it into perfect condition for the race.'

All this is above and beyond anything that might reasonably have been expected of any leading actor, and it betokens enormous energy, intelligence, and, of course, seriousness on Laughton's part. None of these qualities would have guaranteed a good performance of the role, but the whole episode lends credence to his later statement that 'acting in the movies takes up about a tenth of my energy.' He was overflowing with unfulfilled creativity.

As for the script: it was handed over to Lajos Biró, who made a tentative camera script, which he and Wolfe then worked on. A director of photography was engaged (von Sternberg's cameraman, Lee Garmes; nothing but the best); noses were made (Christopher Morahan recalls his father, Tom, the production designer, making dozens of false noses, until one was finally settled on and ceremonially unveiled).

Agate had lunch with Charles and Korda during this time: 'Charles who is a great baby as well as a genius delightedly showed us the mechanical arrangement for Cyrano's cock-a-hoop bearing which are to enable him to give all his attention to Cyrano's crowing. He is to have the heels of his shoes shaved and the soles raised, and illustrated this by means of two books which Korda threw on the floor. One was by Lytton Strachey and the other by Eisenstein.'

But the inherent uncommerciality of a film in verse about a seventeenth century Gascon knight with a large nose must finally have daunted even Korda, who, as so often, simply moved on to a new enthusiasm: a life of Rembrandt. Warner Brothers were beginning their cycle of biographical movies with Paul Muni, so Korda had better get on with it quick.

Humbert Wolfe was left stranded and baffled, clutching an unwanted manuscript. 'Weeks passed during which my hopes were proved dupes, and my fears were emphatically not traitors. Silence brooded over the waters, and whatever doves I sent forth to Denham, elsewhere, returned.'

Korda finally sold the rights in the play to Stanley Kramer, who made a dull film of it – in prose – with José Ferrer. There is however a ghostly glimpse of Laughton's performance at the beginning of a Deanna Durbin vehicle of the late forties, *Because of Him*, which opens with Laughton's *curtain-call* as a ham actor playing Cyrano for the last time; some kind of private joke, no doubt.

The 'upper-part in Gordon Square' that Wolfe had visited was the new flat Elsa Lanchester had found for them. The impression of this flat created by photographs is one of austerity. The architect of the reconstruction was Wells Coates, creator of the notorious Permanent Setting at the Old Vic, and one of the most fashionable architects of the day. He emphasised the straight clean line of the walls, and introduced sliding doors in between the two main rooms. These doors were decorated, flora on one side, and fauna on the other, by the Laughton's witty friend John Armstrong. His delicate poetic touch would have added a cool pastel dimension to the impact of the place, but essentially it remained plain, going on austere. The most lavishly decorated section of the flat was the servants' quarters, which Laughton, typically, had commissioned Heal's of Tottenham Court Road to furnish. This means that they would have been the acme of sober luxury – very different from the nearly Oriental starkness prevailing below.

Laughton's solicitude, not to say anxiety, in matters relating to his domestic staff verged on the comic, and had its obvious origins in his own experience of *service*. He loathed anything resembling command, on his side, or servility, on theirs, and went to great lengths to avoid unduly troubling them. Elsa Lanchester's description of their household in the mid-30s is richly funny. It was evidently a somewhat Chekhovian establishment, with Nellie Boxall, the cook (inherited from Virginia Woolf, so quite unfazed by raffishness), and a housemaid, 'a communist', according to Lanchester, up in arms for one reason or another, calling the Laughtons 'idle rich'. The Laughtons countered this by referring to the servants as 'serfs' or 'slaves'. 'A mad house – but spotless and efficient, and – according to Charles – as well run as any household he knows.'

Very likely. His sense of management was in the blood and in the bones. The starkness of their personal accommodation does, however, come as a surprise, though in fact it is entirely characteristic. Neither he nor Elsa enjoyed luxury or clutter. The 'tree-house' in Stapledown was similarly plain and unadorned, and the subsequent American houses followed suit. The luxuriance of Laughton's physique and the juiciness of his persona lead one to expect a corresponding expansiveness in his environment, but his girth and the amplitude of his characterisation are in that sense deceptive. His acting was highly selective, made up of strong clear strokes – nothing messy or impressionistic about it; it was, if anything, expressionist, strong bleeding colours applied with incisive directness. His mind was similarly clear and as far as one can judge, uncluttered. When he knew a thing, he really knew it. Later, as a director both in the theatre and on film, he proved to be above all a sterling editor and shaper: he had a wonderful sense of selection and placement. He and Elsa were both passionate flower lovers, but he was supreme as a flower arranger (a skill he preferred to keep quiet about, telling Elsa to claim responsibility). In one of the photographs of the flat, there is a bowl with a strikingly arranged bunch of twigs. Constance Spry was a best friend, and they would fight over adjustments of a millimetre. In the light of this, it is hardly surprising that Laughton should have been drawn to Japan: Hokusai, the tea-ceremony, flower-arranging, and that the most satisfying image of him should remain the collage Brecht made of him as a Zen master on a pony.

From his youth, painting, sculpture, drawing, all that is called Art, were his great passion. There was nothing artsy-fartsy about it: there was real, intense, physical response to line and form and colour. His relationship to painting was not intellectual, but sensual. On another level, however, it was an *essentially* intellectual response, because it was the abstract qualities in it that so mesmerised him. There are many accounts of Laughton's ability to stand, or preferably sprawl on the floor, in front of a painting for literally hours, till every inch of the canvas penetrated his consciousness. It's very striking that it was not representational art, which in a literal sense can be very useful to an actor, but an art of pure forms that meant so much to him – doubly striking in that he constantly strove somehow to inform his acting, transform his acting, with its qualities. This is a task some miles removed from 'playing the truth of the character in the situation', and other such reductive prescriptions. For Laughton, to adapt Pater's phrase, all acting should aspire to the condition of art, the highest, the purest art; neither photography nor the work of Madame Tussaud falling, in his opinion, into that category.

His career as a collector had started early, in Scarborough, where he was able to decorate the Pavilion with engravings and paintings by at first local artists, then artists whose work he'd seen in London. Once established as an actor, he bought carefully and with great discrimination. Lanchester describes how they would put paintings on the wall at Gordon Square for a couple of months, then cupboard them, putting up other paintings in their place, after Gertrude Stein's advice to stop the paintings 'melting into the wall.' For a brief while, Laughton even ran a little gallery displaying the works of actors; Bernard Miles showed in it.

But it was in 1935, in New York, that Laughton met the man who decisively influenced his taste, and put him into the big league as a collector: Dr Albert Barnes, owner of a substantial collection of impressionists. He it was who encouraged Laughton to shell out the $36,000 being asked for Renoir's *Judgement of Paris*. It remained the centrepiece of Laughton's collection, bought, I am inclined to believe, more out of deference to Barnes than his own taste, its candy floss treatment of the subject being unlike anything else Laughton ever owned. Barnes' other tip, the black American primitive painter, Horace Pippin, seems more in Laughton's line. He already had a Douanier Rousseau, and a Matthew Smith, works of weird poetic intensity, and continued to cultivate, for the rest of his collecting life, side by side with the abstract, works which embodied the naïveté and simplicity which became his ideal in life.

In *Rembrandt*, he had the opportunity to surround himself totally with beauty, to immerse himself in a painter's life, to try to imagine the sensation of looking through a painter's eye. He bought every book written about Rembrandt, he saw every possible canvas painted by Rembrandt, he studied every likeness made of Rembrandt. He and Korda went back and forth to Holland, where the curator of the Rembrandt Museum assembled a private show of all the available paintings, drawings and engravings; they studied treatises on painting and architecture; they found and shipped over Dutch furniture and pots and cloths.

Just before filming started, he undertook a little jaunt which must have seemed like a delightful idea but turned into a living nightmare. Maurice Chevalier invited him to participate in a gala at the Comédie Française to raise money for the family of a suddenly deceased *sociétaire*. He was to be the first English actor to perform at the Comédie since its foundation; he would, of course, perform in French. He enlisted the aid of his old teacher, Alice Gachet, and they chose an extract from Act Two of Molière's *Le Médicin Malgré Lui*. So far, so jolly. Meticulous as ever, Laughton learned his part down to the last perfectly pronounced syllable, and in due course, he and Gachet flew to Paris, where the full horror of the thing began to sink in, as it is inclined to do on galas. No matter how good the cause, regardless of the fact that you're not being paid, you are still, you suddenly realise with a sickening churn of the stomach, about to stand on a stage in front of a lot of people who have paid a great deal of money to see you practise your art. All very well for singers, dancers, players of the marimba: they just have to get up and do it. The actor has to create some kind of reality, play some kind of character, say lines which are often quite unfamiliar to him. There's never sufficient rehearsal, and the run-through is always abandoned just before they get to your bit.

If playing in a foreign language, multiply all these factors by a hundred. If playing with the regular company of the Comédie Française in 1936, just lie down and weep, because they have played this particular scene at least a million times, and their idea of rehearsal is to flick through their speeches at top speed, indicating movement and business with fluttering hands and daintily impressionistic foot movements. Add to this the news that the gala is due to start at midnight, that you are on last, and that you will be preceded by Serge Lifar and Maurice Chevalier, and you don't even have to be Charles Laughton to want to kill yourself.

Charles Laughton wanted to kill himself very much indeed. According to Elsa Lanchester, he lay on his back and moaned, then he lay on his front and moaned. He kept this up with little variation until four o'clock in the morning, when his time finally came. The lights went up, he spoke, the other actors spoke. The audience did not speak. They did nothing. Were they still there? One surefire gag succeeded another in perfect silence – masterly inflection and perfectly timed pauses made no difference. The piece ended. The curtain fell: to ecstatic applause. Strangers embraced Laughton in the wings, down the corridors and in his dressing room, telling him how *funny* he'd been; never was seen such glorious comedy. Each gesture, each inflection was analysed. Laughton was presented with Molière's walking stick, Sganarelle's purse, Cyrano's signet ring (irony!). He went off, dazed, into the night; or rather morning, it being 5 o'clock by now. The French papers told him that he was a great comic genius, and the English papers jubilated over '*Mr Charles Laughton's Brilliant Paris Triumph*'. 'Everybody said Charles was marvellous, and considering he is an Englishman who had only four days' rehearsal, he was marvellous. But he knows, and I know, it was not a thoroughly good performance.' (Elsa Lanchester)

Back, with relief, to *Rembrandt*. As only before on *Henry VIII*, Laughton was closely involved in every detail of the filming, present at design discussions with Korda's brilliant brother, Vincent, at lighting discussions with the melancholy but inspired cameraman, Georges Périnal, and at casting sessions, where he put forward the names of many of his erstwhile associates at the Old Vic – Roger

Livesey and Marius Goring among them. Elsa was to play Hendrickje Stoffels. (Other members of the strong cast include John Clements, Raymond Huntley, and, in one of her few film roles, Gertrude Lawrence.)

The shoot was not easy, and Korda suffered greatly with Laughton. 'It has been a terrible film for me and Alex,' he told a newspaper. But for once the problem was not one of interpretation, nor was he filling himself with ugly and painful emotions; the problem on *Rembrandt* was simply to attain the utmost simplicity. 'How we fought and suffered in the first weeks when we were still feeling our way. It had to be so simple, so serious, never a sign of acting.' It is that rare thing in Laughton's output, a naturalistic performance. Of course, it is supra-naturalistic as well: magnified, intensified, crystallised. But for once (twice, actually: in a later film, *This Land is Mine*, he attempts the same thing) he doesn't isolate elements of his experience to create a concentrated model of a soul gone wrong; instead he simply exists – a man, complicated, many faceted, living and breathing. Unlike other Laughton characters, he seems to have a life off-screen. Acting was not a dirty word for Laughton, and he knew exactly what he meant by it: the projection of great and warring forces onto the framework of a character. In *Rembrandt*, he wanted to do something quite different. He wanted to celebrate his own love of beauty, his creative aspirations, his sense of humanity. His Rembrandt, I believe, is an idealised self-portrait; just as Albert Lory, the character he plays in *This Land is Mine*, is another self-portrait, only a critical one.

His Rembrandt is a detailed, sensitive, heart-breaking performance, quietly pitched, with not a trace of exaggeration. It is also one of the very few filmed recreations of an artist that actually convince. Laughton at the canvas is possessed by the concentration only ever seen in a painter's eye. He took up painting during the making of the film, but the external details are the least of it: what he astonishingly conveys is the act of translation, the process by which the object depicted becomes line, form, and colour. Every scene he plays is filled from within with complex reality: his exasperated, uncomprehending dealings with the burghers, his tenderness with the blind beggar he uses as a model, above all in the scenes with Elsa Lanchester as Hendrickje Stoffels. She never did anything better; they never did anything better. His grave playfulness is perfectly matched with her radiant openness, and the scene in which she suddenly dies is as poignant as the pointless death of some small animal.

Korda, Lanchester reports, grudgingly admitted that she had

played the part well. She felt, with understandable bitterness, that Korda didn't like her or her acting, and that she was only ever useful to him as a bait for Charles. He even went so far, she claims, as to set up, and even begin to shoot, a film with her in the lead which he immediately abandoned when Laughton signed his contract for *Rembrandt*. That seems to be going to lengths. Miss Lanchester also believed that Korda was chief among those, 'the Laughton-snatchers,' who wished to keep Charles and her apart, and that it was the Laughton-snatchers who finally poisoned their relationship. She looks on the period of *Rembrandt* as a happy time for them. She had recently had what was to prove the greatest success of her career, the double-role of Mary Shelley and the bride in James Whale's *The Bride of Frankenstein*. From now on, everything was to be in the shadow of Charles. She observes, *en passant*, that she wrote the little tune that Hendrickje sings, and that Charles had advised her not to take credit for it; people would think she was trying to be grand.

It would appear, despite what she felt, that the processes of mutual destruction which increasingly characterised their relationship were well under way.

The film in which Laughton gave his exceptional performance, was not a success, either critically, financially, or, in the last analysis, artistically – despite Korda's enterprising marketing: he offered a free ticket to anyone owning a Rembrandt. It was greeted with respect by the critics, and the undoubted success of the design – a stylisation of Dutch seventeenth-century engraving, a kind of black and white toy town – and the lighting – Rembrandt's and Vermeer's tones and textures somehow conveyed in black and white – were acknowledged. But it's poorly shaped, the rhythms are dull, and there is a flatness about the whole thing. All this must be laid at Korda's door. He was disheartened by the failure; that and the struggle with Laughton temporarily killed his interest in directing (he didn't attempt to do so again until *Lady Hamilton* in 1941). In reality, he wasn't ever interested in making films as Laughton understood the job. If it wasn't going to be fun, what was the point? He preferred to swap jokes and stories with Gertrude Lawrence, who regarded film acting as a quick way to make cash; to the extent that she hadn't bothered to learn her lines, having them written out on the sleeves of her cuff. Such was the shrieking and the howling proceeding from Lawrence and Korda that Laughton had screens put round the soundstage where he was working. Dreary and pompous, they must have thought him; and in a way he was. But he was trying to do a very difficult thing. The final film tells it all: Gertrude Lawrence plays Geertje Dirx as a conventional stage shrew, a harsh-tongued villainess, while Laughton . . .

'Only by laying himself bare to the bone could any actor hope to play the part. Only Laughton, I believe, of all screen actors, could hope to play it so movingly and so well . . . he has taken the golden passages like a psalmist. Rembrandt is his great part, his matriculation; full of the intimate moments that test an actor's integrity to the highest . . . probably the finest acting performance ever recorded on celluloid.' (C.A. Lejeune.)

But the film disappoints, because, despite many fine passages in the script (by several hands, but principally attributed to Carl Zuckmayer, already author of *The Captain of Köpenick* and *The Devil's General* (although the memorable scene in which Rembrandt reads the Bible was, predictably, interpolated by Laughton), the scope of the film is circumscribed by Korda's boulevard instincts. The film should have been titled *The Private Life of Rembrandt Harmensz van Rijn*; structurally, it is simply an account of the painter's relationship with his various women, through which certain other episodes are woven. By the end of it one feels cheated of a full exploration of the central character. Which is frustrating, because Laughton, in this film, offered the perfect raw material. In a newspaper interview, Charles took the unusual step of criticizing Korda for not having the courage to show Rembrandt's circumstances as they really were; for sentimentalising.

No doubt Korda was eager to get the Laughtons off his hands for a while. After the film he gave them the permission he had withheld a year earlier (they were both under contract to him) to play in *Peter Pan* in the West End. Laughton had seen du Maurier in the original production times without number, and had for many years longed to do it himself; was perhaps keen, too, for Elsa to have a leading part. At first Barrie was opposed to the Laughtons: principally to Laughton, who, he feared, would 'terrify the children.' A call from Elisabeth Bergner, however, allayed his doubts, and they proceeded. He attended a rehearsal, at which he squabbled with Elsa Lanchester over the changes she wanted to introduce into the conventional conception of Peter. She saw him as – in her own words – 'a dominating little snit who orders people around' and had drawn a most surprising comparison with the now (1937) fully risen Hitler – 'another little dictator'. This was the 'something' which Agate found had 'gone wrong' with her Peter, 'which she has obviously conceived along the lines of her Ariel. It is not elfin but eerie, like some little boy cut off in the blossom of his youth, untrousled, disappointed, unanealed. A sinister green make-up hasn't helped matters.' As for Charles: 'his Hook falls short both in the pictorial and the scarifying quality. There should be something of eighteenth century dandyism about this master pirate. Hook should look like some old print, and doesn't.'

It seems that this was an instance (almost unknown up to this date but later, alas, to become more common) of a half-hearted performance on Charles' part. The problem with the Laughton method is that it requires total commitment to come off. Almost without exception his failures are failures of involvement, resulting in soporific, underpowered performances, which are lamentable, but by no means hammy (the usual criticism of him). The opportunities for hamminess in Captain Hook are unlimited; clearly Charles availed himself of none of them. The reasons may be many; Barrie's injunction not to terrify the children could be one, though it would be unlike Laughton to be cowed by a mere living author (only dead ones really inhibited him). He almost certainly *would* have been inhibited by attempting a part which he had seen performed many times by his idol, du Maurier – a terrible burden on any actor, trying to shake off another actor's inflexions, business, interpretation. Of all the motives for accepting a part, admiration for what someone else did with it is the most treacherous. Curiously, too, Laughton didn't perform the great double of Hook/Darling, thus depriving himself of Barrie's most trenchant stroke, the nightmarish underpinning of his superficially fey tale: father is really a monster; the monster is really father.

Close reflexion on the nature of the role reveals why it is, in fact, a rather unsuitable part for Laughton altogether. It is, as Agate suggests, a high comedy role, a parody of the very stage villainy that Laughton had spent the great part of his career startlingly transforming into genuine evil, with roots in pain and frustration. Real evil in that sense would be completely out of place in *Peter Pan*; and Laughton wasn't on the kind of terms with himself that would allow him to stand apart from his own creations to the extent of sending them up – yet. A self-relishing villainy, eye-glinting, lip-smacking, villainy, celebrating its own wickedness, was not something Laughton was able or interested, at this stage of his life, to do.

Perhaps after all, it was Barrie's observation that did it, because if Laughton had let go, had inhabited and transformed Hook as he had done Bligh, he might have given the little ones some very nasty nightmares; and if he had begun to submit to Hook's fear of the crocodile, he might have given them to himself. So he put the brakes on, and was neither fish nor fowl.

Guthrie later wittily wrote of the production: 'Hook, a heavyweight Don Quixote, became the hero of the evening. It was when Peter Pan came on that little children hid their faces in their mothers' skirts and strong men shook with fear.'

Elsa then went off to frighten children in the regions, with a different Hook (George Hayes); and Charles moved on to the next project Korda had found for him. Having failed to animate a *Ruggles*-like venture called *The Ghost Goes West*, which René Clair was to direct – indeed later did, with Robert Donat – and another, to be based on Romola Nijinsky's book about her husband, with Charles as Diaghilev and Anton Dolin as the dancer, Korda finally found a property quite perfect for his resident genius, which at the same time had sufficiently spectacular elements to woo back the great international audience he had been courting since *Henry VIII*: Robert Graves' masterpiece, *I, Claudius*.

Crisis

The rest is history, though as told, a somewhat enigmatic chapter thereof. The chapter can be written from several viewpoints: *I, Claudius* represented the conjunction of many separate crises: Korda's financial crisis (with, as a sub-crisis, his amorous difficulties with Merle Oberon); the growing crisis in Laughton's acting; and the crisis in Josef von Sternberg's mind: not to put too fine a point on it, his nervous breakdown.

Korda had no intention of ever directing Laughton again. His first impulse had been to engage William Cameron Menzies, fresh from his double triumph as director and designer of *Things to Come* (though not a box-office success, one of the few enduring masterpieces from Korda's stable). But he had run into trouble with Marlene Dietrich on *Knight without Armour*: he had not been able to lay hands on the balance of $100,000 that he owed her. She had agreed to waive the outstanding amount if he would use von Sternberg, the mentor she never failed to acknowledge, though estranged from him as a lover.

Von Sternberg, she implied, would perhaps do for Merle Oberon what he had done for her; that is, make her immortal. Korda needed little prompting on either count. His innovative business principles of bluff and blather and charm and cheat had resulted in a number of very interesting films and monstrous debts, and he simply could no longer raise Marlene's $100,000. Moreover, his love affair with Oberon was entirely dependent on his advancing her career in a decisive manner. He persuaded her that *I, Claudius* was being mounted for her and that von Sternberg would arrange her entrée into the Gallery of Fame.

Laughton, too, was delighted. Quite apart from the eternal debt he owed him in the matter of the phantom spirochetes, he admired von Sternberg as an artist; one of the few American film-makers to explore the possibilities of film as a visual medium. Moreover, his well-sustained reputation as a Svengali attracted Charles, too. Having received, as he felt, no help whatsoever from Korda, the toast of the green-room, he was eagerly on the look-out for someone who would help him through the increasingly difficult agonies of creation; someone, at the very least, who would share his perception of the task; in short, a fellow-artist. Surely von Sternberg, who had already shown himself to be kind and practically considerate, as well as an artist of the most demanding sort, would be the very man.

So Laughton went blithely off to the London Clinic where von Sternberg happened to be installed, a large bunch of grapes and a History of the Roman Empire in his hand, a smile on his face, and love in his heart. He told von Sterrberg that he longed to work with him. He admitted that he was difficult to direct, but that he, von Sternberg, would have no difficulties, 'his difficulties would vanish into thin air.' And off he went.

Why was von Sternberg in the London Clinic in the first place? His memoirs simply state that he had been flown over from Bali to be operated on by 'the King of England's surgeon.' It was an interruption of a tour of the Far East he had abruptly undertaken after the completion of the eccentric house he built in the middle of the American desert: 'No sooner was the house completed than I knew that it was not far away enough from everything I wished to leave behind, and I looked around to see where else I might find refuge from the etiolated ogres I had evoked.' In other words, he was on the run.

In seven years and seven films he obsessively worked through his complex relationship with Dietrich, creating a series of versions of her, ravishingly framed and set, in which her fatally passive beauty was seen to have destroyed the ruined men who loved her. The cycle came to an end with *Capriccio Espagnol*, banned in Spain, and retitled *The Devil is a Woman* by the head of Paramount, Lubitsch, who then sacked its director. His always rocky relationship with Dietrich came to a full stop. Sternberg's emotional and physical exhaustion must have been extreme. He then executed two journeyman pieces, a *Crime and Punishment* with Peter Lorre, quirkily played in modern dress (with a ludicrous Mrs Patrick Campbell as the pawnbroker); and *The King Steps Out*, a Fritz Kreisler operetta starring Grace Moore, which betrays no single trace of von Sternberg's touch.

'I had had enough,' he quite understandably writes. He went and found the 'barren and forlorn landscape', in which he built the house of steel and glass to which he withdrew. 'While it was going up, I planted a thousand trees.' But, as he says, it was not far enough away. So he fled as far as he could go, to the other side of the world.

And then he came to London, to hospital, for reasons of health, possibly physical and possibly mental, the man who, born Jo Stern into an ordinary Viennese Jewish family, had, by his absolute mastery of the technical elements of film-making, become king, emperor, dictator; who had uncompromisingly used the screen to dramatise his claustrophobic, obsessional view of life and, more particularly, love. He was now an emperor without an empire and he had no screen on which to inscribe his bleak message. His old friend Alexander Korda, disheartened by the failure of the film he directed, creatively run down, offered him 'full partnership in all his enterprises,' which von Sternberg declined, and the script of *I, Claudius* to direct, which he accepted. It was a subject that interested him: 'to show how a nobody can become a god, and become a nobody and nothing again, appealed to me.'

If he'd discussed this view of the character with the actor who was to play it, he would have met opposition, for Laughton's view of men and life, though pessimistic, was neither reductive nor negative; but he didn't. Why should he? Laughton was an actor, a not very remarkable one: 'who was this comparatively minor actor whose antics had to be taken so seriously? An actor is rewarded with attention out of all proportion to his services. An actor is turned on and off like a spigot, and like the spigot, is not the source of the liquid that flows through him. The intelligent actor knows this and submits without a question. The problem was only to see that the values that bounced back from the material were under my control. And these values rarely depended on the actor. What became visible was produced by an interplay of light and shadow, of foreground and background, point and counterpoint, inclusion and exclusion of content, a balance of pictorial and acoustic impact. And how is that to be conveyed to an actor?'

It is almost comic to contemplate the prospect of the author of these sentiments approaching the actor who was trying to make acting rival painting and music as an art, and who, in all innocence, was looking forward to a unique creative collaboration.

Von Sternberg, as Elsa Lanchester said, rose from his bed 'like the phoenix,' on the run no more. He was back in harness! Into the jodphurs and boots he climbed, on went the turban acquired en route in Java. He took the reins in his hand and drove like the very devil. Korda had not left him much time, but he strode about, galvanising every one, issuing commands, bullying, harassing, getting results! Making people jump! And every so often, this fat and shambling and self-opinionated actor would come up to him and ask him how he saw the character? And should he limp with the left foot or the right? And what did he think was the meaning of this speech, or of that? These trivial and tiresome questions were answered with injunctions to read the script, to read the novel, to go away until the shooting began, when he would receive his detailed instructions. But the actor wanted to *talk*. Intolerable. Von Sternberg, calmly, patiently, humoured him. 'I was opposed to no method he might think valid for impersonating himself.'

Impersonating himself. The phrase expresses everything von Sternberg's approach implied. 'I became somewhat suspicious when he became a mystic. Apparently he was attempting to imbue his characterisations with meanings that an actor should not attempt to express, intent on soaring into a rarefied air where he could pass Dali, Picasso, Kandinsky, and Chagall in full flight . . . with genuine diffidence, Laughton asked how one should address the gods. I decided to test other methods and be as devious as was possible outside of a lunatic asylum. In order to address the gods, I said, if the words he was to haul out of his intestines were to be effective, he must make the audience feel that the hull of the galley was encrusted with barnacles that impeded its speed. As if galvanized, Laughton understood at once, and vouchsafed that every barnacle would be heard in every syllable, and that he could bring into his voice the brine, the tang of the salt in the air, seaweed, two or more dolphins, and the screech of the seagulls. He stormed out of the office as if chased by the

Furies, and it appeared that now everything was in good shape, *except perhaps, the director.*'

The lines for battle were well and truly drawn, the director, straining at the leash, waiting to whip into shape this story and these actors (by now including Flora Robson, Emlyn Williams, and Ralph Richardson in the part Raymond Massey had turned down, according to von Sternberg, because 'nothing on earth' would persuade him to work with the actor he had directed in *The Silver Tassie*); and the actor, still, despite some rather unfriendly and patronising behaviour from his old friend the director, looking forward to their partnership in trying to give life to the hapless vocal and physical cripple he hoped to embody. He had already given some excellent help in the scene in which he had to address the gods, an almost impossible thing to get the feeling of: the ancient Roman gods so personal and so near, and yet still gods. Von Sternberg's note had been excellent; neither intellectual nor technical: it had done what a note should do: it had released something in him.

He had, moreover, himself hit on something which conveyed some of the anguished, romantically bruised dignity of Claudius: King Edward VIII's abdication speech: 'the woman I love,' and so on, recently released on a best-selling gramophone record. It was a key. It worked. Who knows why? It was a comfort, a little nudge into the part. Every day he played it, dozens of times, in his caravan, on the set, at home.

Thus armed, battle commenced. From the beginning it was evident to Laughton that he could expect nothing but cold command from von Sternberg. Still genuinely grateful for the kind services rendered at the time of the fistula, and respectful of his skills, Laughton never raised his voice against his director, never created a scene, was never once 'difficult'. He simply couldn't work in the conditions von Sternberg had created. The words of the part became meaningless to him, he was standing outside himself, nothing was filling his being: like his mind, it was a blank. He could hardly remember a line; he, who had been word perfect a week before, when he and von Sternberg had gone through the script together. Von Sternberg had been worried that he seemed expressionless, that his face had seemed amorphous, empty. He had (rightly) attributed this to the actor's 'artistic pregnancy'. Elsewhere he speaks of him 'squirming like a woman in labour'. Now that Laughton wanted to deliver, he received no help. He would repeat the same scene over and over again, always losing his lines or suddenly being distracted by some trivial thing – an odd note in his voice – a light – a movement. Self-consciousness kills any inner life. Laughton would try desperate remedies: moving to another set for a different sequence, trying new moves to break the pattern. Nothing availed except momentarily. A kind of blushing modesty, a feeling of nakedness overtook him.

All of this was incomprehensible to von Sternberg. His greatest praise for Dietrich had been her ability to translate his 'instructions' into actions without explanation. His word was her command. 'Given the proper motivation and some guidance, acting is nothing remarkable, providing of course, that the actor is an actor and has the necessary shamelessness to expose his emotions and antics to inspection. To give face to expressions used by millions of human beings all around us, day after day, requires only a relatively minor ability to mimic.'

Von Sternberg had discerned 'a tendency toward masochism' in Laughton and decided to test it. He set up a scene in which Claudius would walk down a street surrounded by a jeering mob, and specially chose the ugliest, most evil-smelling extras he could find, directing them to howl abuse at Charles as he passed. The lighting was specially designed to highlight their savage expressions; they were placed to hem Laughton in. 'We began what everyone thought to be a rehearsal only. My diagnosis proved to be correct. The scene was fine and Claudius superb.' Not surprisingly, as von Sternberg had at last done something actually to help Laughton. Of course it could have been done mechanically, by skill alone, by the actor working in isolation; but it is hard to believe that the scene would have been as charged as the performance revealed in the footage assembled by Bill Duncalf for *The Epic That Never Was*, his television documentary about the failed project. Thank God for Laughton and for what he was trying to do as an actor that this footage exists. Otherwise von Sternberg's account and the insidious rumours of the detractors would have convinced us that all that was going on during that doomed shoot was a monumental case of primadonna-ism, an actor self-indulgent to the point of buffoonery wrecking the work of his fellow-workers.

Instead we can see that Laughton was struggling to give life to a performance of unprecedentedly searing pathos, to show a man mocked and spurned though sensitive, gentle and intelligent: a simple enough character who, by the intensity of his inner feeling, he was transfiguring into a paradigm of pain, a Dostoevskian creation, almost too painful to watch.

The twenty-five minutes or so of surviving footage are painful to watch in another way: it is almost embarrassing to eavesdrop on the public humiliation of this struggling man, constantly breaking off – 'I'm sorry, I've lost it', or 'that's the broadest London accent you ever heard in your life' – as the extras and his fellow-actors shuffle nervous and bored in the background. When he does forget a word or a line, von Sternberg, off-camera, shouts it out – always a terrible reproach. If the *director* knows the line and you don't. . . what's curious is that as far as one can see up to the point Laughton breaks off, he seems to be giving a wonderful performance. Something obviously snaps in his brain, the thread is lost, belief is suspended. Self-consciousness overtakes him. Very often when an actor forgets his lines, it is because a voice inside his brain has whispered to him, 'Wouldn't it be dreadful if you forgot the lines?' And that voice has generally entered the brain at the moment the actor loses contact, however momentarily, with the character in the situation, and, looking back to examine this or that line, turns, like Lot's wife, into salt. And *this* often happens when there is no contact between actor and director, and the actor becomes convinced that every time he opens his mouth it is a further source of displeasure. This shortly becomes paralysing, and unless the actor can get hold of some form of self-confidence (most likely anger against the director), it will only get worse; until, in the theatre, the director goes away and the performance can begin to exist. But of course, in a film, the director never does go away.

From the evidence of what has survived, Laughton was desperately in need of support because he had chosen to walk a very high tightrope indeed. The physical gesture of the performance is enormous: the stutters and the tics are nearly incapacitating, and the limp is one of utmost deformity, like a man walking along with one foot in a trench. The point is not that people do have just such terrible distortions in life, which they certainly do, but that behind them, inside them, is a quite different person, not a loon or a cripple, but a gentle, wise, and humorous man, a scholar and a poet, who has remained untarnished by his physical disadvantages and people's crass and cruel reaction to them. It is this gap which creates the scale of the performance – the huge obstacles surmounted by a witty and shrewd spirit, and which makes the climactic speech in which Claudius finally takes command in the Senate such an overpoweringly emotional experience ('One of the greatest performances in the history of the cinema'', Dirk Bogarde says in his commentary to *The Epic That Never Was*). We see the spirit totally overcome the flesh. It is a moment to bring forth cheers from an audience, because it celebrates, as Charles Laughton liked to celebrate, the triumph of reality over appearance. It becomes an epic moment because of the actor's choices. Another man might have striven to show Claudius' pain and suffering, which would have created sympathy, but would not been remotely as moving as what we see, because then we would have become involved in what Claudius was feeling instead of seeing what was being done to him. Equally, another actor might have tried to minimise, to rationalise, his physical distortions, to join the two sides of the character closer together. What Laughton does is to sound the furthest notes of the octave as loud and clear as possible, and thus to strike the chord of maximum resonance.

No such task was ever attempted by any actor in any other von Sternberg movie, except, of course, Jannings in *The Blue Angel*; but any comparison of the two performances leaves Jannings behind in a morass of face-pulling and sentimental manipulation. The *actuality* of Laughton's performance remains shocking today.

But to von Sternberg the success of the scene was his: he had tricked the actor, as so often before, into giving a performance. Well, perhaps the trick would work again. He scoured the script for other instances in which Laughton's alleged masochism could be activated in the film's favour. And he found a scene in which Claudius had to be kicked through a door, fall on his face and say – it was his bridal night – 'This is not how I would have chosen to appear before you.' Laughton asked for someone actually to kick him into the room. 'My assistant gladly volunteered to perform this service.' Laughton was kicked into the room. He fell. And then he dried up. He couldn't remember his line, his one simple and obvious line. The scene was repeated. Same thing. And again. If Laughton's masochism was being given a night out, so was the assistant director's sadism. Finally, they broke for lunch. 'Laughton went off to eat as if nothing out of the ordinary had happened.' After lunch, same thing. And again. Von Sternberg sent for Korda; 'my peculiar type of wizardry, if such it be, had come to an end.'

Korda's quite different wizardry was equally unavailing. Filming was abandoned for the day.

Even if this account is, as usual with von Sternberg, both one-sided and distorted, there is no doubt that Laughton was behaving strangely. If so, it is hardly surprising. Constitutionally incapable of 'just getting on with it,' he had somehow, up to this point, been able to engineer situations in which he was able to function as a creative artist, somehow finding the equation between self-exposure and the technical frame within which to shape the material thus mined. Faced with an absolute refusal to acknowledge let alone abet the processes by which his creations were achieved, he was thrown into a state of paralysis. Temperamentally incapable of standing up to the harsh dictatorial style of von Sternberg, he adopted a defensive posture: he retreated into babyhood. In what amounts to a satirical parody of how von Sternberg wanted him to behave he was in effect saying: you want to tell me what to do? All right, tell me: everything, every movement, every gesture, every word, tell me when to get up and when to sit down. Tell me when to breathe. Obviously you feel that my brain, my contribution, are of no value, so I will withdraw both. Then you'll really be in charge. This posture of Charles, a typical one, simultaneously passive and taunting, drove von Sternberg into a frenzy; it was a mockery of him and his methods; above all, it was an abrogation of his authority, as he had, finally, to admit by calling in the producer.

It was a terrible confrontation which, the moment it became a battle of principle, could be won by neither antagonist. Laughton wept the bitterest tears of his career every night when he went home; he was in agony; but he never gave up his stand: that the actor's work, in its complexity, difficulty and sheer human cost must be acknowledged and abetted. It was the spigot's revolt. Laughton was insisting that, as he had proved in innumerable dull and clichéd scripts, he was both the conduit and the source of the liquid. Von Sternberg, implacably opposed to the notion of a co-creator, could not allow this heresy to flourish.

The point of no return had been reached. The final showdown never happened, however, because of the famous car accident in which Merle Oberon, driving home from the studio one night, was injured. At first Korda, despite his love for Oberon, frantically called Hollywood to try to acquire the services of Claudette Colbert; but she wasn't available. Meanwhile it became clear that the wounds Oberon had sustained were much less than at first appeared; but she was still hysterical from shock, and refused to continue shooting. She was calm enough to receive a visit from Herbert Wilcox, as reported by Philip Jenkinson. Wilcox was surprised at the modest extent of her damage: a facial bruise and a slightly twisted ankle; and more surprised when she said that shooting would have to be abandoned, not because of her, but because of 'poor Joe'. 'Where is he?' Wilcox wanted to know. 'Charing Cross Hospital Psychiatric Unit.' Wilcox finally managed to contact him there, asking if he wanted to be visited. 'Absolutely not,' said von Sternberg, 'I'm sick.'

So Korda pulled the plug. Oberon's accident satisfied the insurance company; Korda was not the loser, financially. He nursed hopes for a remake of the film the following year. He told Robert Graves that it would have to be without Laughton: Korda, said Graves, 'complained bitterly of Laughton and his intellectualism. It was worse with von Sternberg, who did not humour him.' Laughton must obviously have been relieved; there was no question of him remaking any of the film, because when his contract expired a couple of weeks later he was due to take up a new contract immediately after, a contract which promised an entirely new direction in his unhappy career: he was to be co-producer of a new company, Mayflower Productions, with Erich Pommer, ex-head of the great German studio, UFA, and, by a nice irony, producer of von Sternberg's first great success, *The Blue Angel*.

After leaving the Psychiatric Unit, von Sternberg continued on his travels: back to the Far East, above all Japan. Then, somehow, he found himself in France, trying to cast a London-based film of *Germinal*; at the same time he was setting up a film which would restore Austria's good name in the world. In the grip of demonic energy, he returned to London. 'A great surge of strength and power had taken hold of me; I was like an electric bulb which gleams with an intensity, too bright a moment before it is burned out . . . it is not difficult to perceive that I had wound up my inner spring too tightly . . . I looked out of the window to think it might not be a bad idea to take a little walk; but there was no time to waste, and I turned back to my desk. A few minutes later the concept of time ceased to exist for me, something within me had snapped like an elastic that had been stretched too far.'

Slowly he recovered ('a human being has reservoirs of energy deeper than the deep seas'); but his remaining career, except for his Japanese film *Anatahan*, is a dismal record of hack-work and co-direction. His main project after the war was a script he had written but which no one would back. It was called *Seven Bad Years*, the years of the title being the first of a man's life, which, according to von Sternberg, determined the whole of the rest of it; the rest of one's life was effectively run by ones's seven-year-old self. Laughton may have been a mess, and difficult to handle; but his pathology was quite normal compared to that of the tiny emotionally stunted autocrat in whose nervous crisis *I, Claudius* is but an episode.

Mayflower

Mayflower Productions was started with the utmost seriousness and the highest hopes. Pommer, in flight from Hitler, originator of the films (*Caligari, Mabuse, Die Nibelungen, Metropolis*) that had made the German cinema the most vital and the most beautifully produced in Europe, was a guarantee of integrity and high production values: Caroline Lejeune had written, in 1931, that 'it would not be possible to present a complete impression of the better movie in Europe and America without some mention of Erich Pommer. He is that phenomenon so dear to the brighter journalism, a 'mystery man'; the public does not know him, and even the men most closely associated with studio politics find it difficult to agree on the subject of his activities . . . his name across a film stands sturdily for box-office value, but it carries with it, at the same time, a definite promise of intelligence. It represents a certain scope of thought, a certain novelty and audacity of treatment; it represents a standard set high through many years of film experience, a product rigidly maintained above a certain demarcation line.' In associating himself with Pommer, Laughton had scored a coup.

Laughton's intention was to revolutionise film-making. He was no actor-manager, planning a series of vehicles for himself; on the contrary, reported *Film Weekly*: 'he believes and hopes the star system will gradually die out'. Instead 'team work among actors in films should develop . . . if a permanent company could work together as in a repertory theatre they would create something new and exciting.' He believed, moreover, that the writer was central to the development of the medium, that Shakespeare, Molière and Chekhov had written their immortal plays for a known company of actors and actresses. The same system should exist in films. 'When the new medium starts to produce its own writers, then will begin the period of great movies.'

As for himself: 'I'm not going to play any more emperors or figures of genius. I don't like it – 'exposing the extraordinary instead of illuminating the ordinary.' I'm going to look for more human parts to play. The Blighs and Barretts can have a rest for a while.'

So the great experiment began. He flung himself into the unaccustomed role of executive, appearing daily at his office, sporting tie and suit and shoes not merely laced up but actually polished. He and Pommer (a third partner, the shrewd Scot, John Maxwell, who had built up the ABC chain and was a central figure in many deals of the British film industry of the thirties, was not concerned with artistic policy) assembled a programme with a distinctly middle-brow slant. Writers, if not exactly Shakespeare, Molière or Chekhov, were well represented: Somerset Maugham (*Vessel of Wrath*); Clemence Dane (*St Martin's Lane*); and Daphne du Maurier (*Jamaica Inn*). There was some semblance of a permanent group of actors: Robert Newton and Tyrone Guthrie, for example, would appear in two films each, as would Elsa Lanchester; and Laughton, though a central figure in all three (he was, after all, the company's main asset) had surrounded himself with very good actors in sizeable and meaty roles.

Things started well enough with *Vessel of Wrath*. The adaptor of the Maugham story, Bartlett Cormack, was also designated director, but the strain of a major location shoot led him swiftly to the bottle, and Pommer took over. The result is the most visually stylish and most coherent of the Mayflower films – rather beautifully shot, in fact, both on location in the South of France, and on Tom Morahan's convincing jungle sets, with Jules Kruger's photography creating the shadows which were the hallmark of UFA films. Robert Newton, in the days before the words 'Arr, Jim lad' had ever passed his lips, makes an interestingly world-weary district commissioner with a fitful French accent; Tyrone Guthrie plays a bird-like caricature of a missionary, madly exaggerated but funny and vivid; while Lanchester plays the missionary's sister, the longest, most central role of her career. Happily, it's also one of her best. Laughton is Ginger Ted, the beachcomber of the American title, an agreeable sot and reprobate, who spends most of the film avoiding Elsa's reforming ministrations. Their relationship – again with an autobiographical thread: it was she who had put Charles into the suit, tie and shoes of his producer's uniform after all – is played with some passion and realism, and does rise to a real encounter between the opposed forces of hedonism and Christian do-goodery (much hated by both Laughtons). His perform-ance, in particular, is a real celebration of easy carnality as the native women of the island to which he is exiled caress and pamper him. The film contains an indictment of colonialism of a romantic kind, as Lanchester strides through the milling natives, trying to force Christianity on them. Its last scene presents a witty reverse of the film's main situation when Ted and Martha (Lanchester) return from the East Indies to run a hotel in suburban England – strictly teetotal, at Ted's insistence.

All in all the piece is charming and fun and very well made and perfectly honourable. The Brave New World of Film it wasn't, however. Laughton made a point of admiring his Ginger Ted in preference to other characters he'd played: 'I think it is my most significant role to date'. Which is just silly. 'I am a little weary of playing heavy, humourless characters,' he said, quite understandably, but the part lacks the tension of Laughton's relationship to it – as in *If I Had a Million*, for example – and thus fails to be memorable.

His account of the genesis of the role is interesting in this connexion: '*Vessel of Wrath* resolved itself into a much broader comedy than we at first intended. I thought, when I started work on the characterisation, that the pathos and the humour would be fairly divided, but Ginger Ted turned out to be a much funnier character than we had anticipated . . . I have learned never to force a characterisation into a specified mould, but allow the character to build itself up from the material. Ginger Ted, I discovered, evoked more laughter than sympathy, so I let him go his own way.' It is hard to imagine Bligh, or Rembrandt, or Nero being arrived at in this way.

Producing as well as acting in a movie (or play, for that matter) is a curious and unsatisfactory combination of duties. It requires the development of a sense – the planning, budgeting, organising sense – which is best left to another person. Directing and acting in the same film, though not without its disadvantages, is simply a bringing together of two complementary aspects of the creative work. The producer has to concern himself with how that creative work can be realised with the minimum compromise; the word compromise should not even be in the vocabulary of the other two. For Laughton, however, Mayflower must at first have seemed an ideal opportunity to divert his huge energies away from the exhausting and nearly dementing labour of giving birth to *major performances*; acting would be just one of his activities; the pressure would be off.

He was right: the pressure was off – but was also gone from the centre of his performances. This still left a lot, but it meant that they became particular rather than universal, and Laughton became a character actor, purveyor of personality studies instead of matrices of the human experience.

Contemporary criticism of Laughton was generally enthusiastic ('he is first-rate' said the *Spectator*); 'he carries nearly the whole burden of the film, moving through an almost visible fog of alcohol and perspiration'. 'Grand all through it,' said Otis Ferguson, 'he got into his part with such relish you could almost smell him.' These tributes to his fleshliness had a particular significance in 1938. 'There is great skill in (Laughton's) insolence and a nicely calculated vulgarity which is very near that gusto we have been missing so much in British films. Viewed as a comment, not on missionaries, but on those wretched Women's Leagues of America who have been taking the corpuscles out of American films, Laughton's performance has a certain importance,' wrote John Grierson in *World Film News*. Otis Ferguson too observed that 'part of the blessing of this film is its unbounded appreciation of some joys of life to which movies are making us rapidly unaccustomed.' But in England, particularly, the film was judged by tougher criteria than usual, because much hinged on the outcome of Laughton and Pommer's experiment. 'With the continued storm over the new Quota Act the moment is critical for British films. If at this juncture our studios can prove their mettle, much will be done to restore City confidence in the future,' Stuart Legg observed in *The Spectator*. He continued: '*Vessel of Wrath* has many desirable qualities. It is sanely and economically produced, its technical standards are high, but it lacks the vitality of the big films.' Grierson wrote even more sharply in a article that amounts to a public warning to the partners:

I like Laughton very much, for he is a brilliant fellow, but I like the future of British films even more. He will not mind, therefore, if I suggest an elementary lesson in the categories. The trouble with Laughton is that he is good at several very different things. He has skill in tragedy and has an ambition to play King Lear. He speaks rhetoric with a flair almost unique among modern actors, and though there may be mannerism in the way he slides across a full stop, no one will forget his reading of the Bible in *Rembrandt*. He is, moreover, a dangerously good and upsetting showman in his capacity of lagging on a cue and exaggerating an acting trifle behind the back of his director. No scrum-half ever played the blind side of a referee more knowingly. Add to these talents the equally various ones of being good at comedy and quite brilliant at slapstick and you have a deadly mixture of virtues.

In any single film you can't possibly have the lot. Lear cannot possibly at the same time act the Fool, and Macbeth take his place among the porters. That precisely is what Laughton is forever doing. He does not understand economy and, by the mere process of being everything in starts and nothing long, is the greatest saboteur a film could have. It may all come from his anxious desire to add everything of himself to the value of the film. But the damage is certain. Laughton one at a time would be the wonder of the day. Five at a time he is a producer's headache.

I have quarrelled a great deal with people over *Vessel of Wrath*. But I soon found we were quarrelling over very different things. I viewed it as principally slapstick and was prepared to forgive the odd departures into drama and sentiment. My arguers had viewed it as drama and were bewildered by the fact that it was mostly slapstick. See the film as, nearly, in the category of Laurel and Hardy, and you will see *Vessel of Wrath* at its best. But this does not absolve Pommer and Laughton from making up their minds more decisively next time. Knowing Laughton a little, I think he should come through. A strategic retreat from his own talents is what is called for.

This trenchant analysis foreshadows Laughton's increasing reluctance to play *a* character, his yearning somehow to play *all* the characters, to play the whole film.

Their next offering, *St Martin's Lane*, had much less coherence than *Vessel of Wrath*, stemming from failures of both writing and direction. The idea – from Charles – has a certain charm: set in the community of West End buskers, it charts the rise of one of them to stardom and riches, while another remains behind, lost in hopeless love. The notion of popular entertainment was always close to Laughton's heart, and the sections with which he's connected – the busking scenes – are full of affection and fun. The film is one of the first to have scenes shot on location in the centre of London, which lends it atmosphere and authenticity. Clemence Dane, the writer, said: 'We desired to make a classic of London street life, so that everyone should cry out: "This is home!" "This is the true London!"' And to some extent they succeed. Tom Morahan's St Martin's Lane itself is a brilliant recreation. Things begin to go wrong with the arrival of Rex Harrison – despite a delightful performance by him (Laughton had visited him backstage at the Criterion Theatre where he was playing in *French Without Tears* telling him: 'you're very good in this Rex, you play the part as if you were wearing a sword' – an interesting, and, Harrison felt, a perceptive remark). He plays an improbable upper-class songwriter who falls in love with the girl busker of the group, writes a musical for her, makes her a Great Star, and marries her. Laughton's busker watches her from a distance, she having rejected him, then auditions for her next show, but he's no good, and he tails sadly away. All are somehow reconciled by the last frame.

For all the success of the low-life scenes, the high-life scenes are so poorly written, crazily plotted and played, and the musical sequences are so tackily botched, that the entertainment quotient of the film is slight. Even the busking sequences are rendered somewhat bizarre by the presence in them of Tyrone Guthrie, a credible if burlesqued missionary in *Vessel of Wrath*, but here an almost expressionist figure, gangling, hawk-eyed and apparently possessed of no busking skills whatever. He is very striking, sitting up in bed in his lonely attic when the girl comes looking for Charlie (the Laughton character) and delivering himself of a stinging rebuke on the nature of friendship, but it's utterly out of key with the tone of the film – insofar as it may be said to have one. Essentially it's a mess – which must be laid at the door of the director, the genial, bottle-happy Tim Whelan, an American in London, ex-script-writer and sometime director to Harold Lloyd (which, given Laughton's constant hankering after slapstick, must have been what got him the job). His grip on the film is, to say the least, loose: in the musical sequences, positively slack.

But how could Laughton and Pommer – with their avowed sense of the central significance of the script – have gone into production with such a hodge-podge? Well, of course, a thousand reasons, the usual thousand reasons, but it was ominous that their high ideals should so swiftly have produced a film which is as inconsequential, as ill-thought-through and as inept as the general output of the film industry. It failed exactly as they failed, from the same causes and the same waste of time and money. Clemence Dane, in a letter to Pommer, catalogues the unceasing vacillations of the partners. They didn't really know what they wanted.

There are consolations in the film: one is the almost spectrally suave performance of Harrison; a second is the girl: Vivien Leigh, not at the very outset of her career, but sufficiently unknown for this film, trans-atlanticized into *The Sidewalks of London* (no wonder it was a flop!) to be her calling-card to Hollywood (it was after a viewing of it that Selznick decided on her as Scarlett O'Hara). Her performance is, on one level, inept beyond words. The Cockney accent is quite unaccept-able, she plays peevishness and petulance throughout, she can't really sing and lurches from one emotion to another without even a gesture towards character. Against this must be set her astonishing face, a squeezed rose, exotic and fresh at the same time, unconventional by standards of the time but flawless. Moreover, she contains within her a spirit of anarchy, a real danger and unpredictability, that is almost

Lulu-like: a daemon, a siren, a pussycat with the sharpest claws and a tongue that spits like a lynx.

She is phenomenal; which is always better than being competent or solid. She does nothing to help a shaky script, however. Some of the phenomenality of her performance could derive from the life-style which her biographer, Anne Edwards, charts. She was at the passionate start of her affair with Olivier, and most of her nights were filled with things other than sleep – this may account for the hectic quality of her acting. She was apparently repelled by Laughton, and dreaded a sexual advance which she would have to reject; he for his part was deeply shocked by her liberal use of four-lettered words. His sense of propriety was and remained essentially Victorian: he didn't like to hear words of that kind used by someone who belonged to the same sex as his mother.

His performance of the oddly named Charlie Staggers is beautifully judged, human, warm, funny, sentimental, real, in fact surprisingly modern. His is the only Cockney accent in the film that would be acceptable today, or recognisable even, and the whole pitch of the performance, particularly considering that he's playing a performer, with all the limitless potential for mugging that offers, is exceptionally restrained. It's touching, too: Charlie knows he's not good-looking, but he dares to hope. The scene where Leigh tells him to 'look in the frying-pan' which he uses as his mirror if he wants to see why she could never marry him, and the scene in which he auditions for the swanky West End backers of her musical and quietly wanders away to spare her embarrassment, bring a tear to the eye. In its economy and accuracy the performance is a complete refutation of any accusations of self-indulgence or trickiness. It is, especially in its context, an admirably straightforward piece of work.

The delicacy of Laughton's performance was noted – 'one of the finest, if not the best – sympathetic performances Charles Laughton has ever given on the screen . . . Mr Laughton is the meticulous, sensitive artist in this instance.' (Richard Sheridan Ames); though the resistance of some critics was not to be overcome by any such crude expedient as his giving an excellent performance: 'Whether he is really a finished actor or no I leave to you. I have thought sometimes in the past that Laughton was acclaimed for much of that specious, arresting but obvious, grossly physical playing. This is a comparatively restrained and certainly a felt performance. Yet it seems to me the actor still puts physical mannerisms in the way of our seeing inside the character, so to speak. Be that as it was, few actors could bring to the role what Laughton does,' Bert Harlen told readers of *Hollywood Spectator*. You can't please some of the people *any* of the time.

Despite decent notices and a stupendous première at the Odeon Leicester Square, at which 5,000 people massed for the arrival of the stars, it did only moderate business. Much hung on the success of the third film, *Jamaica Inn*. Laughton drew on his personal acquaintance with him to sign Alfred Hitchcock, on the brink of his American career, to direct it. It was a coup. Hitchcock was the man of the hour, having completed *The Man Who Knew Too Much*, *The Thirty-Nine Steps* and *The Lady Vanishes* in the past three years. He brought a sense of tautly-controlled style quite lacking from contemporary British films – not least those produced by Mayflower. Curiously, he seems to have accepted the film before having read the script. The moment he did, however, he tried to get out of his contract; was, it is said, prepared to sell his house in order to do so. But Laughton cajoled and persuaded and begged; and finally, Laughton prevailed. A new script was commissioned – Clemence Dane had been responsible for the despised first version – from Sydney Gilliatt, Hitchcock's collaborator on *The Lady Vanishes*; but that was not completely satisfactory, either. The problem was Laughton's character, the squire, Sir Humphrey Pengallan. To avoid offending the church-going section of the population, the parson could not be the villain, as in the novel; so Sir Humphrey became the smugglers' master-mind. Much re-thinking was called for, to which end, J.B. Priestley was put on the payroll, to work exclusively on Laughton's part. Once again, the prophets of writers' cinema were embarking on a film without that essential, a coherent and workable script.

A very good cast was as usual assembled, Robert Newton, this time a pirate at last, but only a pretend one, Emlyn Williams (a Laughton veteran), Leslie Banks (a Hitchcock veteran), Marie Ney, a veteran, *tout court*. The discovery was Maureen O'Hara, eighteen years old, fresh from Dublin and luxuriating in her colleen loveliness, hair a-tumble, eyes a-sparkle, lips a-pout. They all do their best, acting with gusto and inventiveness, but very little sense of purpose or style. The result is, alas, not far short of ludicrous. They are nothing abetted by the sets, an uncharacteristic exercise in semi-expressionism by Tom Morahan. Half-hearted expressionism is almost a contradiction in terms (*in*expressionism, it seems more like here): 'the inn looks as though it had been painted on cardboard by an admirer of Vlaminck,' observed Agate. The staging of the film and the entire look of it suffer from this same half-heartedness: it's sloppy, stiff, unrhythmic, ugly, and there are terrible, laughable errors of continuity. The director's lack of enthusiasm for the project is established: but what were the producers up to? It is almost inconceivable that those perfectionists Laughton and Pommer should have allowed the mess that is *Jamaica Inn* to go out under the name of Mayflower.

They were, of course, in crisis.

Vessel of Wrath, re-named *The Beachcomber*, had failed to create any impact at the American box-office, and had not, in fact, done very well in England. *St Martin's Lane* was no great shakes under either of *its* titles. Money was short. John Maxwell, the only professional financier among the three, agreed to put more money into the company only if he could have exclusive title to Laughton's services as an actor. Laughton summoned his brother Tom, a sounder business-man than he – but then almost anyone would have been – to speak for him, which he did, at least to the extent of wangling unconditional completion money out of Maxwell. The enterprise was stumbling; as was the film in question. Laughton and Hitchcock were not really hitting it off; and Laughton was stuck.

The two men were not locked in conflict; nor was one trying to dominate the other. There was not even a great temperamental difference. In fact their superficial similarities are very striking: two portly scions of Jesuit colleges, not quite gentlemen, sexually complex, and closely involved in their work, with the darker impulses of humanity. Their self-presentation, however, and above all their artistic means, were radically different. Hitchcock all laconic containment and ellipsis, Laughton naked exposure and bold statement; or, in the simplified terms in which the confrontation was perceived, Hitchcock the pro, Laughton the amateur.

Laughton's block was due to the absurdity of the newly-confected character, which he tried to fill with some sort of meaning. At first he was completely stumped, and wouldn't go before the cameras at all: the film had to be shot around him. Then, according to Tom Laughton, he got drunk one night, came to the studio hungover after a sleepless night, and was suddenly able to play the character: a hangover can indeed often dispel self-consciousness, as can tiredness, and being in love: concentration is by no means always achieved by concentrating. But, though he'd devised a satisfactory make-up, and had a sense of the man he was playing, he still couldn't find how he should walk, so he persuaded Hitchcock to shoot him only in medium close-up: that is, from the chest up. Desperation again; then, his old

Scarborough acquaintance Eric Fenby, who was composing the score, happened to hum the lilting waltz measure from Weber's *Invitation to the Dance*. That was it! He could walk. Now Hitchcock was permitted to shoot the whole of him.

This behaviour was, quite understandably, beneath contempt to Hitchcock. 'The only way to prevent a complete disruption of communication between the director and the star was for Hitchcock to indulge his own fantasies at key points in the narrative,' writes Donald Spoto in *The Dark Side of Genius*. 'Thus he instigated the appalling exaggeration of a sadistic scene in which the deranged Laughton, protesting how much he is in love with Maureen O'Hara, binds and gags her. "I am primarily interested," Hitchcock said at the time, "in the the Jekyll-Hyde mentality of the squire."' These scenes, as Spoto says, 'were the only ones filmed with passion.'

In a much-quoted phrase, Hitchcock later said: 'It isn't possible to direct a Charles Laughton film, the best you can hope is to act as referee.' Laughton 'wasn't really a professional film man,' he told Truffaut years later, 'it wasn't serious, and I don't like to work that way.' He made many public comments about Laughton, all devolving on the question of his 'professionalism'. 'There are many, many artists in the world who are extremely talented and are geniuses, but they never become a pro. I think that was one of his problems – Charles never became a craft professional. He was always an artist and a genius, and he worked that way, so it became a disordered lack of control . . .'

The question is whether it is more professional to refuse to commit a mediocre performance to film, to whittle and to dig and to probe until something worthwhile has been achieved; or to simply get any damn thing onto the screen, good, bad, indifferent, but *there*. Because that is what Hitchcock did in *Jamaica Inn*, a film whose only possible redeeming feature is the performance by the 'artist, the genius' (obviously words of the deepest opprobrium for Hitchcock), Laughton.

It is an uncomfortable performance – uncharacteristically uncertain verbally, with many an um and an ah in the middle of phrases – and it is not a searching one; but it is fun, and it is quite enterprising. From behind his false nose (his first since *Sign of the Cross*) and false brow, he attempts an eighteenth-century feeling, like something out of Fielding: an elegant grossness, gallant and sardonic, and underneath it all, quite, quite mad. There is a flicker of something very nasty in the scene where he attempts to tie up Maureen O'Hara; and when he is cornered there's a certain grandeur to his defiance. It's not a masterly performance, but it's an original and, in its strutting, sneering self-satisfaction, a memorable one.

Agate put his finger on the quality it lacked in an ominous analysis presaging an unhealthy development in Laughton's acting: 'The whole performance seemed to me to be 'screen', by which I mean the film equivalent of 'stagey'. It had obviously been put together in the studio at the same time as the eyebrows and the nose. Perhaps what most precluded my belief in the character was the actor's obvious delight in his own creation. One was conscious not of Sir Humphrey revelling in Sir Humphrey's gusto, but of Mr Laughton revelling in Mr Laughton's actorship.' Wonderful phrase: although, of course, it only *seemed* that way. It was a display not so much of bravura as of bravado. Not having found the goods within himself, he was drawing heavily on external skills and invention and, forceful personality and resourceful actor that he was, it is eminently watchable. But Laughton had been worth more than that. 'Whatever the reason, I had no belief that Mr Laughton's Sir Humphrey was alive and doing this and that nefarious thing in Cornwall, in the way in which I believed in the theatre that his *Man with Red Hair* was actual and up to the monkey tricks indicated by Sir Hugh.'

That was what set Laughton apart from other actors. The cost of such performances (and the less satisfactory the script, the more absurd the situation, the more demanding they were) was, however, inordinately high, and, with Sir Humphrey, he just couldn't perform the miracle. It was some while, in fact, since he had performed that particular miracle: the transubstantiation of lath-and-plaster ciphers into flesh and blood. Perhaps that was one reason for his eager embrace of RKO's offer of the part of Quasimodo, the hunchback of Notre Dame. Another, no doubt more immediately pressing, reason was that he was now heavily in debt over Mayflower, and RKO volunteered repayment of those debts as part of the five-picture contract they were proposing.

So Laughton sailed off in the tense summer of 1939, away from troubled Europe, away from his aborted career as an actor-producer, towards Hollywood and one last, glorious offering up of his guts and his bowels on the altar of his cruel god. This journey was towards an end of something, not a beginning.

The Hunchback

It had been Thalberg's idea, originally, to re-film the famous novel. Lon Chaney had had his greatest success in the 1923 version, directed on spectacular settings by Tod Browning. Chaney's performance is touching, only moderately deformed, and, of course, silent. The performance is in a line of tough losers in which the older actor specialised. RKO actually used the sets from the 1923 film, but in every other respect it was intended to be, and was, totally different.

William Dieterle was the director chosen by Pandro Berman, head of the studio. He came fresh from a string of biopic successes starring Paul Muni, and there is a didactic strain in his writing about film that is prominent in his approach to *The Hunchback*. 'Film art is yet in its childhood. As time goes on, the motion picture artists, not the directors alone, will continue and eventually win their fight for creative freedom, for the benefit of better pictures, to enlighten intelligent audiences.' Sentiments that could equally have been uttered by Pommer and Laughton. The difference, of course, was that Dieterle had a studio behind him, and within its limitations, he produced honourable work for them. He was a Reinhardt man, acted for him (opposite Elisabeth Bergner), and finally co-directed the film of *A Midsummer Night's Dream* with him. Like all of Reinhardt's disciples and colleagues – like Reinhardt himself – he had a keen sense of the actor and his contribution. 'All I can say now is: the personality who is not an actor is to me impossible – I prefer the actor with personality. It should never be necessary for the director to compel an actor to create something that is not in him.' Dangerous words from someone about to work with Laughton, who had no interest in *personality* and whose conception of the task of acting was all to do with releasing something in himself that may well appear not to be in him. However: 'the director must achieve a proper creative state, which will help the actor to the birth of inspiration. The rest will come about subconsciously – by nature. Not the actor alone, but all co-operators, whom I consider as important as the director himself, give of their best only in a favourable atmosphere, which is the supreme task of the director to create. How can anyone, not to mention an actor, work, if he is embarrassed, or if he feels a sense of inefficiency, or failure? To create success one has first to create the spirit of enthusiasm; that is, the spirit of success. This works miracles.'

These are exemplary sentiments, and quite rare in Hollywood,

1939. Dieterle was firm but courteous. His image as 'von Sternberg and water' seems misplaced and perhaps derives from his sinister habit of wearing white gloves to direct – because, he claimed, in his days in the Berlin theatre when he was acting or directing he was frequently called upon to shift the furniture. As he had a neurotic fear of dirtying his hands, he adopted the gloves. It seems to have been his one eccentricity. No suffering on Charles' part can be laid at his door. If Charles suffered – and he did, hugely, titanically – it was because he needed to, because he wanted to – because he had to. Something in the part and the project drew him hypnotically towards the pain it contained. This was over and above the pain of Quasimodo's predicament, his sense of ugliness, his sense of rejection, his physical suffering. It was all of these, with which Laughton could of course so readily identify – but it was something more: some kind of world-pain, world suffering that was sucking his soul out of him. He was not conscious of political events but even he was aware of the impending conflagration. His memories of Flanders 1919 were still vivid and frightening, and informed the emotional state that was welling up inside him.

The make-up, that famous mask of mangled features, had taken months to evolve under his impatient direction. Perc Westmore, inventor and perfector of modern movie make-up, and ten kinds of a swine, was Laughton's personal make-up expert (Jack Warner lent him to RKO for $10,000). He produced version after version for Laughton, only to have them rejected after a moment's consideration. Charles knew what he wanted; and finally he got it. But he and Westmore were at loggerheads from almost the beginning. Laughton had spoken to him of the need for the hump to be heavy: Chaney's, made by himself, had weighed a ton; Laughton wanted the added input of that extra burden – every extra ounce of pain, from whatever source. 'Why doncha just *act* it?' says Mister Westmore, and Laughton roared at him: 'Don't ever speak to me like that again, you *hired hand*' and stormed out. And indeed, it was an intolerable impertinence on Westmore's part. He committed the offence Laughton could never forgive: he belittled Laughton's labours. 'Get on with it,' he was saying. But Laughton's taunt hit Westmore's raw nerve: 'hired hand'! Westmore had laboured since he was thirteen to establish respect for what he rightly considered his art.

So once again, Laughton was fighting a battle of principle. He had a ruthless and powerful opponent in Westmore. When the make-up, both face and hump, were finally ready to both their satisfactions,

Westmore called up his kid brother Frank and told him to skip school for the day: there was something he wanted him to see. So Frank came with his brother to Laughton's caravan, where he was introduced as an assistant. Laughton (as Perc had promised) got down on his hands and knees ('like a pig,' said Perc) and struggled into the hump – an aluminium scaffold filled with foam rubber, over which a thin layer of elastic was stretched. Perc started to fit the mask. Laughton was by now sweating copiously. Everything was going just the way Perc said it would. 'I'm thirsty, Perc. Give me a drink, will you?' says Laughton, right on cue. 'Sure,' says Perc, approaching him with a 7-Up bottle which he shakes up and down. 'No Perc, no, you wouldn't!' cries the kneeling and trapped actor. 'Oh yes I would,' says Perc, and sprays the contents of the bottle over Laughton's face. Then he goes round to the other side of Laughton, and kicks his arse. 'That's for all the grief you've given me,' says Perc. 'I brought my brother today because I needed a witness to say this never happened, if you try to say it did. But you won't, Mr Laughton, you won't.'

Frank Westmore, the kid brother in question and Perc's admiring biographer, doesn't record Laughton's reaction to this somewhat unusual development in the relationship of actor and make-up expert. Perc Westmore, on his brother's evidence, was clearly something of a brute (he drove his father out of the family business), and Laughton, of course, must have made many people feel they *wanted* to give him a good kick, but this is *hors limites* as far as any tension in working relationships go. And yet Laughton said and did nothing. He took it, just took it, languishing in the limbo between *his* pain and humiliation and Quasimodo's, topping up the misery levels on every possible occasion.

'Charles started the part with a kind of theatrical idea, which he carried around inside him as a pregnant woman does her baby,' wrote Dieterle. 'He was not able to play his part until it was ripe within himself.' Almost von Sternberg's words; but this time without irony. Perhaps there was Sternbergian sarcasm in his voice when, on the first day of shooting, with a thousand extras ready and costumed on the old Universal lot, and the entire massive team poised for action, Laughton said that he was unable to play the scene: 'please, Charles, the next time you are not ready, let me know it previously so I can plan accordingly.' But Laughton's reply obviously struck him deeply: 'Sweltering under his heavy rubber make-up Charles muttered in a tormented voice, "I am sorry, I am so sorry, but I thought I was ready, but it just did not come, but it will come and will be good."'

The burning sun that summer broke all records; 100°F was the average temperature. Laughton suffered and suffered under the make-up, and there was no relief when, bruised and weak with exhaustion, he stumbled home; it was so hot that sleep was impossible. The wet sheets they draped their bodies with to keep cool were bone dry in ten minutes. He had, anyway, to get up at four o'clock in the morning to start the make-up.

Even that, though, was not enough. Westmore reports that in the scene on the wheel where he's lashed while the crowd jeers, he asked the make-up assistant to take his foot and twist it. 'More, more,' he screamed, 'twist it more.' Elsa Lanchester reports that Charles was upset by a remark of Dieterle's: on the sixteenth take of the scene, Dieterle – 'in the intimate tone directors use to confide their tricks, their genius, their wares and ideas', she says, with magnificent contempt . . . 'leaned over to Charles and whispered: 'Now, Charles, listen to me. Let's do it one more time, but this time I want you . . . I want you to suffer.' For this,' she says, 'Charles never forgave Dieterle.' That may be so; but, in view of Laughton's state of mind during the film, it seems to have been a very sympathetic and even helpful thing to have said – really entering into cahoots with him.

The awareness of events in Europe so far, far away, hung heavily over the making of the film: and the day war was declared, Dieterle wrote, 'the tension on the soundstage was unbearable. The scene in which Quasimodo rings the bell for Esmerelda, high in the bell tower . . . was supposed to be a kind of love scene between these two, but it developed into something so powerful, that everybody including myself forgot that we were shooting a film. Something super-dimensional happened at that moment, so that I forgot to call "cut" according to custom as the scene ended. Laughton went on ringing the bells after the scene was really over. Finally, completely exhausted, he stopped. Nobody was able to speak, nobody moved. It was an unforgettable thing. Finally, in his dressing-room, Charles could only say: "I couldn't think of Esmerelda in that scene at all. I could only think of the poor people out there, going in to fight that bloody, bloody war! To arouse the world, to stop that terrible butchery! Awake! Awake! That's what I felt when I was ringing the bells!"'

This is what acting can be. In *The Hunchback of Notre Dame* every scene that Laughton plays is informed by this sense of relation to the whole of mankind's life. Of the scene on the wheel, Dieterle wrote: 'when Laughton acted that scene, enduring the terrible torture, he was not the poor crippled creature expecting compassion from the mob, but rather oppressed and enslaved mankind, suffering the most awful injustice.'

Two years before, Laughton had gone to see Laurence Olivier play *Henry V* at the Old Vic. Going back to congratulate him after the performance, he asked Olivier if he knew *why* he was so good. 'Because you *are* England, that's why,' Laughton told him. Elsa Lanchester claims that the remark is apocryphal, uncharacteristic of Charles. On the contrary, it is exactly what he believed: that acting could transfigure the raw material of the actor and the character into the embodiment of huge ideas and human realities.

But the intensity of feeling that was the pressure behind his work, that was the source of its size and richness, was never indulged in the performance; quite the opposite. His Quasimodo is rarely seen to suffer at all. One of the most striking images of all is of the hunchback turning round and round on the wheel as the lash falls, expressing no pain, simply turned to stone, the suffering motionless, as eternal as a negro spiritual or the tombs of Belsen, numb, vast, fathomless. Then he glimpses Frollo, who may be coming to rescue him. His eyes light up with a dog's mute yearning – but Frollo passes on, followed by the still yearning eyes of Quasimodo. Esmerelda climbs onto the wheel. She offers him water. He pulls away. She persists. He drinks, knowing he can trust her. He gobbles it greedily. He's released from the wheel and limps alone back to Notre Dame. He goes in through the great door, locks it carefully behind him. He sees Frollo. 'She gave me water,' he says, with the utmost simplicity.

Every moment in the sequence is simple, direct, precise. Its emotional impact is overwhelming, because of the suffusion of every cell of the actor's being with the essence of the character's experience. The character's gestures, actions, utterances reveal this essence at every moment. There is no need for the actor to try to be moving, or impressive, or to show why he does this or that. The doing is enough. When Quasimodo approaches Esmerelda with a bird in a cage and having given it to her tries to tell her of his love, he places his hands, very simply, over his face. It is almost impossible to watch the scene, such is the piercing expressiveness of this gesture; but it is simplicity itself.

In the bell-ringing scene, his laughter as he compares himself to the man in the moon stems from very deep indeed, and is sustained so long that it becomes a laugh at the whole idea of deformity, at the idea of appearance at all.

In short, Laughton does with acting what great creative artists attempt: to sound the deepest and the highest notes of human possibility, to exalt the human soul, and to heal the damaged heart.

It is absurd to speak of Laughton's Quasimodo as a *great performance*, as if that were some quantifiable assessment. It is acting at its greatest; it is Laughton at his greatest; it is a cornerstone of this century's dramatic achievement; it is a yardstick for all acting.

At the time, some people liked it; and some didn't. It was his third and best gift to impressionists the world over; and it was the last time he risked madness and physical collapse to fashion from his own psyche an image of the human condition. He decided, instead, that he would join the human race, and try being Charles Laughton instead of Philoctetes, the bleeding, smelling patron of artists, exiled to his island with his wound and his bow.

Now he wanted to like himself, and to be liked; to create, certainly, but from materials that lay outside his own body. He climbed down from the cross, pulled out the nails, and made with uncertain steps for real life.

PART TWO

Change of Life

There is no evidence that Laughton saw his career as falling conveniently into two halves – the first, everything up to Quasimodo, the second, everything after it; there is no evidence that he took any conscious decision to find his ultimate fulfilment elsewhere, or to find a different channel for creative expression. The fact remains, however, that if all record or mention of his work up to 1939 were lost, the remaining performances would seem intelligent, well-observed, powerful, striking, often moving, and always, even at their very least inspired, watchable; but – with two remarkable exceptions over the twenty odd years left to him – in none of them does Laughton function as a primary creative artist, as he did in Nero, Bligh, Barrett, Quasimodo, even Phineas V. Lambert. In short, from now on he put his talent into his acting, his genius elsewhere.

The factors involved in this re-routeing of creative energies are complex, but principal among them is a change in Laughton's attitude to himself, whether *on account of* his experience playing the hunchback, or merely *after* it. It can hardly be coincidental that all the new elements which entered his life during the next few years – teaching, public reading, directing, and having love affairs – were activities which focused on him as himself, rather than as a character. It may be that he had exorcised his self-loathing in taking on, not merely the hideousness of feature of Quasimodo, but the lunatic self-destructive urges of all mankind: as Elsa Lanchester so vividly put it, 'he took physical torture over and above what was needed – a sort of purging of his human weakness and general guilt. Not guilt for any piddling little act. Just guilt for an overall insufficiency of perfection in life and work.'

Elsa Lanchester had joined Laughton just before the start of filming, in the weeks of tension which preceded the invasion of Poland. When war did break out, they, like the rest of the Hollywood Brits, were advised by the British Ambassador, Lord Lothian, to stay in America where they would be of most use in making out the British case. The pro-German lobby was powerful and vocal, and every positive image was needed to counteract it. So they, and most of the English actors, stayed. Some, like Laurence Olivier, defied the ambassadorial advice and stole away in secret, passionate for action.

The rest, feeling oddly guilty, were as conspicuous in England's cause as could be. In the end, they undoubtedly did more good where they were; but back home, there was a widespread feeling that they had got off lightly. Most of them were well beyond enlisting age; many of them, like Laughton, had seen action in the First World War. The feeling in England was that, fighting or not, an Englishman's duty was to be inconvenienced. In fact, during the blitz, the Laughtons' house in Gordon Square was hit by a stricken divebomber – the only house in the square to suffer. 'I should be glad to sacrifice twenty houses if German divebombers would smash themselves to bits on them. To hell with the cash if they can bring down the Junkers. It was a glorious end for the house' Charles told the *New York Times*; but a lurking impression of malingering persisted.

His first assignment after *The Hunchback of Notre Dame* was, one might guess, specially chosen by him as light relief: an adaptation of Sidney Howard's Pulitzer Prize-winning play, *They Knew What They Wanted*, a genial piece set in the Italian community in the Napa Valley of California. Laughton plays Tony Patucci, the simple, good-hearted but unprepossessing vineyard owner who, on a rare visit to town, falls in love with a waitress (Carole Lombard) whom he hasn't even spoken to. He proposes to her by post, sending her a photograph, not of himself, but of his handsome employee, William Gargan, with whom she then, of course, falls in love.

It's a classic Laughton character, and a classic Laughton situation: too classic. How much longer could he go on re-cycling the same complex? As long, presumably, as he needed to. But now, it would seem, the wound was healing. His approach to the rôle reveals a marked reluctance to tear the scab off again. Other actors could have made a great deal of the touchingly written part of Tony – indeed they had, in the two previous filmed versions (one starring Edward G. Robinson) and in its musical apotheosis, Frank Loesser's *Most Happy Fella*; Laughton could only have done something remarkable with it by living through every painful step in the character's journey through hope, doubt, self-hatred, pity, anguish, to the final hard-won happy resolution. On this occasion, and increasingly hereafter, he declined. The result is a performance in which, despite occasional flickers of intense expression, the actor appears to be sulking. This unattractive quality sadly pervades a great deal of his work in the two remaining decades of his career.

By chance, we have extensive documentation of this unsuccessful

performance in this unimportant film, because it was directed by
Garson Kanin, whose career as a chronicler has long since eclipsed his
career as a creator. His account of the filming rivals von Sternberg's
chapter on *I, Claudius* as the most vividly one-sided portrait of
Laughton. It appears in his book *Hollywood*, and like von Sternberg's
account, it presents its author as the epitome of sweet reason and
patience, bewildered by the antics of the child-monster, Laughton. In
fact, Kanin was something of a boy-monster himself at the time of
filming: twenty-seven-years-old, flushed with his, as it turned out
short-lived, triumph as a director (*The Great Man Votes, Bachelor
Mother, My Favourite Wife*, all within a year), ex-jazzman, hoofer,
vaudevillian and finally Broadway actor, quip-happy, bursting at the
seams with what on the cocktail circuit passes for intelligence, he
viewed the fat, battle-weary veteran of the unequal struggle to forge
Art from unyielding life with brisk amusement going on affection:
'C'mon, cuddles,' he'd say to him; or 'C'mon Chuck.' Faced with the
complex inertia of the man of a million quivering impulses, he tried to
josh him into giving a performance. This was a miscalculation.

Added to Laughton's usual pre-natal apprehension at the start of
any project was a particular displeasure at the casting of his co-star,
Lombard. He and she had proved to be out of sympathy in *White
Woman*. He found her broad, 'one-of-the-boys' social style impossible
to handle, and her preferred dialect, Anglo-Saxon, offended him
deeply. To Kanin, on the other hand, she was a model actress: he
admiringly recounts how she simply picked up her page of dialogue
before the shot, learned it, and then spoke it with perfect naturalness.
Well, if that's your definition of acting, of course Laughton would
seem to be making a lot of fuss over nothing. The fact that in the
finished film she gives a performance of unrelieved one-dimension-
ality seems not to excite Kanin's censure; she had a great personality,
she learned her lines, she looked pretty. What else is there? Laughton,
on the other hand, was slowly circling the dreaded task. His preparation was oblique, as ever: oblique because the undertaking was not a
simple one. He was not aiming for verisimilitude: he was erecting the
derrick which would enable him to drill for the deep black oil which
was lurking – even *hiding*, he may mournfully have thought – inside
him; the substance which would turn Tony Patucci from a chap with a
girl-problem in some Californian valley into an icon of the
transcendence of physical limitations, the transforming power of love
– whatever. Who knows what Laughton might have made of Tony
Patucci? He never got there. It wasn't worth the effort.

'From now until the first day of shooting, I propose to study the paintings of Michelangelo, listen to nothing but Vivaldi, and read aloud, in the original, the epic poetry of Dante.' How Kanin's friends must have *shrieked* with laughter when he reported to them this remark of Laughton's. What had any of that to do with Tony Patucci? Just learn the lines, Chuck, it's all there. After all, Sidney Howard won a *Pulitzer Prize* for them. What point explaining that by touching some essence of Italian-ness, he might release a dimension in Tony Patucci that would resonate through the whole film, enriching its character beyond recognition?

Kanin complains that from the first day, Laughton seemed to want to 'take charge.' Certainly he must have attempted to define the parameters of what he was going to attempt; and certainly, he wanted help. In his assault on yet another mountain, he wanted a partner in imagination, a companion, a comrade. He did *not* want someone shouting 'Get up that mountain!'; nor did he want some loon burbling 'It's not a mountain, Chuck, it's easy.' He *did* want acknowledgement of his contribution. When he emerged from the make-up room after the first tests, totally unrecognisable, he presented himself to Kanin with the innocent joy in his transformation he always revealed on these occasions. 'They've done a very good job,' said Kanin, carefully choosing his words. '*They?*' replied Laughton, '*they* simply *did* what *I told* them to do.' It is an arrogant reply, but essentially truthful. Most make-up artists – Perc Westmore, the Charles Laughton of maquillage being a notable exception – place their considerable skills at the disposal of 'their' artist, who, they assume, knows more about the character than they do. Achieving the desired result is of course their department, and endless the virtuosity and inventiveness that goes into it. Kanin's remark was a calculated denial of Laughton's responsibility for his own work. Carole Lombard, of course, would have acknowledged her make-up artist without hesitation; but then as that artist's task was confined to the most direct presentation of her bone structure, the question of creativity did not arise. To Laughton, his creativity was the central issue in his work, and he was fiercely jealous of it.

Before Kanin had administered his little put-down, Laughton had been capering around, doing a tootsie-fruitsie Italian accent. Kanin panicked: was Laughton really going to do it like that? He bearded Laughton about it. Laughton turned suddenly nasty: did Kanin think he was auditioning for the part? He'd been fooling around with the accent – obviously he wasn't going to do it like that. Kanin said he just wanted to be certain that Laughton had a method of acquiring an authentic accent. Of course he had, said Laughton, grandly: the Michelangelo-Vivaldi-Dante method. Kanin, he claims, was impressed – until the read-through, when Laughton's accent was so incomprehensible that he had to stop the proceedings and send him off to a voice coach. After a few hours' tuition, says Kanin, he had found an accent that was not merely accurate, but entirely personal to the character.

Of course there was an element of old mullarkey in Laughton: an obstinacy, sheer Scarborough cussedness. And there was also an element in him of masochism, of welcoming the big stick when it was finally wielded – that at least has the advantage of relieving one of personal responsibility. At the read-through, Laughton may have been groping towards some deep immersion in the sensations provided by the experience of strange sounds passing through the mind and the mouth. Or he may just have been being difficult, protesting in a general way against the Lombard – Kanin axis, the *pros*.

Kanin observed: 'Laughton enjoyed being difficult not because it disconcerted others, but because being difficult made him special, the centre of attention.' Not even his worst enemy has ever accused Laughton of being ordinary, or having trouble commanding attention. Why would he bother to engineer what he already had? Where he was 'difficult' was in bringing his problems with the part to rehearsals, instead of concealing them, or solving them in the bath at home, à la Laurence Olivier. He was also obviously intensely self-absorbed in a way which left him little energy or inclination to engage in the good-humoured banter usual and, to most mortals, indispensable on the studio floor. He did like people to know what it was all costing him. In this way he was like someone who has a bad headache and won't let you forget it – wants his nobility in being there at all to be recognised. This is not the most charming of traits; but it is a mitigating factor that he *did* have a headache; that he was, that is to say, engaged in painful and frustrating efforts to reach a result which was substantially more ambitious than what most of his colleagues were even attempting.

There was little sympathy for his approach from his fellow-players. William Gargan, playing the handsome hired-man, wrote,

> On the set, he was the most difficult man I've ever worked with. An inveterate scene-stealer, not at all subtle, without any of the charm of Barrymore (or his talent), he was a grubby man who fought and clawed for every inch of celluloid. In an early scene, as I would say

something, Laughton would begin to writhe, his heavy face hanging over my shoulder like a full moon. Every line I'd speak, he'd growl, grimace, wipe his nose, lick his blubbery lips; he'd grovel, rub his hands, do everything but have a fit. Finally he had his fit as well. So did Garson Kanin . . . he was a fine director, perhaps the finest I ever worked with . . . but Laughton needed no direction (Charles knew best); Laughton would take no direction (from an American!).

Gargan, who, in the film, gives a constricted and charmless performance, may well have resented Laughton's inventiveness and force of personality; it was hard for any actor to keep up with him in those regards. Laughton had but to walk into the same frame as Gargan and the scene was stolen.

Kanin dubbed Laughton a 'privy player': one who works on his rôle in private and is then unable to adapt his performance to the needs of the moment. 'Giving a direction to Charles was like offering him a cup of hemlock.' Laughton never developed the technique of appearing to accept a suggestion in order to consider it at leisure. Having indeed worked (and worked and worked) on his rôle in private, he had begun to create something rather complex. Any 'direction' requires some accommodating, unless, of course, the director is deeply in sympathy with the actor's aims and methods. What is clear is that Kanin had sympathy with neither. Like von Sternberg before him, he couldn't see what the problem was. As far as he was concerned, Laughton was talented and well-cast. End of story. He describes an incident which demonstrates, according to the angle from which you view it, either Laughton's determination to go to any lengths to achieve something new and alive, or his grotesque obstinacy and perversity. Interestingly, Kanin's account begins with him failing to find anything 'wrong with the scene or with Laughton's attack on it' and ends with how he 'saw and heard and felt great acting' in what was 'perhaps the best scene in the whole picture' (it would be truer to say that it was the *only* scene in the whole picture.)

As told by Kanin it's a very funny story: how Laughton was unhappy with a scene he was due to shoot the next day, how he went to Kanin to talk about his difficulty, how he persuaded him to go up to the vineyards with him though it was nearly midnight, and, then, striding about, waving his arms around, finally broke through. 'All at once the quality of his voice changed. Laughton disappeared. Tony Patucci replaced him . . . we had stopped in a clearing. There was a certain amount of moonlight. Laughton's genius turned it into sunlight.' Actor and director were equally thrilled. They went back to their respective homes. Next day, Laughton had lost it again. Shyly, tentatively, he asked Kanin if they could go back to the vineyards. 'There are people who possess strange powers. Laughton was one of them. He had the power to draw one into the orbit of his pattern of thought, sense of feeling and mode of behaviour.' Kanin agreed. Laughton found it again. They returned to the set. Kanin was allergic to the crop-spray, and started to sneeze, ruining a take. Laughton lost it again. He and the production secretary went back to the vineyards. Kanin stayed behind, taking soporific anti-allergy tablets. Laughton returned, did a number of takes which Kanin, drugged to the eye-balls, barely saw.

It may have been 'perhaps the best scene in the whole picture,' but the price was too high, both for the film and for Laughton. He never again made that kind of fuss over a performance, because he never again tried so hard. Except for *This Land is Mine* and *Advise and Consent*, with both of which he had, for different reasons, a strong personal identification, he increasingly saw films as a source of easy money – 'paying for ice for father's piles,' as he and Elsa Lanchester used picturesquely to describe it.

Laughton made a significant remark to Kanin at the rather subdued end-of-shoot party. 'What's so terribly, terribly sad about all of this is that some day you'll come to know what a damned nice fella I really am.' He was beginning to like himself – wanted to be liked by others. His art of acting, which consisted of driving himself relentlessly to reveal unpalatable aspects of his personality, was not calculated to endear him to anyone. So he began to withdraw from it. To be loved was more important. Perhaps on *They Knew What They Wanted* he was already looking for release from the behaviour his relationship to his art demanded of him. Some years after the film, he and Kanin were both at a supper party. Kanin, asked how he handled difficult actors, 'heard the pompous side of me take off,' he says. '"Well Frances," I said, "Take charge. Never lose control, not for a moment. Let them know that either they're going to do what they're supposed to do, or else get rid of them at once. That's the only way."' Charles looked up from his soup and said, "Why *didn't* you?"'

They Knew What They Wanted was produced by Erich Pommer; it is the last fruit of his unhappy collaboration with Laughton. 'Mayflower', the name of their company, turned out to be oddly prophetic: they had both emigrated to America. Pommer stayed for a few more years until, in 1946, he returned in U.S. uniform to

Germany to help reorganise the shattered film industry. Elsa Lanchester reports that Pommer's son claimed that he had been killed by Laughton's impossible temperament. If so, it was a long-drawn out death: he outlived Laughton by four years.

Charles' next film presented a very different face of Laughton, both as actor and as man: *It Started with Eve*, whipped cream topped with sugar and drenched in chocolate sauce. It's not a very agreeable experience, watching it today, but Deanna Durbin, whose vehicle it was, is pleasantly straightforward on the plump brink of womanhood, and Charles is larky. He seems to be having fun; indeed, there is every evidence that he *was* having fun. He got on famously with Durbin – another daughter substitute, like Maureen O'Hara and, later, Margaret O'Brien – and they liked to play practical jokes on Henry Koster, the good-natured director, a Durbin veteran (*Three Smart Girls*; *One Hundred Men and a Girl*; *Three Smart Girls Grow Up*). 'Thanks to Charles,' Deanna wrote, 'I discovered that making pictures could be fun, lost my tenseness, and discovered that Hollywood and making pictures were not the most important things in the world.' It was exactly what Laughton had been discovering for himself. The result in his case is a performance which is fun, but not funny – not *seriously* funny at any rate, so his work becomes a mere diversion. This is a new development in his work. It is the flip-side, the Bank Holiday, as Oscar Wilde might say, of his sulking. It is still a formidable talent, but frivolously used.

He plays an aged millionaire who is revived on his deathbed by the life-enhancing sight of Miss Durbin, apparently his nephew's fiancée. She isn't, is in fact a last-minute substitute for the real one, but when he's back on his feet, he demands to see her. The film resolves into the story of his attempts to bring her and his nephew together. He effects this with great twinkle. It is, in fact, a considerable physical transformation on his part – he seems tiny, thin and incomputably ancient: the very image as it happens, of the late Lord Stockton (Harold Macmillan). It is said that Deanna Durbin wasn't introduced to him by name on the first day of filming and passed the entire day wondering where Charles Laughton was. There are many good physical gags (with cigars, and, particularly, an up-ended sofa) and he finds a wonderful wavering voice for the character. The performance is suffused with the quality that is said always to have eluded him: benevolence. It is, in a word, charming.

The Tuttles of Tahiti, which followed *It Started with Eve*, is more dispiriting, as the talent itself is in question. Jonas is a sleepy, mildly whimsical descendant of Ginger Ted, surrounded by his enormous family of toothsome Tahitian youths, distant descendants, perhaps, of Fletcher Christian (the film is based on a novel by Nordoff and Hall, authors of *Mutiny on the Bounty*) but hardly of the irredeemably Caucasian Laughton. There are, of course, pleasant interludes, especially in his scenes with Florence Bates, an amateur actress, with whom Laughton, always attracted to the simplicity and directness that eluded him in his own personality, struck up a friendship. There are the obligatory eating and chase scenes – showing him, as usual, in the one, shamelessly indulgent, in the other, comically fleet of foot, but there is no animating spirit. He acts like a little boy persuaded to play, but determined not to enjoy it. Laughton is often accused of mugging, implying a certain relish, an actor unrestrainedly indulging his favourite tricks, but that is a false definition of the word. Mugging is what an actor does when he is not engaged. He manipulates his mug into shapes, instead of reconstructing the impulses which would create those shapes. In *The Tuttles*, Laughton is mugging. There is, moreover, no connection between his performance and the *ideas* of the piece (such as they are). Generally, good acting spontaneously engages with the ideas of the script: Laughton, in his performances of the thirties, evinced a positive genius for doing so. His Jonas, alas, is a mere blur of hastily assembled characteristics.

Again, as in *They Knew What They Wanted*, the sense of resistance comes off the screen. Neither physically nor as a personality was Laughton capable of being dull or routine. Unsatisfactory as a performance, his Jonas nevertheless exists as a substantial phenomenon: another actor's discomfort in a rôle might pass unnoticed, but Laughton's is palpable. It is as if, like one of Woody Allen's characters in *The Purple Rose of Cairo*, he would like to step out of the screen and be released from his celluloid prison. It is, indeed, as if playing this character in this film were an indignity, a humiliation that had been imposed on him.

This *dégringolade* did not pass unnoticed: 'Why,' asked the *New York Times*, 'has he been permitted to dissipate his talent in arrant mugging within the past few years?' What is astonishing is the speed of his decline, both actually, and in critical favour. 1939 (the year of *Hunchback*), a genius; 1941 (*It Started with Eve*), a joke (Garson Kanin reports that he and a friend went to see the film. In the opening sequence, Laughton, apparently on his death-bed, says,

'I'm so happy'. 'Don't you mean *hammy*?' whispers Gar's chum, and they crack up); *The Tuttles* is a low-water mark. *Tales of Manhattan*, also 1941, is an honourable exception in the decline, though the *New York Times* didn't think so: 'he is farcical in a manner which violated the mood.' Seen today, his performance in this compendium movie is the most effective of all the half dozen stars, each with their own episode. The thread between episodes is a tail-coat, worn in turn by Boyer, Fonda, Laughton, Edward G. Robinson and Paul Robeson. Laughton plays an impoverished composer who finally gets a break when the Toscanini-like martinet (Victor Francen), in whose orchestra his best friend plays, agrees to programme his *Scherzo*. He conducts it himself, wearing the tail-coat his wife has bought for him from the pawnshop. As his baton-waving becomes more vigorous, the coat starts to split at the seams. The audience starts to titter, then to laugh; finally, in the Hollywood Manner, the entire auditorium is roaring with uncontrolled hysteria. Laughton, shattered by this, stops conducting and sits pathetically on the edge of the podium in his shirt-sleeves, having torn off the remains of the tail-coat. Francen-Toscanini has been watching all this from the box with icy rage. Suddenly, he stands. The audience falls silent as he takes off *his* tail-coat. Slowly at first, then increasingly quickly, every man in the audience does likewise. Laughton picks up his baton and resumes the *Scherzo*. Ovation, in the Hollywood Manner.

Laughton's performance is delicate, precise, and touching. The character is one of his ordinary little men (to underline the point he's called Charlie Smith) and he handles the part as cleanly and simply as his earlier Charlie in *St Martin's Lane*. As before, his emotional honesty is affecting: his hopefulness while the conductor examines his score; his joyful communication of the good news to his family; his nervous anxiety before the concert; his exhilaration as he hears the score for the first time; and, supremely, his despondency as he sinks to the floor amid the derision of the audience – all this is truly and lightly played. It is, in fact, an excellent performance, full, as well as all its other qualities, of genuine high spirits. It never attempts the concentration of gesture and intensification of feeling that make his performance of Phineas V. Lambert in *If I Had a Million*, for instance, so deeply funny. It is a study of one little man which never reaches out to encompass all little men, but it is clearly the work of an immensely gifted player. It is hard to see what the *New York Times* was aiming at in its imputation of farcicality – apart from certain helter-skelter moments – but even these are entirely within the framework of the character and the situation.

There is no record of Laughton's relationship with Duvivier, the director. In an extensive career, beginning and ending unremarkably, Duvivier had a middle period of the most glorious splendour, including some of the masterpieces of the French cinema: *Un Carnet de Bal*, *Fin du Jour*, *Poil de Carotte*. He had achieved outstanding success with what amounted to a regular company of actors, including one who had a certain resemblance to Laughton, Michel Simon, and who, like Laughton, was haunted by what he conceived of as his physical unattractiveness. Many of Simon's performances seem, also like Laughton's, to embody titanic emotions to a degree that shifts them from psychology into mythology. The resemblance with Laughton ends there, however, because Simon, after a brief brush with emotional relationships – an abortive marriage – became more or less a recluse (which Laughton never was) – and devoted himself to acting quite single-mindedly, even after a disastrous experiment with make-up which left him nearly blind. Acting was Simon's destination, whereas Laughton was en route somewhere else.

It is pleasing, however, to imagine that Duvivier approached Laughton with some sensitivity – he was used to actors trying for complex results – even if the work they produced together was not among its respective authors' very finest. (Elsa Lanchester, incidentally, gives an unusually affecting performance as Charlie's tough, good wife.) The film in fact made a great deal of money and led to another, less successful compendium film, *Flesh and Fantasy*, with Boyer and Edward G. Robinson, directed again by Duvivier. But Laughton was not in it.

For Laughton, 1942 was dominated, cinematically and in more important other ways, by the war. America had joined the Allies in December 1941. Laughton had done everything in his power to promote that course, and now he threw himself with extraordinary passion into the drive to sell War Bonds. He went on a selling tour in August of 1942; on 1 September he took part, along with other stars in a series of rallies; and on 30 September he talked himself hoarse on a phone-in broadcast during which, starting at seven o'clock in the morning and ending at midnight, he sold $298,000 worth of bonds. His passion was evidently persuasive. He ended the broadcast with the exhortation that it was 'a duty and a privilege to buy bonds – the last chance to save the flickering flame of democracy. God help you and your children if that flame goes out.'

The ideals of democracy, and particularly, it may be said, American democracy, meant a great deal to Laughton; also, like many wartime expatriates, he wanted to do everything he could to contribute to the war effort, 'from guilt', as Elsa said, 'of being in the Hollywood sunshine'. Behind the passion of his commitment to these drives, however, lies something else: the desire for communication with the audience, direct communication, unmediated by a play or a character. He wanted to communicate what he had learned and was learning (for he never ceased to learn; to question was his supreme passion); and that was a sense of values. He had neither politics nor philosophy, but he had a most vivid apprehension of beauty and the rightness of things. Most of his career as an actor had been spent in exploring the disorders of the human spirit, exhibited in his own person. Already in his films he had started to quote, wherever possible, great statements about the human condition, the Gettysburg Address, of course, and the Bible. At these moments – in *Ruggles*, and *Rembrandt*, particularly – he departed almost entirely from character and even situation to celebrate great truths clothed in gorgeous rhetorical raiments.

In a 1937 article (in which he was once more defending himself as an actor), he recounts how on one of his journeys home from America, a crowd gathered to bid him farewell – 'not, you understand, confirmed autograph hunters, whom I detest, but just a normal crowd of Americans, come to see their friends and relations off.' They cheered him affectionately. 'This obvious feeling of goodwill impressed me not a little, but far more important was the fact that, time and again, I found they were shouting out expressions from my films which I had gone out of my way to impress upon them. I felt that my work had not been wasted, that they all knew exactly what I had been striving after.' That sense of communicating something important and memorable came to seem to Laughton the most valuable thing he could do – added to which, it made the work so much less lonely and painful. It was a worthy vocation and it was in touch with the human race, of which, Lanchester wrote, 'he really never felt himself part.' His work as an actor had gained him a kind of co-opted membership of it as a tragic fool, a court jester whose maimed body served as a means both of facing misfortune and laughing at it. Quasimodo was not only the culmination but also the paradigm of what he had been doing. Now he wanted to approach mankind from a different angle, bearing gifts of beauty and wisdom. He wanted to be a teacher and a prophet – and a lover.

. . .

After the completion of *They Knew What They Wanted*, he began to see how he might reach people directly. Dreading the usual promotion tour – receptions, parties, interviews, autographs, 'well, Mr Laughton, what do you think of our little town?' – he had suggested that he do some readings instead. It had been his habit to read out loud at the slightest prompting, or at none. Having neither capacity nor inclination for small talk, he would prefer to spend the time usefully by sharing his discoveries in the literary field – not by talking about books (that would be more small talk) but by actually quoting them. His physical relish of words was as great as, and identical in kind to, his passion for paintings. Sound, texture, rhythm, tone, shape were what he responded to with an aesthetic appetite that was both sensuous and spiritual. It was this, more than any meaning contained in the words, that he sought to transmit. He wanted to direct people's attention to the beauties readily available to them.

The perhaps slightly surprised citizens of middle America took very well to his readings on that promotion tour. Laughton simply read a couple of poems, a section or two of the Bible, and, inevitably, ended with the Gettysburg address. The experience lodged deep in his brain. Peddling beauty, exalted thoughts and heightened language was much more agreeable than struggling with some squalid character, trying to invest paltry phrases with truth and force, and being publicly humiliated in the process. The isolation of the life, the feeding off himself, the constant revelation of his ugliness: all of this could be avoided. He could give the audience delight and enlightenment; they could give him acknowledgement and, yes, admiration; and the words themselves would give him all the inspiration, all the energy so patently absent from filmscripts.

The thoughts marinated in Laughton's mind, taking – as did everything with him – their own good time before they were matured. He carried on reading privately – to Henry Koster, for example, the German director of *It Started with Eve*, forbidden by the curfew on aliens from going out at night; to Jean Renoir and his wife Dido (to whom he read Shakespeare); to soldiers in hospitals; and, something that made him 'very happy', according to Elsa Lanchester, to crippled and retarded children. He found to his delight that his auditors, whether famous artists like Koster and Renoir, or wounded GIs and backward kids, were spellbound and eager for more; eager, too, to find out more about the authors. He started to satisfy their interest; and so, in time, he became a teacher.

Routine

Meanwhile, there was money to be made, and that meant films. *Forever and a Day* was officially a war charity film – the first of them – the idea for which came from Cedric Hardwicke, and his prestige helped to persuade the seven directors, twenty-one writers and seventy-eight featured actors to participate. It was the Hollywood Raj's big do, and in fact it made rather a lot of money, almost all of which went to various good causes.

Nothing else favourable can be said of the film. The many episodes are tenuously threaded together by the theme of 'the great house', in which, over the centuries, the several stories are supposed to have taken place. In his episode, Laughton plays a most peculiarly attired butler, circa 1850, attending on a household in which a new-fangled bath is being installed by a pair of comic plumbers (Cedric Hardwicke and – one rubs one's eyes – Buster Keaton). 'Comic' is an indication of intent rather than achievement. 'Is there no one at RKO to tell Cedric Hardwicke when he is being unfunny? Or Charles Laughton when he is being plain bad?' Agate's exasperated comment is typical of those who remembered Laughton's stage career. They felt something like bitterness at the apparent squandering of gifts. Of the film itself, Caroline Lejeune wrote in *The Observer*, 'The most imposing thing about it is its harmonious consistency – the fact that so many diverse talents could work together to achieve something so monumentally and homogenously dull'.

American critics were more generous, condoning the absurd implausibility of the depiction of English life on patriotic and escapist grounds. 'The story proves nothing in particular, except that old British mansions have fine ghosts and that there'll always be an England so long as there is one sentimentalist left.' (Bosley Crowther, *New York Times*)

There were no such kind words from the same source for *Stand by for Action*, Laughton's next film, a most peculiar concoction concerning battleships and babies, which may have given Charles the cue for his performance of the Rear Admiral, 'Old Ironpants', as 'a character out of *HMS Pinafore*'. 'This is the sort of mock heroics,' says Crowther, 'which insults our fighting men.' Charitably one assumes a sense of duty as the motive behind Laughton's (and the other actors') participation in the wretched farrago. That is exactly what is conveyed by the playing: a dutiful passage through hoops. There was nothing, absolutely nothing, for Laughton to engage with in the part; his performance remains dutiful until the last scene when (surely this must have been at Charles' suggestion) he recites the entire Declaration of Independence, very well indeed. He suddenly connects. It, its sentiments and its language, obviously impassioned him; the character, never too sharply focused, simply disappears, and one is left with a great orator. Charles' interests are quite nakedly displayed.

The movie (referred to privately by Laughton as 'Fun Among the Holocausts') was directed by Robert Z. Leonard – a studio workhorse who in his time had held together films such as *Susan Lennox* (with Garbo and Gable), *The Great Ziegfeld* (Myrna Loy, William Powell) and *Pride and Prejudice* (Laurence Olivier, Greer Garson) – and produced, inauspiciously enough, by the Brothers Dull: Leonard and Orville, Mrs Dull's little boys. They and Robert Z. were responsible for Laughton's next film, *The Man from Down Under*, which he retitled, in a letter to Perry Charles ('if you show or mention this letter to anyone else, I shall personally crawl to New York City and will wring your God damned neck'), *You Can't Keep the Wallace Beery Tradition Down*. Theodore Strauss reviewed it for the *New York Times*: 'In the curious, clumsy and oddly lifeless story of a reprobate old Australian warrior and two refugee children adopted in the First World War, even Mr Laughton's outrageously ebullient spirit seems tamed and listless. Perhaps it is his comment upon the naivetés of the story, but the fact is that for once in his life, Mr Laughton is giving a performance that is simply ordinary. And certainly the film has little else to recommend it.' Caroline Lejeune was more censorious, shocked, like many of the London critics, by the poor quality of Charles' recent work: 'One of the most painful screen phenomena of latter years has been the decline and fall of Charles Laughton from the splendid actor of *The Private Life of Henry VIII*, *Mutiny On The Bounty* and *Rembrandt*, to the mopping and mowing mug in *The Man From Down Under*.'

Straight on to the next one. There was no lack of demand for his services; but clearly Laughton had embarked on that fatal road which starts with the need to make money and the fear that one will never be asked again. The road leads to steadily declining fees and dwindling demand: the more you are prepared to play any old thing, the more any old thing is all that is offered you. From having parts specially constructed for you, you are called in to redeem underwritten parts: the result is almost always an appearance of strain, of contrivance, above all, of over-acting, which of course is exactly what it is. If the writing is under, the acting will be over – over and above the part. In Laughton's case, such was the power of his screen presence that merely casting him, simply having him in the frame, places a weight on many of his characters that they can't take. As Peter Ustinov later put it: 'When Laughton was sitting quietly in a chair, not speaking, he was doing too much.' In most of his films of this period – indeed, in *most* of the rest of his films, he was doing the bare minimum, hardly engaged at all. But it was still too much.

In *The Canterville Ghost*, he partly engages; with the paradoxical result that he seems to be doing less. This may have something to do with his having demanded, and secured, the dismissal of the director, with whom he claimed to be unable to work. This hapless individual was Norman Z. McLeod, veteran of the Marx Brothers (*Monkey Business, Horse Feathers*) and later to direct (is that quite the word?) Bob Hope (*Road to Rio*) and Danny Kaye (*Walter Mitty*). Laughton generally worked happily with comics' directors; but not this time. It is an indication of his weight as a star that he was able to have the director removed. Not for much longer.

The replacement, possibly at Laughton's suggestion, was the thirty-year-old Jules Dassin. He had been assistant director on *They Knew What They Wanted*, but was presumably not tarred with the Kanin brush. Laughton was co-operative and full of good, discreetly delivered suggestions. He took time and trouble with Dassin, and evidently taught him a great deal. This was a relationship in which he always thrived. The performance remains unfulfilled – the absurdities of the adaptation, pointlessly travestying Wilde, cannot have made the part easy to play – and there is a not wholly inappropriate air of a slightly tetchy uncle forced somewhat against his will to dress up for the children's amusement. His scenes with Margaret O'Brien are affecting, however, and endowed, like similar encounters with Deanna Durbin and Maureen O'Hara, with the father-daughter tenderness which came from somewhere deep inside him. [Elsa Lanchester has recorded her decision, after discovering Charles' homosexuality, not to have children by him. 'A woman feels these things,' she says. Later Laughton reproached her bitterly. By this stage, however, sexual relations between them had long ceased.]

The Canterville Ghost was well-enough reviewed. (James Agee, who later became Laughton's friend, then collaborator, then enemy, dissented: Charles, he said, played the ghost in 'the mock-pansy, mock-Shakespearian style,' which is true enough, but not necessarily a bad thing. Wilde would have liked it.) It seemed, however, to

Left: *The Importance of Being Earnest*, Old Vic, 1934, with Laughton as Chasuble and Lanchester as Miss Prism.

Below: 'Laughton bestrides the Atlantic', a fantasy from the *Sketch* of 20 February 1935, showing Laughton with puppets of his most famous roles to date: (l. to r.) Nero; Henry VIII; the Murderer in *Payment Deferred*; and Moulton-Barrett in *The Barretts of Wimpole Street*.

Charles at Waterloo Station
leaving for Hollywood and
arriving (with Elsa), March 1935.

Laughton as Rembrandt (1936).

Picturegoer
The Screen's Most ~~Popular~~ Magazine

2d
WEEKLY

Charles LAUGHTON
& *Vivien* LEIGH

Laughton and Vivien Leigh
in *St. Martin's Lane*, 1938.

Preparing *Jamaica Inn*: Charles lunching with fellow-actors in November 1938; and with J. B. Priestley (left: screenwriter) and Erich Pommer (centre: producer) in December 1938.

Five Years After

A LMOST exactly five years ago Charles Laughton's first starring vehicle, *Payment Deferred*, had its English première. This week his latest film, *Vessel of Wrath*, is showing in London.

Payment Deferred was a grim, highbrow little picture, rather full of self-conscious subtlety—but *Vessel of Wrath* is a near-slapstick comedy.

When this latter film was in its last weeks of production at Elstree I received an invitation from Laughton to drop in at the studio and have a chat.

I arrived in the middle of an hilarious comedy sequence in which Charles, in the part of the rascally beachcomber, Ginger Ted, was informing the prim sister of the missionary (Elsa Lanchester) that she would have to spend the night alone with him on his island.

"Well, what do you think of it?" Laughton asked when he had completed the scene.

"Looks like low comedy to me," I said.

"That's good," he replied. "That's what I want it to look like."

He went away to collect a dressing-gown, then came back pensively to where I was sitting and offered me a cigarette.

Weary of Heavy Characters

"Probably," he said, "you are wondering why this, the first picture which I have personally produced, should be a comedy."

"Maybe it's a psychological kink," I told him. "The comedian always wants to play tragedy—and I suppose this is the case of the tragedian wanting to play comedy."

"I am a little weary of portraying heavy, humourless characters," said Laughton. "And I have come to the conclusion that pure melodrama is not very effective on the screen.

"I find that I am far more affected by Borzage, with his mixture of humour and pathos, than I am by such purveyors of stark drama as Fritz Lang and Josef von Sternberg.

"Of my own past characterisations I like Ruggles best and find him much more interesting than the little bank clerk in *Payment Deferred*—or Mr. Barrett, or Captain Bligh.

"In *Vessel of Wrath* the humour is broader even than in *Ruggles of Red Gap*, but my characterisation of the dissolute Ginger Ted has a leavening of pathos.

"The critics may disagree with me, of course, and I may be entirely wrong—but I think this is my most significant rôle to date.

"Being a film star for five years has altered my outlook. When I first went to Hollywood I was still comparatively young and had all the 'correct' ideas about drama.

"I talked of 'pure' cinema, was a little contemptuous of many modern plays and films, and believed that *King Lear* was the final test of any actor."

Laughton shrugged his shoulders.

"Nowadays, I believe that Gary Cooper is doing a far greater service to mankind than the highly-elocutionate Shakespearian actor playing Shakespeare is really nothing more than a piece of scholarship."

Wasted "Subtle" Gestures

"Gary Cooper, on the other hand, is part of the twentieth century. *Mr. Deeds Goes to Town* was certainly not a great work of art, but at least this picture was full of virility and modern spirit—a perfect mirror of contemporary life in the United States.

"When I first went into pictures I intended to make some money and then return to the stage. I had no intention of allowing Hollywood to rob me of my 'correct' opinions.

"*Payment Deferred* was just a pot-boiler. All the same, I thought it well above the ordinary standard of films.

"Having made several more pictures I discovered during conversations with other people, that my 'subtlest' and most penetrating gestures often went unnoticed, and that the things which really stirred the public were little human incidents, often quite spontaneous.

"I had still been a star for only twelve months or so when I found myself in a hospital in New York, recovering from an operation on my teeth.

"One afternoon the door of my room opened and a man, whose wife was lying desperately ill in the next cubicle, asked me, as a favour, whether I would slip in next door and see whether I could brighten her up.

"Seeing a real live film star did, in fact, brighten her considerably. The experience affected me deeply.

"Who was I to sneer at this powerful instrument of stardom which had been thrust into my hands? If it enabled me to bring a little colour into drab lives, and perhaps a few significant ideas, who was I to lay it aside in favour of more conventional drama?

"Which was more important—to please or to play Shakespeare?

"Some months later, while I was in England I was invited to attend a play produced by the Oxford University Dramatic Society. After the show the students sat me down in a corner of a room with a glass of wine, and began to air their 'correct' opinions about Ibsen, Molière and the rest.

"It was just so much hot air, so many words. To them I was a ham actor who had sold his soul for gold.

"Acutely that evening I remembered my experience in the hospital in New York. Films had really meant something to that woman. Probably in the whole of her life she had never developed a single theory about anything—but what emotions she did feel were nevertheless real, and her appreciation of movies was genuine.

"I began to see that the emotional sincerity of the masses was infinitely more important than the 'correct' ideas of a few sophisticates. By stimulating the emotions of the great film public one might achieve tremendous artistic heights.

"After my performance in *The Private Life of Henry VIII* one critic accused me of playing to the gallery.

"'Quite right,' I told him, 'the people in the boiled shirts don't interest me. My public is in the shillings.'"

Highbrow Snobbery

"Don't think," Laughton added quickly, "that I despise true intellectuality, but I believe this is to be found more in the works of scientists and philosophers than in the cinema.

"Fundamentally, both cinema and theatre are places for emotional relaxation and most of the theories aired by highbrows are nothing more than snobbery.

"By the time I made *Ruggles of Red Gap* I had lost all my 'correct' opinions and my sole concern was to loosen and stir the emotions of the rank and file of the film public.

"This picture possessed a simple, tragi-comic theme well within the reach of everyone, yet I have the critics' word for it that it was stimulating and significant entertainment.

"*Ruggles*, I think, succeeded because he was a real person and because his predicament was true to life.

"It was only natural that, when I started my

Payment Deferred—1932

If I Had a Million—1933

The Private Life of Henry VIII—1933

White Woman—1933

The Barretts of Wimpole Street—1934

6

CHARLES LAUGHTON

discusses the past five years and
their influence on him as an actor
in this exclusive interview with
J. DANVERS WILLIAMS

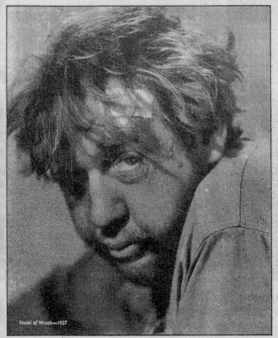

Vessel of Wrath—1937

too much ever to ignore them,' he told me. ' Some
of my best sequences of film have been the
result of their suggestions.'

"The entertainment value of Capra's films is
due as much to the mass-enthusiasm which
invariably exists in his studio as it is to his
own individual craftsmanship.

"He makes his assistants feel that this is their
picture and that any ideas they have will be
gratefully received.

"Of course, some directors find it impossible
to work without a carefully-prepared scenario.
They feel that if they stopped to consider the
suggestions of others, the final picture would be
just an awful muddle.

"But there is no danger of this happening
when Pommer is working on the set. A man
with a remarkably clear head, he can build up
a film as he goes along, capturing that all-
important feeling of naturalness and spontaneity."

Comedy-Drama of Soho

"How about *St. Martin's Lane?*" I inquired.
"Is that going to be as fiercely humorous as the
present picture?"

"I doubt it," he answered. "The busker will
be a mixture of humour and pathos, but I have
a shrewd suspicion that, when we come to make
this picture, we shall find that pathos is the
dominating influence.

"A poor street singer forced to wander the
crowded pavements of London hasn't the comic
potentialities of a really degenerate old soak who
has gone native in the South Seas.

"*St. Martin's Lane* should be quite an exciting
comedy-drama. When I was a young actor I
would often frequent the café bars of Soho and
see these happy-go-lucky minstrels singing for
their suppers.

"I always used to think that, if only a good
author troubled to get to know and understand
these people, he would have the material for a
really terrific book.

"Behind the lights of the West End, up dowdy
streets and narrow alleys, dramatic things are
happening all the time. Each evening there must
be any amount of interesting little plots worked
out among the crooks, artists, street girls, and
all the flotsam and jetsam who have drifted into
the happy, careless life of Soho.

"I can never go into the back streets around
the West End without being assailed by a feeling
of excitement, and our ambition in *St. Martin's
Lane* is to capture some of that excitement in
celluloid form."

own company with Erich Pommer, it was with
the idea of continuing along the lines suggested
to me by Ruggles.

"As a matter of fact *Vessel of Wrath* has
resolved itself into a much broader comedy than
we at first intended. I thought, when I started
work on the characterisation, that the pathos and
the humour would be fairly equally divided, but
Ginger Ted turned out a much funnier character
than we had anticipated.

"I have learnt never to force a characterisation
into a specified mould, but allow the character
to build itself up from the material. Ginger Ted,
I discovered, evoked more laughter than sympathy, and so I let him go his own way.

"Making this film we did not adhere strictly
to the original scenario. Pommer produced the
picture from behind the camera and although we

followed the bare outline of the story we made
many innovations as we went along.

"I have come to think that this is the most
satisfactory way of making a motion picture.
Some years ago I visited Frank Capra while he
was working in the studio."

Capra Tries Everything

"He was about to retake a difficult scene when
one of the electricians, suspended on a cradle high
above our heads, shouted down a suggested
alteration.

"'O.K.,' said Capra, ' we'll try it.'

"The sequence turned out considerably worse
than before, and I asked Capra why he had
troubled to take the man's advice.

"' I rely on the judgment of these fellows

Ruggles of Red Gap—1935

Les Misérables—1935

Mutiny on the Bounty—1936

Rembrandt—1936

St Martin's Lane—1938

7

A spread from *Film Weekly*, February 1938.

Hollywood. *Les Misérables*, 1935. *Mutiny on the Bounty*, 1935.
The Hunchback of Notre Dame, 1939. *They Knew What They Wanted*, 1940.

suggest another ominous development: he, who had given flesh and blood to the most genuinely terrifying ogres of the screen, monsters from the collective unconscious, becoming a star of children's movies, a sort of harmless ogre. In itself a perfectly decent performance, *The Canterville Ghost* cannot have reinforced Laughton's self-respect.

In the circumstances, the telegram he sent to RKO on receipt of the script for *This Land is Mine* ('what a tremendous challenge for a tired old ham!') is fully understandable, if a trifle self-dramatising. The 'old' ham was in fact forty-four years old, and had been a professional actor for no longer than seventeen years – a modest period in the light of John Gielgud's estimate that it takes twenty-five years to make an actor. It is an eloquent testimony of the low opinion of himself that Laughton had reached. He had lost contact with his vision of acting and with his sense of his talent. He was flailing around, adrift in celluloid.

He was right to be grateful for *This Land Is Mine*. The script (by Dudley Nichols) is clear, strong and intelligent, if structurally unbalanced; the central character, Albert Lory, is complex and touching; and the director was Jean Renoir. Laughton had known Renoir for some years; his ownership of *The Judgement of Paris*, Renoir père's huge canvas, had been the starting point of their friendship. He was a witness at Renoir's wedding, and had read Shakespeare to the French couple during their American exile. (This unusual service was apparently available to anyone, particularly those of foreign extraction. No one seems to have questioned it, simply settled down for regular infusions of blank verse, with occasional light relief from the King James version of the Bible. They were very serious sessions. Renoir entertainingly recalls, in his autobiography *My Life, My Films*, that cats and clocks were banned: absolute concentration was the order of the day.) Evidently the generosity of Renoir's personality warmed Laughton, whom he regarded as a genius – a thing much more evident to Europeans than to Anglo-Saxons – Walter Slezak, who plays the Nazi Commandant in the film, wrote in his vivacious memoir, *What Time's the Next Swan?* (he had been a *Heldentenor* in his earlier years): 'I saw him seven times in *Payment Deferred* on Broadway. I had known nearly all the great actors – Kainz, Bassermann, Werner Krauss, Raimu – to me, he topped them all.'

Renoir's purpose in making the film was 'specifically for Americans, to suggest that day-to-day life in an occupied country was not so easy as some of them thought.' His central character embodies the predicament of ordinary people. He intended the part for Laughton from the beginning; whether the actor influenced the writing or the concept is not recorded, but he might well have done, so personal is it to him. The performance is, with Rembrandt, the most simply human, as opposed to projected or heightened, he ever gave.

Lory is a coward, a nervous, pampered, overgrown child, tied to his mother's apron strings, a teacher unable to control his class, hopelessly in love with a fellow-teacher (Louise Martin, played by Maureen O'Hara), terrified of the air-raids and unquestioningly obedient to the demands of the occupying force. The film charts his growth from cowardice to resistance, demonstrating the need for political commitment. In intent, it has an almost Brechtian feel to it, a kind of liberal and humanist version of Brecht's play, *The Mother*, in which an essentially unpolitical woman learns that she must pledge herself to revolution. Of course, this being Renoir, the enlightenments are all given a personal and emotional base; nevertheless, the re-education of an unlikely subject is what *This Land is Mine* shows, and Laughton's performance admirably clarifies this.

He plays with the utmost restraint: Albert Lory is, after all, a shy and inhibited provincial schoolmaster. The scenes with his mother at breakfast are miracles of observation and subtlety: as she smothers him with a kiss, he, still reading the paper, absently mouths a kiss back at her. He manages to maintain a conversation with her on the subject of her rheumatism while never skipping a word of the article he's absorbed in. He suggests the combination of weakness and power that underlies relationships of emotional dependency. As the mother, Una O'Connor (the veteran Irish actress and a survivor, like Laughton, of the 1928 *Silver Tassie*), doesn't match his particularity or precision. She is, however, the physical type to perfection, and bears a strong resemblance to photographs of Mrs Laughton, Charles' mother, who was dominating in another vein, not smothering but exacting. Most remarkable in Laughton's delineation of the relationship is his ability to suggest that underneath the vexation and the obsessiveness lies genuine love.

In the street on his way to school, he meets the girl he secretly loves. Her brother, pretending to be a collaborator, shows a copy of the underground paper to passing soldiers. Laughton's attitude of barely daring to breathe, just hoping the whole incident will go away, neither being ingratiating to the soldiers, nor in any sense suggesting association with the ideals expressed in the paper, is the exact expression of the situation of the silent majority. His attitude is rendered even more vivid by the presence of the girl, in whose eyes he realises he has discredited himself.

What's quite remarkable is Laughton's communication of the man's situation. As if in an X-ray, we see the whole problem: the political reality complicating what is already a difficult moment for him: trying to impress the girl. We see his paralysis, the result of a number of given factors, among them his personality. It's moving and memorable not because we feel with him, but because we exactly understand his position.

At the school, he's given a number of excisions the Germans have demanded from the textbooks dealing with Greek theories of democracy. Meekly, he passes them on to the class which he anyway can barely control: the kids are daubing a star of David on the face of a Jewish pupil. Lory is deeply distressed, and seems on the point of some kind of decision, some kind of protest, when the sirens wail. A spasm of terror passes across his face. As the rest of the school rushes out to the air-raid shelter, he runs to find his mother, who, he says, is terrified of the bombs. He finds her striding purposefully and fearlessly through the streets and we see the fear is his. He rushes with her into the shelter, fat little legs scurrying down the road. The scene in the undergound shelter is the most extraordinary in the film, and one of the most extraordinary things Laughton ever committed to the screen. The stoicism of the teachers, the defiance of his mother, the high spirits of the children, the radiant idealism of Maureen O'Hara, are contrasted with the abject terror of Lory: the fear of a child in the dark, a whimpering, bed-wetting, snotty and tearful terror, the sort of thing a grown man does not own up to – the sort of thing a grown actor doesn't generally like to show. Laughton shows it so unabashedly that it is almost impossible to watch. It is cowardice made flesh, not the idea of it, but the actuality, and it provokes nothing but compassion, as if someone had found a way of demonstrating the pain of a migraine. All one can say is: how awful! What a burden. It is not exactly moving; it is, rather, enlightening.

Laughton preferred never to speak about his war, his time in the trenches. It seems inescapable that he chose this moment to exorcise some nightmare. His experience of war seems to have consisted of more than the simple ghastliness of death and killing. He seems – like so many – to have had to face something in himself. Maybe this was it. Certainly Laughton was not brave in many areas of his life, emotional, political, sexual. Perhaps at the centre of him was terrible physical fear. It is hard to know how otherwise he could have achieved the stabbing painful truth of this sequence.

In several scenes hereafter, Lory is shown finding a little courage: when the soldiers take the headmaster away, Lory, who has revered him as a father, spontaneously hurls himself against them, ineffectually hammering them with blows from his plump fists. His outburst is rewarded with a peck on the cheek from Louise. With a gesture that only an actor in total command of his expressive means would risk, he allows his hand to drift slowly towards the cheek that was kissed, as if it was drawn to it by magnetic impulse, while he stares fixedly ahead, only the slightest, the very slightest, flicker of what might be a smile, hovering about his lips.

Again, he's having supper with Louise, when her hero brother bursts in, demanding that she and Laughton cover for him. The soldiery arrives; Laughton, having accepted a cigarette though he doesn't smoke, manages, through coughing fits, to back him up. The coughing highlights his ineptitude at this kind of game.

Eventually, he's put in prison under suspicion. He's unexpectedly released the next day. When he returns to his mother, he's a slightly different man: gentle, soft-spoken, but some spark has been struck in him. He and the headmaster were in adjacent jails, and talked the night through about liberty and democracy. The disarray of his clothes and unaccustomed stubble on his chin testify to his loosening up. He runs next door to tell Louise and her brother that he's free but the brother has been killed, and Lory's release leads them to accuse him of having traded the brother's life for his freedom. His new expansiveness shattered, he runs out to the street, where his mother confesses that she shopped the brother. He runs to find the only man who could have put his mother in touch with the authorities: he breaks into his office to find him dead. He picks up the gun, and is immediately arrested for his murder.

The film now passes from the realistic, if slightly schematised mode, to something more overtly inspirational. Lory appears in court, starts falteringly to defend himself. He starts to speak some home truths. The prosecution demands an adjournment; Lory is visited in his cell by the Nazi Commandant (Slezak), who silkily expounds his vision of the Aryan future. He promises to release Lory, so that he can get on with the great task: teaching the children of the future. Lory seems to agree; but then, from his prison window, he sees the headmaster being shot. The next day when he appears in court, he dismisses the attempt to, as it were, un-frame him, and makes a passionate speech urging the necessity of resistance. He is acquitted; and returns to the classroom, where he starts to teach his openly-weeping pupils from the American Declaration of Rights. He only gets to Article 6, when the soldiers come to take him away. As he goes, O'Hara takes up the book: Article 6: 'The law is the expression of the will of the people.'

Naked and improbable though this ending is, against the odds it almost works largely due to Laughton's performance. Contemporary reviewers all noted the absurdity of a Nazi court calmly listening to twelve minutes of alien propaganda. Renoir's (and Nichols') point was to show that the French, or occupied Europeans in general – the geographical location is never specified – were capable of heroism and resistance. So here, Lory's appeals to the (native) judge are sustained when he is shamed by Lory's accusations of spinelessness. In any case, Laughton varies the two speeches from the dock in the most masterly way. His command of the *tirade* was never more in evidence. He has Lory start nervously, groping for what he means to say, then surprising himself with his own eloquence. After his scene with the commandant, for which Laughton finds a new tone of amused politeness, and the glimpse of the headmaster being shot, he returns to court a changed man – an inspired orator. It is a far-fetched development in the character; but it is emotionally powerful, and indeed intellectually cogent. The radiance with which his newly-found convictions fills him, his new faith in himself and certainty in the need for action ('We must stop saying that sabotage is wrong, that it doesn't pay . . . it does pay. It makes us suffer, starve and die – but though it increases our misery, it will shorten our slavery') is an astonishing transformation, and his acquittal is genuinely exciting because it means not only has he been freed, but the court and the people have regained their self-respect. It is fantasy, but it inspires: and the final scene in the classroom, more and more improbable, is deeply touching. In the circumstances of the film's production, the words of the Declaration of Rights have a special resonance; but again, Laughton's presentation of the new Lory, walking tall, strong and clear, the same character but radicalised from within, is what carries it. 'Goodbye, Citizens,' his parting words to the children, are the summation of the film.

Renoir wrote:

He was intelligent and he wanted to know why he was being asked to do things. He had every right to know, and I appreciated the

concern and concentration he showed all during the filming . . .
Charles was both intelligent and gifted, with an instinctive genius
for acting.

Renoir had only one crisis with Charles during the work: in the scene
where Lory sees the headmaster being shot, he has to cry out, holding
onto the bars of his prison window, 'Professor Sorel, Professor Sorel!'
First of all, Laughton grasped the bars so passionately that they came
away in his hands; but once they had been shored up, he became
blocked: 'Where is he? Where is he? I can't see him.' The cut-away
shot of the Professor was of course shot at a different time and place. A
real impasse seemed in the offing, but Renoir was inspired to say, 'In
your head, Charles.' It satisfied the actor, and the shot was done in
one. In the final film, this is the least convincing moment in
Laughton's performance. Some large emotion is certainly going on,
but it seems inappropriate. The printed screenplay offers this direction: '. . . he opens his eyes and looks, the frenzy going from his face
which seems to fill with strength and resolution. It is as if the
explosions of their rifles had smashed through a window in his mind
and now he sees a new and unknown world.' This is one of those stage
directions that writers compose in their attic; any attempt to realise
them would only end in osteopathy. (They so often, as here, read like
reviews of the performance before it has been given.) The general drift
is clear, however, and it is most distinctly *not* what Laughton does.
Possibly this was a rare instance in this film of his old malady: a loss of
belief in his own ability to believe. With him it was almost a moral
thing: he felt ashamed of not connecting imaginatively. Not for him
the latter-day cry of 'I can't *feel* it!' No, his imperative was to *see*.
Actors, awash, for the most part, with emotions, are often deficient in
the area of connecting with meaning. Never, or rarely, Laughton.

Slezak, who 'adored the man', offers a colourful glimpse of
Laughton aged forty-four: my dear boy this, my dear boy that, very
much the grand old man, dispensing advice, short lectures on wine
and art, readings from the classics, a little heavy-handed professorial
humour ('You need help with the scene? What's the matter – *no
talent?*'). One thread of observation is especially interesting:
Laughton's ability – uncontrollable urge – to play all the parts. 'A
torrent of emotion burst out of him, he laughed, he was menacing – he
lived every part. It was a dazzling display of virtuosity.' On another
occasion, Slezak asks for help with a scene. Laughton suggests an
approach. It's brilliant. Renoir accepts the first take – very rare for
him, apparently – and Slezak thanks Laughton. 'Of course, my boy,'

says he, 'there are several different ways of doing it,' and he reads it three more times, each with a different attack, a different interpretation, and a new characterisation. 'I was ready to turn in my Equity card.' There is no sense in this report, or other similar ones from other actors over the years, that Laughton was showing off, but rather that the myriad possibilities were teeming around inside him and had to be let out.

Slezak relates a most striking incident. He, Slezak, was doing the close-up shots for a scene they'd just done together. Laughton stood alongside the camera, as he needed to, not in the shot at all. He insisted that Slezak must be able to see his eyes. 'I began my close-up, which was practically a monologue, and saw that Laughton's eyes were filling with tears; he pressed a hand against his mouth as if to prevent himself from crying out. His face became contorted, and when the scene was over he collapsed in his chair with a groan. I rushed over to him. 'Charlie, are you all right?' I thought he was in pain. He looked up – worn, exhausted, spent – and whispered: 'Oh, my dear boy, it's so difficult to keep it simple!'

Keeping it simple is what Laughton supremely does in *This Land is Mine*. It amounts to a new sort of performance, prefigured, I suggest, by his Rembrandt. In it, maximum expressiveness, the intensification of the image, the iconisation of the experience, is not the aim. His Lory is not an archetypal figure but a model of behaviour. The personal connection which Laughton obviously made with the character has, if anything, enabled him to achieve an exceptional clarity. Instead of fashioning colossal statues, he has here made something much more life-scale. If this was a pattern he was going to follow, he would more than before be dependent on good scripts, because his giant projections of the pre-war years were largely made by his own flesh and blood. This more analytic, more conscious approach could only apply to a text which offered material for analysis, for demonstration. With one modest exception, he never found those texts; not in film. He had to look elsewhere.

The reviews of the time, though generally well disposed on account of the worthiness of the enterprise, and the standing of Renoir, fail to notice any change in Laughton's style. Agate was cutting: 'I regard this film as dull, prolix and unamusing. It ends with Laughton reading the American Bill of Rights to his pupils. I fear Charles' habit of reading the Magna Carta and such-like manifestos is growing on him; some one should break him of it. At the same time, it is the best thing he does in the present performance, which for the most part is boring, unattractive and even unappetising.' Agate had never spoken of Laughton like that. The film's relative neglect in the Laughton oeuvre is serious. It is one of his most interesting and best, a new road sadly unexplored.

'In my heart of hearts,' wrote Charles to a friend, 'I think that it is the most important thing written on the war to date in any form at all – novel – movie – play – political treatise or what have you . . . I am hoping that public thought is sufficiently advanced to take the lesson it has to teach on the chin . . . the film flouts all rules laid down for a successful picture. There is a hell a lot of talk – not Shavian – that is to say, not pure argument, but talk brought out of people by the pressure of their situation and their suffering.' To the same friend he wrote: 'There is a love story in me and Maureen O'Hara, and as I go to my death at the end of the picture, Maureen kisses me, not in daughterly devotion, but with physical passion.' In the picture, Lory achieves beauty through courage; and so does Laughton. In an ironic aside he writes 'I remember reading a note on Thalberg's desk, upside down – I have trained myself to do that, have you? It bore the legend, "Laughton must never get the girl."'

Another new road opened up before him during the making of *This Land is Mine*. His friend Perry Charles suggested that he might have a radio programme of his own. Laughton was mightily tempted: 'Frankly, I am very ambitious about the radio.' He had considerable experience of the medium, with his friend Norman Corwin, who produced the series *Pursuit of Happiness*. Corwin wrote 'in radio, only Orson Welles and Martin Gabriel were in the same class when it came to handling rhetoric and language that flexed the imagination.' Moreover 'I had no hesitation in casting Laughton, an Englishman to be cicerone to material as American as hotdogs and the teaparty, for he had the capacity to be as lyrical or as colloquial as the texts required, along with other qualities between, above and beyond.' But this offer of Perry Charles was different. He was to talk as himself. 'I feel that I have something to say . . . that I could develop a definite point of view toward people, as myself. (You are one of the only two people in the business who know that I can hold an audience in my own personality). I don't of course mean standing up and knocking the ———— out of them.' He was reaching out for some new form of expression. He had something to say, and he wasn't being allowed to say it in his other work. But he decided against it on characteristic grounds. 'I have three pictures to do next year, and a radio script really and truly is a full-time job. You can't just sit back and leave it to writers. You know yourself people like Allen, Benny, Bergen, and so on, spend all their energy on their radio scripts. You may say that Benny and Bergen make pictures, too, but they make pictures with their left hands . . . and you know, Perry, I am the kind of guy that can't do anything with his left hand.' His movie commitments took up five or six months of the year. They didn't satisfy him, but he couldn't do them part-time. 'The whole problem of leading a decent self-respecting life in the movies is one of how to keep one's functions exercised and occupied without over-straining yourself so that you are done for in a few years.' He was desperately looking for a new outlet; but this was not to be it.

The reception of *This Land is Mine* did nothing to halt the decline of Laughton's reputation; nor did his next film, *The Suspect*, directed by Robert Siodmak, which both Laughton and Lanchester, and indeed Siodmak, regard (wrongly, I believe) as one of his best performances.

Charles Higham recounts the curious working relationship that prevailed between Laughton and the director, later a great friend and member of the Bard-reading circuit. Siodmak, it would seem, decided to pre-empt any possible temperamental outbursts on the part of his star by having an even greater one himself. The strategy evidently worked: Laughton regarded him as insane and was watchful in his presence. This strange situation may account for the generally subdued tone of the film, which is very well shot, rather well acted (particularly by the admirably caddish Henry Daniell, wolf-featured, with a corrugated mouth running from ear to ear) but just a bit of a damp squib. Given the propensity of the script to avoid actual drama, and to build teasing fragments of tension which quickly disappear, it is somehow unfortunate that Laughton should have chosen to play the central character quite as damped-down as he does. The result is overall somewhat monochrome, a psychological thriller with neither thrills nor psychology. Admittedly Laughton's restraint finally pays off: his poised inscrutability under questioning becomes rather fascinating; and the film's ending, in which Marshall, Laughton's character, is tricked into thinking that an innocent will hang for his crime, is genuinely gripping. He slowly leaves the boat on which he and his family were about to escape to Canada. His slow impassive walk across the pebbled quay is beautifully shot, and ends the film with a memorable image of a born loser, doomed by his temperament not to be able to take the steps necessary to relieve him of his misery.

In general, however, the *New York Times'* verdict stands: 'Too genteel.' The *Manchester Guardian*, admiring Charles, said: 'He has never been easy to cast. In spite of a long list of middling films, he can still emerge as a fine player of complex characters.' In other words, not bad for a tired old ham. The list wasn't *that* long. Yet. The *Guardian* concluded its review with praise so faint it is almost inaudible: 'interesting without being too clever.'

Charles' real creative focus, in any case, was elsewhere. Late in 1943 he at last formed a professional relationship which demanded of him everything he knew and was longing to give. He met Bertolt Brecht.

Brecht

'It was soon after returning to Santa Monica in March 1944 that Brecht met Charles Laughton, who fell in love with him,' states Ronald Hayman, unequivocally. Salka Viertel, at whose house in Maybery Road they met, writes that Laughton was 'hypnotised' by Brecht. Conversely, James K. Lyon in his definitive *Bertolt Brecht in America* describes Laughton as 'the single most important person for Brecht in his American exile'.

Certainly they fell on each other with the passion of two people who want something only the other can give, something desperately desired and long lacked: in Brecht's case, a production, in Laughton's, a rôle. Brecht, at this point in his exile, would have collaborated with any star he thought he could hitch a production to (he had been speaking to Luise Rainer, star of *The Good Earth*, about putting on *The Caucasian Chalk Circle* – had indeed written it on the basis of her enthusiasm to play in Klabund's original *Chalk Circle*) whilst Laughton was pining like some great animal denied proper exercise.

What began as mutual self-interest, however, quickly turned into something infinitely rich and rewarding, both personally and creatively, if not, in the last analysis, professionally.

The very fact that their meeting took place at the Viertels' salon might have suggested to Brecht that Laughton was not like the common run of American actors; but Laughton, though not easy socially, always wanted to be near artists – painters, composers, poets, playwrights; and Salka Viertel had somehow created a space where that most un-English and largely un-American phenomenon, the community of artists, could flourish. The only other Englishman he might have met there was Chaplin, who knew Laughton well, but with him, much as he admired his comedic techniques, Brecht could find no rapport. As so often, the admired does not recognise himself in the admirers' description. Chaplin had no hunger for ideas: he liked to talk, and had, as Norman Lloyd, then a young actor-producer, observed, 'living-room routines, designed to dazzle.' Laughton, who had no small talk, would only speak when he had something to say. Brecht was a man of few words, conversationally, but those words were precise, pithy, provocative. Laughton detested cant and pomposity; he loved intelligence and frankness. The authentic voice was what Laughton was always listening for; through the hubbub of the dispossessed intelligentsia of Europe, he must have heard it loud and clear from Brecht's mouth.

In a very simple sense, the man from Augsburg and the man from Scarborough understood each other. A certain bluntness, a certain cussedness, a penchant for questioning, an impatience with sartorial and social observances were theirs in common – as were capacity and inclination for hard work, admiration of craftsmanship, love of learning. There are further points of connexion: each had a wife who ran the house, while lovers hovered in the background, occasionally awkwardly entering the domestic frame; each was dependent on collaborators, preferring to work in harness than alone; neither had the gift of friendship. There was work and there was sex, and everything else was somehow a waste of time; only learning and its concomitant, teaching, could claim equal status, to make up Reich's famous trinity, Love, Work and Knowledge.

But there were differences. The greatest difference was crucial: self-confidence. Through years of revilement and exile, Brecht never for a second lost faith in his work, nor in himself. 'Do you know who I am? *I am Brecht!*' he screamed at Luise Rainer, 'and you are nothing.' She was at that moment one of the most famous actresses in the world, and he was an unperformed and penniless emigré. This self-confidence of course extended to his sexual life, and must, indeed, to a large degree, have accounted for it. The confidence enabled a ruthlessness which often appeared in the guise of slyness or disingenuousness. All this was very different for Laughton. He was certain of nothing, not even his acting. Elsa Lanchester reflects that now Laughton's films are being shown again on television, his performances seem much better than he considered them at the time. 'It is sad that he always denigrated himself.' Nothing was any good, neither when he was making the film nor when it was finished. Sexually it was worse. Never was he able to approach a man sexually without the expectation of rejection. He was plagued with feelings of guilt and inadequacy.

The balance sheet of difference and similarity serves as a prelude to a consideration of how it is that Charles Laughton and Bertolt Brecht, on the face of it radically contrasted artists, should have collaborated so happily. Who would imagine that Charles Laughton would be held up by Brecht as consummate exponent of his acting theory; or that the creator of Captain Bligh and The Hunchback of Notre Dame would say of Brecht: 'I believe there is Shakespeare and then Brecht'? The matter is of interest in illuminating both Laughton's acting and Brecht's theory. Towards the end of his life, Brecht, impossible as ever to pigeon-hole, wrote: 'My theories are altogether more naïve than one might think – more naïve than my way of expressing them might allow one to suspect.' He was dismayed by the academic industry that had grown up around him, still more by the dreadful work it had engendered. 'It must be due to my way of writing, which takes too much for granted. To hell with my way of writing!' The long years of exile from theatre practice, coupled with an attempt to systematise the New Theatre which would make the New Society possible, resulted in a body of theoretical writing of great beauty and intellectual excitement, but of limited applicability. The terminology itself – Verfremdungseffekt, Gestus, Epiktheater – has thrown a sometimes impenetrable veil over the plays. It's particularly interesting, then, that Brecht said of Laughton: 'He didn't need any kind of theoretical information about the required "style." ' Laughton was a spontaneous Brechtian actor.

Brecht had admired Laughton's work before he met him, especially his Captain Bligh and Henry VIII. He was very struck by the chicken-eating scene. It is, as it happens, a little sequence which contains a number of elements that might be described as Brechtian. The king, speaking about the decline of manners, greedily scoffs chicken legs, discarding the bones over his shoulder. It's funny because of the contrast between what's being said and what's being done – the contrast draws attention to the incident, puts the speech in special focus. This is a classic Verfremdungseffekt – nothing to do with the mistranslated alienation (for which the German is Entfremdung), Verfremdung being the-making-strange, the-making-foreign, seeing in a new way, from a different angle. There does exist an English word for this, but it is unlikely to gain wide currency, even though it was coined by Dickens. 'Mooreeffoc', it is, and it's simply the word 'coffeeroom' seen from the other side of the glass pane on which it's written. In conversation Brecht gave another very clear notion of what we should perhaps just call *V*, as the German seems so formidable and unfunny: 'in order to see one's mother as a man's wife we need V; this is provided, for instance, when one acquires a stepfather.' In the case of the chicken-eating interlude we're dealing with a *Gestus*; in Martin Esslin's definition, 'the clear and stylised expression of the social behaviour of human beings towards each other'; in Brecht's own formulation, 'a theatrical conception: what Garrick did when as Hamlet he met his father's ghost; Sorel when, as Phèdre, she knew that she was going to die . . . it is a question of inventiveness.' One might bring it even further down to earth and call it 'business' – *significant* business. This particular business in *Henry VIII*, like some wonderful shorthand, tells us that the king is a man of appetite; that notions of what manners are thought to be have changed over the centuries; that there is a class of persons waiting to pick up the royal débris. It's memorable, it's clever, it's meaningful. The moment also fulfils the central requirement of epic theatre. Epic theatre, says Brecht, is where the spectators don't cry out (in Needle and Thomson's formulation) ' "How true!" but "How surprising!"; not "Just as I thought!" but "I hadn't thought of that!" ' Even fifty years after its première, when all social attitudes (to monarchy, for example) have transformed and the risqué elements in the film no longer shock, this sequence creates a frisson, catches the audience by surprise. And finally, but perhaps most Brechtian of all, it is definitely Laughton doing it. Remarkable though the physical transformation is, there is no sense of the actor losing himself, Stanislavsky-style, in the rôle, or placing a mask over his own face (something that Laurence Olivier was much inclined to do). We are not merely witnessing, we are being *shown* something. It is not being explained to us – we have no idea why the king behaves like this or what he feels about it – it is simply being dangled in front of us: 'what about this, eh?' Later, in Zurich, in his dense and sometimes abstract *Small Organum for the Theatre*, Brecht enunciated a principle: 'the actor appears on stage in a double rôle, as Laughton and as Galileo; the showman Laughton does not disappear in the Galileo he is showing; Laughton is actually there, standing on the stage and showing us what he imagines Galileo to have been.'

This is the heart of the matter. Laughton delighted Brecht by two different answers to the question why he acted. One, quoted by Eric Bentley in his *Brecht Memoir*, was: 'Because I like to imitate great men.' It is the word 'imitate' that so pleased Brecht: an imitation is always a critique, a comment on the original. Laughton might have said: I like to become great men; or I like to forget myself by becoming great men. His choice of word was precise and intentioned. The other reply was the one Brecht made famous in his magnificent *Building Up A Part: Laughton's Galileo*: 'Because people don't know what they're like and I think I can show them.' Brecht goes on to say 'he had all sorts of ideas which were begging to be disseminated about how people *really* live together.' That is no doubt true and no doubt Laughton did feel that he knew what people were like. That is not why he proved such a perfect vehicle for the Brechtian approach. His instinctive grasp of it stems from his relationship to himself, his critical account of himself. He was profoundly ill-at-ease in society, in his profession, even, perhaps especially, in his own body. He didn't like himself, felt himself to be wrong, odd, unlovely. This is common with actors. The usual method, however, is to change oneself into someone one does like and display that (star acting), or keep escaping into different characters, and thus elude oneself. Laughton does something different. He knows what he's like, and he painstakingly displays it. He doesn't ask us to identify with it, because *he* doesn't identify with it: he is the subject of his own demonstration. His performances never console nor do they sedate: we are moved by the naked truth of them, and by the courage and self-expenditure of the man giving them. In the best of them we are moved, like Brecht's ideal audience, to cry out: 'These things should not be allowed!' His attitude to what he is demonstrating is personal and often painful; the demonstration is passionate, passionate from a lifetime of observation and struggle. As it happens, his attitude, his stance, his viewpoint were not the same as Brecht's – 'in political matters he was indifferent (indeed, timid)' – but the all-important thing as far as Brecht was concerned was that he didn't want to drug the audience (as in the 'culinary theatre' he abhorred); he urgently wanted to tell them something they might not know.

Not to *prove* but to demonstrate; not to *explain* but to state the thing that needs to be explained; not to tie up the ends, but to expose the contradictions. This, as Brecht was at pains to indicate, meant no loss of warmth of emotion or reality, indeed, the more, the better: the thing being shown *must* be real. And the fact that he greatly admired

Laughton's acting is a guarantee that he wasn't interested in anything dry or cerebral: flesh and blood, alive and real, was what he was after: but capable of change. Brecht was distrustful when 'there is a complete fusion of the actor with his rôle that makes the character seem so natural, so impossible to conceive any other way.' Laughton never suggested that; though he did draw short of any political solution. 'We must find means of 'shedding light on' the human being at that point where he seems capable of being changed by society's intervention.' There the collaborators parted company. Laughton might have felt, with Kierkegaard, that 'an artist cannot change society; all that he can do is to express that it is sick.'

The course of their relationship is charted in Brecht's *Arbeitsjournal*, his work diary. Shortly after they met, Brecht showed Laughton one of his innumerable unperformed plays, *Schweyk in the Second World War*. Laughton fell for it, was 'really enthusiastic.' He read it out loud to Brecht, Eisler and Hans Winge. 'We laughed uproariously. He understood *all* the jokes.' The thought of Laughton in that particular part is mouth-watering. His grasp of the indestructible Bohemian would have been absolute. 'He got *all* the jokes.' Reading out loud, already a familiar mode of communication for Laughton, became central to his relationship with Brecht. 'L. reads to us from *Measure for Measure* and *The Tempest*. He reclines on a white couch before a magnificent grandfather clock in Bavarian baroque, his legs crossed, so that his Buddha-like tummy is openly visible and reads out a short piece from a small book, partly like a scholar, partly like an actor, laughing at the jokes, occasionally apologising for not knowing lines . . . he reads the part of Caliban with feeling.' On that occasion Laughton talked to them about how badly actors are treated in England: apparently his Bond Street tailor only agreed to make his suits if he kept it secret, otherwise he would lose his Tory customers. 'You get no respect here,' he said, 'but you get money. Where else can an actor live like this?' – pointing at the antique furniture, the park with lawn, and the Mexican heads of Medusa.

Barely three months later, in August 1944, as if to mock him, a large piece of his lawn slithered away into the ocean. Laughton immediately succumbed to apocalyptic intimations: it will be all over the papers, he'll be a laughing stock, it'll damage his career. He told Brecht that he was widely regarded as a ham, and feared not being able to make enough money, that he was old (45, in fact). Brecht in his journal observes that he looks old. As a sort of consolation prize, he showed

Laughton the poem he had written for him: 'Garden in progress', a celebration of the flowers and statues so lovingly installed by the actor. It was at once his greatest comfort and the most direct outlet for his creativity – every plant had been chosen personally by him, carefully placed, and expertly bedded. The Mexican and pre-Columbian statues (Laughton was among the first serious collectors of these) were likewise positioned with infinite care. All this Brecht saw and celebrated in a poem of exceptional charm and perceptiveness:

Wherever one went, if one looked
One found living projects hidden

He told Laughton: 'Your garden will be a myth based on a legend.' In view of the calamity, he appended a last verse which completes and extends the images of the poem:

Alas, the lovely garden, placed high above the coast
Is built on crumbling rock. Landslides
Drag parts of it into the depths without warning. Seemingly
There is not much time left in which to complete it.

Laughton could hardly have failed to cheer up on receipt of the lovely Horatian poem; but it was only the first part of Brecht's consolation: the second was the play *The Life of Galileo*, which Brecht now showed him for the first time. He had written it in 1938 at the suggestion of his collaborator, Ferdinand Reyher. Initially it was to be a film-script, but it quickly turned into a play, which Brecht provisionally entitled *The Earth Moves*; by the time he completed it, in 1938, in Denmark, it had acquired the present title. Brecht and Reyher had high hopes of an American production of it; in a sense it was always destined for Broadway, though in fact the first performance of this version took place in Zurich, in 1943. As early as 1942, though, Brecht had tried to interest his friend Oscar Homolka, now established in Hollywood, in playing Galileo, suggesting that he had written the part with him in mind; nothing happened.

By contrast, the moment he read it, Laughton knew he must do it; the rôle, the play, the subject all demanded it. But perhaps the most alluring prospect was that of active participation in the writing of the play itself. His sense of language was acute, but his own use of it dismayed him. 'I just can't get myself down on paper,' he writes to a friend; 'I just can't put two words together on paper,' he writes to Elsa Lanchester. In almost every one of the few letters he wrote, he says 'Jesus, what a stinking letter I write,' or 'What a bloody awful letter I write. It reads simply bloodily.' But perhaps in collaboration. . .

He spoke no German, and first read the play in Elisabeth Hauptmann's literal rendition. A version of the play was then commissioned from two young MGM writers of Laughton's acquaintance, Brainerd Duffield and Emerson Crocker; it was evidently satisfactory as far as it went, but he and Brecht decided that they should make a new version. In late 1944, they started the unique process of play-making which resulted in a radically new version of the play, and which dominated both their lives for nearly three years.

Brecht was always perfectly happy to share his authorial activities with others; his confidence, again, spared him any anxiety about his creative potency. Any useful input was accepted and absorbed. The relationship with Laughton was evidently entirely congenial to him, all the more for its unusual form. Because Laughton spoke no German, it was necessary for Brecht to offer a rudimentary translation of each line, which Laughton would then convert into idiomatic English. Brecht would then re-work that to further precision, and Laughton would make final adjustments. 'This system of performance-and-repetition had one immense advantage in that psychological discussions were entirely avoided' – anathema to both. Laughton was, however, deeply concerned with the shaping of the scenes, the making of points, the overall impact of the play; and many of his suggestions were incorporated into the text. Together they conducted what would now be called a workshop: Laughton would bring in scenes from other plays so as to learn from them – especially Elizabethan ones ('Although L.'s theatrical experience had been in a London which had become thoroughly indifferent to the theatre, the old Elizabethan London still lived in him, a London where theatre was such a passion it could swallow immortal works of art greedily and barefaced as so many texts'). They shared a passion for the mechanics of playwriting: how is this effect achieved, what is the best way to handle such and such a relationship? Both were learning, both were teaching. They'd rush off to the museums and the art galleries for clues. Laughton amassed a collection of sometimes no more than tangentially relevant material – 'I could see L. would only make marginal use of it' – in order to discover the world of the play and its embodiment: 'he obstinately sought for the external: not for physics but for the physicists' behaviour.' 'For quite a while, our work embraced everything we could lay our hands on.'

As Brecht paints it, it was something of an idyll for both of them. 'We used to work in L.'s small library, in the mornings. But often L. would come and meet me in the garden, running barefoot in shirt and trousers over the damp grass, and would show me some changes in his flower beds, for the garden always occupied him, providing many problems and subleties. The gaiety and proportion of this world of flowers overlapped in the most pleasant way into our work.' It *was* a kind of love affair, for Brecht an extension of other similar collaborations, for Laughton the discovery of a new and wonderful world. At last he knew what he had been preparing himself for, all these years of reading and studying and looking and learning. Somehow it had needed association with another mind, one he deeply respected, to give him courage to create something. 'I have many times tried to write very simple stories, but they all looked and sounded terrible the next morning,' he wrote, years later; and Elsa Lanchester wrote that 'Charles was never a creative playwright, but he was a master cutter. He would have liked to have been a writer, because in fact he really knew how to build a dramatic house. And Brecht spotted that. Beyond acting, Charles' chief talent, I think, was construction. You might call it editing.'

For Brecht it was simply a treat to have the total engagement of this huge and complicated spirit whose commitment to the play, and to Brecht himself, was unqualified. No doubt with the constant overview of wanting to get the thing on, this touchiest of men was astonishingly compliant; moreover there was a sense in which, despite Laughton's political 'indifference', his suggestions, both for cuts and additions, sharpened the play's political impact 'on the simple grounds that passages in question seemed 'somehow weak' to him, by which he meant that they do not do justice to things as they are.' Willett and Manheim in their critical edition examine in detail the changes made from the 1938 original text. The most significant with which Laughton was involved were, to take two examples, quite specifically political: it was he who urged Brecht to make Lodovico, Virginia's fiancé, into a nobleman; and it was his idea to have a dummy of the Pope thrown in the air by the crowd in the carnival scene. Laughton had obviously entered into the mind of author: 'driven by his theatrical instincts, L. is fervently expounding the political aspects.' His greatest influence, of course, was in the area of the character of Galileo. Interestingly, his suggestions to Brecht were all to do with rendering the character more culpable: 'L. is for throwing the character to the wolves . . . he insists on a complete portrayal of depravity, stemming from the crime that brought out Galileo's negative side. Only Galileo's brilliant mind survives, functioning in a void, found redundant by its owner, who now desires mediocrity.'

Laughton's identification with not merely the outward characteristics of Galileo – his sensuality, his passion for learning, his cunning – but also with his moral situation gave his work on the play particular intensity. His nameless, undefined guilt immediately homed in on the matter of Galileo's treachery, his betrayal of science, of the people. Brecht reports: 'he reveals this idea most clearly when he is called a 'scab' for crossing a picket line in front of the studio; this hurt him deeply, no applause here.'

The film being picketed was *Because of Him*, one of the five films he made during the period of his collaboration with Brecht. Though mostly forgotten now, each of the films contains a rather refreshing performance from Laughton. It may not be fanciful to suggest that the work with Brecht, in restoring Laughton's self-respect and stimulating every part of his creative faculties, did in fact somewhat restore his enthusiasm for acting itself. It was, of course, necessary for Laughton to keep breaking off from the work in order to make money. In an eloquent phrase Brecht compared Laughton's lifestyle with that of his friend Peter Lorre: 'like Laughton, he lives in shameful poverty with four houses and his own Japanese gardeners in a $50,000 villa.' Laughton did indeed maintain a substantial establishment – though his principal expenditure was on the vast consolation of great art. He was beginning his collection of modern masters, and it wasn't cheap. It is a measure of his new-found sense that life was, in Rimbaud's famous phrase, 'elsewhere.' He was acting in order to surround himself with great art; to surround himself with it, rather than to create it. But now he could use the indifferent films he was offered to underwrite the Great Project: *Galileo*. So perhaps that too affected his general demeanour in the making of them.

Captain Kidd, the first of the five films, is generally regarded as a woeful demonstration of the depths to which Laughton had sunk. Certainly in point of production values, the picture, in common with so many at this period of his career, bears no comparison whatever with the films of his great period, the MGM and RKO films. There was neither time nor money to aim for the kind of finish and detail and intelligent shaping of script that had characterised those films. The producer on *Captain Kidd*, Benedict Bogeaus (better Bogeaus than Dull, no doubt), seems on the evidence of the drab costumes, fake interiors and palpably plastic ocean, to have confined himself to cutting corners. The director, Rowland V. Lee, veteran of costume action dramas, shoots without inspiration; while the script is a preposterous travesty of history and verisimilitude alike. There are a number of attractive performances, however. John Carradine is forceful, Gilbert Roland poses the dago threat to Barbara Britton's Lady Anne with some flair and Randolph Scott does his usual poor man's Gary Cooper routine with panache. Henry Daniell, Laughton's mocking neighbour from *The Suspect*, without either lines or character, fails to make that elusive monarch William III live; but Reginald Owen, with whom Laughton had agreeably sparred in *The Canterville Ghost*, makes a brilliant foil to him here. Their scenes, valet and master, are the best thing in the film. It is tempting to believe that Laughton had a hand in the writing of them, because they so stand out from everything else. They are, for one thing, *about* something: class. Laughton's Kidd aspires to social improvement and hires the valet to instil the appropriate behaviour into him. There is much dry correcting of vowels and adjusting of syntax and murmured sartorial advice, with Laughton torn between the desire to learn and the impulse to kill his mentor. 'Pity about the hair,' says Owen, surveying Kidd's matted locks, 'I suppose you've tried everything?' Their first scene together has an almost Brechtian quality to it, a demonstration of attitudes and behaviour with distant parallels in several of the plays, in which a character is re-made: *Arturo Ui*, *Man Equals Man*, and, indeed, *Galileo* (the Pope dressing scene).

Laughton's Kidd is splendidly centred, the most straightforward character, barring only Henry VIII, that he ever created – strong, clear, forceful, dangerous. His assumption of a slightly off suburban London accent is witty and appropriate; his revelation of the depth of his ambition quite chilling; his rage and pride at bay when finally confronted, animal and fearsome. Reservations only apply to the final *tirade* at the gallows, for which one might have expected a severe reproach from Agate; but no: 'Laughton is grand throughout; he shows again one of the first qualities of the great actor, whether of stage or screen – that power of compulsion which makes it impossible for you to take your eyes off him.' So he was a 'great actor' again. The *New York Times*, regarding the film as 'strictly Charles Laughton's vehicle' applauds him for being 'as much the posturing comedian as the blood-thirsty buccaneer.' The performance is full of relish (which is something of a relief after his most recent offerings) but it's no spoof; is rather, a vigorous and realistic account of a criminal confidently expecting and working for ennoblement. There's no record of whether Brecht ever saw the film or what he thought of it if he did, but Laughton's demonstration of the interaction of the criminal with the Establishment mentality might have idly led him to speculate what kind of a Mackie Messer the Englishman might have made.

It is a prime example of what might be called Laughton's second period as an actor. Comparison with his mariner from the first period, Bligh, makes the development of his approach to acting very clear. Bligh became a universal symbol of the cruelty bred by repression, a kind of Francis Bacon-like image of distorted emotion and warped authority. Expressionist is the word for the impacted power, the concentration and intensity of that performance. Kidd, by contrast, is entirely linear, the character laid out for examination, a prototype rather than an archetype of behaviour. Brecht was fond of citing *Richard III* as an example of the way in which his characters functioned, celebrating and demonstrating the way in which he achieves his ends, which is exactly what Laughton does here. Instead of Bligh's soul, we are made privy to Kidd's mind. It is a most remarkable development.

Because of Him is another matter altogether, Laughton's reunion with Deanna Durbin. Again directed by Henry Koster, the film, like Miss Durbin, is much less nimble than its predecessor; but it is of exceptional interest in Laughton's output for a number of reasons, most of them quite unconnected with the film itself. In it he plays a classical actor of some expansiveness, an extraordinary amalgam of Donald Wolfit, Beerbohm Tree, and, well, Charles Laughton. The opening of the film is itself a Laughton connoisseur's item: 'John Sheridan''s last performance of Cyrano de Bergerac. We get only the last few lines in longshot, a curtain-clinging bow, and a scene in the dressing-room where he hangs his nose up for the last time; but there is a distinct frisson about all this in view of his close involvement in the part for a good two years in the thirties. Similarly, when Sheridan spends the weekend holed up with an old chum he regales him with quotations from *King Lear* – the play which obsessed Laughton for many years. There is moreover a fascinating scene in which he rehearses a play: he is shown as both temperamental and searching; the director/writer finally walks out on him – another sly insertion of Laughton's? Earlier, too, there's a preposterous but funny scene in which he rises from his sickbed to confront reporters with a nearly Joycean stream of boulevard cliché. For the rest, the film is pawky, Miss Durbin sings her way out of trouble in the usual manner, and spends an excessive amount of time in a state of plump tearfulness.

'On the whole, *Because of Him* is a pleasant enough divertissement, chiefly because Mr Laughton had the wisdom to toss restraint out the door,' said the *New York Times* (Thomas Pryor). 'His performance is magnificently expansive. In less polite society it might be whispered that Mr Laughton is hamming all over the screen, but his grandiose acting is in keeping with the general exaggerations of the plot.' In fact, seen now, the effect is not at all hammy; his John Sheridan, vast bulk swathed in a cloak and topped by a fedora, is more of an affectionate *hommage* to the actor-managers of Laughton's youth, an Oscar Asche, perhaps, or, indeed, Tree himself. Certainly, in the rehearsal scene, he is shown to be a serious and scrupulous artist. By now, however, the label had stuck: ham it was, and everything he was to do from now on would be judged by that: it might be good ham, it might be bad ham, it might be indifferent ham, but no matter what subtlety, delicacy, or indeed harshness, he might introduce, it would never be detected, because hams aren't delicate, subtle or harsh: they are just hams.

For self-respect he turned eagerly back to Brecht. Finally, at the end of 1945, they had a version which satisfied them. Brecht being Brecht, there would be more re-writes, sometimes behind Laughton's back, which would then be re-re-written by Laughton and Brecht, but essentially the text now arrived at, radically different from its first (1938) version, was ready for production. The crucial changes resulted from Brecht's strong reaction to the dropping of the A Bomb at Hiroshima, an event which he felt epitomised the divergence of science from the life of the community. He grafted this perception onto *Galileo*, tracing the split to Galileo's recantation. Laughton, whose initial response to the news of the bomb had been ruthlessly protective of the play ('Bad publicity, old man'), was passionately disgusted by the unleashing of this terrible power – he used to tell an ironic anecdote about an encounter with a man who said he didn't go to the theatre because he couldn't stand the bad language. 'And what do you do for a living,' asked Laughton. 'I'm a nuclear scientist,' the man replied – but he resisted laying the blame at Galileo's door. There remains in their version a slight uneasiness in this area; but essentially, it's an excellent, playable, tight piece of playmaking. The notes they made, according to James Lyon, show that Laughton, 'a proponent of the mighty phrase, tended to inflate or elevate the text, while Brecht attempted to reduce the language to its leanest form.' The combination of these two modes produced a version which, unlike many translations from Brecht, is neither jejune nor stilted;

neither self-consciously plain, nor self-consciously poetic.

From now on the main task was to get the play on. Brecht created a beautiful memorial to their collaboration in 'Letter to the Actor Charles Laughton':

Still your people and mine were tearing each other to pieces when we
Pored over those tattered exercise books, looking
Up words in dictionaries, and time after time
Crossed out our texts and then
Under the crossings-out excavated
The original turns of phrase. Bit by bit –
While the housefronts crashed down in our capitals –
The façades of language gave way. Between us
We began following what characters and actions dictated:
New text.

Again and again I turned actor, demonstrating
A character's gestures and tone of voice, and you
Turned writer. Yet neither I nor you
Stepped outside his profession.

Galileo

In December of 1945, Laughton started private readings of the version of *Galileo* over which he and Brecht had so long laboured. He read, in wonted fashion, to anyone who would listen: 'wounded servicemen, fellow actors, millionaires, agents, lovers of art' according to an entry in Brecht's journal. 'Not a single boo or reservation, so it seems.' The reaction at these impromptu and perhaps unlooked-for sessions were noted and adjustments were made. Other more formal gatherings were convened; one for Eisler, the Viertels and Feuchtwanger among others; another, more importantly, for Orson Welles, who immediately expressed an interest in directing it. Brecht liked him and his response, and was confirmed in his enthusiasm by a visit to Welles' spectacular and, in the event, spectacularly disastrous production of *Around the World in Eighty Days*. With half a mind on the carnival scene from *Galileo*, Brecht was thrilled by the circus sequence Welles had introduced, complete with animals and acrobats. Laughton apparently shared Brecht's enthusiasm, although he had privately sounded out other possible directors, including, unimaginably, Alfred Lunt. 'The nearer the hour to rehearsal, the more scared I become of being directed in the play by anyone but an actor.' Did he regard Welles as an actor or as a director? Despite the débâcle of his relationship with Hollywood, the collapse of his political career, and the over-ambition of his present stage venture, Welles was very much the thrilling young man in a hurry, still only 30, the boy genius, the Renaissance man *de ses jours*. Whatever the temporary setbacks, his confidence and charm were supreme, carrying all before them. This must have been very hard for Laughton to handle.

So!' wrote Welles in a jaunty postscript to one of his letters to Charles 'you find my confidence in my own charm overbearing, do you? Go fuck yourself!'

Powerful, rich and famous though he might have become, Laughton's caution, intellectual inferiority complex, and slow-moving cussedness remained intact. What position could he adopt in relation to this whirlwind? He could be neither teacher nor pupil. Welles would simply make him feel dull and old, blinking foolishly as Welles performed his verbal, artistic and actual conjuring tricks with Laughton not quite seeing how he did it but obscurely sensing a fraud somewhere. From the beginning of the venture, there seems to have been a sense of strain. Welles became impatient with Brecht's obstinacy: 'Brecht was very, very tiresome today until (I'm sorry to say) I was stern and a trifle shitty. Then he behaved.' At first Welles resisted Laughton's participation as co-producer – upon which Brecht was properly insistent – then acceded – but he kept becoming involved in various other projects and putting off *Galileo*. Laughton and Brecht in, it must be admitted, a fairly amateur way went behind Welles' back and did a deal with the impresario Mike Todd, who was to supervise the entire production. Laughton, with his perennial insecurity, urged Brecht on: 'That's protection. That's what you need'. They had either failed to check out or not thought important Todd's previous dealings with Welles, which had been extremely abrasive – Todd had pulled out of *Around the World in Eighty Days* and precipitated Welles' never-ending financial problems with it. Welles refused to be involved in the venture if Todd was, and told Laughton so; or rather, told his assistant to tell Laughton so. Laughton's reply ('I do not appreciate your habit of using a third party to do the calling') complains of the procrastination: 'Either the play was going on on the earliest possible day or I had to do a movie. Time at my age is dear.'

Laughton was 47. Money, rather than time, was the real issue. The parts and the emoluments were dwindling. Laughton wrote to Welles: 'The rest of Mike's letter seems plain nonsense, including a passage which says 'When Orson does a play (I speak from experience) he really does it.' I was under the impression we were to collaborate all three on the idea of production and so on for the new and difficult play, otherwise how could I also function right? You are an extraordinary man of the theatre and therefore I flatly do not believe that you cannot function as a member of a team.' This utter misjudgement of Welles is equally an illumination of Laughton: he *was* a genuine team-worker, partly from fear and insecurity and dread of the aloneness and responsibility of creation, partly from his sense of the vastness of the task – any artistic task. Welles' Promethean dynamism was quite alien to him. Had he not stumbled badly with Prospero?

'You are the best man in the world,' he goes on, 'to put the Church of Rome on the stage, to mention only one aspect of the play. This appears to me to matter. Cannot this important thing between you and Todd be worked out? Todd has never spoken ill of you to either of us. The strongest word he has used is 'afraid.' That also is nonsense when there is the play to be told. Brecht greets you, Charles.'

Whether the word 'afraid' was Todd's word or Laughton's may be doubted; but there's no doubting the passion and sincerity of his last phrase: 'there is the play to be told' – a fine phrase that Brecht would certainly have approved of. The telling of the play was Laughton's whole ambition, to which everything else was subservient. To Welles, it may have seemed exciting, fun, a challenge, 'one of the greatest productions of the contemporary theatre', in other words, more glory; but for Laughton it was the way forward for the future – the future of the theatre, but equally, perhaps, the future of mankind. To Alfred Lunt Charles had written: 'It seems that Brecht is our man and is launching the theatre back to us on the old Elizabethan terms.' 'This is a new play, and it is of such stature! It is as important as, if not more important than, reviving the classics.' He and Brecht had sustained such a productive collaboration on the basis of their common vision of the importance of the theatre; Welles, it seemed to Laughton, was a playboy. On that their partnership foundered, not on Mike Todd (who, as it happens, decamped shortly afterwards, when Brecht and Laughton discovered to their horror that he sought to costume the play with Renaissance sets and costumes hired from the studios).

During these one-foot-forward, two-feet-back manoeuvres, Laughton looked to films to provide income, not only for himself, but for Brecht, too. Drafted onto *Arch of Triumph* to replace the unwell Michael Chekhov, Laughton demanded substantial re-writing of his rôle as a sadistic and drunken SS officer in pre-war Paris. In order to lend some particularity to the stock figure of Harry Brown's script, he proposed an intensive examination of *Mein Kampf*, which he undertook with Norman Lloyd, the director's assistant, and a bottle of whisky. The results of their research were then turned over to Brecht. Not a line of what Brecht wrote found its way into the script; that wasn't the point: he got paid, as did Hanns Eisler, hired as German accent coach, also at Laughton's suggestion. Alas, neither accent nor script have the remotest vestige of authenticity, let alone interest. The film, Lewis Milestone's reunion with Erich Maria Remarque (director and author of *All Quiet on the Western Front* together again) is a limp saga, possessing distinction only in the visual sphere, the responsibility of William Cameron Menzies, greatest of all Hollywood art directors. 'In this slow, expensive film Charles Laughton is absurd as the Nazi brute' (Bosley Crowther). Not absurd, but severely out of focus, like the Eisler-taught accent, which seems in its burr Dutch rather than German; or the odd, rolling walk. The monocle flashes sadistically away, but there is neither menace nor sympathy, because this Haake is neither a monster nor real. Something looks as if it might happen in the drunk scene, but nothing does. It seems that Laughton had seen the potential for something interesting which he had neither time nor perhaps encouragement enough to achieve.

The search for a director for *Galileo* continued, from Elia Kazan, who, Brecht said, seemed promising because he admitted he hadn't the least idea how to do the play ('so he might learn') to Harold Clurman. But Brecht distrusted Clurman ('a Stanislavsky man'). 'You will try to get "atmosphere"; I don't want atmosphere. You will establish a "mood"; I don't want a mood . . . you cannot possibly understand how to approach my play'. 'At this,' says Clurman, 'I roared, "My name is Clurman!"' Despite the mastery of emigré exchanges evinced by this last reply, he was clearly not going to hit it off with Brecht, who turned instead to Joseph Losey, Laughton's one-time stage manager from *The Fatal Alibi*. Losey was one of the first Americans Brecht met, in Moscow, in 1935. Their acquaintance continued during Brecht's first American visit, when he saw and admired Losey's Living Theatre productions, thoroughly Brechtian in manner at least. He was staying in the apartment in New York Brecht had taken with his mistress Ruth Berlau during the second half of 1946, so perhaps seemed like the bluebird in Brecht's backyard; doubly so when he introduced Brecht to Edward Hambleton, a young Maecenas from Texas, who agreed to put the play on.

By curious coincidence, Losey had a Laughton connection as well: he had been stage manager on both London and New York productions of *Payment Deferred*, and had stayed around to work on *Last Alibi*, the Broadway version of *Alibi*. His relationship with Laughton seems not to have been especially warm, but he admired him both as an actor and as an intelligent man, and seems not to have resented the clear indication that although he would be the nominal director, Brecht and Laughton were very much in charge. This somewhat surprising fact, in view of Losey's considerable track record in both theatre and radio, and his current contract with RKO, whose enlightened head, Dore Schary, had released him on full pay to do the play, is a measure of his admiration for the play and his respect for both men. He was, after all, not a baby – thirty-seven – and notoriously strong-willed and peppery. In the extensive preparation that followed he acted as handmaiden to the two doughty collaborators. This work, the casting, designing, composing, continued through to the middle of 1947. It might have been possible to go ahead earlier, but Laughton had a film offer which he felt obliged to take. He needed the money urgently: again his garden was crumbling, more ominously than ever this time: it carried a pre-Columbian wind god with it. He set vigorously to work on *The Paradine Case*, his reunion with Alfred Hitchcock after their unhappy experience of ten years before. Hitchcock was no happier with this film than the earlier one, but this time his displeasure had nothing to do with Laughton, who was now neither leading man nor producer. The trouble this time was David Selznick, the film's producer and, as it happens, screenplay writer, who had vexed Hitchcock deeply by imposing Alida Valli and Louis Jordan on him in the central rôles. His interest was confined to constructing the Old Bailey setting in such a way that he could shoot scenes simultaneously from various angles. The scenes between Laughton and his wife (a magisterially compassionate Ethel Barrymore) and Laughton and Ann Todd are the ones that seem to engage Hitchcock – presumably because of the misogyny at the heart of them, to which Laughton gives full weight. His Lord Horfield is a concentrated study of malevolent authority, both on the bench and at the supper table, threatening and mocking, the glinting monocle deployed once more to good effect (though it had to wait for *Witness for the Prosecution* to reach its apotheosis). Nonetheless the performance doesn't quite live. There's something soporific about it (quite possibly intentional) that does nothing to counteract the lethargy instilled by the rest of the film, an expensively half-hearted effort.

Laughton's billing was very firmly and very conspicuously below the title on the posters, in there with the supporting character players like Miss Barrymore and Charles Coburn. His salary was commensurately in decline; nevertheless, he was generous (or guilty?) enough to offer Brecht $5,000 dollars as compensation for the delay in producing *Galileo*. There was to be one more delay before rehearsals could start: Edward Hambleton had proposed the play to the Pelican Theatre Company, run by his friend Norman Lloyd, actor, producer and assistant director on *Arch of Triumph*, and *his* friend, John Houseman, whose association with Brecht went back, like Losey's, to the mid-thirties and a plan to stage *Round Heads and Pointed Heads*. Lloyd and Houseman were rashly trying to establish a base for serious live theatre in Los Angeles. They embraced the idea of doing *Galileo* with great enthusiasm but judged it too difficult a play with which to open their first season. The play they chose to do this with was *The Skin of Our Teeth*, the Thornton Wilder extravaganza, and *Galileo* was scheduled for the end of May, to open on 1 July 1947. Laughton went away again to make another film, *The Big Clock*.

Laughton's Earl Janoth, the newspaper proprietor who murders his mistress, is an adroit creation, witty and vivid. If in *It Started with Eve* he seems somehow to have foreshadowed the elderly Lord Stockton, in *The Big Clock* he appears to have anticipated Edward Heath, Broadstairs vowels, heaving shoulders and all. He plays the newspaper magnate as a Napoleon of print, master-minding his empire with an eagle eye for detail ('there's a bulb been burning for days in a cupboard on the fourth floor. Find out who's responsible and dock his pay, will you?') and an obsession with time – 'I'll give you six minutes to reconsider'. He's both impassive and dynamic, tripping statistics off his tongue as he suddenly makes his staff jump with a single pointed observation; fastidiously fingering his lips as he dismisses unsatisfactory proposals for the increase of circulation ('our aim is to sell magazines, not to pay our readers to read them'); gliding at top speed from room to room. The performance is a technical tour-de-force of high-speed throwaway, comic and powerful at the same time. The voice rarely rises in either pitch or volume – flick, flick, flick goes Janoth, even under extreme pressure. The scene of confrontation between Janoth and his mistress is the only eruption from Laughton, and even that is almost stylised: he plunges into a jealous reproach, puffing mechanically away at his cigarette, as she rounds on him, mocking his ugliness and undesirability (almost *de rigueur* in Laughton movies). His lip begins to twitch – only his lip, as if it had a life of its own. The camera witnesses this in extreme close-up. When the lip can twitch no more, Janoth picks up a heavy object and hurls it across the room, killing his mistress. He stands just as impassively over her, upon which the scene cuts to him quite impassively and drily confessing his crime to his assistant. Janoth has been demonstrated to us. We know nothing about how he feels, or why he is the way he is, but we know everything about what he is, and how he works – like a clock, as it happens, the image that dominates and unifies the whole film. Laughton seems to be drawing attention to the robotic heartlessness of big business. Without a trace of remorse or morality, he allows his guilt to be transferred in turn to not one but two other people; that's how he functions. It's a quite fascinating performance, ending with the unforgettable image of Janoth tumbling backwards down the lift-shaft as impassively as he has done everything else.

The film itself has been as unjustly neglected as Laughton's performance. Directed by John Farrow, the reliable Australian director of any number of unremarkable films, it has a great elegance and flair in a style that might best be described as nearly *noir* – visually the film is dominated by the big clock itself, a massive tower within the Janoth building which would not seem out of place in Fritz Lang's *Metropolis*. The play of shadows is handled in a masterly way; while the plot with its inversions and convolutions (Ray Milland as a crime detective spends much of the film trying to track himself down, as does Laughton) presents an image of nightmarish reversals. Milland, Maureen O'Sullivan (the director's wife) and Henry Morgan as a psychopathic masseur are sharply focused. Elsa Lanchester provides rather un-comic relief as a whacky lady painter; for once, her work seems out of key with both Laughton and the film.

Richard Maybaum, the producer, reports a curious incident, a week before shooting began: Elsa and Charles appeared in his office at the studio with long faces. 'Dear Mr Maybaum,' said Elsa, 'it's so terribly sad, but we can't be in your film.' 'Oh' said Maybaum. 'No,' replied Lanchester. 'You see, we don't know who we are, and we never take anything on unless we know who we are.' And they left. A few days later, they burst in on Maybaum, who had – wisely in the event – just decided to sit tight – to announce joyfully, 'It's alright! We know who we are!' 'And who,' asked Maybaum, 'are you?' 'Dorothy Parker and Colonel Macormack,' Elsa replied. Maybaum accepted the news phlegmatically. Their performances in the film bear no resemblances to these prototypes, but obviously it made them happy. Or one of them, at least. Maybaum drily observes that Laughton said nothing whatever at either meeting, and he was never certain how seriously he took it. Interestingly, on this film Laughton's fee – $100,000, a very decent whack – included Elsa's fee, as clear an identification as could be imagined of the disparity in their respective standings. Even Charles, however, had been an unattractive casting proposition to the front office and was only finally given the rôle after every other possibility had been considered. When the film was released, he was held to be a liability in certain areas: in Nebraska, his name was actually taken off the marquee in deference to local disfavour.

Filming complete, Laughton returned, refreshed, to *Galileo*. Brecht and he continued last-minute revision on the play up to the very last minute – and beyond. (They were still revising when the play transferred to New York.) They spent hours in the libraries and museums looking above all for visual stimulation both for the characters and for the settings. They gave a young actor whom they were trying to interest in the part of Lodovico, for instance, a reproduction of the magnificent Bronzino *Portrait of a Young Man*, gazing coolly and almost insolently out of the canvas, his finger marking the place in the book he was reading. It is claimed that Brecht did not have a high degree of visual awareness but his perceptive account of, for example, the Brueghel *Fall of Icarus* (the same painting that inspired Auden's 'Musée Des Beaux-Arts') seems to give that the lie:

'Tiny scale of this legendary event (you have to hunt for the victim). The characters turn their back on the incident. Lovely picture of the concentration needed for ploughing . . . special beauty and gaiety of the landscape during the frightful event.'

Clearly Brecht felt that the painter's technique was similar to his own; that is, a method of drawing the eye to what was important, to what was new. He puts it even more clearly in his comment on the same painter's *Flight of Charles the Bold*:

'The fleeing commander, his horse, his retinue and the landscape are all quite consciously painted in such a way as to create the impression of an abnormal event, and astonishing disaster. In spite of his inadequacy the painter succeeds brilliantly in bringing out the unexpected. Amazement guides his brush.'

Laughton too studied painting not merely sensuously but to learn, and to learn about his own art. He spoke feelingly about painting on many occasions, but one particular observation is worth repeating: 'Figures should in fact be depicted in such a way that you want to change places with them.' Both men looked to the visual for enlightenment. Brecht, in particular, relied on his designers, (above all Caspar Neher) to suggest stage pictures which expressed the crux of the scene, groupings, to which all the stage movement should lead. He and Laughton commissioned John Hubley, an ex-Disney animator and later close collaborator of Losey's, to make sketches for each scene. It's a concept of pre-planning the placing of a scene which is rarely practised in the modern theatre, where placing is held to 'evolve'; but it's an interesting measure of the degree to which both Brecht and Laughton were concerned with the expressive impact of the staging: no question here of actors 'just standing around', taking up the most convenient position; on the contrary, the placing of the actors was gestic: a crystallised manifestation of the thing to be shown.

Brecht and Laughton also seem to have done the casting themselves: a few emigré actors, like Hugo Haas, as the Pope, quite a number of serious young Hollywood actors, acquaintances of Laughton (Frances Heflin, sister of Van, for example), but for the most part, in James Lyon's phrase, 'both Laughton and Brecht wanted unspoiled, teachable, younger people.' Many of these they found in the recently defunct Actors' Lab, including one, Bill Phipps, who, as it happens, became Laughton's lover, a troubled but none the less sustaining relationship. He played Andrea, though Eric Bentley, for one, reckons he was overparted. In general, the company they assembled was young, eager and talented.

By mid-June when official rehearsals began, many of the cast had already done a great deal of unofficial and unpaid work – not that there was much money around for anyone. Laughton and Edward Hambleton had each stumped up $25,000 dollars: not peanuts, in 1947, but not a great deal, either, with a cast of nearly 40, innumerable scene changes, a band and a huge wardrobe requirement. Laughton and three other actors were on $40 a week, three more were on $20, and the rest on little or nothing. The 265-seat theatre could never have made enough money to pay for all that; this was a labour of love, in three cases above all: Helene Weigel, Brecht's wife, who, though one of the greatest actresses in the world, offered her services as wardrobe mistress; Ruth Berlau, Brecht's current mistress, who took the many production photographs (which still survive, giving a clear indication of what the play must have looked like); and Laughton himself, suddenly very nervous at the prospect of actually doing the thing he had dreamed of for three years.

Rehearsals were dominated by Brecht. His rage was famous and terrible, but seems to have been reserved for the technical aspects of the production. Houseman observes: 'his attitude was consistently objectionable and outrageous . . . he was harsh, intolerant and, often, brutal and abusive. The words *scheiss* and *shit* were foremost in his vocabulary . . . that he was almost always right in his judgements did not diminish the pain and resentment he spread around him during the long, intense weeks of rehearsal.' It seems to have been Laughton who worked most closely with the actors. Houseman again:

'throughout his own rehearsals, and in his relations with others, he was consistently modest, sensitive and understanding. He appeared in every scene but two of the play; yet his preoccupation with his own rôle did not prevent him from spending hours of patient unselfish work with his fellow actors.'

Brecht himself, in *Building a Rôle*, echoing that judgement, adds:

'the playwright was impressed by the freedom he allowed [the younger actors], by the way in which he avoided anything Laughtonish and simply taught them the structure. To those actors who were too easily impressed by his personality he read passages from Shakespeare without rehearsing the actual text; to none did he read the text itself.'

No doubt to balance Brecht's terrifying ways – as when, for example, he screamed at the choreographer Anna Sokolow that he wanted none of her 'tawdry Broadway dances', after which she was replaced by Lottie Goslar – Laughton consciously brought the temperature down. This directing-in-tandem may well have suited him very well: relieved of the anxiety of supreme responsibility, he could gently and doggedly pursue the truth and the life of the play. His own performance, however, was a slightly different matter.

Norman Lloyd observed that in rehearsals, Laughton would be 'like a baby. "You're just being a big baby," Losey would say. "Yes, I am," Charles would pout. It was just games.' Losey later said of him:

'Charles was very mannered. One of the things that I tried to do . . . was to make him not use his mannerisms. He was an extraordinary actor. Extremely sensitive, extremely moody, very intuitive but with an excellent mind, tremendously moving when he got it right, often undisciplined, finding it difficult to keep something when he got it.'

The young physicist Morton Wurtele, scientific adviser on the production, reported that Laughton handled the instruments used in the experiments 'with remarkable ease for someone without scientific training.' There are no reports of any crisis in Laughton's understanding or realisation of the character, and clearly no problem with realising the physical aspects of the part. The rising panic was fear of exposure: first of all in such a progressive and provocative piece; secondly to an audience at all. It had, after all, been ten years since his last stage appearance (in *Peter Pan*). Houseman reports that he kept his panic perfectly under control until a dress rehearsal at which Ruth Berlau was taking photographs. Suddenly Laughton released a howl of rage followed by a wave of abuse as he threatened to murder her if she did not desist at once. She fled.

'Laughton's outburst that night was far more than an actor's tantrum: it was a desperate act of revolt against a man he loved and revered . . . the man for whom he was about to expose himself, after so many years, to the horrifying risk of personal and professional disaster on the stage.'

Brecht continued to rail at technical deficiencies: the opening was postponed by a week to July 30; at the last minute he threatened to cancel the first performance because the set had been coated with shellac. It was duly stripped 'to reveal the grain of the wood', as he required. Laughton had retreated to the caravan he'd had drawn up outside the theatre to serve as a dressing room. Here, according to Houseman, he fell into heavy psychosomatic slumbers 'from which it became increasingly difficult to rouse him'. There had been a crisis at a dress rehearsal when Weigel, appalled by Laughton's unconcealed fumbling with his scrotum during the early scenes, had sewn up his pockets. Laughton was enraged and his access to his organ was restored. Whether he continued to fumble is unreported, and indeed reports vary as to Brecht's attitude to the whole episode: was this particular *gest* beyond a joke, or did he privately admire the audacious connexion Laughton was apparently making between thinking and sex? It seems a perfectly Brechtian notion.

The first night arrived, more than usually terrifying. The audience contained among others Charlie Chaplin, Billy Wilder, Ingrid Bergman, Gene Kelly. 'Turn out for the Theatah,' crowed *Variety*. 'Cinema Intelligentsia and just plain folks flocked to the Coronet Theatre last night to see Charles Laughton do his stuff as Galileo.'

Galas are ten a penny in Los Angeles, but the cross-section in the audience that night is remarkable. It was a blistering summer. Brecht reports 'Laughton's chief worry was the prevailing heat. He asked that trucks full of ice should be parked against the theatre walls, and fans be set in motion "so that the audience can think."' No doubt; it was not perhaps Laughton's *chief* worry. 'Am I doing a terrible thing?' he asked Elsa Lanchester. 'I have to do this. It is right. I know Larry's company is wonderful' – the Old Vic, then at its height under Olivier – 'but I must do this play. This is a play for now,' he said to Norman Lloyd, as he sipped soda water and burped – going back to babyhood, Lloyd thought. Brecht, for his part, left the theatre with the memorable phrase, '*Ich muss ein 7-Up haben.*'

Just before the show began, Lyon reports, Laughton received a telegram from Orson Welles saying that he would reveal him as a fraud: he, Welles, happened to know that the play had not been translated by Laughton at all but was the work of his, Welles', friends, Duffield and Crocker. Welles had planned the arrival of the telegram for the minute before the curtain went up. Small surprise that Laughton is described by some reviewers as being nervous during the first scenes.

The notices, were, in a sense, irrelevant. The play was already, in the words of Oscar Wilde, 'the most enormous success.' It had sold out the moment booking opened. Admittedly, there were only seventeen performances. Interest seemed equally divided between Laughton, Brecht and the theatre company itself, Pelican Productions. And in fact, though Brecht represented the reviews as being universally bad, they were mixed; even when favourable, however, they were uncomprehending, trying to deal with the play in terms of history, biography, 'art theatre', even propaganda. 'An arresting footlight event' (*L.A. Times*); 'It will start as many theatre discussions as anything paraded across the stage in years' (*News*). The *Los Angeles Examiner* found it 'a juvenile fussy harangue'; *Variety* said: 'There is a symbolic bit of business in the final scene of Bertolt Brecht's new play. Galileo, investigating the laws of motion, rolls a small metal ball down an incline and measures its ability to roll up the other side of the U-shaped chute. It doesn't make the grade. Neither, unfortunately, does the script.'

It's hardly surprising that the critics, good or bad, missed the point. They still do, after thirty years' exposure to Brecht's plays and the theories. Curiously dour and fragmentary it must have seemed. As for Robert Davison's sets and white curtain and all the rest of the

Brechtian stage apparatus (a more or less faithful impression of what Neher, had he been able to be present, would have done) they were thought to be the result of thrift ('in the abbreviated, implicit Shakespeare mode – altogether pleasing'). Eisler's music, again, failed to create atmosphere, which is surely, they felt, what theatre music is for? Expecting high drama, confrontation, thrills, an evocation of the Renaissance, the critics were disappointed: 'the production somehow lacks the impact implicit in the story. It seems barren of climaxes and even sparse in stirring moments. Hardly a sigh of sympathy is inspired when Galileo's scientific determination cuts off his daughter's romance. His recantation comes out cut and dried.' (*Variety*). Little had been done to prepare them: Laughton in an interview before the première had said that the purpose of the play was 'to bring that mysterious personage who works in the laboratory out into the light.' The audience, public and critics alike, at the Coronet Theatre simply had no idea how to respond to this play. Bred on Aristotelian (or more likely culinary) theatre, as far as they were concerned this was merely wilfully unengaging. If they had known that Brecht spent every hour, when he wasn't working, eating or making love, reading thrillers, they might have approached his work differently, more like Gilbert Adair's brilliant account of the thriller writer and his reader, 'like two players hunched over a chessboard, they lock themselves in combat, each acknowledging his adversary's existence and skill'. What could be a better description of the ideal member of the audience of an epic theatre than Adair's: 'not for an instant does he [the reader] identify with the characters or their motivations; in a sense, he identifies with only one character and his motivations, [the author herself]'? But the sharp-questioning state of mind of Brecht's ideal audience, taking nothing for granted, 'cigar in mouth, sitting on the edge of their seats,' as he described them, was not to be found in Los Angeles that summer. They weren't interested in engaging with the author. They had come for Galileo and Laughton.

Laughton's performance was a bit of a poser for them. The reviews spoke, in their routine way, of 'personal triumph' and so forth. He was thought to be 'an appealing figure' but 'over-zealously underplayed'. He is 'honest and intelligent', but there is a sense of their being cheated of those big moments that his name and the character's would seem to promise. One review speaks of 'the greatest and most restrained performance of his career'; even John Willett, years later, speaks of how Laughton 'resisted the temptation to overact'. This tells us what the performance was *not*. There is little evaluation of what the performance was. Happily, Brecht, in his long and affectionate account of their work together, has left a detailed and analytical description of it; coupled with Berlau's photographs, and a charming recording Laughton cut to relay the New York re-writes to Brecht, we can form a vivid impression of it.

His sensuous impact in the photographs is considerable. 'He was able to unfold the great physicist's contradictory personality in a wholly corporeal form . . . he had enough taste not to make any distinction between the supposedly lofty and the supposedly base, and he detested preaching.' Brecht observes that, for Germans, thought must always be stripped of sensuality: 'reason, for us, implies something cold, arbitrary, mechanical, presenting us with such pairs of alternatives as ideas and life, passion and thinking, pleasure and utility.' Laughton's great achievement in the rôle, his great originality, was to show intellect as an appetite: which is exactly what it was for him. His hunger to know, to understand, and then to teach, to re-communicate, was at the centre of his life. Eric Bentley, an enthusiast neither of the play nor of Laughton in it, wrote: 'It is unlikely that anyone again will combine as he did every appearance of intellectual brilliance with every appearance of physical self-indulgence.' 'He could,' Bentley says, in a review of another, later performance, 'effortlessly portray a self-indulgent guzzler; second, he was able to seem an intellectual, even a genius. The *combination* of physical grossness with intellectual finesse was theatrical in itself and of the essence of Brecht's drama.' This ability of Laughton's to seem a genius is a further function of his capacity to play great men, to 'imitate' them, as he says. It has something to do with the size of the screen upon which he was able to project his inner activity; but also the precise connection between his brain and his being. Bentley makes a very sharp point: 'In regard to playing the intellectual, this too should be said. It is not done by playing intellect itself. It is done by making the characteristic attitudes of the intellectual live – emotionally. For instance, Laughton would always bristle when he talked with bureaucrats or businessmen: his Galileo was allergic to them. Conversely, when talking to his students he made it clear how much he got from their admiration of him.' Bentley also draws attention to the contradictions Laughton was able to convey: he is a great teacher, yes, but he's vain, too. He's cunning and in need of money, but his congenital distrust of businessmen leads him to lose what they could give him. The audience is thus given no easy answer to the character, they are denied their moments of sentimental gratification ('the great man surrounded by his adoring pupils,' 'the genius oppressed by shopkeepers').

At the time, in order to promote Brecht's work, Bentley praised Laughton's performance in the highest terms ('it is an astonishingly beautiful and instructive thing, and something different in kind from even the best thing one sees on Broadway'. He later had substantial reservations to make. 'The way in which Laughton "stood out" from his part is not quite what the Brechtian theory bargains for. For it was through actorish narcissism that he kept aloof . . . actorish vanity allowed him to let the brilliance slide over into drawing-room comedy smartness. Narcissism prevented him from even trying to enter those somewhat Dostoievskian depths into which Brecht invites the actor of the penultimate scene.'

Bentley is the only commentator of the slightest stature (apart from Brecht himself, to whom we must shortly return) to have offered an account of Laughton's performance, so we must listen to him very seriously. However, there is a background to their relationship which Bentley freely admits by quoting a letter Laughton sent him in response to a request for an endorsement of his translations:

My dear Bentley, I owe you many apologies for not replying to your appeals about Brecht before. I believe him to be the most important living dramatist. At the same time, I have never been able to understand either yours or anybody else's translations of his plays. As far as I have got is to be able to dimly see the great architecture. I also understand that you didn't like my translation of *Galileo* so the situation between us is not an easy one. If I allow you to say, 'I believe Bertolt Brecht to be the most important living dramatist,' and if the general public is anything like myself, they will see my name stuck on something they cannot understand, which is somewhat of a black eye for me. At the same time I feel all kinds of a heel for not doing everything I possibly can for this great writer. I would certainly like to be a help, not a hindrance.

   Suggestions, please, and very warmest personal regards
   Sincerely yours
   Charles Laughton.

This cautious, canny, sensible letter reveals its author on several levels. The tendency to squirm which it represents is wholly characteristic, but it must also be said with regard to Bentley's translations (as opposed to his masterly exegetic writings), it is absolutely true. Laughton's was the first, and for some time, until Willett and

Manheim set to, the *only* version of a Brecht play which seemed like the work of a real writer, instead of a demonstration of certain theories. Laughton had laboured for two years to understand what Brecht meant, and to translate that into practice. Brecht himself was in no doubt about the value of their version. Interestingly, Laughton, in a postscript to the letter, says: 'I feel the actors as a whole failed the great man miserably in our production.' Does he include himself? He goes on to describe how he has formed a group of young American actors to train them 'in the business of verse speaking and prose speaking . . . I am doing this solely with the aim of getting a company together that can play Brecht's plays.'

The seriousness with which Laughton took the work is not in any doubt. It is *possible*, of course, that his 'narcissism' was so overwhelming that it surpassed even his devotion to the play, the other actors, and the ideal of the theatre. Brecht's account of his performance suggests something very different. He records innumerable delicacies, subtleties and inventions all designed to reveal the man and the play:

> Whenever Galileo was creative, L. displayed a mixture of aggressiveness and defenceless softness and vulnerability.
>
> L. demonstrated how for Galileo learning and teaching are one and the same thing.
>
> L. conducted the exchange with his friend at the telescope without any emphasis. The more casually he acted, the more clearly one could sense the historic night; the more soberly he spoke, the more solemn the moment appeared.
>
> Vis-à-vis the court scholars who refuse to look through the telescope, what L. acted was not so much anger as the attempt to dominate anger.
>
> L. was able, in a manner the playwright cannot describe, to give the impression that what mainly disarmed Galileo was the lack of logic.
>
> Words cannot do justice to the lightness and elegance with which L. conducted the little experiment with the pieces of ice in the copper basin.
>
> The way in which L. caressingly emptied his glass of milk while he said it was enchanting.

Perhaps what distressed Bentley was Laughton's evident pleasure in what he was doing. Brecht himself approvingly quoted Laughton's remark: 'before you can entertain other people, you must entertain yourself' and stated: 'Egocentricity is fun for me if it is expressed vividly.' 'What the spectator – anyway the experienced spectator – enjoys about art is the making of art, the active creative element' – another element of Laughton's performance. Brecht and Laughton were so at one in their approach that the actor even outstripped his author by suggesting, as Bentley reports, that the lights in the auditorium should always be up because 'in a "thinking theater" the actors need to see the audience's eyes.'

The only section of the play where Brecht expresses dissatisfaction with Laughton's performance is in the penultimate scene, already referred to in Bentley's criticism. 'L. could not accept the playwright's argument that there must be some *gest* simply showing how the opportunist damns himself by damning all who accept the rewards of opportunism.' Interestingly, this famous scene, whose failure Brecht attributed to Laughton, was equally unsatisfactory when Ernst Busch, an actor of a very different colour from Laughton, played the part with the Berliner Ensemble in 1957. What both actors gibbed at was Brecht's determination to condemn Galileo for his action – a sudden departure in the play which, as Bentley and other commentators have observed, seems to be as much Brecht's revenge on the character he created for having somehow developed a life of its own as anything thematic in the play. As with several of his characters – Mother Courage is another – Brecht attempted to pull the carpet out from underneath Galileo's feet; to put him in his place. Though Laughton embraced every other aspect of the theory, he drew the line at breaking the character completely. There must be continuity. As for Galileo's despair, *pace* Mr Bentley, it was a job *stopping* Laughton from entering into 'Dostoievskian depths'; he needed no encouragement. It would scarcely be emotional timidity that created his resistance, which is very clear on the gramophone record he cut to send as a sort of letter to Brecht before the New York opening. He and Losey and George Tabori had reworked the scene, using some of Brecht's notes, to make the transition easier, but the re-working simply muddies it further. Laughton tells Brecht on the disc that he's tried every other possible transition, but nothing except this one works; it is however, very clear that once he's cleared the hurdle of 'Welcome to my gutter, dear fellow scientist and brother in treason', he becomes convinced, and the performance is very fine.

The play transferred to New York in the winter, a small theatre again, again sold out. Laughton did readings to try to raise money for a further transfer, but the amount needed was too great for him to raise singlehanded. He refused the offer of a management who required that they cut the carnival scene (one in which, Brecht notes, 'Laughton had always taken a great interest,' though of course he wasn't in it) so the play closed after four weeks. Plans to take it to London also collapsed; discussions for a possible film, to be made in Italy, similarly came to nothing. So *Galileo* was over for Laughton. Brecht was by now in Switzerland, having given his famous testimony before HUAC, the House Un-American Activities Committee, in which he may be said to have run smoke-rings round his interrog-ators. He knew that the political climate made it impossible for him to stay any longer. On the day he left America, he noted in his work journal: 'Meet Laughton a.m., who is growing a Galileo beard, and is glad that he requires no courage to play the part of Galileo. As he says: no headlines on me.' As the subpoenas started flying, Laughton became very alarmed, and perhaps was glad to be rid of the dangerous play. As for Brecht, he had got what he wanted: a satisfactory American production of a play of his. He had stayed in America for two years more than he needed for just that. It was Laughton who had made it possible for him. He had been unstinting of time and money (his own tailor, to take one small example, had made Lodovico's costume), and had given a performance which deeply pleased him. There had passed between them, too, a time of great stimulation and nourishment, their '*zweijähriger Spass* [two years' fun].' Laughton's gain from it, in artistic self-respect and intellectual confidence, was enormous. There was a strong emotional thread to it, as well, something like hero-worship, a crush, almost. Whether one could go so far as to describe it as sexual in quality is doubtful, but both Brecht and Hans Viertel record Laughton reading stories from the Bible and certain scenes from Shakespeare of a decidedly homosexual flavour; Brecht notes that he read the parts of Osric, Jacques and the Clown in *Antony and Cleopatra*, 'whom he wants to play homosexual.' Laughton wanted to reveal his homosexuality to the man he admired so much. But Bentley, sharing with Ruth Berlau his disapproval of Laughton's boyfriend being cast in the rôle of Andrea, wondered why Brecht said nothing: 'Because,' said Berlau, 'this is a subject [homo-sexuality] that cannot be brought up with him.' And again, 'he was never accepted, *chez* Brecht, as what he was, a man trying to be honestly homosexual.' It may be that the various ladies of Brecht's seraglio wished to believe that their pasha was homophobic, but in his earlier years this does certainly not seem to have been the case, on the evidence of the diaries of 1920–22, and the early plays such as *Baal*.

Brecht wrote a very tender but by no means sexual poem for

Laughton, which in its affectionate and celebratory tribute to the body which caused him so much misery, must have moved him deeply. The poem speaks of great intimacy.

Laughton's belly

All of them, the way they carry their bellies around
You'd think it was swag with someone in pursuit of it
But the great man Laughton performed his like a poem
For his edification and nobody's discomfort.
Here it was: not unexpected, but not usual either
And built of foods which he
At his leisure had selected, for his entertainment.
And to a good plan, excellently carried out.

Brecht wrote one last poem for Laughton. It is short and harsh:

Epitaph for the actor C.L.

Speak of the weather
Be thankful he's dead
Who before he had spoken
Took back what he said.

Brecht had heard of the paragraph in Kurt Singer's book which read:

'The play opened in the autumn of 1947. At first it had seemed destined for success. The New York drama critics hailed Laughton's performance and admired the skill with which he adapted the original text, which was rather ponderous and wordy, into a fast-moving, stirring drama. However, the production soon ran into snags. Berthold Brecht was a dyed-in-the-wool communist . . . Laughton had gone into the project in complete innocence. He had more or less been kidnapped by the communists, who were very happy to have a person of Laughton's stature to lend prestige to one of their propaganda flyers . . . When the facts of the matter were put before Laughton by his manager, Charles saw that he was playing into the communists' hands. He had fallen into bad company. There was nothing for him to do but withdraw from the production of *Galileo*.'

How this piece of nonsense came to Brecht's attention is not clear: it may have been through Joe Losey – he bitterly denounced both the book and Laughton, whose authorised biography he supposed it to be. The Laughtons in turn denounced the book, claiming that they had never even met the author. Losey then accused Laughton of possibly betraying Brecht to HUAC, a grotesque thought. This is the background to the premature 'Epitaph'. Certainly Laughton and Brecht never communicated after *Galileo*. Perhaps Brecht was too strong, too overwhelming a figure for Laughton. In his task of liberating himself from the fat little boy he still felt himself to be, a father, or at any rate big-brother, figure was not what he wanted. The story ends a little squalidly: when Brecht died, Laughton received a cable from the East German Culture Ministry asking for his reaction. He contacted his lawyer, who contacted the FBI, saying CABLE RECEIVED FROM RED COUNTRY. The FBI indicated that there would be no repercussions if Laughton sent a telegram of condolence. So he did.

At the end of his recorded message to Brecht, Laughton (always calling him 'Brecht') says that he can't wait to start work with him on another play. He never did, of course, which is a great shame for him and for Brecht. He had even started translating the *Caucasian Chalk Circle*. But there was no Azdak. No Schweik. No Schlink. No Arturo. His students never did perform a Brecht play. He never read any story or poem by Brecht in his reading tours. He omitted Galileo from his list of rôles. Brecht seemed to vanish.

Teaching

The Girl from Manhattan is one of the more enigmatic films in Laughton's output, though not quite as enigmatic as its predecessor, made in between the Los Angeles and New York runs of *Galileo*. Entitled either *On Our Merry Way* or *A Miracle can Happen*, that film had four directors, three directors of photography, two art directors and a large and fairly prestigious cast, among whom the name of Charles Laughton does not appear, because his episode, for reasons shrouded in mystery, was cut. David O. Selznick, it was rumoured, offered to buy the deleted episode and destroy the rest, but the offer was not taken up. Laughton had become involved only on account of his growing friendship with Burgess Meredith, the film's producer. *One* of the film's producers. The other was, somehow inevitably, Benedict Bogeaus, who was also to be the producer of *The Girl from Manhattan*. The enigma of *this* film consists largely in its having been seen by no one. There is an awful silence about it, though a no doubt apocryphal anecdote from the filming would have brought a grim smile of satisfaction to Agate's lips: there is (apparently) a baby in the story, and this baby would not stop crying. Finally Laughton went over to the baby and murmured something into its ears. Immediately the baby fell asleep. On being asked what he had so effectively whispered, Laughton answered: 'The Gettysburg address. It has such a wonderful rhythm, you know.' For the rest: the film was directed by the veteran Alfred E. Green, who had just made *The Jolson Story*, and was soon to make *The Eddie Cantor Story*; it was written by Howard Estabrook, screenwriter on *A Bill of Divorcement*, *Cimarron* and *The Bridge of San Luis Rey;* and it starred Dorothy Lamour, who was also in *On Our Merry Way/ A Miracle can Happen*. Most writers on Laughton pass rapidly over *The Girl from Manhattan*, and it seems the only sensible thing to do.

Certainly it must have seemed very small beer after the intoxication of *Galileo*. Fortunately for Laughton, he was able to come down gently from that experience. A succession of *Girls from Manhattan*, or worse, no work at all (which once unimaginable eventuality was becoming increasingly feasible) would have destroyed everything that he had gained in the years with Brecht. Instead, he had met a young actor called Bill Cotrell, who had had some pre-war experience with the Oregon Shakespeare Association. In attempting to establish something similar in Hollywood, Cotrell had been deluged by 1500 applications, which he whittled down to twenty or so. At first the plan, devised by him and Kate Drain Lawson, Houseman's associate at Pelican Productions, appears to have been to involve various teachers, but at one of the sifting sessions, before the group's composition had quite been decided on, there was a clash of titans between the two heavyweight older actors present – Laughton and Thomas Gomez, a renowned movie villain. In avoirdupois, there was little to choose between them; but Laughton put on a brilliant display, reading a great chunk of *A Midsummer Night's Dream* – all the parts, of course – till Gomez, cursing, retreated into the street. From then on, it seems pretty much to have been Laughton's class.

This is the group referred to in the postscript of the letter to Eric Bentley. In full, it reads: 'I have started a Shakespearean group, training a bunch of American actors and actresses in the business of verse speaking and prose speaking. We have been working together some 8 or 9 months, three evenings a week for three hours, and I believe that in another year (it will take no more, but will also take no less) we shall be the best team of speakers in the English language. I am doing this solely with the aim of getting a company together that can play Brecht's plays. I want to see *Galileo really* performed, and *Circle of Chalk* and *Mother Courage*, and the rest of them. I am devoting all my spare energies to that end.'

Nobody in the group seems to have been aware that their ultimate goal was to become the Berliner Ensemble of California; but otherwise it was just as Laughton says. Very hard, methodical, regular and committed work; methodical, that is, in its thoroughness – there was no system. The group assembled three evenings a week, in the so-called schoolroom at Laughton's Pacific Palisades house – the very room where he and Brecht had wrought their version of *Galileo*. There, buried deep in his armchair, surveyed by a Vlaminck, a Utrillo and a tiny Douanier Rousseau, he talked to his students, in Elsa Lanchester's words, 'with feeling and passion about being able to relate one art to another, and it was there for them to see'. Billy Wilder suggested that the classes served 'to make them *think*, to live, to understand more – to *initiate* them.' And years later, Shelley Winters, briefly one of the class, telegraphed Laughton: YOU GAVE ME THE DISCIPLINE AND LOVE OF THE THEATRE THE RESPECT AND BELIEF IN MYSELF THE UNDERSTANDING OF THE POETRY THAT CONNECTS ALL MANKIND BUT FOR YOU MY FATE MIGHT HAVE BEEN THE SAME AS POOR MARILYN'S.

Clearly what was being imparted was as much inspirational and spiritual as technical or academic. Certainly there was no question of Laughton passing on skills or tricks. He of all actors was the last person to attempt that – not that he lacked either; simply that that was not his conception of acting. It was a vision of acting that he wanted to convey, not a formula. Lanchester says that he was an alchemist who wanted to pass on his secrets. That, no doubt, is true; but his powers of transmutation were not to be worked by mechanical means. They called for a state of mind. What Laughton was propagating, in short, was art, not craft. He was trying to awaken in his students an awareness of – well, yes, in Miss Winters' phrase – 'the poetry that connects all mankind'.

He did have, it must be admitted, an *idée fixe*, which was both technical and academic, and must have seemed odd to his students in the light of everything else he seemed to stand for. This was The Iambic Pentameter, which, since his outright rejection of it fifteen years before at the Vic, he had now elevated to a central place in his conception of Shakespearean acting. With ruthless rigidity he imposed it on his class. The metronome dominated the room.

Sometimes he even made them bounce a ball as they spoke: ti *tum*, ti *tum*, ti *tum*. It was as if, having been criticised in the past for failing to observe the rhythm, he had said: 'You want iambic pentameters? Right, I'll *give* you iambic pentameters!' Another sort of sulk.

In his teaching, as in his work, his best results had not been, and never would be, in Shakespeare; but his engagement with the problems and the challenges of verse drama was of inestimable value to his life as an artist. It is doubtful whether a day in Laughton's life went by without him speaking a line of Shakespearean verse, resounding it in his mind, turning it over, questioning it, trying to make it release its truth to him. It could even be that Shakespeare meant too much for him ever to perform the work successfully. Sensing the potential in every participle, unable to choose between the thousand alternative interpretations, trembling with delight at the sensuous beauty of each word, he was, like an over-ardent lover, doomed never to consummate his passion. His love was almost an end in itself.

Better, however, to love unproductively than not to love at all.

The form of the class was always the same: it started with an unstructured question and answer session, a general discussion, not necessarily related to acting; then they moved on to the session proper, in which they would work on various texts. Charles obviously strove to make the class as unpredictable as possible; he'd suddenly ask someone to read something, or he'd read something himself, now analysing the structure of a part, now looking for its *key*. He'd talk about types of actor: he divided them into, on the one hand, presentational (personality actors, stars, of whom Gary Cooper was the supreme example, who were more pure as actors because nobody else could do what they did; they were thus vertical) and, on the other hand, *re*presentational. These were horizontal; they were less pure because they encompassed aspects of other people; they were always intellectual, because they were obliged to analyse and break down their rôles. Or he put it another way: some actors put a coat on and it looked perfectly natural on them; others put on a coat and changed physically because of the coat.

Whatever the value of the teaching to his students (and at the very least, they came away from his classes with an exalted sense of the dignity and importance of the profession, and of its interconnectedness with the other arts), its value to him was enormous. As he taught, he learned: the experience of all teachers. But, listened to raptly by the eager young, he began to believe in himself; began to believe he was worth something. And watching the seeds he was sowing begin to flower satisfied both his creative and his paternal impulses. Elsa Lanchester notes that he boasted of his students' achievements like a proud father – 'mother' might perhaps be more appropriate – nurturing them, tending them, binding them to him with strong emotional ties.

Ernest Jones had predicted that teaching would calm his soul: and indeed, 'he became a happier, more contented man. He was less morose and actually seemed to enjoy his other activities more' (Lanchester). Producing had been an attempt at creating something outside of himself. It was not a good choice. Throughout the forties his creativity, so vastly engaged in his performances of the previous decade, went subterranean as he grew towards a new means of self-expression. Teaching was one of the few visible outlets for it; in some senses it was the prototype of his later activities, all of which were to some degree heuristic.

On the classes went, calmly and dedicatedly. From time to time, he had to go away to make some money; bit by bit, too, the more famous members of the group (Suzanne Cloutier, Robert Ryan, and, of course, Shelley Winters) drifted off to pursue their careers. But a solid nucleus stayed together, and – a sure mark of seriousness – even continued working while Laughton was away.

His first departure was to make another film for Robert Leonard, produced, this time, by Pandro S. Berman, who seems to have ensured a higher standard of production than Laughton was becoming accustomed to. The film is *The Bribe*, little known now, little liked then, but in fact a rather good film with a distinctly wow finish – a chase through a fiesta, against a backdrop of exploding fireworks. (It is unkindly suggested that this sequence was in fact directed by Vincente Minelli. It's worthy of him.) The tone of the film is interestingly impassioned beneath its fast pace and terse dialogue. Its failure with the 1949 critics was precisely in its refusal to send itself up. 'The Bribe is the sort of temptation which Hollywood put in the way of gullible moviegoers about twenty years ago – without one little wink at the audience or the slightest protrusion of tongue in cheek' – complained Bosley Crowther in the *New York Times*. Paradoxically, its seriousness makes it seem, at this remove, not dated, but surprisingly modern. The moral and emotional mess in which the characters work out their destinies is thoroughly familiar to us. The slight blankness (woodenness is the standard term) of Robert Taylor in the leading rôle only contributes to the sense of modernity. Ava Gardner, as the singer with whom he falls in love, entirely lacks the self-mockery of a Lauren Bacall, say. *The Bribe* is neither romantic nor hyper-dramatic: there is a veil of ambiguity over its events. This forms a perfect context for Laughton's J.J. Bealer, a performance of Graham Greene-ish complexity: a broken-down sot, pawn of circumstances, craven, weakly aggressive, ingratiating, threatening. R.R. Anger writes: 'It is Charles Laughton's great triumph that he tears this acknowledgement of J.J. Bealer's humanness from our unwilling selves, as we watch Bealer plot, betray and extort, driven by the basic and simple need to be relieved from pain.' Surely something like the opposite is true: it is the pitiless revelation of Bealer's moral bankruptcy which is borne in on us, made the more piercing by the human and ordinary weaknesses with which he is endowed – his bad feet, for example, or his hunger. The man Bealer is constantly begging for sympathy, pleading special circumstances; it is the actor's triumph to stop us from being deflected from the utter corruption they mask. 'Inside this moral cripple, Laughton is saying,' continues Mr Anger, 'is a man.' On the contrary, inside this man, Laughton is saying, is a moral cripple. This ruthless exposure is accomplished with strokes so deft, so accurate that a whole new possibility for Laughton's acting suddenly opens up; never, alas, to be pursued.

If the performance was perceived by contemporary filmmakers the way it was by the critic of the *New York Times*, it's scarcely surprising: 'Charles Laughton simpers and fidgets as the scummy "fixer" who has considerable trouble with sore feet.' That's it. Simpering and fidgeting are words that come up in Laughton notices with monotonous regularity. These things become critical reflexes: Laughton? Simper and fidget, of course! If that's what you're expecting, that's what you'll see. In his next film, *The Man on the Eiffel Tower*, his worst enemy couldn't accuse him of simpering or fidgeting. Unfortunately, he does nothing at all, as far as the eye can detect. His Maigret, which might have been rather interesting – his Poirot having been such a triumph – is soporific to the point of catatonia; a somnambulistic performance which does nothing to clarify or expedite a severely turgid plot. After a while, he totally abandons the accent which he half-heartedly essays at the beginning. It is only in the final chase sequence that he shows any life, and then he becomes very dynamic, but not, unfortunately, any more interesting. It is one of the few performances in his output which has almost nothing to recommend it.

The film, however, is of great significance in his career, because with it he made his directorial début. According to Charles Higham, he found it impossible to work with Irving Allan, the designated director (who was also the producer), so Franchot Tone, whose company was making the film, decided to attempt a bold experiment in co-operative film-making: the actors would take over. Burgess Meredith would take overall responsibility and direct all the scenes he wasn't in; Charles would direct all the scenes *he* wasn't in and Tone would do anything left over. This arrangement left Charles in charge of the beginning and the end of the film: as it happens, the only parts of it worth watching. The final chase is exciting enough, and uses the Parisian streets to very good effect (the credits, quite properly, end with 'and the City of Paris'); but the film's opening sequence has real flair and menace, as the camera slowly takes the scene in. The director of photography was Stanley Cortez, Welles' cameraman on *The Magnificent Ambersons*, and he must have offered advice to all three tyro directors. It is only here, though, at the beginning, that anything approaching an expressive frame is achieved. For the rest it's visually efficient, no more. 'Everybody left Paris to catch a ship, leaving me and Charles behind to do the finishing sequences. That's when I got to thinking Charles would make a good director,' wrote Cortez later. 'I saw Paris through his eyes, all of Paris; and he knew Paris better than most Frenchmen.'

Laughton had evidently lost all interest in acting while absorbed and challenged by the new medium. Certainly the actress he introduced into the picture, Belita, at that time topping the bill at Les Ambassadeurs as an ice-skater, had enormous time and thought lavished on her in her rôle as the lens-grinder's wife. He took her to Les Halles to pick exactly the right skirts for the layers and layers of clothes he decided she must wear – pointed out possible models for her character in the streets. He offered her all his enormous concentration and power of inspiration, leaving none over, it would appear, for his own performance.

Back in Los Angeles, he deemed his group of students was ready to work on a play for public presentation: or perhaps he deemed he was ready to direct a play. He was nearly fifty by the time he came to this point: his contemporaries in England, Gielgud and Olivier, had started directing without a moment's hesitation almost as soon as their names appeared above the lights. It was the tradition – the obligation, one might say. To lead a company, to put plays on, was synonymous with directing. They staged the most complex plays in a matter of weeks, with themselves in vast and difficult leading rôles; both Gielgud and Olivier, for example, had directed themselves in *King Lear*. Such a thought would have been inconceivable to the young Laughton: his self-consciousness would never have allowed him to organise or control other people; besides, his own performances were all-absorbing. For the older Laughton, the problem was that he saw so much in the play, was aware of such depths and resonances, all of which he wanted to capture, that the ordinary conditions available for staging it would simply be inadequate. In time, he would find that no longer true; for the present, teaching with the group offered an ideal halfway house. He knew them, he trusted them, they had plenty of time. Perhaps they could begin to do justice to some great play . . . and, providentially, at that moment, Eugénie Leontovich, who, after her great triumphs in *Grand Hotel* and *Twentieth Century*, had also established a teaching group with whom she had been performing plays at her own Stage Theatre (a converted hat-shop) approached Charles and suggested that they collaborate. She would contribute the theatre, he would direct, and *his* students (none of hers) would form the company. He and she would play the leading parts. And so, after due consideration, *The Cherry Orchard*, a play which Charles by now knew rather well, was settled on.

Rehearsals were spread out over three months. The pre-rehearsal symposium was maintained, now followed by work on the play. Charles' method was straightforward: everybody was expected to know their lines, he placed them and then worked line by line on the scene. He was a hard, hard taskmaster. He directed, on the whole, by demonstration, a daunting procedure if there were any expectation of imitation, but what Charles was aiming at was a physical shorthand, the most vivid way of suggesting the inner sensation of the character, the suggested route for the transformation. He never gave inflexions or line readings; what he was attempting to suggest was another way of being. His demonstrations were complete transformations: when he was working with actresses he would become more feminine than any of them, with actors he revealed unexpected athleticism. Belita, who had begged to be allowed to join the group, and finally did after a six-month apprenticeship of making coffee and doing the tidying up – at a time when she was the most famous ice-skater in the world! – was amazed by his physical freedom. 'He'd sort of stretch out and his whole body, which you know was quite large, would sort of get thin.' He wanted to bring Marcel Marceau to Hollywood to give the group lessons. He'd already laid on – at his own expense – voice classes with a celebrated voice coach of the day, Margaret Prentice MacLean. He was, as he said to Bentley, training the group. If he was an actor-manager, it was in a completely different sense to the familiar English one; it had more in common with the French tradition, of men like Copeau, Dullin, Jouvet: actor-philosophers, proponents of a new way. It is hard to say what that new way was, in Laughton's case. His theoretical musings have the air of being elaborate rationalisations of intuitive understanding. He used many techniques – an exercise called 'tell me a story,' for example, in which he'd stop rehearsal and have the actors tell stories, any kind of stories, to restore their sense of narrative – but what he stood for was simply deeper and deeper exploration into the characters and the rôles until the hard nugget of the real was struck. Laughton has so often been described (not least in these pages) as a realist, and so he is, but what he was after, both as actor and as director, was not in fact realism; *reality* was what he sought, the location and presentation of the real. Not verisimilitude (if that's the criterion, then he frequently fails), but something which has its own life and truth; which is its own reality.

He didn't probe or delve into the personalities of his actors, he simply goaded them on to deeper and deeper depths. In the rehearsals he created a strongly emotional feeling, which could easily dissolve into laughter or tears. In his notes he was often, says Richard Lupino, a young English member of the group, 'on a knife edge of cruelty' – but 'if you fitted in with his crusade of the moment, you were part of him. If he saw something he loved he would make it part of him.' He expected unflagging work till all hours of the morning, and you wouldn't be surprised if he called you up at four in the morning because he thought he'd discovered something new in the script; or wanted to show you a Japanese print he'd just bought.

There is an unavoidable sense of ego-massage in all this, which is not denied by his pupil/fellow-artists' love of him and of his approach. What matters is that it worked. 'Steadily the century turned and the globe and, in spite of all, the time and place became Chekhov's. The audience laughed, was hushed, and wept. Hearts were touched, minds fired, emotions disturbed. It all added up to as pure a piece of theatre experience as I have ever known,' wrote Ruth Gordon of his *Cherry Orchard*. Her husband, Garson Kanin, with all the reason in the world to find nothing pleasant to say about it, wrote: 'He had assembled a group of unemployed and unemployable players . . . and directed the whole company as though he and they were truly Russian. It is a play I go to see performed at every opportunity, but I have never seen its quality as fully realised as in Laughton's production, not even by the Moscow Art Theatre.' In addition to Leontovich, he had recruited the distinguished Italian actress-manager Maria Bazzi to play Charlotta Ivanovna, had persuaded Harry Horner, one of Hollywood's most famous art directors (*Our Town*, *The Little Foxes*), to design the play, and Karl Struss, the great lighting cameraman (*Sign of the Cross* and *The Island of Lost Souls* amongst many others) to light it. He had given minute attention to every aspect of the production. His own performance as Gayev – genial, melancholy – was held to be very fine, and the performances of the company, as Kanin implied, were better than they knew themselves capable of. It was an ideal cornerstone for an ensemble. 'The future is bright,' wrote Ruth Gordon in *Theatre Arts*, 'there will be tours and a repertory company. And perhaps, one day, a theatre of their own. And new actors, perhaps directors and playwrights as well. All because an urge to move forward was somehow crystallised, because an unselfish man took a courageous chance, because work and achievement came before gain, because the theatre is a living treasure, and because there are still the stage-struck.'

None of it was to be. The reasons are several, but they come together in the striking person of Paul Gregory, agent, hustler, manager, promoter, producer, who leaped into Laughton's life from nowhere, and played at different times the rôles of fairy godmother and demon king.

New life

The forties had been a period of germination, of slow exploration of new possibilities. Paul Gregory seemed to act as a catalyst on Laughton, turning possibilities into actualities. Within a couple of years of the new decade, Laughton, up till then apparently drifting aimlessly but generally downward, had become one of the best-known, best-loved, most formidably creative and respected figures on the American scene. This transformation of fortunes was largely wrought by Gregory, who shrewdly and with flair exploited some of the vast resources of his unique property. A junior agent at MCA, the giant artists' agency, he had seen Laughton read the Burning Fiery

Furnace episode from the Book of Daniel on television (the *Ed Sullivan Show*, in fact) and had suddenly conceived a brilliant and fully-fledged notion: Laughton should devise a whole evening of readings and tour the country with them, playing one-night stands in auditoria – they needn't even be theatres – all over the country. It would cost nothing whatever, and he could ask very substantial fees – perhaps 2,000 dollars a show. When he finally got to see Laughton, he proved very persuasive, and, in early 1950, they went out on the road for the first time. It was a huge success, beyond even Gregory's enthusiastic projections. Charles then returned to Hollywood, to work on *The Cherry Orchard*. It ran for nearly six months, and, true to the group's programme for the future, they started to rehearse another play, *Twelfth Night*, in which Charles was to play Toby Belch. They reached a fair state of readiness, too, when Gregory (who actually managed *Cherry Orchard*), pulled the plug on it. His reasons were mainly financial: Charles could be making a fortune on the road; at the Stage Theatre, he, like everyone else, was on an Equity 'Little Theatres' minimum salary of $10 a week. And Charles needed the money very badly. Gregory, moreover, felt, as he revealed some years later, in a somewhat hysterical interview for Barry Norman's profile of Laughton in the *Hollywood Greats* series, that the teaching 'was just an ego-trip for Laughton. He fancied himself with people following him around adoring him'. Several members of the group felt that Gregory was implacably hostile to it, with a hostility that went beyond mere financial self-interest. He was impatient to get on with handling Laughton. His creative energy was roused by the thought of what he could do with Laughton; he felt, in some way, that Laughton was *his*. Gregory has been described as demonic, even diabolic, and the young actors of the group felt that this startlingly handsome young blond was Charles' dark angel.

Norman Lloyd and others have suggested that Laughton was in love with Gregory, which is both possible and understandable; what is certain is that he was only too willing to be handled, to have someone lick his life into shape – provided, of course, that it was a shape he approved of. In the case of the readings, it most certainly was. He had found (Gregory had found *for* him) an ideal medium for his gifts.

At the heart of the enterprise was his passion for story-telling. In his introduction to the compendium, *Tell Me a Story*, that he published in 1957, he writes this touching account of that passion.

As I am not an inventor of stories – I have many times tried to write very simple stories, but they all looked and sounded terrible the next morning – I have become a teller of stories. I would like to become the man who knows all the stories . . . That can never be, because no man will ever know all the stories. When I go into a good book-store or library, I often feel sad when I see the shelves of books of all kinds that I know I will never be able to enjoy. I think of all the wonderful tales I will never know and I wish I could live to be a thousand years old.

For him, 'story-telling' (the term was a comprehensive one for him, embracing poems and psalms and plays alike) had always been the most direct means of communication. He had read to all and sundry over the years; he had been especially moved by the response of wounded GIs to whom he read regularly during the war. He was shy and self-conscious initially, uncertain of how they would react.

I read sentimental and innocuous things which I thought would please them. I read three times a week, but one day I tried something heavy and tragic, and there was an immediate response. They started to talk about their own problems – being in bombers over Germany, or in foxholes, or how they felt after they had been maimed. And so I found that serious literature was a great help to them because other people in centuries gone and in the present had had all the experiences there are to be had, and the GIs felt they were not alone.

When he extended his reading to large halls in front of a thousand people, or more, the sense of communication and the cancellation of loneliness, was just as powerful. 'We all do the same thing together – laugh or wonder or pity – and we all feel good and safe because the people around us are the same as we are.' This was something quite different from acting in plays, where the actors and the audience must perforce be separate. Here he was sharing something that meant a great deal to him. 'When I was reading from all the books I loved, I found the business of reading aloud was a matter of making the effort to communicate something you love to people you love.' During the war, the GIs had protested when he started to read to them from the Bible. 'They did not want to hear anything from a dull book. The Bible was not dull to me, but I had to prove to them that it was not dull. I used every trick that I had learned and they liked it and they asked for more.' How to tell the story in the clearest, funniest, most vivid way was the simple task that Laughton took to with such relish. It returned him to a sense, so vital for his self-respect, of the importance and dignity of his job. In a moving phrase, he writes: 'I found that people had – contrary to what I had been told in the entertainment industry – a common shy hunger for knowledge.' He took the task of trying to satisfy that hunger very seriously indeed.

To describe Laughton's performance as 'reading' is not, strictly speaking, accurate. For one thing, he had actually memorised all the material and used the book as a mere prop – as he freely admits during the course of the performance. But the readings anyway comprise only about half of the show; the rest is linking material – one-liners, anecdotes, introductions. The experience of listening to the records he made of the show is very pleasing, like spending time with, not a professor, but a lover of art and life. It's cunningly constructed for variety of tone and for fruitful juxtapositions. And behind everything is a sense of points being made; nothing is there without a reason. In the gentlest, least patronising way, it is a kind of lecture, or, rather, perhaps, an introduction to culture. Because it is done with such love and modesty, it communicates directly. Although Laughton flatters the audience to some extent, there is never any question but that there is someone real there, not a mere front-man. He obviously knows what he's talking about, and it obviously matters to him. It is above all generous.

It started with him shambling onto the platform in an overcoat from which, balefully eyeing the audience, he would remove books, one by one, making a pile out of them. Then the overcoat would come off to reveal him attired much as he would be in the street, i.e., shabbily. He'd chuckle: 'Here we are again – an actor and an audience . . .', and he'd be off, with the first reading, after which, 'I'll tell you a story,' he'd suddenly say, and it might be a four-line gag about a little boy he spoke to in Athens, Ohio, or it might be an anecdote about Henry Moore. He was at great pains throughout to humanise contemporary artists, to explain why they paint or sculpt the way they do. His range of readings, too, goes from the Bible to Shakespeare to Shaw to Jack Kerouac. 'The spirit goes on,' he says, after a reading from *The Dharma Bums*. The readings themselves vary in quality; he is prone, when faced with a lyrical or emotional text, to use what Brecht described as 'the well-known international clerical tone'. With a dramatic text, like the Burning Fiery Furnace story, the characterisation of each separate character, and the evocation of action, amounts to great virtuosity. He reads the whole of the oration scene from *Julius Caesar*, playing all the characters, not least the crowd, and makes a very vivid job of it. Now that authors no longer read their plays to the cast on the first day of rehearsals, it's a novel experience to hear a play read by one person – stage directions and all. It proves to be strangely satisfying – you 'get' it very strongly. This was an art form that Charles had perfected over the years. He reads a passage from Plato's *Phaedrus* dialogue, loosely and speakably translated by Christopher Isherwood. It is a section about the lover and the beloved that might be thought to be very close to Laughton's heart; interestingly, though, he chooses neither to characterise Socrates, nor to connect very strongly with it emotionally: he is concerned to pick his way carefully through the difficult material, striving for clarity rather than expression; and he succeeds. It's completely lucid. The most remarkable – and laudable – thing about it is that he chose to include it at all.

It is not an exaggeration to say that the heart of the show lies in his less formal linking comments and stories. One of them, about Chartres Cathedral, and his encounter with the curator, Étienne Houvet, is a little masterpiece, like something by de Maupassant: he went to Chartres when he was nineteen, and had the good fortune to be shown all of its wonders by the curator, a very old man. Twenty-five years later, he returned, and as he gazed round the building, a voice came out of the dark: 'Where have you been for 25 years?' But the exceptional feature of the story is his description of the cathedral: 'There are blues and greens in that window like you've never *seen!*' he cries. 'This building was built by the trade unions of the day, ordinary men and women, craftsmen, traders.' He uses his voice at its most thrilling in such passages, the rallentandos on crucial phrases, the shouts of joy as he describes something particularly beautiful. It's easy to believe that he may have been a very good teacher, not from his analysis, or from intellectual stimulation, but from his ability to open one's eyes to beauty, to the wonder of things. He renders aesthetic emotion highly attractive, and so he works his ends by example. The public got an absolutely true encounter with the impassioned aesthete that was Charles Laughton, with only the dark and the pain edited out.

'You looked so beautiful tonight,' said Paul Gregory to Charles after he'd given the show one evening. Laughton wept. 'You bastard, you bastard,' he kept saying, 'what did you tell me for?'

It exhausted him, but it exhilarated him. 'I believe this is something people want,' he told Elsa after the first tour. 'You look very tired and fifteen years younger,' she told him. He continued doing the show to the end of his life, visited every part of the country of which, since April 1950, he and Elsa had been citizens, became a national figure, made a great deal of money (soon he was earning $4,000 an engagement) and above all was a triumphant ambassador for beauty. It was all missionary work, a kind of one-man peripatetic university. 'Charles believed that in America people never stopped wanting to learn,' wrote Lanchester. 'That was one of the things that attracted Charles to America in the first place: the eternal student point of view.'

The energy which had for nearly a decade only fitfully found a channel was now fully engaged. He no longer looked to movies for artistic activity; now – by an exquisite irony – he looked to them to publicise his reading tours. It was in this spirit that he made *The Strange Door*, a half-hearted, half-baked adaptation of Robert Louis Stevenson's story, 'The Sire de Maletroit's Door.' Joseph Pevney directed it, Irving Glassberg wrote it and there is nothing that can be said in its favour. Boris Karloff, an old colleague, though never a friend, gives a grey, dull performance, whereas Laughton himself does exactly what he was so often (and so often unfairly) accused of: he messes sloppily around, pulling faces, slobbering, leering, chuckling, wheezing, a nightmarish display of an acting machine out of control. Even the obligatory eating scene is perfunctory, as he crams the grub mechanically down his gullet. He plays a wicked nobleman who's imprisoned his own brother for twenty years. The character (insofar as there is any character at all) emerges as a blend of Squire Trelawny from *Jamaica Inn* and Captain Kidd with none of Trelawny's incipient dementia or Kidd's rough amorality. Evidently it satisfied Laughton's purposes, however: it did decent business, it kept his name before the public until he reached them in person, no doubt very surprised that the coarse ham of the film was the same person as the eloquent, passionate votary of the muses that addressed them so ardently from the stage of their town hall or social club. As it happens, and perversely enough, the performance was in some quarters (*Time* magazine, for example) hailed as return to form. 'How good it is to see Mr Laughton enjoying himself again.' In fact there is no shred of enjoyment in the performance; it is ice for father's piles with a vengeance. *Monthly Film Bulletin* assessed the film more drily: 'A costume shocker which is by no means devoid of atmosphere. Charles Laughton appears to overact – perhaps to assure us of the Comte's insanity. The other players perform in the usual convention.'

It was again Paul Gregory who turned Charles in the direction of his next venture. Seeing the extraordinary impact of Charles, unaided by scenery or props, he asked why not two actors? Or more? Perhaps reading a play, or part of a play, or even something non-dramatic: Shaw's Prefaces, for example. Laughton suggested the third act of *Man and Superman*, known as *Don Juan in Hell*. And they knew they were onto something. It was Gregory who insisted that it would best be performed on a bare stage, in front of podia, in evening dress, instead of the cloaks favoured by Laughton, and that Charles Boyer should play Juan, which Laughton had fancied for himself; and in all these things Gregory was right.

Cedric Hardwicke was recruited to play the Statue, and finally Agnes Moorehead was cast as Doña Ana. Laughton wrote to Shaw for permission to perform the piece and received a reply of characteristic lucidity and pertinence from the nonagenarian writer, giving the performing history of the rarely performed Hell Scene, and entering a note of discouragement: 'It is such a queer business that I cannot honestly advise you to experiment with it . . . as you know it is customarily omitted, and was never meant to be played. I fear that audiences will think it nothing but a pack of words.' But the Drama Quartette, as they had named themselves, were not to be daunted, and how right they were. Starting gently, at Claremount, California, they gained momentum till by the time they reached Los Angeles they were an unstoppable force. 'One of the most exciting experiences of this and any other season,' said *Variety*. When they reached New York, the acclaim was unanimous. The box office was more remarkable even than that for the one-man show: they were playing vast auditoria, with capacities of three and four thousand. Gregory's every calculation had been impeccable: the stars were all in difficulties with their film careers, and all of them were hungry for serious work in the theatre – Boyer had just played in Sartre's *Les Mains Sales* in New York, while Hardwicke was bitterly cynical about Hollywood: 'I believe that God felt sorry for actors so He created Hollywood to give them a place in the sun and a swimming pool. The price they had to pay was to surrender their talent'. But they were still hugely popular in the provinces, which is where their main audience was to be found; there was a dearth of live theatre in those places; and there was something about being read to which seemed to feed a deep appetite in the audience. Perhaps Laughton was right when he said, à propos of his one-man show, 'there is something about reading aloud to a group of people that turns them into children.'

Even sophisticated judges, however, felt that the Drama Quartette was a breakthrough: 'Within an organism which continues to shrink and rot at such a rate as does America's commercial theatre,' wrote John Houseman in *Theatre Arts*, 'every evidence of fresh growth and renewed vitality invites not only congratulations but also careful examination.' J.B. Priestley thought they had invented something new, and proposed to write a piece for them. 'I got excited about it. I saw there was in it the basis of a new form. You couldn't call it drama – perhaps heightened debate or oratory.' It is hard, and no doubt wrong, to judge the performance from the gramophone recording they made later. The four actors, possessed each of very distinctive voices, speak the lines with great intelligence and flair. In Boyer's case, his characteristic French accent verges on the comic, but there is no other ground to find fault. Exciting, though, it certainly isn't, and it is impossible to discern the *virtuosity* so commonly attributed to the performance. It is undramatic in the extreme. Of course, that is in the nature of the piece, whose author doubted its dramatic, as opposed to literary, worth. It is an intellectual exchange, a tennis match of ideas. Whether the ideas themselves are really very searching is perhaps beside the point; or perhaps not. Sir Thomas Beecham said of the English that they didn't like music, they just liked the noise it made. It may be that the American audiences didn't like the ideas, they just liked the noise they made.

At the time, Eric Bentley wrote: 'Praising the Drama Quartette, people are saying how nice it is to do without scenery. I do not share their disdain for stage design, but I am not surprised at it. What surprises me is the assumption that, when a play is read to us, nothing is missing but the décor . . . It is a mistake to regard the Drama Quartette as a solution to our problems. We can settle for nothing less than acting, as it was, is, and ever shall be.' Charles Laughton would not have shared that view. He was finding a new way in the theatre. Certainly he was finding a new way for himself; coming quite soon after the first New York performances of his one-man show, *Don Juan* clinched his return to form. He was an actor re-born, for critics and public alike. The accolade of a *Time* magazine cover was awarded him. The profile within, entitled 'Every Night is Amateur Night', and subtitled 'The Happy Ham', was couched in somewhat ironic terms; but there was no hedging the phenomenality of what he was doing and how many people wanted to see him do it. He was now, irrevocably, the Word Man.

His directorial work on *Don Juan* did not pass unnoticed. Its calculated simplicity sounds cunning, and may have effected the mysterious transformation of non-dramatic material into something genuinely theatrical. Jed Harris, the awesome figure of the twenties and thirties, by now a more or less spent force, had this to say about it: 'By appearing to read, but actually knowing their parts by heart, they make the whole thing come alive. In a theatrical production, the power of illusion would be much more difficult.' Under pressure of the urgency of any particular speech, any one of them might suddenly leave the podium and stand in the centre of the space. There's an interesting tension in that, as if the actors were pushing against the formal constraints of the setting and staging. Laughton himself said of his staging: 'Every movement of the body, even the turning of the pages, becomes important. You mustn't move, except for a startling effect.' He himself introduced the evening: 'Playing the part of a modest, jovial, scholarly fellow in a well-cut but loosely worn tuxedo, he invites the audience to share with him and his associates the pleasures to be derived from a public reading of one of the lesser known masterpieces of contemporary literature. Disarmingly he warns that it will not be roses all the way: it will require concentration and effort on the listeners' part too. Eagerly,' continues Houseman, 'the audience accepts the challenge, and the show is on.'

It was on for a year, a triumphant progress from campus to stadium to concert hall in every town big enough to have one. 'Audiences throughout the US – in Oakland, New Orleans, Salt Lake City, Syracuse and Williamsport, PA. – have been eating it up. Businessmen and bobby-soxers, college students and clubwomen have jammed theatres and auditoriums and high-school gymnasiums to hear the Devil and Don Juan swapping epigrams,' according to *Time*. *Variety* drooled: 'STICKS OUTSHINE BROADWAY.'

Only once was the triumphant progress checked, and that was in England, where the Drama Quartette had been invited to participate in the Festival of Britain. Once there, it transpired that they were to be confined to the provinces; John Clements was putting on *Man and Superman*, and Laurence Olivier, as executive officer of the theatrical arm of the Festival, ensured that the rival group never played against him. 'I would no doubt have been on John Clements' side as he was a closer friend of mine than Charles, and Charles seemed to be coming home rather too late to make any claims upon the loyalties.' So the production limped around the provinces, unheralded and overpriced. Cedric Hardwicke: 'They had expected to see Hollywood stars glittering with wisecracks. They got the four of us . . . we played to half-empty theatres which normally resounded to the gurglings of rock-and-roll singers. I was glad for only one thing – that the author was spared this sorry spectacle.' It saddened and enraged Charles to feel that he was regarded as a foreigner; his espousal of American citizenship had been an act of love for that country, not a renunciation of England. It also crystallised a vague antipathy he had for Laurence Olivier. In an interview he gave to Kenneth Tynan at the time, he criticised Olivier's approach to Shakespeare: 'You've got to bring *today* into Shakespeare. That's what Olivier never does. He is the apotheosis of the 19th-century romantic actor.' Whether this is actually an insult is debatable, but Laughton certainly thought that Olivier would think it was, because he wrote him an apology, which Olivier gracefully brushed aside, writing: 'I was only distressed that you were bamboozled into giving the little fucker an interview.'

Laughton and Lanchester loathed it, but the little fucker's profile of Charles is characteristically elegant: 'A few weeks ago, Charles Laughton returned to England, a Prodigal son bearing a strong resemblance to the Fatted Calf . . . the man of fifty looks a mere boy of 40, a lordly urchin playing a hard game of marbles with his own talent. He is as ageless as Humpty Dumpty'. It contains a brilliant verbal cartoon of his physical impact: 'He walks top-heavily, like a salmon standing on its tail. Laughton invests his simplest exit with an air of furtive flamboyance; he left the hotel for all the world like an absconding banker.' 'Furtive flamboyance' is very fine. But the piece offers more than natty phrase-making. Tynan goes on to analyse Laughton's art:

> The secret of his freshness possibly lies in his boredom with anything that has gone before. As an actor he goes to fantastic lengths to avoid the obvious: called upon to express simple love or hatred, he will offer instead lechery or disgust. His style is circuitous, and rarely steps onto the direct highroad to an audience's heart. In this he is like the man in Chesterton's poem who would travel to John O'Groat's by way of Beachy Head. Laughton arrives at his characterisations panting, having picked up a hundred oddments on the way, and the result is always a fascinating and unique mosaic.

The critics who did come to see the show at Manchester or Birmingham were as enthused as their American colleagues, and in similar terms: 'It was an unforgettable spectacle. Through this Quartette, Shaw is himself again. The Drama Quartette has done something remarkable for the cause of theatre by their bold, pioneering spirit' said the *Evening Dispatch*. Manchester's *Evening Chronicle* found it 'sheer delight. The relish with which Charles Laughton licked the lines and turned and twisted was the Laughton the world loves.' Despite the box-office flop, and the show's non-appearance in London, Laughton himself was perceived to be renewed and revitalised. In Tynan's words: 'He looks the reverse of tired and disenchanted; Captain Hook has returned in the character of Peter Pan.'

And indeed, the English performances of *Juan* were a brief interlude – after Los Angeles, before New York – in the Drama Quartette's unstoppable progress, which lasted until the beginning of 1952, by which time Paul Gregory reckoned they had played every viable date in the land. It had restored Laughton as an actor to the serious theatregoing audience, and it had introduced him as a director. At the very first preview, Martini-maudlin, he had sobbed that he was responsible for destroying his cast's careers. In fact, he had revived them: theirs and his.

Abbot and Costello meet Captain Kidd is generally held to be the low-water mark of Laughton's career, a proof, if one were needed, of the terrible *dégringolade* this once-great actor had suffered. While it would be hard to argue that the film is a significant work of art, its context offers extenuating circumstances. The film was one of a series – others that Abbot and Costello had encountered included Frankenstein, Dr Jekyll and Mr Hyde, and The Mummy. They were the top-grossing comedians of the decade; were, indeed, regularly among the top-grossing stars, full stop. To be invited to make a film with them was a sort of humorous accolade, just as it was for English legitimate stars like Glenda Jackson and Keith Michell to be asked to appear on television with Morecambe and Wise in the late seventies. Moreover, Laughton, as we've seen, had a great passion for knockabout comedy, here given the freest possible rein. The result, within the limits of Bud and Lou's woefully laboured routines, is by no means displeasing. Laughton really does seem in this case to be having fun, entering into the spirit of things with a performance not so much slapstick as slapdash, but all the more charming for that. There's not a trace of the elaborate contrivance which often mars his comic playing; instead, he hurls himself into the action, recklessly proliferating double-takes, keeling over on the slightest provocation, doing comic walks and comic runs, spending quite a large part of the movie in his underpants, and ending up hanging from the mainbrace. It's all wonderfully game; he even joins in the opening chorus of 'Captain Kidd! Captain Kidd!' (The performance, incidentally, bears almost no resemblance to the 1945 film, nor even to Captain Bligh. It's more like the performance that everyone *thought* he'd given in those roles.)

Laughton usually enjoyed working with old comedy pros, and the director, Charles Lamont, was certainly *that*: veteran of all the Abbot and Costellos, the Ma and Pa Kettle series, and responsible for two films which subsequently – at least for readers of *Cahiers du Cinéma* – attained cult status, *Salome, When She Danced*, and *Frontier Gal*. He seems to have done nothing more than point the cameras at the actors and the drastically tacky sets and painted backcloths. Surprisingly, the cameraman is the great Stanley Cortez, with whom Laughton was shortly to have a remarkable professional association; on this one, he, too, presumably decided to have fun and take the money.

Immediately afterwards, Laughton slipped in a quick appearance in yet another compendium movie, *O. Henry's Full House*; this time, however, it was a proper film (a pretty dull one, too, in the non-Laughton sequences, despite direction by Jean Negulesco and Howard Hawks), in which he gives a more than proper performance: it's rather lovely, in fact. O. Henry was an author whose stories he often read on his reading tours, and this little tale, *The Cop and the Anthem*, is a wry fable that Laughton brings off with much delicacy, almost as if, in fact, he were reading it. He doesn't characterise it with any particular depth of feeling, but he tells the story wonderfully: with winter coming on, Soapy, a tramp, decides to get himself, as usual, arrested and imprisoned for the duration of the cold months. Try as he may, he can't, and in some depression repairs to a church, where he's so moved by the music he hears there that he decides to reform his life. Just as he makes the decision, he's arrested for vagrancy and sentenced to prison. It's deftly directed by Henry Koster, Charles' partner in schmaltz on *It Started with Eve*, and still with another fifteen years' film-making in him (*The Robe, The Story of Ruth, The Singing Nun*). This charming little film becomes immortal in a breathtaking moment when Charles' elaborately courteous Soapy approaches a girl in the street in the hope of being run in for propositioning, only to find out that she's a streetwalker by profession. The girl is Marilyn Monroe in her last rôle before stardom hit in a really big way. It's a brief but electric couple of minutes of celluloid. Marilyn had informed her friend Shelley Winters that Charles was 'the sexiest man she'd ever seen'; perhaps a suggestion of that informs their little exchange.

Laughton's other film for 1951, *The Blue Veil*, was almost a compendium film. It charts the journey of Jane Wyman, a bereaved mother who finds fulfilment in looking after other people's children, through the lives of her many infant charges. This results in a number of more or less self-contained episodes starring, among others, Joan Blondell, Don Taylor, Everett Sloane, and, in the first episode, Laughton. He plays a genial widower with a tiny baby, to whom Wyman takes an immediate shine, which leads Laughton, in a scene of some delicacy, to propose to her. Describing himself as 'the fourth largest corset house in the East' and – a first this – 'not the plainest man who ever lived', he invites her to share his life, but she, with the restrained calmness which characterises virtually everything she does in the film, gently refuses him. Instead he marries his secretary, who sees no further use for Wyman's services. She moves sadly off to the next child, and on to the next episode. The film is solidly put together by Curtis Bernhardt, with a literate and sober script by Laughton's friend, Norman Corwin. Perc Westmore did the make-up, but this was largely confined to supervising Miss Wyman's forty years' ageing, so his contact with his one-time foe was limited. Though receiving top billing after Wyman, Laughton's importance had much declined, almost in direct proportion to the decline of the importance of film in his own life. But the performance is charming, skilful and benevolent in a way not usually associated with Laughton. 'The most sympathetic role of his career' wrote *Picturegoer*, 'and he makes the most of it.' He does, but it is a slight use of a great talent.

Back to serious work: the theatre. Gregory was eager to push Charles' career as a director as hard and fast as it could go within the context of the new form that they had pioneered. They had discovered America's appetite for being read to; almost accidentally, they had also discovered the aesthetic as well as the economic gains of having little or no setting. Gregory's suggestion of Stephen Vincent Benét's *John Brown's Body* as the next project was as shrewd as his notion of getting Tyrone Power to lead the company. The Pulitzer Prize-winning verse epic of the Civil War is admirably suited to distribution among several voices; its celebration of America was guaranteed a welcome on the new Chatauqua circuit Gregory and Laughton had opened up; and Power was a loved star, almost a national hero, whose film career was, however, on the wane, and who desperately wanted to prove himself as a 'serious actor'; 'to pay his dues', as he put it, 'to the theatre,' into which, as the son of a famous stage actor, he had been born. Gregory's commercial calculation in the choice of stars was masterly: he knew his audience perfectly and, as Elsa Lanchester points out, by creating a groundswell of excitement around the country before attempting the metropolis, created the conditions for a triumphal entry; which is what, once again, happened. With Judith Anderson and Raymond Massey as Power's partners (Laughton confined his efforts to adapting and directing), the production was hailed as 'refreshing the whole conception of theatre.' After its sold-out tour of sixty cities, it played sixty-five sold-out performances at the New Century Theatre in New York, before going off to another eighty sold-out performances all over America, including places where, as Raymond Massey wrote, 'Lincoln had not yet been canonised and fiery crosses on the lawn were not unknown.'

Laughton had encountered Benét's poem before; he and Elsa and others had performed excerpts from it on the radio in the late thirties, and it is precisely the sort of work which appealed to him: a grand evocation in varied verse (and sometimes prose) forms, infectiously rhythmic, essentially straightforward in its poetic method, depending neither on complex metaphor nor on sophisticated verbal manoeuvres. It is, most of all, a story; a story about America which celebrates the land and the people, almost equally divided in its sympathies between North and South. Its peroration identifies the death of the Southern ideal as the necessary condition for the birth of industrial America, and there is in this a quality of lament.

Bury the purple dream
Of the America we have not been,
The tropic empire seeking the warm sea,
The last foray of aristocracy
Based not on dollars or initiative
Or any blood for what blood was worth
But on a certain code, a manner of birth,
A certain manner of knowing how to live,
The pastoral rebellion of the earth
Against machines, against the Age of Steam.

Sentiments with which Charles Laughton was perfectly in sympathy. His version, a skilful digest of the nearly four hundred pages of the original into a two-hours' traffic of the stage, preserves all the elements, the folksy, the lyric, the epic and the philosophical, in a shape which maintains the overall pulse of the poem. 'Charles knew the poem,' wrote Massey, 'with a depth I had not anticipated. He loved it with the appreciation of a scholar, with the patriotic fervour of newly-acquired citizenship and with the admiration of a theatre man for a great play.' A *play* is exactly what *John Brown's Body* isn't, and

Laughton made no attempt to make it into one. It is a narrative epic, an American *Odyssey* or *Aeneid*, to which it was compared by no less a Virgilian than Dudley Fitts; it demanded a form that reinvented the public utterance of the epic poet, the balladeer, the séanachai.

In creating *John Brown's Body* for the stage, Laughton's skills as an orchestrator match his editing skills. Sharing the piece between three contrasted voices, he makes them pass the narrative baton around, sometimes in the middle of a sequence; sometimes one or the other will take a single line for emphasis; sometimes, when Benét draws a character, Massey, say, or Anderson, will play that character, but then Power might take over. All this is cleverly varied, and keeps a constant narrative energy which can never tail off into introspection or emotional indulgence. The stroke of genius, however, was the decision to frame the three narrators with an *a capella* chorus of twenty men and women, creating immediate changes of scene, imitating the sounds of nature or of a battle, moaning like the wind, or stamping on the floor like an advancing army. The score – written by William Schumann – is an achievement of the greatest virtuosity, melodically inventive, but equally impressive in wordless, tuneless melismas. Then the chorus breaks up into its components and becomes a group of twenty individuals, sometimes chanting *en masse*, or interjecting a shouted line, or grimly reiterating 'John Brown's Body lies a-*mouldering* in the ground,' toneless, threatening. The culmination of their contribution comes at the work's end, when, as Benét's metre changes for his evocation of the New Age, they become machines, tracks, railway engines, with electrifying mechanical stabs and rumblings:

> Out of John Brown's strong sinews the tall skyscrapers grow,
> Out of his heart the chanting buildings rise,
> Rivet and girder, motor and dynamo,
> Pillar of smoke by day and fire by night
> The steel-faced cities reaching at the skies,
> The whole enormous rotating cage hung with hard jewels of
> electric light.

The effect of sudden transformation anticipates by twenty years the violent assault of 'Now' at the end of Stephen Sondheim's *Pacific Overtures*; same motor rhythms, same frenetic energy, same sense of something dreadful and wonderful in its unstoppable triumph. The very last words of the poem ram this home:

> While the prophets shudder and adore
> Before the flame, hoping it will give ear,
> If you at last must have a word to say,

Say neither, in their way,
'It is a deadly magic and accursed,'
Nor, 'It is blest,' but only 'It is here.'

The chorus seizes the last three words from the narrator and spits
them out like nails.

This *is* a new form of theatre, and it is fully-fledged. Cantata and
oratorio-like, in a way, it is also a sensuous and visual form. Though
the staging was of the utmost simplicity (a brown backdrop, a little red
balcony which the actors could sit on or stand behind), with a certain
limited movement by the chorus, the production had come on a long
way from the four after-dinner conversationalists of the *Don Juan*
evening. A whole world was on this stage. Laughton's confidence as a
director was now fully up – his first-night remarks to the cast are in a
quite different tone from his tearful lamentation on the first night of
Don Juan though the words are almost identical: 'Well, my dears, you
have done exactly what I asked of you. I think I have ruined my career
and yours!' 'He vanished,' says Massey, 'through the pass-door,
giggling.' He had, in fact, done nothing but good for any of them.
Tyrone Power, in particular, was for the first time perceived as an
exceptional actor; and indeed, in the recording which Columbia made
at the time, his work is far the finest of the three, skilful, felt, but
always specific, unmarred by the rhetorical windiness which Massey
can't quite throw off (too many patriarchs, no doubt; too many Abe
Lincolns and John Browns. He does not always avoid 'the well-known
international clerical tone.'). Judith Anderson, not yet officially a
Dame, but acting as if she were, is somewhat severe in her well-bred
tones, but her voice is a splendid instrument, and she can cut through
the choral textures like a trumpet. For reasons which are not clear, she
was replaced on the second tour by Anne Baxter; she had not been
well, it is true, but Elsa Lanchester hints that there was something
more untoward, and that – as usual – Laughton 'lacked the courage to
do the dirty work himself'.

Howsoever that may be, as a stage director, Massey said, 'Charles
was one of the finest I ever worked with. He lived and breathed
theatre; he was resourceful, sensitive and inventive. He was adapt-
able; he could be firm and also gentle, expressive and taciturn . . . he
made me do just about the most difficult acting job I ever faced.' What
is clear is that this poem of Benét's touched Laughton deeply; like so
much American literature its subject is America's destiny: what is this
country, and who are we? The ontological anxiety at the heart of the
American experience was something to which Laughton was no

stranger. Laughton, like America, took solace in sturdy affirmations drawn from the soil and from the Bible; like America's, his affirmations seem more willed than achieved. The glory of his version of *John Brown's Body* is that it fully reflects his, its, and America's ambivalence.

During the long period of preparation for the Benét, Laughton had lent his weight (that seems to be the correct phrase) to a madly misconceived version of *Salome*, Harry Cohn's idea of a suitable vehicle for Rita Hayworth; which it might well have been, had Cohn not insisted that the star be a) virginal, and b) Christian. The result of these exigencies is that Miss Hayworth here dances to secure, not John the Baptist's death, but his reprieve. Laughton is, of course, Herod. His attempts at ogling are somewhat undercut by the range of kilts, blankets and all-purpose upholstery with which the wardrobe department endeavours to cover his bulk. His performance is largely sedentary, but there is a twinkle in his eye, whether lascivious or merely mocking it is hard to divine; most probably the latter if Stewart Granger, who plays a converted tribune, is to be believed. He reports that Laughton was openly contemptuous of the proceedings, from time to time announcing that he proposed to leave the set and read from the Bible. Filming stopped, and everyone listened. This attitude understandably enraged Granger, who was trying his best to make a wretched script work. He accused Laughton of scene-stealing. 'He didn't like leading men and did everything to screw me up. Much as I admired his acting, I was in no mood to put up with his tricks and told him if he didn't stop them I would kick him in the balls. He stopped.' Laughton simply didn't care any more. When acting was the centre of his life, his salvation and the source of his self-respect, he would have laboured unceasingly to create something significant. He would have re-written the script, conferred with the director, coached his fellow actors. 'He rehearsed with his partners, hoping to improve his scenes,' wrote the director, Dieterle, 'but 'a fencing master cannot fence with amateurs,' was his private remark to me.' Time was when 'amateur' had not been a dirty word to Laughton, but he was a different man now. Now he was in charge of his talent, not at its mercy; its master, not its slave.

Whatever his attitude to the film, however, his performance remains value for money; if anything, it's insolent in its ease, and, as Dieterle observes, his use of the dialogue, such as it is, is impressive. 'I knew few actors who could handle dialogue like Laughton, and none of them was in the cast of *Salome*.' In fact, a couple of actors who could handle dialogue very well indeed were in the cast of *Salome*; Alan Badel, as John the Baptist, charismatic as ever, but lacking weight, and Cedric Hardwicke, giving the sort of performance that Laughton never sank to: mere mechanical efficiency, a shell of a performance, just a profile and a voice. Good, bad, gross or glorious, there was never an absence of inner life with Laughton; *something* was always going on inside him. If he sold himself for money, it was always in order to do something rewarding: teach, direct, or maybe just buy a painting.

His self-confidence was complete, too. He had no fear of never being employed again. He had reached that position of eminence, half-way between being an actor and being a legend, that ensured that he'd never want for work. If it was interesting work, so much the better, if not, *tant pis*; his real creative life was – elsewhere. Thus when Harry Cohn tried to push Laughton as Herod towards a more conventionally tyrannical performance ('being,' as Dieterle pointed out, 'himself a little tyrant who bullied his people in the filthiest tongue') Laughton replied, 'Tell that son of a bitch up there that he must stick to his business and leave the acting to me. Or else.'

The truth is that the Laughton of *Salome* was to all intents and purposes a different Laughton to the Laughton of fifteen years before, when Dieterle had last worked with him, on *The Hunchback of Notre Dame*. Technically, everything was the same; even, perhaps, enhanced. Years of the reading tour had strengthened his voice, and taught him a great deal about phrasing and communication. He knew, in fact, a great deal about acting. But the *need* – that had gone. Not the need to perform; that was a strong and continuing imperative. What had gone was the need to reveal himself – to own up. The need to transform was gone, too. He was at last someone in whom he could believe, someone he could almost like. How deep that self-reconciliation went is hard to say, but at least now when he wanted to escape from himself, he did so by assuming the well-known, well-respected form of 'Charles Laughton', public person, rather than descending into the amorphous sludge of his inner darkness, hoping perhaps to catch a monster or two, and take the pressure off. His 'alliance with the void' (Cocteau's phrase) was off; now he was for the light.

Young Bess belongs to this period, too: a Coronation special, it again starred Stewart Granger, poor chap, and Jean Simmons. Charles betrays no resentment at going over the old ground, and gives a good, straightforward performance as Young Bess's father, Henry VIII, very restrained in the death scene, full of fire and bluster elsewhere.

What is inevitably missing is the sense of discovery and liberation of the earlier performance. This is simply the good work of a very good actor in a dull film, directed competently enough by George Sidney, master of musicals and costume romps. Perhaps the impending Royal Event took some of the *oomph* out of his attack; perhaps the producing presence of Sidney Franklin (erstwhile director of *The Barretts of Wimpole Street*) dampened things down a bit. The script could certainly have been no inspiration to anyone, though for buffs it is amusing to note that it was co-written by Arthur Wimperis, one of Biró's collaborators on *The Private Life of Henry VIII*.

If *Young Bess* took Laughton back twenty years, his next project – immediately after the opening of *John Brown's Body* – took him back yet another ten, to the very beginnings of his acting life. David Lean was to direct *Hobson's Choice* for Alexander Korda, and there was an enthusiastic exchange of cables across the Atlantic between director and actor. Korda hadn't seen or spoken to Laughton since the *I, Claudius* fiasco, though they had an exchange of letters. 'My dear Charles,' wrote Korda, sharply, 'Nothing could please me more than having a letter from you after so many years. I have never stopped having affectionate memories of you and I was really profoundly touched to know that you were thinking of me again. Let's hope that you will not need another letter from somebody else to remind you of a friendship which I shall never forget.' He then wearily refused Charles' request to do something for a young man of his acquaintance: 'Alas, it is very difficult, if not impossible, to do something for all these young people who, dissatisfied with their lot, want to start working in the film industry'. During shooting, he kept his distance from Laughton. Lean, however, was enchanted with his star. A famously unsentimental man, known for his impatience with actors ('I don't really like actors much – I mean, I like having *dinner* with them, but working is another matter', he told Richard Attenborough), he nevertheless had the greatest regard for Laughton, having been at the old Gaumont studios while Charles was shooting *Wolves*, his first film. The pains to which Laughton then went for verisimilitude (it was a fight scene) impressed Lean deeply, as did his ability to fill the frame. He regarded – and regards – Laughton as what a star should be, and is particularly fond of his performance in *Hobson's Choice*, one of his favourite among his own films. It is hard to share this feeling.

While there is no gainsaying the skill of the film-making in a technical sense, it almost completely fails to create the feeling of the original play, whose freshness and reality are overlaid by a heavy coating of stylisation and self-consciousness. In a brilliant study of Lean's films, Michael Anderegg observes that Lean's 'mannered, detailed style turns the film into what might be described as a gothic comedy or baroque farce . . . he borrows stylistically from German Expressionism, employing its elements to lend a patina of the psychological to what started life as a slight portrait of English provincial life. A highly uneven film results, at once comic and grotesque, sombre and light-hearted, psychologically compelling and yet filled with stock characters playing out stock situations.' In fact, Brighouse's play is rather more than a 'slight portrait of provincial life': it's a trenchant account of women's position in a male world, the overthrow of tyranny and the emergence of a human spirit from its chrysalis. It's also very funny and very moving; in fact, everything a play written for Miss Horniman should be. Its impact, however, both comic and emotional, depends on belief in its characters and situations. Here, this belief is denied, killed by excessive love. Lean's camera (and above all, alas, his wonderful composer, Malcolm Arnold) so relish every moment that the audience can never connect with the play for themselves. Look! Lean seems to cry, here comes Mr Hobson. *Isn't* he a funny old chap! Ho ho! Whoops a daisy! He's nearly fallen over now! At which Arnold obliges us with woozy trumpets and farting tubas. It is the film of a man totally lacking a sense of humour. Laughton's performance only compounds matters. Here again is his repertory of comic biz, but now self-conscious whereas in *Abbot and Costello* he had been abandoned. Here he most distinctly is *not* having fun. More serious, however, than the terrible slow-motion poutings and blinkings and shakings of his head in disbelief is the fact that we can't see who he's supposed to be. On no level does he convince as Hobson – neither as a father, as a tyrant, as a shoemaker, even as an alcoholic; nor does he offer any other reality. He never, therefore, seems any kind of match for Maggie, nor does this plight, unlike Willie Mossop's, matter at all. In fact, the situations of the film seem to fall away as we watch two actors who know what they're doing confront another who is severely (and very prominently) floundering. The part didn't need Laughton; it would have been much better for everyone if it had been played by some strong, straightforward character actor. If, however, Laughton had decided really to inhabit the rôle, to penetrate to the heart of his relationships with his daughter and with the bottle, he might have transformed the part and the film. But he didn't. An earlier Laughton would have; but now it just wasn't worth the fag. So he did 'comic business', which delighted the director, who, as Anderegg points out, far from trying to contain or curb him, 'clearly showcases and abets Laughton's interpretation'. Both the opening sequence, where Hobson's entrance is built up to almost spooky tension, and the famous sequence (a technical achievement of the greatest virtuosity) where Hobson chases the moon from puddle to puddle, only render the character less conceivable in any human terms; he becomes a figure of almost poetic menace. The same applies to his alcoholic hallucinations – actual monster mice, who take us into a world of expression as far away from the author's Manchester School realism as one can go.

But at least Lean's stylisation is fully achieved; Laughton appears – this is rare enough in his work to require comment – at no point in the proceedings to have decided what he wants to do. It is perhaps an instance of the man on the way from John O'Groats to Land's End actually getting *lost* at Beachy Head. He had, it is sometimes suggested, a notion that Hobson, with his three troublesome daughters, was a Lear-like figure. It seems far-fetched, but one should never dismiss any of Laughton's insights. The problem is that the idea never manifests itself. The explanations for this failure are no doubt very prosaic. He was extremely unhappy during the making of the film: Korda put him up in a hotel that he loathed because it was near the studio; his old friend Robert Donat who was to have played Willie Mossop had dropped out because of ill health; he loathed Brenda de Banzie, all the more, no doubt, because he must have realised that she was giving a wonderful performance ('Ideal', says Mr Anderegg); he was fighting with Paul Gregory nightly by telephone; and he had boyfriend trouble. Finally, though, the explanation is even simpler: he didn't want to do it. It didn't interest him. He didn't want to immerse himself in that man and that world. He loathed having to play so many drunk scenes ('seen enough of 'em in Scarborough as a lad,' he used to say) and – it was difficult. He was now interested in practising his craft, of which he was a master. He didn't want struggle – not with acting, at any rate. He looked to that now as a source of relaxation and money. And so the performance in *Hobson's Choice* has the appearance of a famous pianist being asked against his will to play a piece at a party: grudging and half-hearted. With a personality of his size and expressiveness, this might seem intentional, might seem to be part of the performance. But it wasn't; it was Laughton, not Hobson.

At the end of an unenthusiastic account of *John Brown's Body* (on grounds of poetic worthlessness and over-complication of staging)

Eric Bentley made a remarkable analysis of Laughton's current state:

> It matters nothing that Mr Laughton's work cannot be defined as good drama or good theatre – provided it be good something. My real complaint is that it is, for this artist, not good enough, and my hunch is that it is an evasion. An evasion of theatre. Mr Laughton walks round and round theatre like a dog that cannot make up its mind to sit down. He tries the movies. He reads aloud in hospitals. He recites the Bible to schools. Or on TV. He invents the Drama Quartette. He trains a Drama Trio. Meanwhile, he falls in love with literature and therefore with Thomas Wolfe. It is all an evasion.

Evasion is certainly the word for his performance in *Hobson's Choice*. As for the rest, he hardly had time to think. He was riding a switchback called Paul Gregory.

Laughton returned to America to discover that Gregory had, for once, overreached himself. His generally reliable instincts had led him to Herman Wouk's best-selling novel, *The Caine Mutiny*, and in order to persuade Wouk to sell him the rights, he signed up Henry Fonda to play the prosecuting counsel, Greenwald; before, that is, he *had* the rights. This proved persuasive, and Gregory then somehow got RKO, who were at that moment setting up the film that Edward Dymytryk directed and in which Humphrey Bogart played Captain Queeg, to allow him to put the play on before the film was released. The setting up of packages was Gregory's special gift and this was one of his best. On the strength of it he booked and sold out 67 out-of-town dates. Despite the large cast, it was another minimally-set, easily-tourable piece of the kind he and Laughton had done so well with. The only difference this time was that there was no Laughton. Gregory offered it to various directors, including Harold Clurman (whether he cried 'I am Clurman!' by way of refusal is not recorded). Finally, he took a gamble on a respected actor who was just starting to direct movies: Dick Powell. The gamble failed, as was immediately evident to everyone in the cast, though, not, as is so often the case, to Powell himself.

The script had been fairly directly drawn, by Wouk himself, from the chapter in the novel which describes the court martial. It read at four hours, and had no dramatic shape. Powell had experience neither of the theatre nor of editing scripts. He seemed not to see that there was a problem, concentrating on tiny details. When he got them right, he'd say 'Print it,' as if it were a movie. Charles Nolte, playing Lieutenant Keith, said that he seemed to be under the impression that if there were any problems, they could all be sorted out on the cutting-room floor. The cast's anxiety was not at all relieved when they saw the unmistakable bulk of Charles Laughton appearing at the back of the rehearsal room. He was Gregory's partner, after all. This could mean the closure of the show before it had even opened. Instead, of course, Laughton took over, the same day Powell was summarily dismissed. 'Dick, I have some bad news for you.' 'Is Fonda going to leave?' 'No,' said Gregory, 'you are.'

Laughton's priority was to get the script right. Over one weekend he hacked an hour out of it. His instinct, according to all reports, was infallible; but his manner was brutal. He shook the play and the cast by the collar, without regard for feelings.

Charles Nolte, keeping a diary of the production, gives a vivid account of what it was like to be directed by Laughton.

He looked out between his puffy skin, and I could only see little slit eyes, cold pale blue, between the folds of flesh, 'You have a terrible vocal habit, absolutely terrible. MUST get rid of it at once. You're UNLISTENABLE, absolutely intolerable. I can't hear a word you're saying when you open your mouth. Utterly impossible, do I make myself clear?' All too clear. I sat rather stunned, while across the table Jack Challee drummed softly with his pencil. Nobody else spoke a word, and I didn't open my mouth. When we read the scene again, he launched into me once more. The others retired discreetly to the TV screen and the World Series, but I felt sure they could hear. 'This upward inflection, where did you get it? Didn't anyone ever tell you about this before? It's something which must be corrected at once. Now I won't harp on this because it'll probably make you feel self-conscious, but you MUST work on it.' We were alone. The blood had drained from my face. 'Say something! Tell me what you did today'. I haltingly started to talk. We got on the subject of sailboats, why I'll never know. He mimicked my voice-pattern, rising inflection on certain words. 'You hear that? It's false. It means I'm not sincere, I'm not telling the truth. It's bad.' And an audience simply WILL NOT listen to it! Rid of it, get rid of it.' He hunched over: 'You must have more than a beautiful body and face to be in the theatre, unless you're content to be a whore. There's more to it than that! You understand me, you understand what I'm trying to say?'

Three cast members walked out; bitter resentment and distrust were engendered in some, not least Fonda, who felt that his friend Lloyd Nolan, playing Queeg, was, as a result of the cuts, being handed a starring part, while he was having one taken away. To placate him, Laughton concentrated greatly on the last scene, a sort of coda to the trial in which Greenwald, having won the case for his client, throws a glass of wine in his face as a mark of contempt for the liberalism and anti-authoritarianism he feels he represents. Fonda both demanded and resented the inclusion of this scene, and indeed nursed a deep sense of grievance against Laughton throughout. This finally broke at a rehearsal on tour when, Laughton having made an observation on some military detail, Fonda said: 'What do you know about men, you fat, ugly, faggot.' Laughton never spoke to him again, even when, in *Advise and Consent* (1961) they acted together.

The play fulfilled its triumphant tour, and when it arrived in town, in June 1954, Laughton received his traditional encomium. Under the heading, 'Austerity the keynote,' George Jean Nathan wrote: 'Integrity and restraint mark Charles Laughton's direction throughout. A man of long experience with 'readings', Laughton has great respect for the author's text. He never overdoes, never sacrifices an honest but straight remark for a cheap laugh, never distracts from the lines by directorial embellishments.' His work on the text had obviously been remarkable. He and Wouk had worked together for hours and days on end until they had a play instead of a script. The published text is dedicated to Charles. In *Tell Me a Story*, Laughton writes about a moment in their work together:

I was feeling uneasy about the play. It was not bolted together. Certain short passages in the play needed expanding to serve as arrows, pointing to the climax. One morning I tried to tell Herman what I was thinking and I failed to communicate with him. It is almost impossible to be articulate about the form of a work of art. You have only to listen to the drivel people talk in front of paintings in a museum to know this. When I am not articulate I sound long-hair-pretentious and impractical. Herman got edgy. I got edgy. And neither of us liked this.

'Let's go and look at pictures,' I said. I have often found the harmony of good painting will restore my balance and I hoped it would have that effect on Herman too. We went to the Boston Art Museum, which has a great oriental collection. We were standing in front of a Japanese screen. The screen is in black and white and the main pattern is composed of monkeys with long arms in the branches of trees. The monkeys are painted in tones of grey. Across the screen from left to right, small birds are flying in a descending arc. The birds are painted in deep black and, so to speak, seal the pattern of the picture.

I said, 'The birds are missing.' I looked at Herman. He was blushing.

'Damn you, Charles, damn you,' he said and he burst out laughing. The screen had said what I had been unable to say.

The following day we had a script with the necessary emphases beautifully written. They contained some of the best thoughts in the play. Then the play held together.

His comment to Wouk is so like so many things he said about his own performances: had it not resulted in remarkable results, it would have seemed like purest bullshit; because it did, it merits attention. He was obviously trying to by-pass the literal brain, both as an editor-director and as an actor; trying to winkle out the organic life. Evidently, with *Caine* he succeeded (it was equally successful when Franklin Schaffner staged the production for television). But in a sense, Fonda was right. It and its world were nothing to Charles. He had functioned as a play doctor, performing his drastic surgery with skill and relish; and, of course, there is a peculiar exhilaration about putting right someone else's mistakes. But his service to the play and its author led him, for structural reasons and in order to keep his star happy, to put his name to a play whose climax appears to be a denunciation of values which Charles espoused, and an exaltation of values he utterly rejected: militarism, command, hierarchy. Eric Bentley was not the only critic to find this last scene regrettable; he put his objections more wittily than most:

> Inasmuch as *The Caine Court Martial* says that a wicked captain deserves a vote of thanks, it might well have been entitled *Captain Bligh's Revenge*. Luckily, Mr Laughton and Mr Wouk are artists, and, as such, have not been able to resist the temptation to make their wicked captain as offensive in the modern (i.e., the neurotic) way as Captain Bligh was in the old satanic-melodramatic way. The result is, they create a character and unfold a tale, which no amount of conservatism, new or old, can spoil.

He had the good grace not, in print at any rate, to wonder what Brecht would have made of it all, though there is a – slightly shaky – case to be made for the apparent confusion of values requiring the audience to try to resolve it for themselves; but, as Bentley says,

> If you don't take the play seriously, none of this matters: the first part is a thriller, the last scene gives you a moral to take home to the kids. That the two sections are not organically related need disturb no one who is unalterably determined to have his cake and eat it.'

Gregory's plans for Laughton had, it seems, only begun. 'I wanted to

bring Charlie into focus as a top director and have him quit performing; the performances were what were killing him; he needed to find
something where he could direct one or two things a year and make all
the money he needed. That was the goal I had for Charles. With me
producing and him directing, and when he didn't direct, we'd be co-
producers.' It was always Gregory who found the projects; he knew
his Laughton, and they generally proved irresistible to him. *The Night
of the Hunter*, a novel by Davis Grubb, had been on the best-seller lists
early in '54, and Gregory snapped it up, seeing the whole project, as
usual, in one. They would make a film of it, Charles would direct, and
the leading character, the murderous Preacher, would be played by
Robert Mitchum. The book was, in fact, right up Laughton's street,
rather self-consciously cadenced prose, evoking a Southern world of
oppressive communities, simple emotions, hymns, picnics, decency
and destruction. He later made a recording of excerpts from the book
in which, backed by the film's soundtrack, he makes a very persuasive
case for its virtues, though it has not, according to those who know,
'worn well'. It certainly tells its tale powerfully and hauntingly;
'American Gothic,' as Carrie Rickey calls it, in which the deadpan,
hypnotic voice of the story-teller is always present. So Laughton was
definitely on; and the moment he offered it to Mitchum, so was he.
The extraordinary combination of these two men was a success from
the start: 'this character I want you to play is a diabolical shit,' said
Laughton. 'Present,' replied Mitchum. He was their banker: United
Artists put up the relatively meagre sum involved ($700,000) on the
strength of his name. Laughton then cast Shelley Winters, his
sometime pupil and recent Oscar nominee (for *A Place in the Sun*), to
play opposite Mitchum, to Mitchum's considerable disgust; but his
trust in Laughton seems to have been absolute.

Laughton had a strong hunch that the appropriate visual world for
Night of the Hunter was D. W. Griffith's, and accordingly re-ran all his
movies. Quite apart from the power of the films themselves, he was
overwhelmed by the work of Lilian Gish who, in her unassailable
virginity, delicate but indestructible, touched some deep place in
him. Charles Higham perceptively describes her as Kabuki-like, and
there is something of the onnegata about her; but Laughton's
response to her was more than merely aesthetic – one of the indelible
memories of his life was having seen her in *Broken Blossoms* in France,
just after the Armistice had been declared. He said he had fallen in
love with her then. Her grace, her girlishness, her lack of sexual threat
may have combined to form an image of the eternal feminine, an

anima, almost, some idealised version of his own feminine self, perhaps. Anyway, he cast her, and when, in her infinitely courteous way, she asked him why he wanted her in the film, his reply would have pleased Brecht: 'When I first went to the movies they sat in their seats straight and leaned forward. Now they slump down, with their heads back or eat candy and popcorn. I want them to sit up straight again.' Their meeting was only slightly marred by the presence of the film's screenwriter, James Agee, in a state of charmless inebriation; but he soon left them. He remained with the film a little longer, just long enough, according to Paul Gregory, for Charles 'to have a vision and some inspiration to write his own script . . . out of the terrible disagreements with Agee'. On the face of it, the author of *Let Us Now Praise Famous Men* was the ideal man to adapt Davis Grubb's novel. His skills as a screenwriter were not to be sniffed at, either, on the strength of *The African Queen*; but everyone in Hollywood except, apparently, Laughton and Paul Gregory, knew that he was drinking himself, in short order, into the grave. The script he handed to Laughton after a summer working by the pool at the house on Curson Avenue was 350-pages long, and, according to his biographer, not an adaptation at all: 'he had re-created a cinematic version of it in extraordinary detail. He specified use of newsreel footage to document the story's setting and added any number of elaborate, impractical montages.' Shooting was only weeks away, so Laughton took on the screenwriting himself. Thus manœuvred into a position of sole creative responsibility, he proved himself a master. The script is good enough to have been passed off for years (in *Five Film Scripts* by James Agee) as the work of a seasoned genius. As a first screenplay it's a triumph both of structure and sustained tone. To put it mildly, he knew what he was doing.

Stanley Cortez was his chosen cinematographer. Famous for his dandyish ways ('the Baron,' he was nicknamed) and his advanced technical experiments, he was happy to share his knowledge with Laughton. 'I used to go to Charles' house every Sunday for six weeks before we started and explain my camera equipment to him, piece by piece. I wanted to show him through the camera what these lenses would and would not do. But soon the instructor became the student. Not in terms of knowing about the camera but in terms of what he had to say, his ideas for the camera.' They understood each other very well. Cortez was something of a poet; something of a wild man, too: 'To hell with all this caution! To hell with this "academic" approach!' he exclaims in *Sources of Light*. 'There are times when nature is dull:

change it.' Like Laughton, he got his inspiration from outside his own discipline. 'I often will revert to music as a key for a photogenic effect.' They spurred each other on. 'Apart from *Ambersons*, the most exciting experience I have had in the cinema was with Charles Laughton on *Night of the Hunter* . . . every day I consider something new about light, that incredible thing that can't be described. Of the directors I've worked with, only two have understood it: Orson Welles and Charles Laughton.'

Laughton was fortunate, too, in his choice of second-unit directors, Terry and Denis Sanders, whose documentary film *A Time out of War* eventually won an Oscar. 'Brother Sanders!' he greeted the twenty-year-old Terry, fresh out of UCLA; 'Brother Laughton!' the young man cried back. He sat them down and drew precise, if spindly, line drawings of every shot he wanted – the relation of everything to everything else in the frame, and that is what they shot, on location in Ohio: the ravishing overhead shots of the children as they drift down the river. All the rest – the haunting nature scenes on the riverbank, owls, frogs, rabbits and all, were shot in the Studio; the tank on Stage Fifteen in the case of the riverbank. 'When I tell people that, they turn white,' writes Cortez. His technical inventions on the film are numberless, and give rise to scenes the like of which barely exist in the American cinema. The results, however, are invariably simple and poetic in feeling; nowhere a trace of conscious virtuosity. The legendary sequence in which Shelley Winters drowns in her car was achieved with extreme ingenuity and much hardware; the effect is simple, lyrical, and haunting.

Laughton's collaborative instincts worked at every level. Terry Sanders recalls his simplicity on the set, consulting, appreciating. 'He spoke very quietly, but you sure listened. He made you feel you were important, and *this* was important.' Lilian Gish wrote: 'I have to go back as far as D. W. Griffith to find a set so infused with purpose and harmony . . . there was not ever a moment's doubt as to what we were doing or how we were doing it. To please Charles Laughton was our aim. We believed in and respected him. Totally.' Elsa Lanchester wrote that 'The filming of *Hunter* was a compassionate time for Charles, and he found that he was able to bring out his compassion in his performers.' Certainly the film is exceptionally well acted. Shelley Winters, despite Mitchum's disfavour ('Shelley got what she deserved, lying there dead at the bottom of the river'), shows, underneath her sweet demeanour, a welling erotic current of a piece with the constant eruptions of sex, real, irrepressible sex that bubble up into the story. Her playing of the scenes themselves may sometimes be questionable, but the intensely expressive sensuousness is a great contribution to the film. As for Mitchum, he has frequently maintained that it's his best performance, and that Laughton was his best director. Laughton's belief in him, his conviction that 'Bob is one of the best actors in the world' is unlikely to have made much difference to this man whose inability to accept praise is notorious; what probably did the trick was Laughton's discovery in him of a private self different from the public one. 'All this tough talk is a blind, you know,' he told *Esquire* magazine. 'He's a literate, gracious, kind man, with wonderful manners, and he speaks beautifully – when he wants to. He's a very tender man and a very great gentleman. You know, he's really terribly shy.' They had recognised in each other a man at war with himself. When Mitchum, incensed by Paul Gregory, had urinated in the radiator of Gregory's car, Laughton phoned him: 'My boy, there are skeletons in all our closets. And most of us try to cover up these skeletons . . . my dear Bob . . . you drag forth the skeletons, you swing them in the air, in fact you brandish your skeletons. Now, Bob, you must stop brandishing your skeletons!' But Laughton brandished his own favourite skeleton to Mitchum. 'I don't know if you know, and I don't know if you care, and I don't care if you know, but there is a strong streak of homosexuality in me,' he told Mitchum as they bowled along the freeway. 'No shit!' cried Mitchum. 'Stop the car!' Who knows what Mitchum's skeletons are – that is to say, what the original skeletons are; there are plenty of acquired ones which have been all too well publicised. The interesting thing is that Laughton, normally ill at ease with uniformly masculine men was very comfortable with Mitchum, and that Mitchum's performance in *Night of the Hunter* is to a striking degree delicate, seductive, soft-eyed. Even in the scenes of greatest menace, there remains a sinuousness most unlike the monolithically machistic performances which form the bulk of his work. The laconic, smiling, almost humorous quality he brings to Preacher in no wise distracts from the menace; it only enhances it.

Interestingly, Lilian Gish was anxious during filming that Laughton might have undercut Preacher's evil, and told him so. Laughton's reply, 'For Mitchum to play this all evil might be bad for his future . . . I'm not going to ruin that young man's career,' though humorously meant (and an echo of what he'd said on two previous stage shows), indicates a certain protective, fatherly feeling, confirmed by Elsa Lanchester's remark: 'Charles was patient with him because Mitchum was going to be one of his children.'

Miss Gish herself brings to her rôle everything Laughton wanted: her scrubbed, sturdy radiance and power of nurture are the perfect polarity to Mitchum's greasiness. She is the spirit of absolution and healing in the film, and discharges her function as no one else could have done, with a kind of secular sanctity which cannot be forged. As for the children, they too are perfect; which is something of a mystery, because Laughton kept as far away from them as possible. His special loathing was reserved for the little girl, Sally Bruce, but he didn't have much time either for Billy Chapin as John after Mitchum had given Billy a note: 'Do you think John's frightened of the Preacher?' 'Nope' said Billy Chapin. 'Then you don't know the Preacher and you don't know John.' 'Oh really?' said Billy. 'That's probably why I just won the New York Critics' Circle prize.' 'Get that child away from me,' roared Laughton. Thereafter, Mitchum directed the boy – with the most remarkable results. Odd paradox, that Laughton should have failed to create any rapport with the children, when it was his vision that the entire film should be a child's nightmare.

Consciously framing the film with Lilian Gish surrounded by children, apparently among the stars, suspended, as she rehearses the comforting and warning words of the Bible, Laughton then shows the novel's story if not precisely from the children's point of view, certainly in the children's terms. It is, in a way, a fairy story ('really a nightmarish sort of Mother Goose tale,' said Laughton): the children's father dies, his place in their mother's bed is usurped by an interloper who threatens them, their mother disappears, they run away from home, all the time hanging on to their real daddy's secret. Finally they are found and rescued by a new mother, a kindly, sufficient mother, the bad daddy is removed, and they live happily ever after, stronger and wiser. That is the backbone of the story; Laughton chooses to tell it in a way which is neither realistic nor arch, but with intense, simplified poetry, which corresponds to the children's state of emotional intensity. It would be more accurate to say *child's* state, because it is John who sees and hears everything: it is John's wide-open eyes which see the wonderful creatures that sit along the riverbank at night; it is John who wearily sees Preacher on the horizon, just as he thinks he's thrown him off. The adults all behave in typical ways, gossiping or getting drunk, or, as in the lynching scene, baying for blood. The escape from the mob of Gish and the children is a scene which was particularly dear to Laughton: the image of Lilian Gish shepherding her cares had some very

Left: Laughton as Captain Hook, 1936 (from *The Sketch*, 30.12.36.)
Below: A hand-made collage by Bertolt Brecht serving as the front cover of a collection of poems he gave to Charles for Christmas 1945 or 1946.

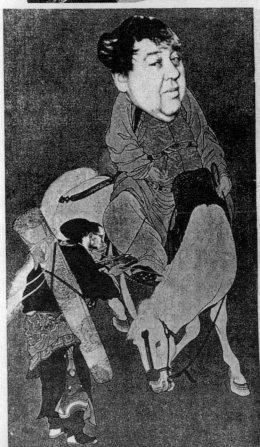

詩人としてブレクトと言ふ私はフワトン上様に
何を自己の危い思潮を甲上げます.

playwright brecht humbly submits some of his subversive thoughts to the great Amerald Laughton

Don Juan in Hell, 1951.
Laughton and Agnes Moorehead.

Left: Laughton briefly encounters Marilyn Monroe in *O. Henry's Full House*, 1952. *Below*: Laughton and, right, Henry Daniell in *Witness for the Prosecution*, 1957.

Members of the
Stratford company,
1959:
(l. to r.)
Laughton,
Leslie Caron,
Peter Hall,
Angela Baddeley,
Paul Robeson,
Mary Ure,
Edith Evans,
Glen Byam Shaw
(on stairs),
Harry Andrews,
Laurence Olivier.

Laughton
as Lear
and Bottom,
1959.

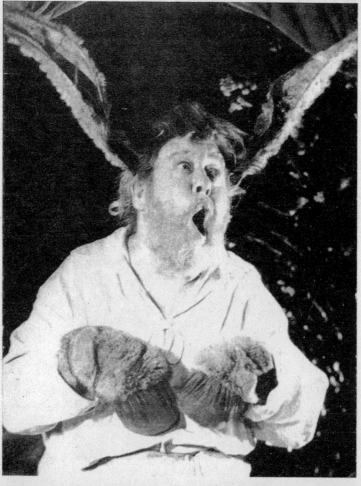

Laughton and Albert Finney
in *The Party*, 1958.

The late films.
The Paradine Case, 1948.
The Bribe, 1949.

Night of the Hunter
(Laughton directing
Lillian Gish), 1952.
Advise and Consent, 1962.

personal meaning for Charles – something to do with mothers, with nurturing and belonging; to attempt to relate it to his bruised psyche would take us into areas we are not competent to explore; sufficient to note the intensely personal feeling which informs the handling of everything to do with Lilian Gish in the film.

Mitchum, the Bad Father, is similarly endowed with mythic overtones, at once attractive and repulsive, the words *love* and *hate* spelt out on his face, just as they are on his knuckles. 'Leaning! Leaning! Leaning on the everlasting arm,' he sings, and, heard in the distance, now closer, now further, it becomes oppressively menacing, all the more so for its neutrality. When the children give him the slip, he becomes momentarily absurd, like a cartoon character, as he stumbles up the stairs, stunned by a collapsing shelf. It's a Tom-and-Jerry interlude, a child's revenge on an adult. Later, at the end of the film, when Preacher has been caught and is about to be lynched, John can't endure the real pain and the real death that Preacher is about to undergo; he throws the precious doll stuffed with ten dollar bills that he's been keeping from him on the ground, sobbing, 'Take it, take it.' And he refuses to testify against him in court. It is in the dreaming child's terms that he has his reward at the picture's end: a watch, which gives him magic protection: 'I ain't afraid no more! I got a watch that ticks! I got a watch that shines in the dark!' And then we're back up in the stars again, Gish exuding love without condition, strength without threat.

These sections, the opening and closing shots, are perhaps the least successful; they are what the film never is elsewhere: sentimental. The stars are partly the cause of that, but the main culprit is the music, elevated and replete with angelic voices of children. It serves a valuable function, in taking the film out of the realistic groove from the very beginning, but the effect is syrupy, not sublime. Otherwise, the score is of the utmost value in creating the overall atmosphere, frequently functioning as a counterpoint to the action, as in the *valse triste* suggested by Cortez for the scene in which Preacher murders Willa (Shelley Winters). The nature music, Honegger-like with its burbling flutes and murmuring strings, is exquisite, and the organisation of the hymns, children's catches, and songs creates a large part of the film's texture. Walter Schumann, who composed the music, had performed a similar service for *John Brown's Body*; his death shortly after the completion of *Night of the Hunter* was a serious loss for music in the movies.

The visual aspect of the film is of course paramount, as it could hardly fail to be, the outcome of a collaboration between two supremely visually-oriented artists. Laughton contributed everything he knew by way of pictorial composition; Cortez ensured the intensification of every image. There isn't an undistinguished frame in the picture; as in Welles' work, every picture tells a story. The famous A-frame of the roof in Willa's death room, the image of Preacher hanging upside down in his bunk in the jailhouse, the strange light which plays on Preacher's face while he tries to ingratiate himself with John, the boat carrying the children gently downstream; this is visual poetry of the most sensuous kind. The abiding impression of the film is its physicality. Sex and nature loom through the film at all points; nature a kind of all-permeating presence, now in the background, now in the foreground, but always palpable, always *there*. Sex, from the first glimpse of Preacher in a strip-club, his eyes clouded with homicidal rage, as the flick-knife in his pocket tears phallically through the cloth, to the intimations of Willa Harper's nubile longings, the dry and brutal talk of Icey ('I've been married to my Walt for forty years and I swear in all that time I'd just lie there thinking about my canning') and the all-bursting, uncontainable sexuality of Ruby, one of Lilian Gish's wards, face painted, lips pouting, irresistibly drawn towards the Preacher. All this sex is somehow threatening, perverted, or disgusting; except, that is, to Gish. Ruby can confess to her: 'I've been bad'. 'You was looking for *love*, child, the only foolish way you knowed how,' Gish tells Ruby, 'we all need love.' In the market she sees two spooning lovers, and says, with affectionate dismay, '*She'll* be losin' her mind to a tricky mouth and a full moon, and like as not, I'll be saddled with the *consequences*.' Love without conditions; strength without threat. As John makes his way through the adult world of murder, rape, theft, poverty and irrepressible, confusing sex, he finds, in the end, a haven which does not deny the existence of all these things, but is a fortress from which to contend with them. Until this resolution, his attitude to the world, a mixture of wonderment and alienation, seems not unlike his creator's.

It is interesting to compare Laughton's astonishing first film with those made by his near-contemporary, fellow actor-director, Laurence Olivier. The hostility between them, which had a few more eruptions yet in it, was as much a matter of principle as of personality. Olivier's films, especially the Shakespearean trilogy, are brilliant achievements, exciting, dramatic, witty. They are in no way personal, however, and have an extrovert energy which is exhilarating but theatrical. They borrow shamelessly from other films (the famous arrow-shooting sequence from *Aleksandr Nevsky*, for example). Laughton didn't *borrow* from Griffith; in some mysterious neo-Platonic sense, their souls united to create something unique. Laughton's film is filled in every frame by his preoccupations, by his poetry. Olivier's film is brilliantly done, Laughton's intensely imagined.

Reviewing the film on its first appearance in France, François Truffaut wrote: 'it makes us fall in love again with an experimental cinema that truly experiments, and a cinema of discovery that, in fact, discovers.' Another way of putting this is that the creative moment remains present in the finished result, what Brecht had called 'the active creative element, the making of art'. That is what had frequently distinguished Laughton's performances in the past; it is supremely true of this film. 'Every day,' wrote Cortez, 'the marvellous team that made that picture would meet and discuss the next day's work. It was designed from day to day in fullest detail, so that the details seemed fresh, fresher than if we had done the whole thing in advance.'

Laughton, had found, it would seem, his métier. Everything in his experience contributed to it: his love and knowledge of art, his gifts in shaping a script, his ability with actors, his deep immersion in all the process of movie-making. The man who loved words but could not write, the man who loved art but could not paint, the man who had authority but preferred to work with collaborators, had found his brush, his pen, his team. He had been brought to it, but once connected with the process, all he needed was encouragement and enthusiasm, and he would surely wreak wonders.

Alas, it was a flop. Critically it did moderately well – misunderstood, treated as a thriller which wasn't quite thrilling enough, or a parable of which the moral was none too clear – but commercially it was a disaster. As far as the box office is concerned, Paul Gregory was inclined to attribute its failure to United Artists' favouring of the *next* Mitchum movie, *Not as a Stranger* (which in fact he had started filming even before *Night of the Hunter* was completed), a much bigger production altogether, five million dollars against *Night of the Hunter*'s seven hundred and fifty thousand for a thirty six day shoot. It is easy to see, however, that *Night of the Hunter* would never be a popular hit. Not only is the subject-matter complex, the movie itself has a poetic and imagistic density which make it somewhat indigestible on first viewing. It benefits enormously from being seen twice, or more – something that can be expected of no popular audience; in fact, it would be correct to say it *needs* to be seen twice. It doesn't grab you by the lapel; it tries to suck you in. Both Billy Wilder and Truffaut drew attention to the inadvisability of starting one's career as a director with such a film: 'The film runs counter to the rules of commercialism; it will probably be Laughton's single experience as a director,' wrote the Frenchman. Another man, however, might have risen above the disappointment; Laughton was neither of the age nor the temperament to do so. It broke his heart. He was, in the words of more than one witness, destroyed by it. After the triumph of *The Caine Mutiny*, it was humiliating to fail in this way; he had put all of himself into it, and it was not wanted. From now on there would be no more great projects. Gregory (ever avid for best-sellers) bought the rights to Norman Mailer's war novel, *The Naked and the Dead*, for him; Laughton went through all the motions, but his heart was clearly not in it. His skill and his application were unimpaired. Mailer wrote eloquently of what he'd learned from him: 'He gave me, in fact, a marvellous brief education in the problems of a movie director, as he would explain to me, sometimes patiently, sometimes at the edge of his monumental impatience, how certain scenes which worked in the book just weren't feasible for the movie.' But the subject was not one to which Laughton warmed. He worked with Stanley Cortez on ideas for the photography, even sent him to Hawaii, to scout locations; and he hired the Sanders brothers to work with him on the script. Their work, Terry Sanders said, was 'leisurely': starting at 10.30 a.m., they would read a bit of the novel, follow a couple of tangents, he would read them a bit of Dickens, perhaps, or Thomas Wolfe, then it would be time for lunch which Heidl the cook would prepare for them, an enormous, many-coursed banquet, after which more readings, and then it was 5 p.m. and time for Martinis, and then the day was over. 'After a while it dawned on me that Charles didn't *want* to finish the script. I felt that we were just sitting around as an audience.' It was 'a great experience', and 'an education', but after six months the sense of aimlessness became unbearable to the brothers: they had their own films to make. One has the impression that as far as Laughton was concerned, it could have gone on for ever. After the brothers resigned from the project, Gregory had backer trouble: how long would it be before there was anything to show for the now nearly half a million dollars which had been spent? Charles produced a script, thought by Gregory to be 'brilliant, absolutely brilliant'. Mailer approved of it, too; but it was clearly far, far too long. It would take, he said, another year before a shooting script was ready. The backer then handed the draft to his chum, George Sidney, late of *Young Bess*, and *that* towering figure's opinion was that it was no good, and would cost $20 million to shoot. And that was that. (Gregory later sold the property, with a new script by the Brothers Sanders, to Warner Brothers, and Raoul Walsh shot it, and it was worse than no good.)

Gregory claims that the backer's withdrawal was a relief; the feeling is that it was a relief for Charles too. Is there an element of Wellesianism here? A Promethean anxiety, the dread of completion? Probably. But also it seemed that with Charles, the more he understood a thing, the more difficult it got. Mailer wrote of Laughton's work on the script: 'I don't think I ever met an actor before or since whose mind was so powerful and fine as Laughton's. No aspect of the novel passed by him unnoticed . . . he wanted me to explain every single last point he did not clearly comprehend for himself.' It is admirable to be so thorough, but there comes a point where perfectionism is procrastination's other name.

It is interesting, though not necessarily related, that it was at this moment that Charles suddenly and irrevocably broke with Paul Gregory. The pretext was apparently a personal one: Gregory had boasted to Charles' then boyfriend that he could get anything out of Charles: if he wanted a car, he could even get that. Laughton went, with cold rage, to his attorney and dissolved the partnership there and then. He never spoke to Gregory again.

The imputation that Charles was Gregory's poodle, that like Uriah Heep he could manipulate him into any shape he liked, must have been very vexing, of course; but theirs was a stormy and openly recriminatory relationship. Charles' pride was considerable, and this may have proved the final unacceptable affront to it. He knew that he was Gregory's main asset, and perhaps wanted to remind him of who needed whom. This too would be fully understandable. What was also true was that Gregory had been the organising energy behind Laughton's professional life for five unceasingly active years: project after project he'd initiated, prodding him, goading him, bribing him with promises of large financial rewards. At the same time, he'd been the voice of his conscience, challenging him to greater heights, reminding him of his great gifts and reproaching him for squandering them. Gregory behaved exactly, in fact, as if those gifts were his own. And it is true, he was responsible for all the artistic successes of Laughton's *anni mirabiles*, the early fifties. Without him, they would never have happened. He had, as he often boasted, rescued Laughton from a backwater. But what if Laughton didn't want to be rescued?

He'd been happy teaching – that 'ego-trip', as Gregory called it. The reading tours were a great inspiration, of course, and lucrative; but Laughton had come to hate them. He carried on with them, nevertheless, for the rest of his life: they were after all, a form of teaching. But the constant draining labour of creation, the pressure to produce results! Paul was the spur: remove the spur, and he could get on with what he most loved: contemplation, paintings, reading out loud, teaching. Many of these activities could be pursued in the presence of handsome young men who would also – sometimes for a small consideration, sometimes not – have no objection to being made love to. The rest was too exhausting.

And so, Paul Gregory went.

Almost Legitimate Again

Life went on, of course: there was life after Gregory. First, he was asked by David Lean to play the character that Alec Guinness eventually played in *Bridge on the River Kwai*. Lean denies this, on the not unreasonable grounds that it would have been absurd for that part to cast an actor of Charles' bulk; besides, he always wanted Guinness for the part. Elsa Lanchester, however, recalls much agonising over the decision on Laughton's part, from which we can conclude at least that he *thought* he had been offered the role. His reasons for turning it down, she says, were to do with the extreme discomfort involved: what would once have been the most persuasive reason for accepting.

Instead he succumbed to considerable pressure from a New York producer who wanted him to direct *Major Barbara* and play Undershaft. He turned it down at first, liking neither the play nor the part; but on reflection agreed, and did what people so often do in those circumstances: he tried to turn it into a play he did like. It was not the argument of the play that he disagreed with; it was the form. His experiments with poetic intensification and with narrated drama made him impatient with Shaw's extremely straightforward dramaturgy. Firstly, he did what is rarely done with Shaw, not so much on grounds of lèse-majesté as of respect for craftsmanship: he re-wrote the play. In collaboration with Herman Wouk (Herman Wouk! Shaw's shade must have been overcome with gratitude at posthumous collaboration with such a master of the drama) Laughton cut a scene here, merged another there, conflated the second and third acts, and ended the play on Barbara's cry of 'Glory Hallelujah!' The intention seems to have been to deprive the play of its undercutting irony, which was felt by the co-adaptors to be anti-climactic. It is, if you're thinking in terms of images, and messages. But Shaw was very careful to embed the dialectical reverses of his plays deep in their structure. Laughton's next decision was to stage the play in a non-realistic manner, to heighten its expressive impact; to intensify the images. Here again, he was on dangerous ground, because Shaw made himself a master of the theatre of his day in order to stand it on its head. If you abandon the conventions in which he wrote, you no longer receive its inversion.

Laughton's production was obviously a very striking account of a different play. The set, by Donald Oenslager, one of the outstanding American design minds of his day, consisted, of, to quote Brooks Atkinson, 'a series of cubes that can be arranged in the shape of a living-room by liveried stage-hands'. Part of the reason for this was economy: the bulk of the budget had gone on an impressive effect for when Undershaft and company descend to the foundry. But whatever the intention, whatever the reason, it can surely have had only one outcome: the destruction of the illusion of solidity that is essential to Shaw's purposes. The effect on the play's rhythms, so finely calculated by the author ('it's music, it's music!' as he so often said) must have been disastrous, too. As for the acting, Laughton had cast it somewhat quirkily – Cornelia Otis Skinner as Lady Brit, Glynis Johns as Barbara, Burgess Meredith as Dolly Cusins – and then imposed on the actors a deliberateness of utterance (for reasons of intellectual clarity) of which he was the supreme exemplar, centre stage. 'Most of the actors behave like well-bred ladies and gentlemen who have studied the craft of educating the public with serious homilies,' wrote Brooks Atkinson in the *New York Times*. Only Eli Wallach and Richard Lupino – from Laughton's original acting class – were exempted. Laughton himself was said to be 'imposing in a style of thoughtful deliberation' – the very thing to be avoided like the plague in Shaw. There was, say the reports, no discernible character in Laughton's playing; he was simply an articulate presence – a much appreciated articulate presence, given an ovation and sometimes a standing ovation every night. But, said Atkinson, 'This is not Shaw. It is not Laughton. It is a stand-off which nobody wins.'

Relations with some of the cast were unsatisfactory: Burgess

Meredith walked out at one point; Glynis Johns was replaced by Anne Jackson a short while into the run. Richard Lupino remembers a baffled Sally Gracie, playing Rummie Mitchems, telling him that Laughton had told her to find the 'key' to her character. This she could neither do nor understand. A few days later, however, she'd cheered up: he'd given her the key. 'And what is it?' 'He says she's an old cunt.' A distinctly un-Shavian insight.

Why did Laughton decide to do the play? Money? Yes, up to a point. He would have been handsomely remunerated, as both actor and director, but, then as now, he could have made a great deal more on even the trashiest movie. Pressure from the producer? This is not to be underestimated in his case: his fundamental passivity was such that enough determination from whatever quarter and he would submit. Pleasure in performing? Least powerful motive. Performing within the confines of a play seemed cramped after the freedom of the reading tours. (Alec McCowen, on Broadway in *The Matchmaker* at the same time, recalls attending a performance at which Laughton appeared on stage in his dressing-gown to urge the gala audience to their seats. 'Shut up!' he said, 'and sit down!' He then proceeded to delight them with poems, limericks and inspirational passages from the Bible. Somewhat reluctantly, according to McCowen, after about half an hour he allowed the play to start.)

The most powerful persuasion to do the play evidently came from a sense of duty, both to his own talent and to the theatre. It's a rotten motive.

His next work was, happily, undertaken much more in a spirit of fun and relish. Billy Wilder, who had long admired him, asked him to play Sir Wilfred Robarts in his film of Agatha Christie's *Witness for the Prosecution*, with – a droll touch – Elsa Lanchester as his vigilant nurse. He was surrounded by other old chums: Tyrone Power (his last film, though he was not to know it), Marlene Dietrich (who had delighted him by saying, in the early thirties, that she would rather play a love scene with him than with anyone) and Henry Daniell, his old sparring partner from *The Suspect* and *Captain Kidd*. The script, greatly improved by Wilder and Harry Kurnitz from the Agatha Christie original, is, despite interesting resonances from Wilder and Dietrich's earlier collaboration, *A Foreign Affair*, hokum, but it is hokum played to the hilt, by no one more so than Laughton, who gives an effortless display of personality allied to technique. It is in a line of tetchy monsters, including Lord Horfield in *The Paradine*

Case, but it has more fun, more élan, and, at moments, more tenderness than he was wont to bring. It demanded nothing of him, and he gave it everything. There is, in the character, no deep note to be struck, but the surface is a brilliant contrivance, flashing monocle, illicit cigars and all. The relationships he creates with Dietrich and Power are clear and telling, though, perhaps inevitably, his best work in this regard is with Lanchester. She is less busily kooky than usual, and their games of cat-and-mouse are both real and funny. They were both nominated for Academy Awards for their work on the film; her second, only his too, after *Henry VIII*. Neither won. By rich coincidence, the Best Actor Award was won by Alec Guinness – for *Bridge on the River Kwai*.

Billy Wilder reports that Laughton's spirits were of the highest during shooting, and that he was endlessly fertile in alternative readings of every line, full of suggestions on every aspect of filming, from costumes to camera angles, and, on a memorable and much quoted occasion, in such good humour that he volunteered to read all the parts for the jury's reaction shots. 'You don't want to do this, Charles,' Wilder told him; 'it's donkey work, the script girl can do it.' But he insisted, and, says Wilder, it was an astonishing display, each character more like the actor who played it than the actor was himself. Wilder says he wanted to shoot the film all over again. This charming little story testifies both to Laughton's superabundant pleasure in acting (except that it isn't exactly acting: nothing depends on it, no one has paid to see it: it is release without responsibility) and to a certain more or less innocent desire for admiration – and why not? If someone picks up a violin and tosses off a couple of Paganini caprices just to be praised, praise them! Wilder was a wonderful audience, too. Exasperated by actors who could hardly say good morning without the aid of an acting coach (he hadn't seen nothing yet: *Some Like It Hot* still lay in the future) he beamed at Laughton's sheer skill. So would von Sternberg have done; Laughton was a different man, now, and the joy of Sir Wilfred for him was that he could lavish all he had learned on him. It made him feel very good; and it shows.

If there are aspects to the performance beyond that, they lie in the area of, firstly, decency – an elusive quality, but which Laughton wonderfully embodies, without a trace of sentimentality – and, secondly, Englishness. Sir William's crustiness and eccentricity are quickly revealed by Laughton to be masking an extreme boyishness, an emotional immaturity which is not without charm. His confusion at Dietrich's overpowering femininity, and the *Boys' Own Paper* feeling about his determination to save her and nail the guilty man, are peculiarly English in feeling, and add a touch of reality to a picture which is constantly threatened by the preposterousness of its events and characters.

Maybe the Englishness of the part kindled some nostalgia in Laughton. At any rate, he accepted an offer to direct and act in a new play in London, which he accordingly did in May of 1958. It was *The Party*, by Jane Arden. It was widely felt at the time that he wanted to associate himself, rather in the manner a couple of years earlier of Olivier's appearance in *The Entertainer*, with the new wave of English writing, and it may be so. He may have felt that modern England was a very different place from the country he'd left behind; a different place, even, from the England of 1951, when he last acted here. There were all kinds of new waves going on: socially, theatrically, in painting, in writing. Class seemed to be breaking down, and it was no longer comic or pathetic to come from the provinces: perhaps it was even an advantage. He was excited to discover a painter like Alan Lowndes in Manchester, and an actor like Albert Finney (also Mancunian) in Birmingham. No doubt he thought *The Party* was another manifestation of the same movement; if he did, he was wrong.

Its author, Jane Arden, had spent her early life in Wales, went – at the age of fifteen – to RADA, and then fetched up in America where, in Greenwich Village, according to her programme notes, she spent her time 'looking around, absorbing all I could – forming new ideas'. There she started writing, but decided she must come back to England because she could only 'write out of her own background'. The play she wrote, far from dealing with contemporary Britain, is heated personal drama, by no means without talent, in fact having a dangerous unstable energy all of its own but which is somehow completely at variance with the setting (a London suburb) and the form – good solid two act drama, three scenes in the first, two scenes in the second, and a resounding curtain line for each. Later, Miss Arden went on to write a neo-expressionist piece, *Vagina Rex*, which is much more itself; not, admittedly, a very nice self, but bold and uncompromised. Laughton was obviously drawn to the life in the play; and indeed the central character, had he wished to fully inhabit it, would have given ample scope for his special gifts. But as a director he strove to do contradictory things with it: to create the illusion of domestic reality (as unnecessary here as it was essential in Shaw, where he sought to abolish it) and to heighten the poetic feeling. His approach was Ibsenite, while the reference should have been to Strindberg.

The whole notion of the play revolves around madness – Ettie, the daughter whose party is being held, is clearly, from the outset, unstable, capricious, heartless, functioning on more or less controlled hysteria. We learn that her father, an alcoholic and worse, is in a home of some sort, having let the whole family down. Her mother, a vapid, kindly woman, still in love with her husband, is planning to invite him back for the weekend. The violence of Ettie's rejection of this idea is already unnerving; when he arrives, she cancels the party. By chance, he meets a potential boy friend of hers; he pretends to be merely a friend, and dispenses wise advice to the lad. Ettie's cold contempt for him drives him back to the gin. Their *scène à faire* follows, in which we learn that their closeness is not based on mere similarity of tempera-ment, but on some nameless – and unnamed – encounter, presumably incestuous.

It is, somewhat in the manner of Arthur Miller, a play about adaptation to the real world: the fallen idol who is the father takes refuge in fantasy and fabulism, enchanting the neighbours, inspiring love and despair in equal measure among those close to him. The father's account of his treatment by electro-convulsive therapy, not yet, in pre-Laingian 1958, an issue, is painful to read. The play actually anticipates a great deal of mid-sixties drama on the subject of society's imposition of conformity. The sense of madness in the play is very real; the author, writing to Laughton in the middle of the run, when he was still trying to extract re-writes from her, told him, 'It is a story of the past, and I haven't been able to make it a living reality: the real story of Ettie Brough and her father is not written because the author was afraid to write it.' In fact, whatever the precise details of the relationship ('Something, I am afraid,' Laughton wrote to Oscar Lewenstein, 'which should remain on the shelf in a medical library'), the strain and anguish attaching to it are perfectly clear. 'I have been through so many evasions from her in the past, and retirings from this workaday world,' Laughton continued to Lewenstein, 'I cannot believe she intends to work at all, until I see some evidence of it.' The struggle to turn life into art was never satisfactorily resolved in *The Party*. Author and director were in many ways similar characters, emotionally demanding, obsessive, depressive. 'Extreme . . . attrac-ted opposites . . . without any real orientation to the adult world, the social world . . . emotionally almost too childlike,' were the words in which Jane Arden described Laughton after his death, but they could be a self-portrait. A few years later, having endured the extreme demands of her temperament for long enough, she killed herself.

It is hard to sense any of this from the reviews. The principal point of interest was the return of Laughton to the stage, and he was greeted with a great roar at his entrance on the first night. 'I found it a fantastically moving moment when, after twenty-two years, a door on the New Theatre stage opened to let him back to London . . . all the lines of his body sagged. The man, we knew, was a failure, and a lonely, defiant, uneasy failure. We never questioned for a moment his past or his possible future. We accepted his cynicism, his remorse, his man-of-the-world wisdom. It was entirely a feat of absorption, one of those occasions when acting is so true and so complete that you do not think of it as acting.' Thus J. C. Trewin, who had followed Laughton from his first performances in the twenties, and who was one of the most eloquent lamenters of his defection to Hollywood to become 'an ordinary film actor'. Most of the other critics extended a welcome back: 'it is good to have him back after his twenty-two years' absence' (*Tatler*); 'a perfect piece of Charles Laughton to the last shrug and the most carefully wrung hand' (*Guardian*). 'He remains, in every way, tremendous' (*Punch*). 'Acting with every ounce of his considerable flesh, he fills in the details' (*Daily Mail*). Only Tynan, in the *Observer*, went for the jugular: 'Mr Laughton offers neither danger nor defeat, just an extravagant booby harmlessly letting off steam. On top of this, he plays the part in a *faisandé* Cockney accent, straight out of Bruce Bairnsfather's Old Bill cartoons. All of which,' he mischievously concludes, 'is fascinating, but nothing to do with solicitors, Kilburn or observable reality.' The accent had caused comment even from Trewin; it is all part of Laughton's doomed and misguided attempt to endow the play with specific detail. As for solicitors and Kilburn, these are the author's contributions along the same lines, and they, too, are doomed, grafted on to a story which would have been better told in abstracts.

The production itself suffered from all these contradictory impulses: something along the lines of Elia Kazan's Miller and Tennessee Williams productions may have served it better. As Tynan did not fail to point out, any attempt of Laughton's to create a realistic English suburban scene was absurd: he knew nothing about it. 'The action seems to unfold in a timeless nowhere. The hero has a wife who speaks perfect Schools Programme English and is his junior by twenty-five years, yet the disparities in age and accent are never even mentioned, let alone explained. They are broke, yet manage, with one lodger, to run the kind of mansion, all bookcases and pale beaming, that you would expect a visiting film-star to take near Henley for the summer.

Their closest friend is a rowdy coquette who talks like the late Suzette Tarri and owns what everyone weirdly calls "the nylon shop".'

Laughton had expended a great deal of time on casting the part of Ettie and, having flirted with the notion of using Maggie Smith (who, he said, 'showed some signs of genius,' reminding him of Laurette Taylor), settled on Ann Lynn, who was then immediately proclaimed a 'discovery' and a 'star in the making'. Laughton was convinced that the character was 'like something out of Barrie, a fairy-tale character, sensitive and delicate,' a description which applied admirably to Ann Lynn, but not at all to Ettie, on the evidence of the play. Similarly, he cast Joyce Redman, vivacious, forceful comedienne, as the drab and downtrodden wife, with Elsa as the proprietress of 'the nylon shop'. Both leading actresses found his direction difficult to take, Redman finding him frankly incomprehensible, Lynn, inexperienced and personally insecure, being overawed by his personal authority; she, too, was baffled by his tendency to speak in abstracts: 'this scene is blue, and it's Bartók,' he puzzlingly told her. He made the cardinal error of any actor-director: he spoke to his cast in terms which would mean something to him, but meant nothing to them. How he might have longed for a director to tell *him* that a scene was blue and Bartok! He had cast the part of the potential boyfriend (vexingly named Soya) more happily: he gave Albert Finney his London début in the rôle, having seen him as Macbeth at Birmingham ('you were bloody awful, but what can you expect at your age?'). He felt a huge paternal warmth towards this Northern lad, direct, unactorish, of the real world. 'Actors are useful people,' he wrote later, 'you can tell a lot about what England is like today from Albert Finney.' Ann Rogers, Laughton's personal assistant, thought that they were 'like Falstaff and Hal together.' Tynan wrote 'Mr Finney shares the play's best scene with Mr Laughton, who rises like a salmon to the occasion; few young actors have ever got a better performance out of their directors.'

As for Elsa Lanchester, who had no faith in the play anyway, she gave her well-known cabaret performance, while John Welsh as the lodger, played, as always, with quiet distinction. The play ran decently enough for its six months, coming off in November. It is, like *Major Barbara*, a curiously mixed episode, neither one thing nor the other. Laughton was clearly searching for some kind of expression, but never found it. No central informing notion seems to have lain behind his approach. Casting was quirky, staging uncertain or misconceived, and his own performance interpretatively somewhat neutral. He could never fail to make an impact, and, even misapplied, his talent was original and compelling. But what was he getting at? He wanted to be part of the modern world, but had none of Olivier's instinctive sense of which horse to back. He had thought long and deep about the theatre and acting, but seemed to have reached a point of complexity in his conclusions where all the many strands of his reflection cancelled each other out, resulting in something, both in his performances and his productions, rather low-key and un-defined. The parameters of his vision were becoming blurred, as if, perhaps, he no longer sought to realise it: the vision was an end in itself.

During the run of *The Party*, however, a concrete proposition was put to him: Glen Byam Shaw, planning the centenary season at Stratford, invited him to play King Lear. 'He didn't answer and said he must be going. We said our goodbyes. He left. Two minutes later he popped his head round the door and said, 'If you asked me to play King Lear here, I should find it hard to refuse.' The formula he chose is significant: 'I should find it hard to refuse.' In other words: 'I have been thinking about this play all my life; I owe it to myself, Shakespeare and the audience to do it.' He went back to America at the end of *The Party* to prepare for it. He also agreed to play Bottom. In the midst of his urgent meditations, he was signed to act in the blockbuster, *Spartacus*. It was only thirteen days' work, but it earned him a welcome $41,000.

The film's producer also played the title rôle: Kirk Douglas. He had assembled his galaxy of stars (Laurence Olivier, John Gavin, Tony Curtis, Peter Ustinov, Jean Simmons as well as Laughton) by sending each a version of the script in which he or she appeared to have the largest, most interesting part. The resulting mayhem, with temperaments being exercised and resignations being threatened, charac-terised the whole period of shooting. The director, Anthony Mann, was the first casualty; his replacement, Stanley Kubrick, remained *hors bataille*, simply arranging the physical aspects of the film as best he might (which was very well indeed: he creates a credible Roman Empire that is more convincing than any epic before or since). The actors, meanwhile, thrashed out the dialogue between themselves. Olivier, with his mastery of backstage politics, had been the first on the scene, with the result that his part was in considerably better shape than most – than Laughton's, for example, who fell into a heavy and suspicious sulk from the first day, convinced that Olivier was out to destroy him. Fortunately, most of his scenes were with Ustinov, who volunteered to re-write them, to which Laughton happily acceded. Together they concocted the scenes that ended up in the film: Kubrick, according to Ustinov, simply shot them.

Laughton's pleasure in his work with Ustinov is palpable. The sensuous liberal senator Gracchus is a character to whom Charles could give himself unreservedly. His oratory in the senate gives him the opportunity to demonstrate his rhetorical gifts at their most vital (and pertinent); the eating scene with Ustinov is a miracle of sly and bashful hedonism. His warm, fleshy integrity makes the perfect balance to his opponent and rival, Crassus, played by Olivier.

The on-screen antagonism was perhaps not difficult for Laughton to summon up. Relations between them on the floor were frosty but polite. 'We got on quite splendidly', wrote Olivier, 'though I was a bit distressed at what I considered to be his discourtesies on the set, and told him so.' Communication between them was limited by mutual wariness. Laughton envied Olivier his physical access to a range of parts that he could never play; Olivier, for his part, envied Laughton's individuality of mind and body. It is perhaps not too much of a simplification to say that Laughton envied Olivier's capacity to do, Olivier was jealous of Laughton's ability to be. Both were essentially character actors, but Laughton rummaged among the capacious folds of his own personality for his rôles, while Olivier built new men on top of his. Olivier, of course, had long ago eclipsed Laughton as a classical actor in the eyes of the world, and yet there was something about Laughton that would never be his. Laughton had followed a private path, replete with cul-de-sacs and dead ends, towards a destination that he could never define, let alone reach; Olivier had bowled down the highway in pursuit of the greatest prizes, which he had easily won. The maddening thing for Olivier was that Laughton, despite having become demonstrably lost, had somehow retained his stature; the intolerable thing for Laughton was that despite approaching art and life like an athlete, rather than as an artist, Olivier had somehow penetrated the secrets of the greatest rôles.

The chance for Godzilla, as it were, to meet King Kong, was lost when, whether entirely seriously or not, Laughton asked Olivier to direct him as King Lear. (Perhaps not entirely sincerely, because it was not in Laughton's gift: Glen Byam Shaw was going to direct it; though no doubt something could have been arranged.) Olivier said no: 'Because I really did not believe that he and I would get on as I really never could understand what he said to me – which meant that I was not intellectually his equal. I never really felt on quite the same level as he. What the hell would be the use of *my* directing *him* if I felt like that.' Instead he offered him some advice: 'If he wanted to play Lear he must go to the top of the hill on his estate every morning when the sun rose and breathe and shout the lines until he was exhausted. He rather pooh-poohed the idea.' Of course; Olivier was talking to the man who, when he phoned Glen Byam Shaw to accept the part, had said: 'Meet you at Stonehenge tomorrow'. *And he meant it*. Olivier's excellent advice – excellent, that is, as far as it goes, like Gielgud's advice about getting a light Cordelia – was anathema to Laughton. Olivier was interested in setting himself difficult challenges that he could crack. He won his greatness by conquering great rôles: Jack the Giant-Killer. Thus he is often to be found belittling his characters: 'Lear is easy, he's just a stupid old fart. He's got this frightful temper. He's completely selfish and utterly inconsiderate. He does not for a moment think of the consequences of what he has said. He is simply bad-tempered arrogance with a crown perched on top. He obviously wasn't spanked by his mother often enough. I mean, to turn away from his favourite daughter like that, what kind of an idiot is he?' The shade of Laughton seems to shudder at the very echo of Olivier's words from *On Acting*. For Laughton, the greatness of the great rôles resided in their unfathomable complexity, the depths of experience which they explored and embodied, and the dignity and importance of acting them was that one attempted to realise some part of that complexity. The horror of acting, and the reason one shied away from it, even, one might say, *evaded* it, was the impossibility of getting anywhere near fulfilling it.

The terrible paradox, however, is that, whatever the vulgarity and reductiveness of Olivier's conception of a part, his physical command of both the text and his own instrument resulted in performances which far exceeded the limitations of his interpretations. The part installed itself in his chords and limbs, and took on a life of its own; whereas no matter how profound and imaginative Laughton's connection with the inner life of the play, the constriction of his physical apparatus meant that the point of ignition never arrived. A further terrible paradox is that Olivier's shorter perspectives meant that he drew energy from the achievability of his objectives; Laughton was wearied by the task before he'd even begun.

Gielgud and Olivier were regarded (principally by Olivier) as rivals, each gifted in ways that the other would like to have been. But their theatre was the same theatre; they were running the same race. Olivier and Laughton, however, could hardly be said to be practising the same art. Laughton the deep-sea diver who had to keep coming up for air, Olivier the surfer whose skill took him to places he never meant to go; they had the sea in common, but that was all.

In *Spartacus*, the two modes can be seen side by side: Olivier, in what is perhaps a trial run for his Coriolanus, which he was about to play in Stratford in the same season as Charles would play Lear, plays Crassus like a knife: it is an entirely linear performance with every point brilliantly made. His glacial patrician manner, his ruthless ambition, his strong desire for his handsome young slave, are all cleanly and sharply indicated; it is as if there were a thin black line drawn around the role. Laughton's Gracchus has no such boundaries, no such definition. It spreads, floats, expands, contracts. The whole massive expanse of flesh seems to be filled with mind – thoughts are conceived, born and die in different parts of that far-flung empire. Sedentary for the most part, Gracchus seethes with potential movement. He is a jelly that has escaped the mould; Olivier's (and Crassus's) sharp knife can gain no purchase on it. Not surprisingly, when the time came for Olivier to shoot the close-ups for his big scene with Charles, he sweetly indicated that he would find it easier to do if Charles weren't actually around. Charles was triumphantly hurt by this.

Olivier was of course right about the *Lear*. How could they possibly have worked together? When *Spartacus* finished, they went off to their separate preparations for the coming season of which they were the twin pillars. Larry went into training to lick a particularly tricky bugger, Coriolanus; Charles took thought, then loaded himself up with the spiritual provisions he would need on his terrible trip to the bottom of the ocean called Lear.

Shakespeare

In a sense, of course, Laughton had been preparing for *King Lear* all his life. From the moment he started giving interviews, he had been alluding to the play, sometimes representing it as the ultimate summit, sometimes as a byword for the irrelevance of Shakespeare to the modern world, depending on how defensive he felt at any moment. He never ceased to feel, from the beginning, that an actor's proper place was in the theatre, playing the classics; but he often felt excluded from the charmed circles where his contribution might be acknowledged. So – and this is typical of his way – he denounced the classics and embraced the movies, claiming for them all kinds of greatness, potential and actual, which would make his involvement in them seem important, would give his life value. In time, however, his passionate attentions to the art of film were received more coolly, until finally, in high dudgeon, he turned his back on them, condescending to return to them only for commercial considerations. By now, his enthusiasm had moved elsewhere: to the touring circuit, person to person contact with the people, spreading The Word. Literally the *word*; people, he discovered, were hungry for stories and the stirring phrases which the movies, with their growing illiteracy, had denied them. And among the stories and the phrases were, of course, many by Shakespeare. Not that he had ever for a moment, in his heart, left off loving Shakespeare, studying Shakespeare, puzzling over Shakespeare. Shakespeare was his breviary, his rosary, his private devotion. Shakespeare was also his crossword puzzle, his unsolved equation, his everlasting riddle. But most of all, Shakespeare was his Great White Whale, haunting and mocking him, appearing tantalisingly on the horizon of whatever waters he might be amiably paddling, or perhaps (his favourite posture for contemplation) floating in, as Peter Ustinov put it, 'like a topsy-turvy iceberg,' and all the roles and all the plays had somehow dissolved before The One, *Lear*. It touched his life at so many points that he had come to see the play as his spiritual autobiography: the man more sinned against than sinning, but who, demonstrably, had brought his fate on his own head; the man engaged in a baffling journey through pain and despair towards – hopefully – some sort of tender resolution.

His preparation consisted as much, therefore, of work on himself as on the part. He co-opted Elsa Lanchester as his assistant and adviser; together they delved the depths. 'The strain had become very heavy but exciting for both of us. He had become Lear. He couldn't sleep at night, not because he was thinking of the words but because he was tortured. Lear was always with him.' They found a thread in the play which perfectly expressed the yearning for resolution central to Laughton and Lear: 'The extraordinary connection and repetition of references to water, climaxed by the great storm scene. It was like an outburst of tears, that storm, because there are so many references to water – water animals, rivers, dolphins. It was like a collecting of water behind the eyes and then the storm comes and the tears, and then tears for the terrible death of Cordelia at the end. So we restudied the water theme. We were learning to stretch the water and the tears so that it would be contagious to the audience, a building up of overflowing sorrow, the pressure of tears.' They spent some time, during this preparation, in Hawaii, in touch with the natural world which so dominates *Lear*, surrounded by mountains, caught in storms, cut off by floods. And Laughton entered there on the island into a most strange and poetic friendship. Lanchester's moving account reads: 'His name was Passio. He was a dancer the like of which I have never seen. His dancing and his gestures were beautiful, but he would rarely come out to be seen . . . Charles by his kindness and gentleness, reached the boy's spirit and helped Passio to dance for a small group . . . on a moonlit night on the beach. Passio danced! He used flaming torches that licked around his whole body and seemed to become part of him. He was the moon and the moonlight on the sea, and it was just the most extraordinary experience that I've ever known.' Filled with all this, they returned to Los Angeles, where Charles amazed Elsa by buying some peyote: "I want to get as far into the character of Lear as I can.' (Later, rather proudly, he reported no effect.)'

Leaving America for England, Laughton told Terry Sanders that he was going to play King Lear. 'But I shall fail, of course.'

The Stratford season, a somewhat spurious 100th anniversary season ('A few people might have done a bit of Morris dancing on the walls a hundred years ago, and said a couple of speeches from *As You Like It*,' said Albert Finney), was the end of Glen Byam Shaw's régime, and he'd assembled an astonishing group of actors and directors to mark it. Paul Robeson would play Othello with Sam Wanamaker as Iago, Tony Richardson directing; Edith Evans would play the Countess in Tyrone Guthrie's production of *All's Well That Ends Well*; Olivier would play Coriolanus, and Charles would play Lear and Bottom. It was a grand flourish which celebrated and brought to a conclusion a very honourable tradition at Stratford initiated by Barry Jackson, brought to glory by Anthony Quayle, and sustained by Byam Shaw: that of the big guns, spending an ill-paid summer playing the parts they would have no chance of doing anywhere else. The director-designate, Peter Hall, was about to effect the transformation Quayle and Shaw knew must come about: the institution of a permanent company, exploring the canon in a systematic and thematic manner, and keeping themselves alive to contemporary resonance by performing new plays as well. This tradition has now itself been replaced by a new free-for-all no longer sustained by a star system. The Jackson–Quayle–Shaw régime begins to assume the patina of a golden age.

In 1959, to judge by the contemporary press, Laughton was the biggest of the big guns; or perhaps he was the greatest novelty. '*Laughton to play Lear*'; '*Charles Laughton to Star as Bottom and Lear*'; '*A Star-studded Stratford: Shakespeare with Laughton, Olivier, Robeson and Edith Evans!*' The headlines can only have filled him with more fear, but it is an interesting indicator of the extent of his fame. The first night of *The Party* had been mobbed. Enid Bagnold, with whom he experienced a brief, intense friendship during his English sojourn, noted this.

His glamour included a touch of the conjuror: an element that needed police cohorts to protect him from crowd-adoration. His 'fame' fascinated me. I know one or two great actors, but they are protected in the street by a quality of invisibility. Laurence Olivier especially. Charles's fame in a mob would take the Duke of Windsor at the height of the Abdication to equal it. His unique ugliness plus the film of *Henry VIII* got him spotted. Spotted in a way that gave him claustrophobia. Old ladies swarmed, holding out pencils for autographs. Women pushing prams swivelled the four wheels towards him. Here on the Village Green tourists nudged each other and walked nearer, as he hurried into the car. It frightened him, he hated it, but he wouldn't have been without it. It was his honey and his cross.

His performances at Stratford would certainly not be protected by a quality of invisibility. For a man sometimes accused of cowardice, it was an extremely brave thing to do. He had not appeared in a classical play since 1933, over twenty-five years; and when he had done, he had been slated. He had not worked within the English profession, except for the odd, unsatisfactory interlude of *The Party*, for twenty-five years, either: he had no idea how his colleagues, and, in some cases, contemporaries would receive him. He was offering himself for inevitable comparison with, in Edith Evans and Laurence Olivier, two of the giants of the modern classical theatre. (A third giant, Gielgud, was absent, and had, as it happens, originated the suggestion that Laughton be invited to Stratford.) The strength and confidence he had acquired in America had come largely from his authority as a teacher and his authority on text; here that did not apply. Here he was an actor among actors, many of whom had much greater experience than he in playing these texts. He was tackling a part that was widely held to be unplayable. But above all, he was going to attempt to do justice to his lifetime of meditation on what he held to be the supreme statement about human life.

No wonder the impression he gave as he approached the Stratford season was one of fearful vulnerability. Fortunately he was not in the opening plays, *Othello* (moderately received) and *All's Well* (in modern dress: joyously acclaimed), and his first part was Bottom. The great challenge was put off to the end of the season. It was an agreeable way to ease himself in; not that that was how he approached it. He had had a long relationship with Bottom, too, suddenly reading his lines to whoever would listen. 'To hear him (unwarningly) change places with Bottom, having played his thickness with hanging lips and idiot delight . . .', wrote Enid Bagnold. Some years before, Eric Bentley, chastising him for his evasion of the theatre, wrote: 'One of the great moments in all my theatre-going was the moment when in a hotel room in Paris Charles Laughton read Bottom's first scene in *A Midsummer Night's Dream*. We write about jaws dropping, but that is the only time I actually saw a jaw drop for sheer surprise and delight; it was the jaw of Charles Dullin. The portrayal of Bottom . . . was sublime; and not just sublime reciting, but sublime acting, sublime theatre.' Jane Arden recalled the astonishing transformation that overcame him when he read the play to her five-year-old son.

Peter Hall, the director of *A Midsummer Night's Dream*, found that, 'like all great actors, he sucked you dry', but 'he wasn't hard to direct, providing that you just released yourself and threw everything at him that you were thinking and feeling'. He had ideas about everything – including a conviction that the play should be set in a kind of Japanese garden – but he eventually conceded the value of Hall's preference for staging the play as a festive piece played in a great Elizabethan house. Laughton's modernistic taste in Art led him at first to reject Lila de Nobili's exquisite 'gauzy, golden, sunlit world', but his sense of the real world of these 'Warwickshire craftsmen' putting on their play for the local nobs, reconciled him to a specifically Elizabethan setting. All his joy in acting, uncomplicated by any burdens of great significance, and all his 'questing, worrying mind' (Peter Hall's phrase), were released in rehearsals: 'he was like some kind of mad dog that had come into the rehearsal room – a wet dog, too, shaking all over the place.' He was not, thought Hall, selfish, but 'I quickly found that wherever I put him, upstage, downstage, he'd dominate the proceedings because there was this vast wonderful moonlight face with these huge eyes; it was like a large mirror on the stage.' His fellow actors, of whom Michael Blakemore was one, found him generous to act with, though perhaps more in the sense of taking than of giving (an underrated form of generosity in the theatre, but surely as great): 'you felt him groping around the stage for other sensibilities to latch onto, to keep him afloat.' Interestingly, Blakemore speaks of feeling that in rehearsals 'he was evading the moment when he actually had to commit to a view of the scene.' The more Laughton entered into a character or a play, the more agonisingly aware of the range of possibilities he became; in *A Midsummer Night's Dream*, however, it was evidently delicious agony.

The production was well-enough received. It was held to lack poetry. The critics should have hung around; they'd heard *nothing* yet. Laughton was welcomed enthusiastically enough, though held, in some quarters, to be rather subdued. As ever, it was hard to believe that rival critics had attended the same performance. 'It's a *Laugh*ton performance', squealed the *Daily Mail*, 'with the emphasis on the *laugh*.' 'J.C. Trewin, dismayed by the loss of the 'haunted night of the Athenian Wood, and of the gleaming moonshine of the verse,' alluded to his one-time idol only briefly: 'inspiration flashes only when Charles Laughton is recalling the wonder of the night's dream.' 'Laughton,' he continued, 'is to act King Lear during August; he must regard his hempen homespun as a holiday exercise.' Tynan was ruthless: 'I confess I do not know what Mr Laughton is up to, but I am sure I would hate to share a stage with it. He certainly takes the audience into his confidence but the process seems to exclude from his confidence, everyone else in the cast. Fidgeting with a lightness that reminds one (even as one forgets what the other actors are talking about) how expertly bulky men dance, he blinks at the pit his moist, reproachful eyes, softly cajoles and suddenly roars, and behaves throughout in a manner that has nothing to do with acting, although it perfectly hits off the demeanour of a rapscallion uncle dressed up to entertain the children at a Christmas party.'

Laughton would never be able to satisfy Tynan whose predilection was for acting which bore the stamp of its maker, just as Tynan could never appreciate the great genius of Peggy Ashcroft, stemming as it did from an overflowing radiance of soul. Where was the *interpretation*? Tynan always wanted a scheme for things, and for all his great gifts, this limited his understanding of the actor's contribution. Personal qualities often eluded him; he must always know what the actor was *doing*. Actors whose genius consisted in being, slipped through his net – unless they were a 'turn', like Bea Lillie, or Sir Ralph

Richardson at the end of his life. Then he was full of appreciation. His review of Laughton's Bottom is perhaps on the edge of this kind of appreciation.

Fortunately, and uniquely, there is a filmed record of the performance by which one can judge it. It is not a complete guide to the performance, of course, because the whole pitch of playing is changed to accommodate the medium. Even detractors of Laughton's stage Bottom grudgingly admit that on film he is glorious. The predominant impression is of energy – passionate, earthy energy – and appetite; but beside the physical energy is an enormous imaginative turmoil, so that Bottom's desire to play all the parts comes not from arrogance or greed, but from sudden visions of himself in the various rôles. His melancholy, as he is denied the chance of giving life to his Thisbe or his Lion, is terrible, but valiantly borne. His London (-ish) accent gives great vigour and bite to his utterances; though it must be admitted that it is oddly at variance with either the mummerset of his fellow-players, or the Warwickshire of his avowed intentions. It also must be admitted that he somehow always finds himself at the centre of the action; whether Bottom or Laughton is responsible for this is all but impossible to say – they are indistinguishable. Except physically. Physically, this ginger-headed, ginger-bearded, apparent forty-year-old bears no resemblance whatever to the heap of flesh that had, no more than six months earlier, addressed the Roman senate, nor to the silver-haired patriarch who six weeks before had addressed the London press. The great paunch is there, encased in a cross-stitched smock, but the whole centre of gravity seems to have changed, and when, after the play scene, the duke calls for a bergamask, it is impossible to believe that the whirling, cavorting figure who leads it can be sixty, fat, and very short of breath indeed. Giles Gordon, as a young boy, was backstage during the interval to visit Cyril Luckham, who was playing Quince, when 'I was vaguely aware of a large presence, like a mountain bear, a great, slow animal. He was vast. He seemed to spread, like camembert or brie, beyond the physical space he occupied . . . he shambled back into the wings, looking as weary as William Blake's Ancient of Days . . . I took my place standing at the back of the stalls. Cyril was benign and gentle as Quince. Suddenly a young actor burst onto the stage, playing Bottom the Weaver. To this day, and I have seen many Bottoms, I haven't seen a more youthful, energetic, lively, eager one. He can't, that afternoon, have been a day older than seventeen. I didn't, of course, need to look at the programme to see who played him.'

The same power of imagination which rearranged the face and physique of Laughton possesses his Bottom, and renders his encounter with the fairy kingdom a thing of great poetry. He is accustomed to visions, so he treats this one with perfect naturalness. Most acceptingly he places his monstrous head on Titania's lap, and greets the fairies with tremendous grave courtesy (and a sudden inexplicable access of mummerset vowels). His translation has left him with huge floppy ears and furry, cloven paws (a make-up devised by Laughton himself) which perfectly suggests the mid-point, half ass, half human, that he has become; these, too, he accepts with great expansive good nature. When he returns to his fellows, their joyous greetings seem wholly genuine and completely understandable. In the play scene, he sports a band around his head, acts with great bravura and dies with many a false death, jack-knifing up and down off the floor. In the final dance, he somehow embodies the true spirit of the Morris dance. It is not merely nimble but almost possessed.

The film lasts 90 minutes, which means that the play is condensed into a little over seventy-five, to allow for an introduction by Laughton, and a glimpse of Peter Hall. Laughton was very much the presiding genius of the enterprise, having set it up in the first place. It was claimed that it would be seen by over 40 million Americans, and that it was the most expensive programme ever, up to that point, made for television. Directed by Fletcher Markle, it's a very decent account of the production, revealing the loveliness of Lila de Nobili's designs, and doing justice to all the play's strata, though, for obvious reasons, the mechanicals get the best of it. As an historical document, the film is a delight, revealing the young Albert Finney (at Stratford at Laughton's suggestion, and none too happy), the young Vanessa Redgrave in a performance so startlingly exaggerated that only a huge natural gift could have sustained it without self-consciousness, Michael Blakemore in a nose, Ian Holm supreme as Puck, which he would play again in Peter Hall's 1968 film, and Mary Ure as a radiantly sensuous but human Titania. Laughton's introduction is a fair sample of his persona as a cultural missionary, genial, humorous, reverent in short bursts ('Who were you, Will Shakespeare?'). He glides down the Avon in a punt, he wanders through Ann Hathaway's cottage, he strolls down Stratford High Street in the company of his brother-in-law, Waldo Lanchester, telling us how he had doubts about cramming *The Dream* into 90 minutes, until he looked up and saw the forest of TV aerials on the roofs of all the houses, and realised that if Shakespeare had been alive today, he would have tried to reach as many people as he could through the new medium. 'Now don't you sneer!' he tells his 'fellow-Americans,' as, quite incongruously, he calls them. 'There was a time when I didn't dig him myself, but the more I read him, the more I dug him, and the more you dig, the more you dig, do you dig me, daddy?' 'Well, you must excuse me because I've got to go and put my make-up on and paint my beard and my hair ginger,' he ends. Against all the odds, it's patronising neither to Shakespeare nor to his 'fellow-Americans'. In fact, it's rather moving.

Bottom was a lull before the storm, an encore before, rather than after the main event. Now it was *Lear* at last. 'At the first read-through,' Michael Blakemore, who was playing Lear's knight, says, 'what was immediately apparent was that he would never really get the huge rhetorical passages, he couldn't really do that, he didn't have the machinery.' He knew that, and had convinced himself that it wasn't necessary; his understanding of *Lear* led him to focus his performance on the second half of the play. In a letter to a young fan, he had described his anguish in the dressing-room; how he 'dreaded going through all the things Shakespeare had written: the terrible journey of Lear to his death.' That was the key-note for him: not the fall from a great height, not the turbulent rage, but the stumbling progress towards death. During the run of the play, he was troubled by nightmares associated with the play. He got his cousin, Jack Dewsbery, a psychiatrist, to come to see the performance: 'I went up to Stratford, and, for reasons which even now are unknown to me, I was struck by the very first speech he made in the play, in which Lear speaks of his coming death and of the need to dispose of his properties. I told Charles that was where I thought the trouble lay . . . I can only suppose that in some way his dreams had foretold the future, and that I had unwittingly put my finger on their meaning.' Lanchester suggests, too, that his desire to take peyote indicated that 'somehow there was little time to reach out and touch some unattainable goal in art'.

Rehearsals were unusual in that Elsa Lanchester was present throughout, sitting at a desk, text spread out in front of her, reminding him of what they'd decided during the preparatory period. Once again, Laughton was full of suggestions, which Glen Byam Shaw, a more malleable man than Peter Hall and less skilled at deflecting the more far-fetched notions, generally accepted, thus, according to a young actor in the company, destroying the production. 'What would have been a grand old Shakespearian production was destroyed by Charles, bit by bit – a year's work, dismantled. This poor weak producer Glen Byam Shaw would say to each of Charles' suggestions, 'You're a genius!' We watched with fascination.' What Charles was striving towards was a visual equivalent of the monolithic, abstract delicacy of the painters Soulages and Manessier, both of whose work he collected and indeed examples of which he had with him in Stratford. It was this monumental simplicity that he sought on his frequent visits to Rollright, the Druidic remains nearby. With the younger members of the cast, he'd go up there at three o'clock in the morning, just trying to absorb that simplicity. It wasn't the primitivism that he wanted; it was the same thing he found in his pre-Columban collection – something essential, maybe mandala-like. In the end, he did persuade Byam Shaw and Percy Harris, the designer, to cut away more and more, just as he tried to cut away more and more from his own performance.

He had imposed (deliberately?) a quite separate obstacle to his work: he had come to believe that Elizabethan typography was the clue to the stresses in the verse. Every time a capital letter occurred, it signified a stress. No arguments about the capriciousness of Elizabethan printers would sway him. It was holding him up terribly, as he struggled to wring significance out of prepositions and participles starting with, for example, a capital T, just because the printer had had a run on his lower case that morning and was obliged to use the upper one instead. Glen Byam Shaw appealed to Peter Hall to help him, but all in vain. 'That was him – all knowledge, all experience was his field, and he would go off on mad crazes and many of them were crazy, but many of them were not.'

He was firmly in the grip of the iron iambic, as well: years in front of a metronome had bred in him an almost superstitious fear of offering any reading of a line which diverged from the rigid da*da*, da*da*, da*da*, da*da*, da*da*. So the audience got Howl HOWL, Howl HOWL, Howl. It says much for his emotional force that this was never noted by any critic.

Ian Holm, his devoted Fool ('I felt I had to love this man'), observed in him a dread of exposing his performance, as if it were something so personal that it might perish. 'Perhaps, like Glenn Gould, he wasn't doing it for an audience.' Blakemore reckoned that 'of all the distinguished people we had that season, all the very distinguished talents, Charles in a way was nakedly the most an artist. You felt that the struggle constantly to achieve something fresh, something unrelated to fame or public acceptance, was going on there all the time.'

Laughton's anxiety as the first night approached was quite unconcealed; he had a terrible shout-down with Byam Shaw in which he threatened to walk out unless a certain actor was removed; Byam Shaw resisted. According to Glen, the dress rehearsal was wonderful; Elsa thought the reverse, and rushed backstage to tell him so, to accuse Charles of using all his old mannerisms, and betraying their work together. 'Charles shouted back at me that I was a killer. He said you've ruined it! I'll never do it now, it's hopeless. You've killed everything!' On the first night, Blakemore looked into his eyes: 'it was like a lot of birds flying round a cage in panic . . . He started badly and did not recover till the last third.'

'CHARLES LAUGHTON IS NOT A GREAT LEAR,' the *News Chronicle* triumphantly informed its readers. There had been a few boos from the gallery, too, but in fact, the performance was received with respect by the majority of the audience and the majority of the press. The consensus that generally develops between the extremes (in this case represented by, on the one hand, the *News Chronicle* and, on the other, surprisingly, Milton Shulman in the *Evening Standard*: 'A BRILLIANT LEAR – BY ANY TEST') said that once the unmajestic opening and the vocally weak storm scenes were over, the performance began to bite, until, at the end, it became deeply moving. 'Mr Laughton's performance,' according to *The Times*, 'is a superb essay in stage pathos. Only at the very end does it attain the level of high tragedy.' Absurd, these Beckmesser-like awardings of points in the categories! How many points for kingship? And for pathos? Four for tragic demeanour, not bad. Pity about lacking the all-important bass notes . . . still, he looked old. Some reviews give more detailed accounts of what actually happened, of what kind of experience was generated, interesting clues: 'Cordelia's 'Nothing' is not a blow struck at his kingly authority. It is a kind of shock that occurs as a dream slides into a nightmare,' said *The Times*. W. A. Darlington, in the *Telegraph*, identified the pathos in the reading as coming from 'the slowness with which Lear comes to comprehend what a wiser father would have known from the beginning.' Young Bernard Levin, not yet shorn of his illusions, wrote: 'In the opening scenes, he bases his rage against Cordelia firmly on disappointment, not shaky caprice, so that when he begins to repent of his decision, the terrible sadness of 'I did her wrong' catches at the heart and stings the eyes even before his madness sweeps our sympathies before it. And how moving and eloquent in this scene is the gesture with which Lear, tucked into a square, high, barbaric throne, turns to each of his daughters in turn to hear their protestations of love . . . if he does not bring humanity up to the level of the gods, he most marvellously brings the gods down to earth, so that when he cries to them not to let him go mad, his passion and pity come down among us, and move us all the more.'

These glimpses of the performance give some suggestion that there may have been something more to the performance than occasional moments struggling against huge technical incompetence; that the fruits of Laughton's thirty years of red-hot searching of the play were worth a little closer consideration than the *News Chronicle*, for example, was prepared to give it. There are, after all, failures and failures. Beethoven's last quartets are monumental failures by any criteria that existed before they were written; perhaps even now, they still rate as failures if you insist that the form should perfectly fulfil the content. Certainly if you approached Laughton's Lear with a fixed expectation, namely that you would be thrilled to the very marrow by the spectacle of a crazy tyrannical king being turned against by his daughters, taking to the wilds where he goes completely mad, and the final dwindling into a sad old man, you would be disappointed. You would have loved the intense physicality of Laurence Olivier's performance; John Gielgud's performance lacked that, but his natural nobility would have made the first scenes acceptable, while there were immense dividends to be gained in his heart-breaking lyricism in the play's second half. In a couple of years, though daunted by the strange, alien world of the settings, you would have recognised the brutish struggle of Paul Scofield, like a prehistoric animal facing extinction.

But if someone told you a completely different story, told you that *King Lear* was not about a decline, but an ascent, you would probably fail to understand the performance at all. It seems that Laughton's understanding of the part was just such a breaking of the mould. The performance is lost forever, exists only in memory and a few scattered accounts. It's a wonderful thing, then, for anyone trying to take Laughton seriously as an actor that a full account of it exists; one of the best accounts of any performance, and it was not written by a critic, or anyone connected with the theatre at all: the young man to whom Laughton wrote that the play was 'the terrible journey of Lear to his death', Ken Carter, a teacher. He offers a view of Laughton's performance that makes sense of all the scattered insights, of what Lanchester has written, and of what seems probable, in the light of Laughton's preoccupations.

Having seen the play Mr Carter wrote to his father who, unknown to him, sent the letter on to Laughton. Carter had cried intermittently, he said, all the way through. During the interval he could hardly speak.

And even now I am only half in this world. Laughton's interpretation was muted – Lear was a small, bewildered man, who became terrific because he started as nothing. The storm emphasised the littleness of man, rather than man battling for all he was worth against the elements – a very gentle rain and occasional lightning flashes with the two puny figures in the middle of this. I can't really explain; only a man with terrific strength and spirituality could dare to play Lear so restrainedly . . . this cherubic little man with more dignity and beauty of soul than one could have thought of. *Un homme ne vaut rien, mais rien ne vaut un homme*. Goodness, I wish you could have seen it. I've never been in a theatre before and heard people crying all round me. I don't know how I had the strength to sit through it, it was so beautiful and harrowing.

Laughton and Glen Byam Shaw were both moved to read the letter. Laughton's reply, written nearly a year later, contained an interesting self-observation: 'It did not seem that the play *King Lear* had anything to do with my will. I found myself doing many things which I had not planned to do . . .'

Later, Ken Carter wrote an analysis of the performance.

The first two and a half acts were making ready for the wonders to come. It was a carefully grounded interpretation, craftsmanlike, with sound, solid preparation (the audience needed patience) . . . the scale, or arc, of his concept was so great that one could sense the death of this Lear right from the beginning. In the quest for unity, Laughton chose as the under-lying emotion bewilderment: a very curious emotion, little-explored.

Carter traces the bewilderment through the play, from Cordelia's failure to pander to his wishes, to the Fool's reproof of him, to the storm's refusal to come to his aid, to the wonder of Cordelia's selfless love, to his final bewilderment at her death.

You could say that Laughton achieved an extraordinary technical feat in sustaining this apparently slight emotion, through so many variations, through the entire length of the play. He found unity of character in childishness. In the first part, he was spoilt, petulant, self-centred; in the second he was innocent, with a sense of wonder, freshness of vision, purity.

Carter describes the various manifestations of this, ending with the death of Cordelia:

Laughton's Lear mourned his dead daughter with all the tragic intensity of a child whose pet rabbit had died – that fresh, stabbing, urgent pain which is only belittled by adults who have forgotten their own childhoods . . . This Lear did not grow madder and madder. Instead, he became less and less sane. The process was so gradual and natural that the audience was caught by surprise . . . an added poignancy was that Laughton could never totally hide the power of his mind. He brought out a curious paradox: this Lear was driven to madness by the onset of a new sanity. From within, there arose an unbidden awareness of other people's suffering, of the condition of humanity, of general principles – in short, an aware-ness of reality and reason. In Laughton's performance, the turning point was 'O! Reason not the need . . .' It was delivered as a suddenly perceived deep insight; not as a tit-for-tat in the chop-logic about how many followers he should have . . . Laughton's performance of Lear's humility was outstanding. Not mere absence of pride: humility. All productions show humiliations being heaped upon Lear; all productions stress that Lear has been humbled, broken, made weaker. No other production has shown Lear *gaining* humility; humility as an asset, as a strength . . . Laughton's humility was the foundation of his humanity. Lear became the best the human race could offer in defence of its existence.

Laughton was lucky enough to find in Ken Carter someone to whom his Lear immediately spoke as he had intended it. He had told a young actor in the company: 'You know why my Lear is the greatest? Because I'm the first actor to play it on a rising graph after the storm.' The young actor had simply stared at him; somehow Carter saw it, experienced it. One critic came close to understanding the perform-ance – Harold Hobson, often wayward but sometimes seeing clearer than anyone else: 'Lear is a very grand play; but grandeur soon becomes dull. Now Mr Laughton is never dull. He is not dull even at the beginning, when he looks ridiculous. But this absurdity of appearance is made the foundation of an extraordinary pathos later on. There is something overwhelmingly touching in the thought that the universe should pour so many sorrows, such a multitude of griefs, upon a head that seems, so deliberately seems, so undistinguished . . . even a sort of magnificence develops from the gigantic disproportion between the punished and the punishment. That the universe should single out so small a figure for its wrath gives a lurid splendour to the performance; it is' (Hobson finds the exact image) 'as if an ordinary man were called to crucifixion.' Of course, Laughton was variable; he *did* lack stamina, and sometimes, Ian Holm has said, he simply didn't try to reach the full range of even his own interpretation. His attitude was almost detached; it was almost like a lecture. 'I know more about *Lear* than anyone living,' he'd mock-boasted, and his performance was a kind of instruction. There is one famous incident which is highly significant in this regard. At a certain performance half way through the first scene, he completely forgot his lines, and asked for a prompt. It came. No, no, he said, back to the beginning of the speech. Again came a line. No, no, he said again, further back. You see, ladies and gentlemen, he said, turning to the audience, this is *plot*. And then he resumed the performance, not at all fazed. The remarkable point, though, is that *neither was the audience*. He had created a relationship with them where they had placed themselves totally in his hands.

Moving and stimulating as Ken Carter's account of the performance is, it is possible that had Charles Laughton stood alone on the stage with a copy of the play in his hand and simply read from it, it might have been just as affecting and compelling. There are many accounts of his readings of the play, the *whole* play. One is by Peter Hall in Hollywood; another by Enid Bagnold ('He rehearsed himself for *Lear* . . . in the library his voice thundered'); a third by Christopher Isherwood: 'I used to sit in that little room and watch and when I see the scene now . . . it's like sitting all alone in the front row of a gigantic movie theatre where a vast face, dozens of times larger than life, is hanging right over you and saying things like, 'When we are born we cry but we come to this great stage of fools' and this kind of thing and I just wept, you know, and I was transfixed'. He had demonstrated to both Peter Hall and Christopher Isherwood how he intended to play the storm scene: 'I remember,' wrote Isherwood, 'his telling me it was very important for him to have in his head the high note of the storm. A characteristic note to which he related the sound of his own voice. In other words he wanted to create the effect of the storm in his own speaking of the verse.' 'Of course in a room it was magic because I was sitting in a room being asked to imagine a storm. But in a theatre it didn't work at all.' (Peter Hall). To Enid Bagnold, 'it all seemed so much smaller in the theatre.' But in a sense, it may have been the whole play that he wanted to do. (Interestingly, Edward Hambleton maintained that Laughton's performances as Galileo in the theatre paled by comparison with his readings of the whole play.) 'At every performance,' wrote Elsa Lanchester, 'he reached out and stretched to solve the mystery of the crucifixion of Lear, but he never did quite touch on that ecstasy. He saw, he felt, he knew what it was about, but he still was not the transmitter of the mystery of the tragedy.' Like so many descriptions of Laughton's failures, her words make one long to have seen it, and yet the final verdict about this Lear is that it was scarcely a performance at all, that it was the unequal struggle that Laughton was offering up, not any definitive result; the spectacle of a great spirit at war with itself and a text. There is something indescribably moving about Glen Byam Shaw's description of their visits to Stonehenge:

> Charles arrived in a large hired car. The rain was coming down hard, but he tied a large woollen scarf round his head which made him look like some strange old woman and we wandered off to Stonehenge. There were a few other people there who all stared at Charles. Whether they recognised him, or just thought he was mad, I don't know.

Next week they went to Beachy Head:

> It was a beast of a day. A very high wind and raining. I parked the car and we struggled to the edge of the cliff. I hate heights and stopped well short of the edge, but Charles staggered on until he was within a few feet of it. Standing there alone battered by the wind and the rain, he looked remarkably like King Lear. When he came back to where I was standing my hands were sweating, but Charles was wonderfully gay and excited.

It is as if this was the experience; as if Charles were himself a character in a play or a novel and that his life was an exemplary life; that his profession, or even his vocation, was Being Charles Laughton On Behalf of Humanity. Actual formal achievements like giving a good performance were almost incidental; the more important task was Being Charles Laughton at deeper and deeper levels. There had never been and there would never be a context in which Charles Laughton would be happy, productive, at one with himself, because deeply imbedded in his temperament was an agitating agent which drove him, like Lear, into the storm at his own centre. In the words of Elsa Lanchester:

> With the death of King Lear, Shakespeare not only knew life, but also the welcoming of death. It is almost as if such a scene as the death of Lear was written from the other side of the grave when Kent says, 'Vex not his ghost, O let him pass, he hates him that would upon the wrack of this tough world stretch him out longer.' If there is such a thing as heavenly music, it makes itself felt at this point. Charles' performance made its power felt at this moment.

Your sympathy reached back and back for his King Lear. I must mark this moment well, for looking back on Charles' life I am forced to feel the relief at the end of his self-made burden.

Laughton was a highly intelligent man; he was also a greatly gifted actor. In a sense, however, these attributes are irrelevant to the central fact about him: his great, if, to use the Shakespearean word, vexed, spirit. His progress through acting was an attempt to find a channel for that great spirit. It reached its culmination in the play that was the mirror of its performer's life; after it, he had little time. His last two years were spent in the shadow of death, while the spirit ebbed.

Last Work

The season at Stratford ended with the last performance of *Lear*. The traditional curtain speech was made by Laurence Olivier. In the course of it, he thanked 'our American visitors, Mr Robeson and Mr Laughton'. This observation, which distressed Laughton inordinately, though it was, of course, technically correct, symbolised his non-assimilation into the company. One of the younger actors observed that Laughton was too self-absorbed, too beleaguered by his own problems, really to connect with the company, despite individual connections (with Roy Dotrice and his family, for example). Olivier, fully in command of his body and his craft, had taken the trouble to memorise the names of the whole company, and found an approach to everyone; this was quite beyond Laughton, who, however, according to Blakemore, was 'very, very egalitarian,' and loathed hierarchies and formal etiquette. He did not, though, lead from the front: we're all in this together, was his feeling, all struggling with the many-headed hydra that was the play.

Peter Hall, though, excited by his contact with Laughton, had asked him back to play Falstaff (the part he had told Agate he'd never play because he'd had to deal with 'too many like that in the hotel') and there was an informal agreement that he would return in 1962, for what became *The Wars of the Roses*. It's a beguiling prospect; but even had he lived, one feels he might have found a way out of it.

Immediately after *Lear*, there was money to be made. *Under Ten Flags* was the way to make it: $100,000 of Dino de Laurentiis' money for an inexplicably dreadful piece of multi-lingual nonsense about the war, with Laughton as a testy admiral, again. (*Stand By For Action* had been the previous incarnation of this performance – but at least there was a war on, that time.) In early 1960, he made a Holocaust drama, *In the Presence of Mine Enemies*, for television, in which he played a rabbi trying to keep alive: he read from the Bible, of course, but there is little else about the role that could have attracted him. His accent (very good when it's good) wavers, and he plays a great deal of the part from under half-closed eyelids, a sure sign with him that he's uncomfortable, as well he might have been: it went out live. 'The under-rehearsed, vast, tragic, virtuoso part of a rabbi was not in his range, mentally or physically. Charles would need at least six months to touch a work like that.' The television age (as he had discovered by a glance at the Stratford sky-line) was upon us, which meant, during his lifetime and beyond, skimped rehearsals and the terrifying ordeal of instant transmission. His performance is muted to the point of catatonia, but when, as occasionally happens, he feels confident enough to let go, the scope and grandeur of his talent suddenly reveals itself, and the other, highly competent, actors (like Arthur Kennedy, for example), look pretty small. The young Nazi officer in love with the rabbi's daughter is played by Robert Redford (his biggest part to date), and the comparison in the two actors' styles is instructive. Redford is impeccably 'truthful': he follows all the Method prescriptions, his action is clear, his inner life ticking nicely over. Laughton, meanwhile, appears to be asleep for most of their scenes together. Then he talks of the dignity of his people, and of the superiority of love to hate, and a huge ocean of feeling is released, and the whole absurd farrago suddenly matters, because he becomes the voice of his tribe, and love's advocate. Redford (who is by no means unskilful in the role) seems, at these moments, to be made of cardboard.

The strain of the whole thing took a heavy toll: shortly after finishing it, Charles had a heart-attack, which was traced to a diseased gall-bladder, for which he was operated on later in 1960. On his recovery, or, strictly speaking, slightly before, he started work on what was to be one of his presents to Elsa Lanchester for her help on *King Lear* – he would devise and direct a one-woman show for her. (The other present was a Lincoln convertible.) He took the show very seriously, and shaped and refined it with the same sense of detail and form he'd brought to all the other shows he'd created. As she wrote: '*Elsa Lanchester – Herself* had a good, solid continuity to it, like a successful conversation, and Charles really was the one who did it. I know I couldn't have tied it all together as he did . . . after almost every single show, people came round and embraced me as if I were an old friend. They really thought they knew me. They'd never met me, they were strangers, but such was the nature of the show that Charles made for me that I was *theirs*. The title that Charles gave the show was good. *Elsa Lanchester – Herself*.' His programme credit read 'Censored by Charles Laughton.' The show was a great hit in New York, and Elsa Lanchester continued playing it for the rest of her performing life. A year later, when Laughton was again in hospital, she filled in the dates that he'd been forced to cancel, and, quickly reviving the show, she and her pianist Ray Henderson decided to drop the third partner, Don Dollarhide, and rework the material to accommodate the change. This enraged Laughton, who, from his sickbed forbade the changes. 'You must not do that! The show is made for three.' 'I suppose,' wrote Lanchester, 'he did not want to change the mathematics of his production for me. Charles created with precision, like making a watch. Every show he did was precision made. As my show was – after all, Charles had created it.' They did, nevertheless, play it as a two-hander; but Charles never saw it. It was all too late by then.

Earlier, in the previous year, he had made several television appearances on various shows, reading the Bible or telling stories. So powerful was his image as The Reader that Ed Sullivan, on one show, had said to him, 'I bet you could read anything and make it sound great,' and Laughton had read out a national insurance form, and proved his host right. On another occasion, he even deputed for Sullivan. As it happens, this was a historic programme: Elvis Presley's first appearance on television. It shows, almost diagramatically, the degree to which Laughton belonged to the old world which Presley and his contemporaries were on the edge of sweeping away. Laughton is charming, in the manner of an accomplished after-dinner speaker: rather long-winded and self-conscious, telling lame jokes, pretending to lack culture (mentions the Budapest Quartet playing Brahms, and makes a philistine face, as if to say: anyone who enjoys chamber music is a bore, a snob and a liar) and is terribly coy, sexually. He introduces a couple of variety acts and someone singing a ballad, quotes a poem himself (Keats, but he makes it sound very steamy) and then tells us that we're going over to Las Vegas, where Elvis Presley is waiting to talk to us. His manner is pleasantly condescending. The moment Presley hits the screen, the entire world of *Saturday Evening Post* niceness and seasoned naughtiness is swept away and – to the tune of uncontrolled squealing from little girls in the audience – we are in the presence of a sexuality so naked it brings a blush to the cheeks. Presley is gauche, casual, rather high, in fact; he seems about to burst out of his clothes. His eyes, his mouth, his whole physical manner suggests recent, or imminent, sexual gratification. His little spiel to the camera is accompanied by a simmering hysteria from the young female audience, which with a thrust of his hips, or a pout, or a wicked wink, he can bring instantly to the boil. When we return to the New York studio, Laughton looks as if he might be going to faint; instead he laughs nervously. Presley has just indicated, as loud and clear as if he's held up a placard with the words printed on it, *fucking is great*. However agreeably Laughton has been discharging his duties on the show, after Presley he can only look shifty. However out of step with society he might have been, sexually, he had spent his whole life trying to give every appearance of not being so. His life had been defined by his world's view of sex. The sexual Bastille was about to be stormed; he, a prisoner inside it, was more frightened of the liberating mob than of his own gaolers. He suddenly, on this *Ed Sullivan Show*, looks like the Victorian he always, essentially, was.

There were two more television acting performances: in an episode of *Wagon Train*, and an episode of *Checkmate*, which had the justifying perk of taking him to Japan, whose art Charles had so profoundly embraced. He did a further reading tour of the midwest, and then Otto Preminger approached him to play the sly Southern Senator Seab Cooley in his film of *Advise and Consent*, the blockbuster in which Allen Drury 'takes the lid off Washington'. The rôle, one of the best in the film, had a special point of interest for Laughton: the character is strongly homophobic. Once more he would offer a portrait of the oppressor by the oppressed. Happily, this, his last performance, is one of his most satisfying. He worked very hard, despite illness, and flung himself into learning the accent (he based it on that of Senator Stennis, whom he watched for some weeks, eventually persuading him to record the whole part into a tape-recorder). His physical weakness he used to characterise Cooley, who has the appearance in the film of a lazy cat nonchalantly playing with a trapped bird. The physical sleepiness of the performance is brilliantly contradicted by its great mental alertness, and the climactic speech before the senate, entirely shot in one take, is as fine a tirade as he ever played. With his baggy white suit and black velvet hat he creates a memorable vision of reactionary charm. Preminger loved him, and he loved Preminger, which is not at all what might have been expected. 'I thought Laughton would not need or want direction from me. Instead he asked for it, and paid close attention to my suggestions . . . I learned a great deal from him.' For all his tantrums, mainly directed at actors of limited gifts (whom he had cast!), Preminger was no von Sternberg: he had run one of Reinhardt's theatres in Vienna before the war, he had been a stage director and an actor himself. He would not have failed to perceive that Laughton was the real thing.

From Laughton's point of view, it may be that his physical condition concentrated his mind wonderfully; he had neither time nor energy to spare for conflict.

Preminger's film, though replete with good performances (Franchot Tone, Walter Pidgeon, Gene Tierney), is ponderous and overblown; Laughton, in his handful of scenes, seems to dominate it. His reviews were enthusiastic, and even a little surprised. It had been a long time since Laughton had hit the nail on the head; when he did, there were few to compare with him.

At the beginning of 1962, though far from well, he undertook another reading tour; at Flint, Michigan, he fell in his bath, and broke his shoulder. It proved to be cancer; he never really recovered. Billy Wilder, late in 1961, had asked him to play Moustache in *Irma La Douce*, which he was planning for the following year. All through Charles' last illness he clung on to the hope that he might yet do so; thus it was that when, on 15 December 1962, he died, he was sporting a luxuriant white moustache.

Coda

Like King Lear's, Laughton's death came from a long way off; and when it came, it was terrible. His health had stood up remarkably well to the demands he made of it. His back was a more or less continuous source of trouble, which may have had something to do with his wartime experience (the poison gas had given him severe hives) and of course, he was vastly too heavy for his size, which can create unnatural strain on the spine. Of his fatness, he wrote: 'I used to say I was fat because there was something wrong with my pituitary gland. A lot of people do that sort of thing but it is always because we eat too much – I don't know why I eat too much. I was told the other day it was because

I must have some deep, basic unhappiness and that I ought to go to a psychoanalyst to find out what it is. But I'm not going to a psychoanalyst. I am not that much interested in myself. I'll go on a diet instead – sometime *next month*!' Although this passage is full of the disingenuousness which characterises his public persona, it is true that Laughton did not seem to want to know about the causes of his behaviour, and, far from trying to counteract any trait which seemed to him unpleasant or regrettable, he seemed to go further and deeper into it. There had been occasions in the past where a part demanded that he should lose weight, and he had been able to do so; but had immediately returned to his comforting padding. He ate hugely and indiscriminately, being as happy with an overflowing plate of corned beef and hash as with the *plus haute* of *haute cuisine*. He would eat at any and all times, though he never drank before five in the afternoon. Then he would consume Martinis at a fairly steady rate. He hated drunks, but his consumption of alcohol was not insignificant.

This way of life took its toll on the gall-bladder, which then provoked his heart-attack. He recovered well enough from that, but was then obliged to have two operations for the infected organ. And to undergo that he had to lose a great deal of weight, which he did. The operations were painful: 'I got an infected wound and had to be cut open a couple of times – without benefit of anaesthetic . . . your crucified son-in-law with a gash in his side,' wrote Charles to Elsa's mother. He barely had the strength to see the first preview of *Elsa Lanchester – Herself*; shortly afterwards, he seemed to undergo some kind of a nervous breakdown threatening to kill himself with pills, or throw himself out of the window. 'I have been deeply disturbed these last months. I have never been sick, and found it hard to conceal from you my stupid state of mind,' he wrote to his agent and friend, Taft Schreiber. Evidently he received a vivid intimation of death. He recovered, however, sufficiently to go to Japan and Hong Kong for *Checkmate*, and to do a reading tour of the South. His health began to concern him again during the filming of *Advise and Consent*, but he flogged himself on. At the beginning of 1962, he had a fall in his bath right at the beginning of yet another reading tour, and in reality, he never got up again. There followed eleven months of increasing agony for Laughton and those who looked on, while the cancer of the bone, initially stemming from the kidney, made its fatal way round his body. At first, the surgeons believed they had contained it by excising a piece of infected bone; but they were wrong. It continued relentlessly, colonising more and more of him. For some months he stayed in the St Moritz hotel in New York, near the hospital; then he was brought back to California, where, in the Cancer Center, he received cobalt treatment. By now he was paralysed below the waist, so he had a spine operation that restored the feeling in his limbs; but he was never able to walk on his own again. His weight fell to 90 lbs – under seven stone. He had to be turned over every half hour; but every movement was excruciating for him. Wonder drug after wonder drug was tried on him; nothing availed. Finally, he slipped away, after weeks of unconsciousness.

It is the usual terrible tale; but it was rendered especially terrible by the power of his actor's imagination. Everything – the pain, the fear, the hope – was multiplied by a thousand. He screamed with agony, begging the nurses to give him his drugs before they were due – 'Charles had shots every two or three hours, but he always wanted more. It was always a race between pain and drugs.' As the drugs swamped his system he became prey to hallucinations – about witchcraft, for example. 'He believed,' wrote Christopher Isherwood, 'the doctor was practising witchcraft and was trying to get control of his mind. 'Of course,' said Charles, 'he can only have it for very short periods.' And I realised that Charles was mixing up this witchcraft fantasy with show business and this became even more evident when he asked me, 'How much do you think I'd be paid as a witch?' 'A great deal,' I told him, and this seemed to please him.' The cobalt treatment room, which he dreaded, released much less pleasing images. He thought that the device used in the treatment was a secret camera and that he was being filmed in the nude. He screamed and wept and protested. A dream he had deeply disturbed him: that Orson Welles and Elsa were watching him perform on stage. They'd told him that they were running away together. As he performed, his bowels gave way, and in front of the audience he shat himself.

Later, he became convinced that *Advise and Consent* had won the best film award at Cannes, and that he would be going to France. To sustain this notion, Lanchester bought new clothes and even had a smallpox vaccination; but by then it was forgotten. And he was certain that he'd be able to play Moustache in *Irma la Douce*. 'Don't listen to whatever they tell you, it's not true. I'll prove it – come and see me at my house,' he said to Billy Wilder. 'I went that lunchtime . . . he had had his male nurse dress him up, comb his hair, shave him, maybe even put a little make-up on him, and he was sitting in a chair by the swimming-pool. He said, 'Now look at me. Do I look like someone that's going to die?' And he got himself out of the chair and he walked round the pool. He must have been in tremendous pain, but he just wanted to say to me, 'Wait'. This was one of the finest performances, I tell you. I was very touched.'

Burgess Meredith visited him regularly, often simply sitting and holding his hand; one day Laughton unexpectedly looked up, and said, with the utmost lucidity: 'Buzzy, I don't think the director knows what he's doing, do you? Do you think I can get out of this picture?' 'No, Charlie,' Meredith replied, 'the director's really not up to his job. You're too big for him.'

When she was told of the terminal nature of Charles' illness, Elsa Lanchester wrote, 'I knew that I was being freed of something, I was a kind of Ariel who was being freed from Prospero.' Elsewhere she writes: 'Charles often associated me with Cordelia – I would speak my mind, as Cordelia did, to the point of hurting.' By the end of his life, their relationship would appear to have declined to less classical models: more like something invented by, say, August Strindberg, or Edward Albee. Charles' conduct as a patient over such a hideously long period of time can have done nothing to modify the underlying tension. Bruce Zortman, Laughton's secretary and amanuensis, who was around all through the illness, reports a resentment bordering on physical violence on Elsa's part – she would prod and shake his diseased bones if he vexed her. But the strain on her mind and her health can scarcely be underestimated. She gave up her life for his last year, but this sacrifice was taken for granted. 'I thought he might occasionally thank me for something I'd done – even for the fish I'd cooked for him. Maybe he was remembering all the resentments he had for me.' She had her resentments, too. 'Inside I really hated Charles for it,' she wrote of a typical incident between them, 'and I would nurse that deep hatred all through the years.' The incident is a sharp insight into the nature of the violence they did to each other: she had bought a mask that Charles had also seen but not liked – 'the greenish head had an erotic expression so powerful that I think Charles was actually frightened of it. It was too masculine, too strong for him. But he said to me: "That's your taste. You like it, all right, that's fine. You should have something you like." As it happens,' Lanchester continues, 'of all the works of art in their house, this was the one visitors were mesmerised by. Charles never explained to them that I had picked it out, that it was mine. Nothing was said.' And then, one day, without telling her, Laughton sold it. 'I only said, "Oh dear." Charles then apologised. "I know I shouldn't have done it." Nothing much more was said about it. But inside, I really hated Charles . . .'

'How they tormented each other!' said Don Bachardy who knew them, at one remove, through Christopher Isherwood, and who preferred to keep it at one remove, 'but they were perfectly innocent that this is what they were doing.' They had become locked into a cycle of mutual cruelty which was synonymous with being alive. 'You must not upset me ever again,' said Laughton triumphantly, after his heart attack, 'it's the old ticker.' He evidently felt that he had scored a very high match point. He resented her apparent licence to criticize him, which, with the souring of their relations, she used indiscriminately and with the accuracy bred of a lifetime's close observation. She was like the little bird who lives on the hippopotamus, except that instead of ridding him of insects, she was now drawing blood. Her instinct to protect him had become perverted into aggression; but the starting point was, without question, love.

They were united by certain common tastes, and by common requirements; they were divided by talent, temperament and sexual inclination. Lanchester was a lightweight, almost a flyweight, as a performer: 'I suppose you might call what I do vaudeville,' she wrote of herself, 'making a joke, especially impromptu, and getting a big laugh for it, is just plain heaven.' Once she started to work at the Turnabout Theatre in Los Angeles, and more particularly when she had *Elsa Lanchester – Herself*, she returned to the kind of material in which she was pre-eminent; it was a tiny kingdom of which she was queen, but it was all her own – as a sort of off-colour Joyce Grenfell, or a Bea Lillie without the genius. In between her days at the Cave of Harmony and this later incarnation, came the years as 'Mrs Charles Laughton,' in which she was made by Hollywood, and indeed, by Pommer and by Korda, to feel out of her husband's league. It is not quite clear to what extent Laughton tried to promote her, but the very fact that she would need 'promotion' must have been unbearable to her. She later expressed her conviction that she and Charles had been driven apart by 'professional separaters,' and it is significant that most of the people on the list are producers. Even when Charles devised and directed her show, there seemed to be some deep-seated professional tension between them: he chose the occasion of her first touring date for *Elsa Lanchester – Herself* to attempt to kill himself. 'Filled with tension and hostility and determined to break through his fit of depression, I slapped his face. Charles became silent and said simply, 'Thank you' . . . I think I said, 'You are trying to kill my show. You want to destroy it and me. How can I possibly stand on that stage and be light and cheerful as if nothing had happened!' Charles said something like 'Yes . . . maybe . . . I'm sorry.' Even on the first preview itself, there had been a complicated emotional atmosphere: 'The audience was very enthusiastic, and I took a number of curtain calls. Charles, out front, suddenly leapt from his seat and ran to the back of the auditorium and pounded on the locked door, trying to get in backstage. Finally someone let him in and Charles rushed through the stage curtains to take a bow – but by this time the audience had left . . . now that he saw how successful our show would be, he impulsively wanted recognition for it.'

Elsa Lanchester wrote a book, very vividly. Laughton never did. (He started to dictate his autobiography to Bruce Zortman: the notes for it – considerably more of them than Lanchester implies – are simply a series of cryptic glimpses of his early life.) The Lanchester Version is the official one. She doesn't paint herself in angelic terms, but her every action is justified and annotated; Charles' remain bare, without benefit of advocate.

She makes very clear, however, that there was a vast temperamental gap between them, although their differences could be said to be complementary: he with his limitless capacity for being hurt, she with her strange gift (noted from her earliest days) for the apt barb. He with his huge emotional response, for and against; she, as her cousin in a memorable burst of familial invective described her, 'like the frost-bitten Lanchesters of whom you are a fit scion'; he evasive, she blunt to a fault; he dreading thunderstorms, she loving them; his epic canvas, her miniature frame. To begin with, these differences were refreshing; with time they became a source of almost continuous aggravation on both sides, though it must be said in Elsa's defence that she looked after him when he was dying, and it is inconceivable that he would have done the same for her. Despite several threats of divorce (originating with him, and swiftly scotched by her) there was never any serious prospect of their breaking up.

Of course the relationship was useful to both of them; Charles was particularly anxious that they should be seen to be together. When he discovered that by chance they were in New York at the same time, he with *Don Juan in Hell* and staying at the Plaza, she just returned from a European tour, in a room at the Algonquin, he told her, 'Look, Elsa, for God's sake, get in a cab and come here at once! This situation must not get out to the press. We'll have to go out and be seen everywhere together.' She also functioned as a kind of running joke in his interviews – a kind of she-who-must-be-obeyed figure, with a no-but-seriously implication that they led a life of hum-drum domesticity.

Which, of course, could hardly have been further from the truth.

Early in 1930, they had married. It was not an event of any great significance, insofar as they had been living together, in the modern manner, for over two years. The wedding took place in a registry office, unobserved by the pressmen who had been sleeping on their doorstep in anticipation of the event (*such* was their fame). Elsa attributes the marriage to Charles' desire to please his ever-formidable mother. (Indeed, the elder Mrs Laughton and Charles' delicate youngest brother Frank accompanied them on their honeymoon. 'My friends thought it was hilarious.') Elsa implies that the further seal of respectability was not entirely unwelcome to Charles, too. They were still living in digs-like accommodation in Soho. Their style remained semi-Bohemian.

They were spoken of and written of very much as 'a couple' – a famous eccentric match. Ethel Mannin interviewed them jointly under the heading 'Portrait of a Strange Pair.' Her 'Impression' conveys a certain unease in their company which was a common response.

'We are both naturally restrained,' he said, 'because we're both self-conscious knowing that you've come to see us specially to write about us. How could you expect us to be anything else?' I could only reply that if their present exuberance was to be regarded as restraint, then normally, when they are alone, a sort of riot must take place . . . The last I saw of this strange pair was when they stood with their arms about each other . . . Elsa's tiny face . . . and Laughton's pale puffy face, pressed 'cheek to cheek', saying good-bye and bidding me come to see them. 'In our untidy little flat.' 'It's only a *little* flat, but *we're* fond of it!' As I emerged, I thought of some of the 'impossible' things Elsa had said, and of Laughton's irrepressible bursts of acting, and the story of the young woman who sat at the piano 'in 'er nood' came into my head, and the verdict on that young woman seemed somehow to apply to the odd pair I had left. 'No, not mad, my dear, but *strainge*, I grant yew . . .'

They seem to have been performing their relationship. There can be no doubt that there was a real bond between them, a magnetic pull, which endured for over thirty years, but its exact nature, as so often, is hard to pin down. Neither socially, sexually, intellectually, or temperamentally did they seem to have any affinity: only a mutual – but quite different – oddity seems to have brought them together; that, and loneliness. It's almost as if they had been yoked together by fate, and somehow made the most of it – sometimes for better, sometimes for worse. They both found the existence of the other useful, not merely as a cover for whatever other activities, but as a public point of reference: 'I asked Elsa if I could,' he'd say, while she'd joke about his scruffiness: to present themselves as 'a husband and wife' and thus give their audience something to hang on to. To normalise themselves.

To what extent during these early years they were trying to pretend to themselves that they were well matched is hard to gauge. We only have Elsa's evidence. But even that seems to point towards a certain strain of unreality. She describes his exaggerated resentment of her going off for an early film-call: and of him suddenly bursting into her dressing-room during the run of a play, expecting to find the romantic lead, Derrick de Marne, in there with her: 'this dramatic suspicious entrance was more like cheap melodrama than flattering.'

Intellectually, they were poles apart. Elsa with her quick, bright brain, formed by the combative political encounters of her parents, sharpened by her experience in revue, reducing things to size and piercing pomposity with her sharp little pins – Charles, with his much less nimble wits, constantly circling round and round ideas, approaching them clumsily, perhaps, becoming ponderous and pretentious, but always searching ('one feels,' reported Ethel Mannin, 'the galvanic working of his mind the whole time, so that being with him is rather like being all the time in the engine-room with all the engines running'). Her chief means of communication was raillery: tremendous fun if you were sure of yourself and in the mood, but apt to make you feel put down, sent up, and finally pissed-off, if you weren't. She was, according to her friends of the period, 'the quickest, wittiest, most mercurial *bitch* you could ever hope to meet. She couldn't help herself. The darts just flew out of her mouth.'

It is hard to think of a worse companion for the awkward, self-conscious, self-doubting, boy-man that Laughton was. He was capable of giving as good as he got, no mistake, and savage blows may well have issued from the mess that was boiling and bubbling within.

Some sexual unsatisfactoriness was noticed by others, too. 'I assumed that they weren't very sexually involved,' said Benita Armstrong, Elsa's best friend of the period, 'from the way they never left each other alone in public. They were always *mauling* each other.' The gimlet eye of Miss Mannin dwelt on this aspect of things, as well. 'Laughton laughed and said he wished someone would say of him that he had sex appeal . . . then he sprang up and embraced Elsa declaring

that she was the only woman who had found any sex-appeal in him
. . . Elsa reassured him, tenderly; she said that the women were 'mad
about him' in *The Silver Tassie*, and he seemed comforted.'

Over that between-shows supper at the Perroquet, Emlyn Williams
had smiled at Charles' 'noisy jokes, some of them slanted towards sex,
an area in which I sensed complexity.'

Not so Elsa, apparently.

Once the sexual bomb had fallen, the pattern for their lives was
established – the marriage would continue, but they would go their
separate ways. This pattern was never articulated by either partner,
but, once the marriage had survived the initial impact, it was no doubt
inevitable. It was not, however, quite as simple as that; it rarely is.
The shock to Elsa must have been enormous: she ceased, as she says,
to trust Charles from that moment because she had been deceived.
She no longer wanted a child by him, either. Their sexual relations
quickly cooled. It looks as if the brittle young woman that she was
when she married him had rather unexpectedly found herself falling
in love with him, only to be made brittle all over again. It is to be
doubted whether his emotional centre was ever really heterosexually
oriented (there is no evidence whatever of any other liaison with a
woman, before or after Elsa) but he did deeply want to have children.
In later years he reproached her with her refusal to have any, and
formed a number of strong friendships with various young actresses:
Maureen O'Hara, Deanna Durbin, Margaret O'Brien, Maureen
O'Sullivan – father–daughter relationships. This longing of his may
have contributed yet another layer to the opaque texture of his Lear;
and Elsa failing Charles as a mother, and Charles failing Elsa as a lover
contributed a layer to the opaque texture of their life together, too.

Immediately after Charles' confession to her of his homosexual self,
and just before rehearsals for *Payment Deferred* started, Jeffrey Dell,
the play's adaptor, and his wife took Charles away with them for a
brief holiday in Salzburg. Elsa refused to join them, hating the
pretence of a second honeymoon, as she put it. Laughton wrote her a
miserable letter on the back of his hotel bill. 'Elsa my beloved' it
starts, and continues 'Through these last two days when we have
arrived at our hotel in the evening, in the mornings, and in fact at all
times when I have been alone, the refrain has been going through my
head: "She's married a bugger, she's married to a bugger, she's
married to a bugger," and then you saying to me, "and to think this
has happened to me," as you did once. And I know Elsa what matters
most in life to me is to face it with you. I don't care and I know now I

never will care so much as I did about doing but only about being . . .
our parting at Victoria was a very sad one this time darling, wasn't it?
We seemed to be reaching out to each other all the time inside. Ever
since I left you the side that belongs to you has been sad and listless.'

The externalisation of their separate sexual development did not
occur till the beginning of the forties, theirs and the century's. There
may have been sexual encounters for Laughton before then, but if so,
they must have been fleeting: his work schedule in the thirties was
almost unimaginably packed. He began to discover the sexual possibilities of his chauffeurs and masseurs and batmen, and then, it
would appear, when he started the reading tours, he became insatiable, a phenomenon which often overcomes men who feel cheated of
their sexual youth. 'Charles was aggressive as a homosexual . . . he
made it more difficult for himself, too, because he wasn't content to
have one, he'd have a ménage of them,' Paul Gregory told Barry
Norman. 'Some of them would end up in prison and you'd get calls
from wardens and letters threatening him . . . they were the dregs,
low class kind of people . . . he'd got this Higgins complex. They'd
come and go. I didn't have too much to do with all that except to write
the cheques for him and hide them from Elsa and his accountants.'
Nothing Paul Gregory says should be accepted without corroborative
evidence, but in this case there is plenty to suggest that Laughton
required frequent refutation of his sense of undesirability. At the
same time the 'Higgins complex' led him to form different kinds of
relationships, often with young men who were bi-sexual and whom he
tried to teach; this was his ideal relationship. His sense of physical
inferiority often led him into somewhat masochistic connections,
socially at any rate. Elsa describes one such set-up: 'While Charles was
performing at Town Hall, I went out and returned later to the hotel to
wait for him. There were full ashtrays in the room and too many
glasses from earlier in the day, so I started to clean up, to put them all
on a tray. As I was doing this, Charles marched into the room with his
road man. Charles was carrying a load of heavy books, and also his
overcoat. The road man, arms empty, was munching on a snack. I
said to the young man, 'Don't you ever carry the books when Charles
is tired?' . . . He said, 'No', quite simply . . . I felt quite angry. I
stood there with a tray in my hands and said to the young man, 'You
should be doing this.' He looked up at me and answered, 'I don't see
why.' So I threw the trayful of glasses and ashtrays right into his
stomach.'

But from the beginning of the forties, there had, too, been a succession of warmer and more reciprocal relationships, young men who thread shadowily through Lanchester's and Higham's pages under a variety of coy pseudonyms, like heroes of a Mills and Boon romance: David Higham and Bruce Ashe and Peter Jones. They were, according to Elsa, as handsome and as masculine and as teachable as could be. They came and they went, some of them staying on to become friends, others getting married and going away for good. There were the usual turmoils, rows, reconciliations, painful break-ups, trial separations, all the ordinary dramas, in other words, of human love, but with the complication that as far as Charles was concerned, it must all remain secret. He and Elsa had a little house in Palos Verdes, to which he would take his lovers. 'As the years went by,' wrote Lanchester, 'I suppose I just came to accept these friends as part of my life with Charles. I worried about him, and I was always glad if and when Charles found a man he was really fond of and who liked him . . . Perhaps,' she adds, 'it was unkind of me not to show disapproval. My acceptance may have been more cruel, in a way, and made Charles feel even more guilty about it all. He was a moral man . . . it made me very sad that Charles should have to feel so guilty about it; that he seemed to need to be so secretive, all the while still wanting to be found out.'

It was Charles' drama, his dark, tragic self, his secret. He loved to tell his secret, and was always amazed and hurt when the recipient of the revelation was unsurprised or unshocked. He would announce (as he did to Robert Mitchum, for example, or Terry Sanders, and even, as far back as 1938, to Larry Adler) that he had 'a strong streak of homosexuality in his make-up'. That was the phrase. It seems that he wanted to claim a certain special status for himself, as if to say, 'life isn't easy for me, you know.' It may have been the same with his now almost legendary sense of his own ugliness. Lanchester wonders whether his constant references to his physical unattractiveness (the most amusing was 'I look like a departing pachyderm') weren't cries for help, whether he didn't actually want to be contradicted. Well, yes, no doubt; but in a way his ugliness was useful to him, too. Don Bachardy expressed it acutely: 'It was a conscious decision of Charles' to be ugly. He found that he could handle himself better as an ugly man. He didn't have to compete for certain things, he could demand certain allowances to be made . . . Charles constantly sought excuses, indulgence: 'This is so *hard* for me.' He wanted approval, encourage-ment.' For someone genuinely ashamed of his own appearance, he made remarkable flaunt of it, tearing off his clothes – *all* his clothes –

at the slightest opportunity, and plunging into his pool, there to float in the manner described by Peter Ustinov, 'like a topsy-turvy iceberg'. People who are truly disgusted with their appearance tend to be crippled by it; for Laughton his ugliness was a way of engaging his whole being with another at the earliest possible opportunity. His ugliness, one might say, was a technique, rather than a condition.

And, in truth, few people found him ugly. Many women have gone on record (Belita, for example) as finding him positively attractive. His face was alive with expression and character. There is no denying that he was fat, and if that was an obstacle for you, you wouldn't be attracted to Laughton. For a homosexual man, it can be a terrible disadvantage not to conform to the prototypes of desirability, but Laughton pre-dated the dubious dawn of gay consumerism. To be fat was not yet 'the cardinal sin of the gay world,' as a witty character in the film *Passing Glances* puts it. He was not undesired; and if there was something frantic about his lusts, that is the legacy of the early disappointments. Making up for missed opportunities is rarely an attractive spectacle, gay or straight, ugly or handsome, but it is one of the commoner manifestations of human unhappiness. What is important is that he never ceased to love, or to try to love; and in love he was tender and giving.

The truth about Laughton and his body is not that he thought he was ugly, but that he knew he wasn't beautiful. *That* was the worm in the bud, the source of his life-long inconsolability. To be attractive was not enough: it must be Beauty. His aesthetic sense was hyper-developed; beauty in nature or in art hit him square in the solar plexus; and he failed his own standards. He was that tragic figure, a disappointed narcissist. He could never forgive the face that stared back at him from the mirror for not adding to the world's store of beauty.

And so he tried to acquire beauty, to surround himself with it, to let it possess him. 'Some people buy paintings, they say, because they have a love for them,' wrote Lanchester, 'but Charles really lived on them. It was not just love, it was a necessity. It was like drinking water or breathing.' In hospital, his only outings were to art galleries: 'Charles would have to be given a shot before the walk, and a nurse would give him a shot at the gallery to get him back.' He must have his beauty. In the same spirit, he would surround himself with young men, feeding off their beauty, hoping that by exposure to it in sufficient quantities, he might catch it, suddenly find himself a member of that exclusive club, the beautiful of the earth. It is a doomed, forlorn hope, especially poignant, perhaps, for a homosexual, because there is direct comparison. In the last couple of years of his life, Laughton and Isherwood (with whom he had become close friends, wanting, as he told Elsa, to be 'with my own kind') were working on a play about Socrates, and had they completed it, and had Charles lived, it might have been his final Testament To Beauty. Charles could not speak the word Beauty without trembling; it is the idea around which his life revolved.

Happily, in the last few years of his life, great beauty entered his existence, in the form of a young man called Terry Jenkins, and the relationship came close to transcending the self-defeating tendency of so much of his emotional life. This was due to the extraordinary goodness and simplicity of nature of the young man, whose open and unquestioning acceptance of Charles began to make it possible for him to accept himself. Terry held up a mirror for Charles in which he saw a new face, one transfigured by love. They had met, propitiously, no doubt, for Laughton, in an art gallery, and the first sexual move was made by the younger man. When they repaired to Laughton's hotel, he simply took all his clothes off. This gesture, Laughton told friends later, had overwhelmed him, the directness and frankness of it. It was a paradigm of the whole of the relationship. Terry Jenkins (a.k.a. the slightly swisher Bruce Ashe in Higham and Peter Jones in Lanchester) was one of that rare breed who is so comfortable within his own sexuality that the terms heterosexual, homosexual and even bi-sexual have no meaning; he was simply someone who communicated best and most easily through sexual means. Laughton made an instant impact on him and he sought to be as closely involved with him as possible. This absence of negotiations must have had a powerful effect on Laughton, a testimony that no amount of words or presents could have equalled. It must have done the thing that Laughton needed more than anything in life: it must have taken him out of himself.

And Terry was longing to learn from Charles. He had not, up to this point, been accustomed to function as a thinking being; Charles appointed himself his tutor, and opened up before his astonished eyes, a world whose existence he had not suspected. 'I had never known such a person in my whole life; in fact, I didn't know such people existed. His mind overpowered me. I found it almost impossible to grasp the mind within him. Being with Charles . . . was better than attending the best liberal university in the world.' Elsa and others in Charles' immediate circle were slightly impatient that he would spend so much time (and money!) on such an ordinary boy. His ordinariness was the whole point. Even his beauty was not exotic or conspicuous: he was perfectly formed, symmetrical, open – a lovely golden boy, his looks an exact counterpart of the straightforward geniality within. There was no subtext, no ulteriority to Terry; and with him, Charles relaxed some of the mass of defences and complexities that both protected and defeated him. Through Terry's intellectual and emotional innocence, Charles regained some of his own. Elsa Lanchester marked his child-like quality. 'He was possessed of the same wonder-struck quality Charles had.' It was Terry and Charles who could say, like Lear to Cordelia, 'We two alone will sing like two birds i'the cage' – not, as she hoped, Elsa and Charles.

Once, only once, according to Terry Jenkins, there was a terrible explosion from Charles, and that was, significantly enough, when Charles decided to show Terry what it really meant to be an actor. Terry was by profession a photographic model, he had aspirations as an actor, and Charles and he had talked about acting as they sat round the pool. Then one day, unannounced, Charles suggested they work on a scene from *Witness for the Prosecution* – the scene in which Tyrone Power breaks down in the dock. They worked on the scene for five hours. 'And I just threw the script down on the floor. I said no, I don't want to do it, I don't want to do it. He said 'Now you've got exactly the feeling you want! Now do, do it.' 'No,' I said, 'I don't want to do it.' And the more I screamed I don't want to do it, the more he screamed at me, Do it! Do it! And of course I did it, and it was absolutely perfect . . . it was the only one time I've ever hated Charles, that day.' He encouraged Terry in his acting career at all times, but only once did Charles try to let him know what a serious thing it was to be an actor. For the rest he preferred that they should sing like birds i'the cage.

'And he and I went to Japan, and it was like two children exploring the world for the first time'. And then they went on a reading tour, which Charles accepted because he wanted to show Terry, who was from a little Bedfordshire village, the deep South of America. And then he was ill, very ill. But 'such was his love for Terry, that he was able to get out of bed and feel well enough to go out on the road again.' Early on the tour was Flint, Michigan, where he fell. Terry was there, and took him to the hospital, and he was with him at the St Moritz, and he was there when they went back to Los Angeles. He was there when Charles, who was haunted from the depth of his terrible conscience by the fear of divine retribution, demanded a test for rectal cancer (he had already anxiously enquired of Terry Sanders whether he thought homosexuals were prone to this complaint); he was there when the results were given to Charles and they were negative, and Charles, more drugged than clear in his mind, had pointed at Terry Jenkins, in front of the nurses and the doctors and said: 'We have touched, but not in our house.' Terry was there, day in and day out, and he flirted with the pretty young Greek nurse, which pleased Charles: 'The fact that she liked Charles' friend showed that his boyfriend was a man, a masculine man, which was very important to him.' Elsa says she was glad that Charles felt strongly for someone, and she found herself buying food that she knew Terry would like. But the bitterness kept breaking in. 'Maybe Charles had some 'how do *you* do?' thoughts for his boyfriends . . . he still liked to light their cigarettes, even if he was standing up, and they were sitting down.' Still: 'It's surprising what you can get used to.'

Terry was not there when Charles died. Christopher Isherwood wrote to him in New York, where he was, that he should stay away, that Charles was in a coma, that things had become messy. He suggested that Terry should stay away from the funeral, too, which he did, and didn't even see Charles' tomb at Forest Lawn for some months. By then, he had married – the Greek nurse with whom he had flirted to Charles' delight. Charles was the bond which somehow kept Terry and his nurse together for just over five years. Charles and Terry had been together for four.

The mess that Isherwood spoke of was nothing more or less than a battle for Charles' soul, conducted over his drugged and etiolated body, with his brothers Tom and Frank ranged on one side, his wife Elsa on the other. The brothers were determined that Charles should return to the church; should die in a state of grace. Tom wrote to John Beary, as 'one of the very few people to whom he has shown his inborn faith,' that he was sure 'that if ever there was a man who had lived his life *"Ad majorem dei gloriam"'* it has been Charlie . . . he has had a strange life, always craving love. I think he is gradually achieving peace. I could only show him how much I cared about his spiritual welfare and when it came to it, I was unable to control my feelings . . . even if Charlie does not receive the consolations of the church as long as he is spiritually reconciled with God, which I know he will be, I shall be satisfied. But if he is received back it will be the greatest joy.' His brother Frank was deputed to ensure that the slightest flicker of interest in God would be instantly gratified. There was a steady stream of priests ('I wish they were more intelligent,' moaned Charles) and it is remarkable that Laughton, in his fevered imaginative state, uttered no recorded remark about either heaven or hell. Elsa was fiercely opposed to him being tricked in his depleted condition into endorsing something he had vehemently denounced all his adult life. She claimed that he was more proud than anything else in his life of having, (just before going into battle) refused communion in the trenches. It is hard to exaggerate the courage and determination of a brain-washed Catholic who rejects his religion. Charles was, if anything, Elsa later admitted, suspiciously boastful of having done so: he made a religion of rejecting religion. The brothers, who well knew his position on the matter, argued that it might still give him consolation to return to the faith, and any consolation was to be seized on. Even the nurses joined in, convinced that the poor barely breathing wraith on the bed needed the ministrations of the church. One evening when Elsa was out, a priest was rushed in, extreme unction was given. 'I think I've joined the gang,' said Charles. He was also under the impression that he had signed away his estate to the Church, and a conference of lawyers and doctors was convened outside his door to establish the likelihood of this, while Charles, from inside the room called out, 'Am I dying? What's the matter? Am I dying?' No signing had taken place; it was another hallucination.

Frank, a gentle, sensitive creature, whose lover, his partner in the Pavilion Hotel, had died of cancer the year before, was sweet and patient with him, and shared a kind of rota with Elsa. Somewhere towards the end, Albert Finney was given a glimpse of 'this Big Man' – 'my first look at death.' Elsa had thought Albert 'sufficiently brilliant' to see 'a Giant going.' 'The top half of his body was twisted on to his left side and his face was pushed into the pillow, but even from that extraordinary angle, one could see that all the flesh had left him . . . somehow, the straggly, messy Wyatt Earp moustache showed that in his mind, when it was lucid, he was going to get up and act again . . .'

He died where he would most have wanted to die, in the school-room of his house, looked down on by his Utrillo, his Dufy and his Matisse. His funeral was shortly afterwards, in Forest Lawn, in a new wing. His brother Frank had negotiated a special cut-price with the cemetery, who were keen to get a 'name' for the first incumbent of the new wing: *pour encourager les autres*. In defiance of Elsa's request that they should not do so, the mournful Unitarian choir sang. 'Death, where is thy sting?' The pall-bearers included Preminger, Isherwood and Jean Renoir; the service culminated in Isherwood's oration, in which he spoke of Charles' *power*, powerful himself, but also 'a vehicle of power, something through which power passed, and was transmitted . . . something was coming through him which was uncontaminated, even by an egotistic kind of personality.' He then read excerpts from *The Tempest*, those lines of Prospero which have such extraordinary resonance at the death of actors.

These our actors
(As I foretold you) were all spirits, and
Are melted into air, into thin air

Prospero's renunciation of his 'art':

this rough magic I here abjure

And finally, the epilogue:

As you from crimes would pardon'd be,
Let your indulgence set me free.

Potent as those lines in that context can never fail to be, their direct relevance to Charles Laughton is limited. *Lear* is the reference, the very line Charles had so feelingly quoted: 'Vex not his ghost, O let him pass, he hates him that would upon the wrack of this tough world stretch him out longer.' Unlike his King Lear, Laughton's end was not 'on a rising graph,' but it was a sublime release.

He had said to Christopher Isherwood that he was appalled at how unprepared he was to die: the only thing that helped him was thinking about some of the Temple Gardens he'd seen in Japan. Something very remarkable happened to Charles Laughton in Japan, something which might have pointed to a new way of being, to a Houdini-like escape from the chains and locks and ropes and gags that constituted 'Charles Laughton.' Terry Jenkins: 'He wanted to live as all people do when they're in love, to live their life all over again with their loved one. He wanted to start all over again. He wanted to go to Japan, because it was a new country that he'd never been to. With one he loved. And he and I went to Japan and it was like two children exploring the world for the first time.' 'I see,' wrote Elsa, 'that Charles when in Japan did as the Japanese did. He felt himself akin to people who searched for and found peace.' Terry:

I remember one day in the gardens of Kyoto, the three, five, and seven stones in the gardens. And he sat for five hours alone and I'd never seen him sit alone before. It was beginning to get sunset then, six or seven in the evening. And he said I just can't take any more. And he didn't talk about what had happened to him during that five hour period. But it was very traumatic to him . . . he had the knowledge, I didn't have the knowledge and together we shared the experience of this knowledge. Me on the receiving end of the knowledge and the giving of what I experienced through Charles' knowledge. And he, for the first time in his life, so much of it was pouring out of him . . . I remember one afternoon, the main shopping street in Tokyo. It was a Saturday afternoon before a national holiday. We were in the taxi, all the women were wearing kimonos and little girls wearing kimonos and he suddenly said stop, I want to, I want to walk. And he'd never been able to walk down a street such as Oxford Street. And together we walked down for an hour, not one person recognised him. He sort of had a half smile on his face, his eyes became almost almond and he said it was like a fantastic massage by humanity. We got to the end. And we sat in the coffee shop and he said I want to do it again, I want to walk back again. And we walked back along the street again. You don't have to look where you're going because so many people are around you, just holding you up. Not pushing you along, you're just being wafted along. And he talked about this for hours and hours.

PERORATION

Some half dozen of Laughton's performances of the thirties are of an originality and an intensity that sets them apart from the work of almost any other actor of the century, however skilled, however truthful, however audacious. The only other actor to whom he can be compared in this area where inner pressure and outer transformation combine to create almost totemic representations of the human condition is Marlon Brando, with whom he shares a number of common features: both 'difficult', both widely imitated, i.e. both synonymous in their age with acting, both held to have become parodies of themselves. The difference is that Laughton found another outlet for the creative pressure that tormented him as an actor; Brando has apparently not.

With these actors it is as if acting transcends the story being told, or the ostensible character being portrayed: it becomes an activity undertaken on behalf of the community to celebrate in a ritual or symbolic way the nature of human life. 'The power of the actor,' writes Michael Goldman in *The Actor's Freedom*, 'may well remind us of his primitive prototypes. He retains something of the strangeness and freedom of a man painted in blood and dressed animal skins howling at the moon, a shaman healing his tribe by allowing himself to be torn apart and reassembled by the spirits who possess his body.' The shaman, according to Michael Harner, 'shows his patients that they are not emotionally and spiritually alone in their struggles against illness and death . . . he shares his special powers and convinces his patients, on a deep level of consciousness, that another human is willing to offer up his own self to help them.' So can the actor. Like the shaman he can make 'a heroic journey'. But for each actor it is a different journey, a different celebration. Laurence Olivier has, like an athlete, celebrated man's triumph over his own flesh, has reshaped, extended and contracted his voice and his body in defiance of any physical limitations nature might try to impose on him. He has made a mockery of nature. Charles Laughton, who thought he *was* a mockery of nature, took a different path.

In the *Psychoanalytical Contributions*, Annie Reich writes about what she calls 'the structure of grotesque-comic sublimation'.

Grotesque is a word that frequently recurs in accounts of Laughton's performances, and, as defined by Frau Reich, it is certainly appropriate. 'The grotesque . . . is characterised by a special form of disguise, that is, by a particular disfigurement and deformation . . . we find exhibition of devaluated parts of the body, of defects, which serves at the same time to unmask rivals. Confession and self-punishment are combined with aggression against others. This combination of aggression and exhibitionism turned simultaneously toward the actor's own body and against a hated rival are typical for all cases of grotesque-comic art.' Her analysis is strikingly applicable to many aspects of Laughton's relationship to acting: 'Probably even acclamation from outside is incapable of preventing anxiety and a deep depression. The forces of the actor's conscience are too strong and therefore he is overwhelmed with anxiety and guilt . . . the grotesque-comic performance is characterised by an extreme sexualisation of the relationship between actor and public. . . Whenever someone is talented in caricature of grotesque-comic acting and the like, a tendency to self-exposure creeps in beside the wish to expose others, and this tendency to exhibit and confess produces the driving force for creation.'

But Frau Reich's analysis, acute though it is, is not the whole story. Laughton's grotesqueness stirs us too deeply for that. Enid Welsford has traced the origins and peculiar resonances of the figure who seems to stand behind so many of Laughton's performances: the Fool, at once damaged and funny, potent and powerless. He is, above all, *different*. 'The fool,' writes William Willeford, 'has antecedents and relatives among a wide range of people who in various ways violate the human image and who come to a *modus vivendi* with society by making a show of that violation.' Bligh, Barrett, Nero, are all outsiders, oddities; they are all imbued with the feeling that Laughton, according to Elsa Lanchester, had about himself: that he didn't really belong to the human race. Like the Fool, he came to terms with his strangeness by displaying it, and the result was the same: 'Grotesques have both positive and negative powers, they are hideously attractive; they should be approached and avoided, abused and placated.' He disturbed and appealed in equal measure.

In order to create what he did, he cultivated this feeling in himself. He went deeper and deeper into it, forcing more and more grit into the oyster, to produce bigger and bigger pearls. As long as he could bear it, it enabled him to give performances that have the force of the great paintings from which he drew such comfort and inspiration.

'Every actor worth his salt,' Laughton said in an interview, 'must create the character he plays out out of his mind, his perceptions, his experience – otherwise he's not an actor at all. Great acting is like painting. In the great masters of fine art one can see and recognise the small gesture of a finger, the turn of a head, the vitriolic stare, the glazed eye, the pompous mouth, the back bending under a fearful load. In every swerve and stroke of a painter's brush, there is an abundance of life. Great artists reveal the god in man; and every character an actor plays must be this sort of creation. Not imitation – that is merely caricature – and any fool can be a mimic! But creation is a secret. The better – the truer – the creation, the more it will resemble a great painter's immortal work.'

APPENDICES

CHARLES LAUGHTON

Reading in Alaska

I am a tourist at heart. I wanted to go to Japan to see the cherry blossoms, the tea ceremony and the geishas, the Japanese gardens, and Mount Fujiyama. And I went to Japan and it wasn't cherry blossom time, and I didn't see a geisha, except clacking along a back street of Kyoto with her attendant holding an oiled paper umbrella over her head in the rain. And the Japanese gardens are not at all as advertised – frail and dainty – but solemn religious exercises in stone and green sculptured bushes, and trees and gravel, which is much better.

The Japanese screens are not pretty-pretty, but grave and comic, and some of them dazzling. I did not get to see Fujiyama, except when we left Tokyo we saw it in the blue distance from the plane, and not as Hokusai or Hiroshige saw it from the ground. And I always wanted to go to Alaska to see the polar bears and penguins and the northern lights.

When I was invited to read in Anchorage and Clear, I quickly accepted, but I saw none of these things – no penguins, there are no penguins in Alaska – no Polar bears, we were not far enough north – and no northern lights, because it was not winter, but light all night long. In summer, the light at night is a pale gentle blue.

One night there was a moon, and the colour of the sky behind the moon was a blue I had not seen before, save in a pretty girl's eyes.

The first day there we went to a place called Portage where there is a glacier that was majestic enough, but there was more to follow. The next day we flew over the mountains to one of the outposts of our defences at Clear, Alaska.

Most everybody flies in Alaska. There are few roads. What roads there are get roughed up in the extreme cold of winter, and many of them are impassable in the spring thaws.

We, all of us, have developed a healthy habit of getting away for the weekend or for Saturday night at least. If you want to get away to fish or hunt in Alaska you fly – but that is not entirely true – when we flew to Clear we flew over the Alaska Railroad which is the only railroad there and runs between Anchorage and Fairbanks. The trip, which takes an hour and a half by plane, takes twelve hours by railroad, for the train stops at any fisherman's request at the spot where he wants to fish and picks him up on the way back.

On our way to Clear, our pilot spotted some mountain goats high up on a cliff and went chasing them. I had to keep telling myself that he was far enough from the cliff, as he was used to judging distances in a plane. But I had to keep telling myself that. 'There they go! There they go!' said the pilot. He would turn around to tell me, and I would have to open my eyes because he was looking at me. There were moving specks of snow which must have been the goats. I hoped that he would not find any more. Then he spotted a moose. That wasn't so bad because it was on flat land, although we went back two or three times at steep angles to take another look.

After the mountains (we had flown by Mt McKinley which is 20,300 feet high), the man-made site at Clear looked minuscule from the air – like a small canning factory. When we were on it, it was a humming city of the future with its vast machines – an H. G. Wells or Ray Bradbury nightmare. The reflector screens are the size of a football field. The corridors are big enough for large trucks to drive down – and they do!

This was the second time I had been among men on one of our far outposts. On both occasions, I noticed that they seemed to be in a solemn and kindly mood. I had been flattered that I had been asked to read to them. I found it hard to concentrate on reading, for I was thinking of them and their machines – and the moose and the bear and the wolves outside for hundreds and thousands of miles in the wilderness. I found it very hard to speak the jokes I have in my programme. I told them about the goats on the mountainside and made a movement with my hands of the plane zooming on its side – and every head in the audience moved with my hands. They knew all right. They laughed loudly – as I did after I got over the zooming. The pilot was in the audience, so we flew straight back the next morning – no tricks! I went to bed to rest up for the evening show in Anchorage.

The two fellows who were with me running the tour inquired into the frontier life of Anchorage while I was resting. From what they told me, there were a couple of bars not too far removed in spirit from the Malamute Saloon – in *The Shooting of Dan McGrew*. One thing the two fellows were very emphatic about – the girls weren't gorgeous like Marlene Dietrich – that is to say the girls at the Malamute Saloon. The other girls at Anchorage looked good, if those who came backstage to see me were any sample. As they tell it to me – in the saloon – a guy came in who literally darkened the doorway. He was the size of a Kodiak bear. He had a voice like a gravel pit, and he leant over Bob Hulter and said, 'Are you a bridger?'

'No,' said Bob.

'Well, I'm a bridger,' he said. He put out his hand and near mashed Bob's hand – and Bob's a hefty guy. He's a big Swede. I can't go to places like that – they spot me. They get overhospitable and I wouldn't get out of the place without downing six or seven rounds – and I wouldn't be able to see Anchorage after that, or do all the reading at night.

The audiences are great. They are building a community theatre and I had to break the ground for it with a spade that was still claggy with gold paint.

The people there must be the most hospitable people in the world, for they do not want to show you off to their friends. They are proud and want to show off to you the lives they lead in their state. So Stanley McCutcheon, who is a lawyer, and his son-in-law, Stewart, flew us into a lake in the 'out-country' where Stanley McCutcheon has a cabin.

The plane in which we had flown up to Clear was a wheel-plane that belonged to a small commercial line. But there are not many landing fields in Alaska and the planes which are privately owned are mostly float-planes, because they use as landing fields the multitude of lakes in that country. In winter when the lakes are frozen over, they change the pontoons for skis.

We flew up in two one-engine float-planes into the lake where Stanley has his cabin. At the take-off we had to rock backward and forward to change the angle of the wings, for Stanley said that we had an extra heavy load of gas. I think he was being a good host and not saying that he had an extra-heavy passenger. We did not succeed the first time and the other passenger had to be ditched and fetched later.

When we were over the cabin we circled it several times, as the day before they had had a bear with two year-old cubs around and the bear got menacing toward Stanley's children. Stewart's large calibre rifle had jammed and Stanley had had to shoot at it with a very light-calibre rifle. The bear had got away into the woods and Stanley was afraid that she might be waiting for us.

However, no bear – and down we came onto the lake. We had been given high-waders, and I found out why when we got there. We waded from the float of the plane to the shore. There were moose and bears – we didn't see any wolves – and ducks and swans and arctic terns, which must be the most beautiful birds in the world. I had never hoped to see a bird whose flight is more beautiful than the flight of a seagull. The arctic tern has a black head and neck and a body of pure white feathers. The tail and wing feathers spread like a fan and they hover upright like humming birds. And there were swallows, the bluest swallows I have seen. The swallows were friendly and swooped around our heads and dived in front of us, and lighted on the ground a yard from our feet.

It is very silent there. And you hear the cries of the birds in perspective from the forest and over the lake. The approaching honk of swans and geese, and near – the cheerful chatter of the swallows.

Later in the day, we set off in the two float-planes. I was in Stanley's plane, and he had arranged to meet Stewart on a lake set in a glacier. When we got near the glacier there was no sign of Stewart, and the rendezvous lake was frozen over. We were running out of gas. I think Stanley had not taken as much gas as usual since one of his passengers was overweight, and he was counting on getting a can from Stewart on the glacier lake. However, we were running out, so we had to land on another lake.

'What a beautiful lake,' I said. 'What is it called.'

'It is an unnamed lake,' said Stanley. 'Stewart will be worried.'

However, after foraging around, Stanley came grinning, saying that he had hit the jackpot. He was carrying a five-gallon can of gas which he had found in the only cabin, which was on the shore of the lake. I thought he was trying to josh me. I thought he knew it was there all the time because afterward I saw an aerial map of the area marked with black dots saying 'Cabin with Gas.' I was having far too good a time to be worried. I learned later that I was wrong. Stanley wrote me that he had been worried. 'The nearest filling station was a two-week trek on foot through some of the wildest part of Alaska. Friends would have found us within two or three days, weather permitting, but Oh Brother, what headlines across the country in the meantime.'

We flew back to his cabin, and Stewart had not been worried. He said that he knew better than to worry about Stanley.

About nine o'clock one of them said, 'What about dinner?' We had brought no dinner. And I was wondering, 'What about dinner?' Three of them went off in a small boat leaving Stanley and me behind. In about half an hour they came back with a mess of rainbow trout. How good they were from those cold waters.

As they were setting off to go fishing, we heard shouts from the boat and ran to see what it was about. There were two bears – the young bears from the day before – out on a spit of land looking for duck eggs about fifty yards away from us. They headed the boat into the shore and yelled, and the bears went away. But Stanley had raised his rifle in case the bears charged. Then I knew why, when you went to the toilet about fifteen yards from the cabin, you always had to carry a gun. When the children go to the toilet (the children were not there that day), someone stands guard outside for them. Living the sort of life I do, I figured I should have been scared by this sort of thing, but I was not. I felt at home in the country of the big animals – I have to get back there! I was scared by the machines at Clear and the knowledge that somewhere in those buildings there was a button that someone might some day have to press.

While the others were out fishing, Stanley told me a story. His cabin was up the hill. The one we were in at the edge of the lake belonged to a trapper – an old-timer – called Tom Krause.

Tom Krause is a trapper and commercial fisherman, and a connoisseur of rocks. They say he is the best petrologist in Alaska. If anyone brings him a rock he can tell its mineral content by 'the smell of it,' as Stanley said. He has little 'book-learning,' but deep knowledge. He goes to his cabin and lives there by himself. Stanley is an old and treasured friend, but after three days of company Tom becomes irritable, and at the end of six days, impossible.

Stanley said to me that I wouldn't believe this story. And that is a good way to begin any story. So this is the story of Tom and Sam, the moose.

It was in the wintertime, and there was twelve feet of snow. Tom had cleared the area in front of the cabin, and the moose was hanging about in the clearing. A moose finds it difficult to get around in deep snow, as it is not equipped with snow shoes. Every time Tom opened the door to go up the path to the chic sales, the moose charged – so Tom had to put on snow shoes, climb out of a back window and go to the toilet over deep snow, where the moose could not follow. And Tom had a Husky that he kept around for company, and to bark at moose and bears. But the dog fell for the moose and slept with him underneath the cache. So Tom lost his only protection. Outside every cabin in Alaska there is a food cache built up on high stilts with sheet metal from old gasoline cans nailed around the stilts so that the bears cannot get a grip to tear the cache apart for the food inside it.

After a few weeks of this, Tom got mad and figured he would settle the moose. He started throwing hunks of wood, but the moose would not go away. So he picked up a big log and crept up on the moose and bashed it over the head, and the moose leaned against the stilts of the cache, bleeding. And Tom retired to the cabin and began to feel sorry for the moose – so Tom fell in love with the moose too. And he began to gather together young willow trees – that is what moose eat. They call moose 'wood-burners.' Tom made little heaps of young willow trees and began to think of the moose as 'Sam.' However, this made his life very complicated and inconvenient, and he figured he had to get rid of Sam somehow. So he made a pile of willow trees in front of the cabin, another a mile away, and another two miles away to lure Sam. And he shut up the dog so that he wouldn't follow his friend. So Sam went away after the willow trees and after a couple of days Tom let out the Husky. And the Husky went after the moose and brought him back. So Tom was stuck with Sam until the spring thaw. And then Sam went away.

Everyone who lives this sort of life lives, in winter, on moose meat, which is hung in the open under the cache because the hibernating bears are not around then. And the next fall it was getting time for Tom to bag a moose for his winter supply of meat. About fifteen yards from the edge of the lake there is a large birch tree, and Stanley was with Tom. And Stanley saw a big moose standing by the birch tree. Tom was carrying a gun. And Stanley said, 'There's your moose.'

And Tom said, 'That moose doesn't look to have particularly good meat. Its ribs are showing. And there will probably be another thaw and the meat will go bad anyway.'

And Stanley said, 'I believe you think it is old Sam.'

And Tom said, 'You're darn right. I know it's old Sam!'

And Stanley showed me a picture taken by Tom of old Sam and the Husky looking at him with loving eyes – and that proved the story, I guess.

After that, Stanley started talking to me about the winters in Alaska. There are only a few hours of daylight. He talked about the sounds in winter and particularly about the northern lights which stretch out sometimes like a curtain draped across the sky – red and green and blue. I asked him how he started the engine of a plane when it was forty below. He said he warmed up the engine with a blow torch, and that one day he had burned up a plane doing that. I said, 'How did you get out of the lake?'

He said, 'After five days somebody came after me.' He also said, 'Once a friend of mine couldn't start his engine because the temperature was eighty below and he had to wait until it warmed up to sixty below before he could start it.'

Stanley talked casually about these things. After all, they are less frightening than the stuff we read in our daily papers.

Living is expensive there. Gasoline – fifty cents a gallon – $1.30 for a couple of beers – hotels way above average, but not bad – and by the Lord Harry, it is worth it. I cannot wait to get back – for July when the salmon are running, and for midwinter.

I want to go to Kodiak Island where the brown bears weigh up to a ton a piece – to the Pribilof Islands which are the breeding ground of millions of seals – to Point Barrow where there are polar bears – to the north slopes of the Brooks Mountains which are enamelled with flowers in high summer – but more than that to meet my first hosts in Alaska again.

Reprinted from *The Fabulous Country*,
an anthology compiled by Charles Laughton
for McGraw-Hill Book Company, Inc.,
Copyright © 1962 by Charles Laughton.

The Plays

The Government Inspector *London*
Barnes, 28 Apr 1926, *writ.* N. Gogol, *dir. and des.* Theodore Komisarjevsky. With: Elliott Seabrooke (Swistunov), James Lomas (Derzhimorda), Dan F. Roe (Luka Lukich), Hanley Drewitt (Amos Fyodorovich), Sidney Benson (Herr Hübner, Abdullin), Kimber Phillips (Artemi Philipovich), Frederick Lord (Bobchinski), Alfred Clark (Anton Antonovitch), Neil Curtis (Ivan Kusmich), Jack Knight (Dobchinski), Hilda Sims (Anna Andreyevna), Stella Freeman (Marya Antonovna), Jane Ellis (Avdotya), LAUGHTON (Osip), Claude Rains (Ivan Alexandrovich Khlestakov), John C. Laurence (Waiter, 2nd Merchant), Brian Watson (3rd Merchant, Gendarme), May Agate (The Locksmith's Wife), Patricia O'Carroll (The Sergeant's Wife).

Pillars of Society *London*
Everyman Theatre, 13 June 1926, *writ.* Henrik Ibsen, *dir.* Sybil Arundale. With: Gilbert Ritchie (Krap), Orlando Barnett (Aune), Milton Rosmer (Dr Rörlund), Margaret Carter (Mrs Rummel), Drusilla Wills (Mrs Postmaster Holt), Barbara Everest (Mrs Bernick), Josephine Wilson (Miss Bernick), Brember Wills (Hilmar Tönnesen), Anne Bolt (Olaf), Marie Wright (Mrs Dr Lynge), Gwendolen Evans (Dina Dorf), J. Hubert-Leslie (Vigeland), LAUGHTON (Rummel), Sybil Arundel (Miss Hessel), Charles Carson (Consul Bernick), Michael Hogan (Johan Tönnesen).

The Cherry Orchard *London*
Barnes, 28 Sept 1926, *writ.* A. Chekhov, *trans.* Constance Garnett, *dir. and des.* Theodore Komisarjevsky. With: Douglas Burbidge (Lopakhin), Stella Freeman (Dunyasha), LAUGHTON (Yepi Khodov), Edith Harley (A Servant), Dan F. Roe (Firs), Gabrielle Castarelli (Anya), Dorothy Dix (Mme Ranyevskaya), Lawrence Hanray (Gayev), Josephine Wilson (Varya), Martita Hunt (Charlotta), Oswald Lingard (Semeonov-Pishchik), W. Earle Grey (Yasha), Wilfred Fletcher (Trofimov), Leonard Calvert (A Tramp, Stationmaster), Gerard Barton (A Post Office Clerk), Leslie Paine (His Son), Monica Stracey (A Young Lady).

The Three Sisters *London*
Barnes, Oct 1926, *writ.* A. Chekhov, *trans.* Constance Garnett, *dir. and des.* Theodore Komisarjevsky. With: Martita Hunt (Olga), Josephine Wilson (Irina), Margaret Swallow (Masha), Stella Freeman (A Maid), Leonard Upton (Tusenbach), Dan F. Roe (Chebutykin), LAUGHTON (Vassily Solyony), Douglas Burbidge (Andrey Prozorov), Gerard Barton (An Orderly, Mihail Petrov), Elsie French (Anfisa), Oswald Lingard (Ferapont), Douglas Jefferies (Vershinin), Alfred Sangster (Kulygin), Dorice Fordred (Natasha Ivanova), Anthony Ireland (Alexey Fedotik), Lionel Redpath (Vladimir Rode).

Liliom *London*
Duke of York's, 23 Dec 1926, *writ.* Ferencz Molnar, *trans.* Osmond Shillingford and Anthony Ellis, *dir. and des.* Theodore Komisarjevsky, *mus. comp. and arr.* Max Deutsch. With: Stella Freeman (Dancer), Beryl Harrison (Marie), Fay Compton (Julie), Violet Farebrother (Mrs Muskat), Ivor Novello (Liliom), Wm. Kendall (Berkovicz, 1st Mounted Policeman), Ben Webster (Police Captain, Sec. of the Magistrate), J. Hamilton Kay (Detective), Margaret Webster (Mrs Kalman), LAUGHTON (Ficsur), Ernest Hare (2nd Mounted Policeman), Dan F. Roe (Young Kalman), Douglas Jefferies (Wolf), Douglas Burbidge (Athlete, Linz), Alfred Sangster (Police Surgeon, Court Policeman), Drew MacIntosh (1st Policeman), Alfred Hilliard (2nd Policeman), Marjorie Mars (Louise).

The Greater Love *London*
Prince's Theatre, 23 Feb 1927, *writ.* J. B. Fagan, *dir.* Fagan and Lewis Casson, *des.* Fagan. With: Charles Bealby (Count Ivan Sergevitch Pestoff), Lawrence Hanray (Prof. Panshine), Brember Wills (Zabalow), John H. Moore (Porphery Micolaievitch), Ronald Kerr (Dr Abramitch), Lewis T. Casson (Polusky, Col. Schultz), Sybil Thorndike (Nadeshda Ivanova), Colin Keith-Johnston (Vassili Ivanovitch), Ada King (Tatiana Sergevna), Chris Walker (Piotr), Henry Hewett (Captain Pavel Kaulbach), Basil Gill (Col. Tzaloff), Doug Thompson (Sergeant), Charles Herriot (Lieut.), Brember Wills (Nuhlin), LAUGHTON (Gen. Markeloff),

Desmond Deane (Col. Almazoff), Wallace Wood (Captain Alexieff), Elliott Seabrooke (Captain Nazernoff), John H. Moore (Officer).

Angela *London*

Prince's Theatre, 14 Mar 1927, *writ*. Lady Bell, *dir*. Lewis T. Casson. With: Dora Barton (Hon Mrs Carr), Jessie Bateman (Lady Hartley), Sadie Speight (Mrs Priestman), John H. Moore (Footman), Lilian Moubrey (Servant), Sybil Thorndike (Angela Guiseley), LAUGHTON (Sir James Hartley), Lewis T. Casson (Valentine Guiseley), Lawrence Hanray (Jack Wilding), Thomas Warner (Mr Priestman), Percy Varley (Mr Lambert), Zillah Carter (Violet Guiseley), Winifrid Oughton (Clare Marriner), Ronald Kerr (Geoff Marriner), Wallace Wood (Mr Wilson), Godfrey Baxter (Clerk), Brember Wills (John Quarll).

Naked *London*

Royalty Theatre, 18 Mar 1927, *writ*. Luigi Pirandello, *dir*. Theodore Komisarjevsky. With: Nancy Price (Ersilia Drei), Allan Jeayes (Ludovico Nota), Florence Tyrell (Onoria), LAUGHTON (Cantavalle), George Relph (Franco Raspigi), Joan Levett (Emma), Elliott Seabrooke (Consul Grotti).

Medea *London*

Prince's Theatre, 27 Apr 1927, *writ*. Euripides, *trans*. Gilbert Murray, *dir*. Lewis T. Casson, *cos*. Bruce Winston. With: Sybil Thorndike (Medea), Lawrence Anderson (Jason), LAUGHTON (Creon), Lawrence Hanray (Aegeus), Lilian Moubrey (Nurse), John H. Moore (Attendant), Lewis T. Casson (Messenger), *and* Zillah Carter, Margaret Webster, Iris Baker, Ursula Granville, Renee Rubens, Grace Poole, Penelope Spencer (Chorus).

The Happy Husband *London*

Criterion, 15 June 1927, *writ*. Harrison Owen, *dir*. Basil Dean. With: Laurence Grossmith (Bill Rendell), David Hawthorne (Arthur Tolhurst), LAUGHTON (Frank K. Pratt), Madge Tetheridge (Dot Rendell), Ann Trevor (Sylvia Fullerton), Eric Cowley ('Sosso' Stephens), Stella Arbenina (Consuelo Pratt), A.E. Matthews (Harvey Townsend), Sheila MacGregor (Ada), Mabel Sealby (Stella Tolhurst), Carl Harbord (A Visitor).

Paul I *London*

(Royal) Court Theatre, 4 Oct 1927, *writ*. D. Merejkovsky, adapt. by John Alford *and* J.C. Dale, *dir. and des*. Theodore Komisarjevsky. With: Carl Harbord (Grand Duke Alexander), Lydia Sherwood (Elizabeth), George Hayes (Paul I), Elliott Seabrooke (Grand Duke Constantin), Arthur Macrae (Lieut. Marin, Ropchinsky), LAUGHTON (Gen. Count Pahlen), Hugh Barnes (Gen. Talyzin), Bramwell Fletcher (Col. Prince Yashvil), Vivian Beynon (Gen. Bennigsen), Ian Davison (Col. Argamakov), Dan F. Roe (Dr Rodgerson, Col. Baron Rosen), Dorothy Green (Empress Marie), Dorothy Cheston (Princess Anna Gagarine), W.E.C. Jenkins (Lieut. Bibikov, Kirilov), G. Vernon (Cornet Gardanov), Scott Sunderland (Prince Platon Zoubov), Barry K. Barnes (Prince Nicolas Zoubov).

Mr Prohack *London*

(Royal) Court Theatre, 16 Nov 1927, *writ*. Arnold Bennett and Edward Knoblock, *dir. and des*. Theodore Komisarjevsky. With: LAUGHTON (Mr Prohack), Hilda Sims (Mrs Prohack), Lydia Sherwood (Susie Prohack), Carl Harbord (Charles Prohack), Juliet Mansel (Machin), Scott Sunderland (Softly Bishop), Frederick Cooper (Ozzie Morfey), Dorothy Cheston (Lady Massulam), Dan F. Roe (Hollins), Arthur Macrae (Tailor's Boy), Elsa Lanchester (Mimi Winstock), Elliott Seabrooke (Sir Paul Spinner).

A Man with Red Hair *London*

Little Theatre, 27 Feb 1928, *writ*. Benn W. Levy, *from the novel of* Hugh Walpole, *dir*. Theodore Komisarjevsky, *des*. Aubrey Hammond. With: Ion Swinley (David Dunbar), Keyo Akimoto (A Servant), J.H. Roberts (Charles Percy Harkness), Gillian Lind (Hesther Tobin), LAUGHTON (Mr Crispin), James Whale (Herrick Crispin), George Bealby (Dr Tobin), Kay Chiba (Another Servant), O. Morai (Another Servant).

The Making of an Immortal *London*

Arts Theatre Club, 1–2 Apr 1928, *writ*. George Moore, *dir*. Robert Atkins, *des*. George Sheringham, *mus. arr*. Sir Thomas Beecham. With: Malcolm Keen (Richard Burbage),

Edmund Gwenn (Anthony Grindle), Edward Chapman (Christopher Fir), D. Hay Petrie (Jack Ford), Billy Shine (Jack Thornley), Brian Glennie (Prenny Lister), Thomas White (Robert Warner), George Brijan (Stephen Frion), Sandford Gorton (Henry Cuffe), LAUGHTON (Ben Jonson), Leslie Faber (Francis Bacon), Charles Carson (William Shakespeare), Sybil Thorndike (Queen Elizabeth), Clement Hamelin, Leslie Coles, More O'Ferrall (Javelin Men), John Laurie, Geoffrey Clark, Cyril Hardingham (Players), Barbara Horder (Maid of Honour).

Riverside Nights *London*
Arts Theatre Club, Sun. 24 June 1928, *writ. and arr.* Nigel Playfair and A.P. Herbert, *dir.* Nigel Playfair, *mus.* Alfred Reynolds. With: Marie Brett-Davies, Joan Carr, Renee de Vaux, Elsa Lanchester, Florence McHugh, Violet Marquesita, D.H. Petrie, Nigel Playfair, Mark Raphael, Scott Russell, Penelope Spencer, Laura Wilson, Geoff Wincott, Fay Yeatman, *and for this occasion only* CHARLES LAUGHTON. (Laughton and Lanchester performed 'The Ballad of Frankie and Johnny'.)

Alibi *London*
Theatre Royal, Haymarket, 12 Nov 1928, *writ.* Michael Morton, *from the novel by* Agatha Christie, *dir.* Sir Gerald duMaurier, *des.* Stafford Hilliard and J. Crosbie-Frazer. With: Lady Tree (Mrs Ackroyd), Jane Welsh (Flora Ackroyd), E. Disney Roebuck (Parker), Basil Loder (Major Blunt), Iris Nobel (Ursula Bourne), H. Forbes-Robertson (Geoffrey Raymond), Gillian Lind (Caryl Sheppard), LAUGHTON (Hercule Poirot), J.H. Roberts (Dr Sheppard), Oliver Johnston (Ralph Paton), Norman V. Norman (Sir Roger Ackroyd, Bart.), John Darwin (Inspector Davies), J. Smith-Wright (Mr Hammond), Constance Anderson (Margot).

Mr Pickwick *London*
Theatre Royal, Haymarket, 15 Dec 1928, *writ.* Cosmo Hamilton and Frank C. Reilly, *from the novel by* Charles Dickens, *dir.* Basil Dean, *des.* Aubrey Hammond, *cos.* Mr Simmons. With: Eliot Makeham (Sam Weller), May Chevalier (Housekeeper), Gypsy Raine (Betsy), Delring Wells (Augustus Snodgrass), Harold Scott (Nathaniel Winkle), Lamont Dickson (Tracy Tupman), Oswald Roberts (Waiter, Mr Jackson, Sergeant Snubben), Wallace Douglas (Mr Trundle, Gamekeeper's Boy), Richard Turner (Bob Sawyer), Denis Mowbray (Ben Allen), Bruce Winston (Tony Weller, Sergeant Buzfuz), Ambrose Manning (Mr Wardle), Kathleen Gelder (Emily Wardle), Kathleen Kelly (Isabella Kelly), Madeleine Carroll (Arabella Allen), Susan Richmond (Rachel Wardle), Jack Corps (Fat Boy), Dotrice Fordred (Mary), J. Hubert Leslie (Mr Perker), LAUGHTON (Mr Pickwick), D.J. Williams (Cabman, Justice Stareleigh), George Curzon (Alfred Jingle), Mary Clare (Mrs Bardell), Billy Salmon (Master Bardell), Eugene Leahy (Gamekeeper, Mr Skimpin), Huntley Gifford (Butler), Rollie Emery (Mrs Cluppins), Anne Esmond (Mrs Sanders), Huntley Gifford (Mr Phunky), Archibald McLean (Mr Dodson), Richard Coke (Mr Fogg), Walton Palmer (Mr Roker), Arthur Bawtree (Job Trotter).

Beauty *London*
Strand, 16 July 1929, *writ.* Michael Morton, *from the French of* Jacques Deval, *dir.* Felix Edwardes. With: Oswald Skilbeck (Gustave), Lady Tree (Henriette Sopite), Morton Selten (Xavier Sopite), Grace Wilson (Mme Vadiche), Gwendolen Floyd (Mme Toube), Ena Grossmith (Berenice Toube), Isabel Jeans (Estelle Duparc), Eric Maturin (Paul de Severac), LAUGHTON (Jacques Blaise), Alex Chentrens (Bonamy), W.E.C. Jenkins (Adolphe), Dorothy Dunkels (Rose), E. Lyall Swete (Prof Flammet).

The Silver Tassie *London*
Apollo, 11 Oct 1929, *writ.* Sean O'Casey, *dir.* Raymond Massey, *des.* Augustus John (Act 2), G.E. Calthrop (Acts 1, 3, 4). With: Barry Fitzgerald (Sylvester Heegan, 3rd Soldier), Sidney Morgan (Simon Norton), Eithne Magee (Mrs Heegan), Beatrix Lehmann (Susie Monican), Una O'Connor (Mrs Foran), Ian Hunter (Teddy Foran), LAUGHTON (Harry Heegan), Billy Barnes (Jessie Taite, 4th Stretcher-Bearer), S.J. Warmington (Barry Bagnal, 6th Soldier), Leonard Shepherd (The Croucher), LAUGHTON (1st Soldier), Ian Hunter (2nd Soldier), Jack Mayne (4th Soldier), G. Adrian Byrne (5th Soldier), Sinclair Cotter (The Corporal), Ivo Dawson (The Visitor), Alban Blakelock (The Staff Wallah), Emlyn Williams (The Trumpeter), Norman Stuart (1st Stretcher-Bearer), Oswald Lingard (2nd Stretcher-Bearer), Charles Schofield (3rd Stretcher-Bearer), Clive Morton (1st Casualty), James Willoughby (2nd Casualty), Hastings Lynn (Surgeon Forby Maxwell), Audrey O'Flynn (Sister of the Ward).

French Leave London
Vaudeville, 7 Jan 1930, *writ*. Reginald Berkeley, *dir*. Eille Norwood, *des*. Aubrey Hammond.
With: Charles Groves (Corp. Sykes), Frederick Burtwell (Rifleman Jenks), Madeleine Carroll
(Mademoiselle Juliette), James Raglan (Capt. Harry Glenister), LAUGHTON (Brigadier-
General Archibald Root), Edward Scott-Gatty (Lieut. George Graham), Emlyn Williams (M.
Jules Marnier), May Agate (Mme Denaux).

On the Spot London
Wyndham's, 2 April 1930, *writ. and dir*. Edgar Wallace. With: Frank Everart (Shaun
O'Donnell), Agnes Somerset (A Nurse), Philip Valentine (A Priest), Julian Andrews (A
Doctor), Roy Emerton (Captain Harrison), Douglas Payne (Patrolman Ryan), LAUGHTON
(Tony Perelli), Gillian Lind (Minn Lee), John Gold (Kiriki), Emlyn Williams (Angelo), Ben
Welden (Con O'Hara), Gladys Frazin (Maria Pouliski), Ben Smith (Jimmy McGarth), Dennis
Wyndham (Mike Feeney).

Payment Deferred London
St James's Theatre, 4 May 1931, *writ*. Jeffrey Dell, *from the novel by* C.S. Forester, *dir*. H.K.
Ayliff. With: Ernest Jay (Hammond), Quinton McPherson (A Prospective Tenant),
LAUGHTON (William Marble), Louise Hampton (Annie Marble), Elsa Lanchester (Winnie
Marble), Paul Longuet (Jim Medland), Jeanne de Casalis (Mme Collins), A.S. Homewood (Dr
Atkinson), *and* Edgar K. Bruce, Ernest Haines (Furniture Removers).

The Cherry Orchard London
Old Vic, 9–28 October 1933, *writ*. A. Chekhov, *trans*. Hubert M. Butler, *dir*. Tyrone Guthrie.
With: LAUGHTON (Lopakhin), Barbara Wilcox (Dunyasha), Marius Goring (Yepi Khodov),
Athene Seyler (Lyubov Andreyevna), Ursula Jeans (Anya), Flora Robson (Varya), Leon
Quartermaine (Leonid Andreyevitch), Elsa Lanchester (Charlotta Ivanovna), Roger Livesey
(Semeonov-Pishchik), Morland Graham (Firs), James Mason (Yasha), Dennis Arundell
(Trofimov), Ernest Hare (A Vagrant), John Allen (The Station Master), Raymond Johnson (A
Post Office Clerk).

Henry VIII London
Wells, 7–18 Nov 1933.
Old Vic, 21 Nov–2 Dec 1933, *writ*. W. Shakespeare, *dir*. Tyrone Guthrie. With: Nicholas
Hannen (Duke of Buckingham), Dennis Arundell (Duke of Norfolk), Ernest Hare (Lord
Abergavenny, Duke of Suffolk), Robert Farquharson (Wolsey), James Mason (Cromwell),
Desmond Walter-Ellis (Brandon), Derek Prentice (A Sergeant-at-Arms), LAUGHTON (Henry
VIII), Flora Robson (Queen Katharine), Philip Thornley (Surveyor to the Duke of
Buckingham), Roger Livesey (Lord Chamberlain), Richard Goolden (Lord Sands, Cranmer),
Christopher Hassall (Sir Thomas Lovell), Bertram Grimley (Sir Henry Guildford, 1st Usher),
Ursula Jeans (Anne Bullen), Peter Croft (A Servant to Wolsey, 2nd Usher), Raymond Johnson
(1st Gentleman), John Allen (2nd Gentleman), Orford St John (Sir Nicholas Vaux), Marius
Goring (Cardinal Campeius, Garter King-at-Arms), Cecil Scott-Paton (Gardiner), Athene
Seyler (Old Lady), Elsa Lanchester (A Singer), Morland Graham (Griffith), Frank Napier
(Earl of Surrey), Evelyn Allen (Patience), Thorley Walters (A Messenger), Peter Copley
(Capucius).

Measure for Measure London
Old Vic, 4–20 Dec 1933, *writ*. W. Shakespeare, *dir*. Tyrone Guthrie. With: Roger Livesey
(Vincentio), Frank Napier (Escalus), LAUGHTON (Angelo), Dennis Arundell (Lucio), Peter
Copley (1st Gentleman), Peter Croft (2nd Gentleman), Athene Seyler (Mistress Overdone),
Lawrence Baskcomb (Pompey), James Mason (Claudio), Ernest Hare (Provost), Elsa
Lanchester (Juliet, A Singer), Marius Goring (Friar Peter, Abhorson), Flora Robson (Isabella),
Evelyn Allen (Francisca), John Allen (A Justice), Morland Graham (Elbow), Desmond Walter-
Ellis (Froth), Cecil Scott-Paton (Servant to Angelo), Ursula Jeans (Mariana), Morland Graham
(Barnardine), Anna Brunton (Mistress Kate Keepdown).

The Tempest London
Wells, 8–20 Jan 1934.
Old Vic, 22 Jan–3 Feb 1934, *writ*. W. Shakespeare, *dir*. Tyrone Guthrie. With: Patrick Ross
(Master of the Ship), John Allen (Boatswain), Marius Goring (King of Naples), Ernest Hare

(Sebastian), Dennis Arundell (Antonio), Clifford Evans (Ferdinand), Evan John (Gonzalo), Ursula Jeans (Miranda), LAUGHTON (Prospero), Elsa Lanchester (Ariel), Roger Livesey (Caliban), Desmond Walter-Ellis (Adrian), James Mason (Francisco), Lawrence Baskcomb (Trinculo), Morland Graham (Stephano), Margaret Field-Hyde (Iris), Flora Robson (Ceres), Evelyn Allen (Juno).

The Importance of Being Earnest *London*
Old Vic, 5 Feb–3 Mar 1934, *writ.* Oscar Wilde, *dir.* Tyrone Guthrie. With: Morland Graham (Lane), George Curzon (Algernon Moncrieff), Roger Livesey (John Worthing), Athene Seyler (Lady Bracknell), Flora Robson (Gwendolen Fairfax), Elsa Lanchester (Miss Prism), Ursula Jeans (Cecily Cardew), LAUGHTON (Canon Chasuble), James Mason (Merriman).

Love for Love *London*
Wells, 6–31 Mar 1934, *writ.* W. Congreve, *dir.* Tyrone Guthrie, *des.* Vivian Forbes. With: Barrie Livesey (Valentine Legend), James Mason (Jeremy), Dennis Arundell (Scandal), Ernest Hare (Trapland), Marius Goring (Buckram), LAUGHTON (Tattle), Athene Seyler (Mrs Frail), Morland Graham (Foresight), Raymond Johnson (Servant), Margery Phipps-Walker (Servant to Miss Prue), Ursula Jeans (Angelica), Sam Livesey (Sir Sampson Legend), Flora Robson (Mrs Foresight), Elsa Lanchester (Miss Prue), Roger Livesey (Ben Legend), Alta Hershey (Jenny).

Macbeth *London*
Old Vic, 2–28 Apr 1934, *writ.* W. Shakespeare, *dir.* Tyrone Guthrie. With: Ernest Hare (Duncan, Seward), Marius Goring (Malcolm), Thorley Walters (Donalbain), John Moody (A Sergeant, 2nd Murderer), Dennis Arundell (Ross), LAUGHTON (Macbeth), Frank Napier (Banquo), Athene Seyler (1st Weird Sister, Gentlewoman), Phyllis Hatch (2nd Weird Sister), Elspeth Currie (3rd Weird Sister), Desmond Walter-Ellis (Angus), Flora Robson (Lady Macbeth), Raymond Johnson (Servant, Messenger), Alan Foss (Fleance), Morland Graham (Porter), Roger Livesey (Macduff), James Mason (Lennox), Russell Waters (An Old Man), Patrick Ross (1st Murderer, Doctor), Stephan Schnabel (3rd Murderer), Evelyn Allen (Lady Macduff), Nigel Stock (Boy, son to Macduff), John Allen (Menteith), Derek Prentice (Caithness), Cecil Scott-Paton (Messenger), John Moody (Seyton), Peter Copley (Young Seward).

Peter Pan *London*
London Palladium, 26 December 1936, *writ.* J.M. Barrie, *dir.* Stephen Thomas. With: Elsa Lanchester (Peter Pan), LAUGHTON (Captain Hook), Peter Murray Hill (Mr Darling), Cecily Byrne (Mrs Darling), Pamela Standish (Wendy), Clive Baxter (John), Paul Dunger (Michael), Wallie Scott (Nana), Jenny Wren (Tinker Bell), T. Best (Tootles), D. Blatcher (Nibs), Charles Hawtrey (Slightly), Robert Holland (Curley), Stanley Axham (1st twin), D. Smith (2nd Twin), Charles Dow (Smee), Harold Scott (Gentleman Starkey), Edwin McCarthy (Cookson), Victor Thornton (Mullins), William Luff (Cecco), Hamilton Hunter (Jukes), Granville Darling (Noodler), Claude Talbot (1st Pirate), Richard Turner (2nd Pirate), Sam Henry (Black Pirate), Garrett Hollick (Great Big Little Panther), Olive Wright (Tiger Lily), M. Milne (Mermaid), Kathleen Weston (Baby Mermaid), Helen Moore (Liza), T. Bray (Ostrich), David Little and Basil Macrae (Crocodile).

The Life of Galileo *Los Angeles and New York*
Coronet Theatre, Los Angeles, 30 July–17 August 1947, *writ.* Bertolt Brecht, *trans.* LAUGHTON and Brecht, *dir.* Joseph Losey, Brecht and LAUGHTON, *des.* Robert Davison. With: LAUGHTON (Galileo), Hugo Haas (Barberini), Frances Heflin (Virginia), Bill Phipps (Andrea), Eda Reiss Merin (Mrs Sarti), Peter Brocco (Old Cardinal), Stephen Brown (Street Singer). Subsequently: Maxine Elliott's Theatre, New York, 7 December 1947.

The Cherry Orchard *Los Angeles*
Stage Theatre, Los Angeles, 6 June 1950, *writ.* A. Chekhov, *dir.* Charles Laughton, *des.* Harry Horner. With: Eugenie Leontovich (Mme Ranyevsky), CHARLES LAUGHTON (Gaev), Carol Brannan (Anya), Belita (Varya), Maria Bazzi (Charlotta Ivanovna), Hal Bokor (Semyonov-Pistchik), Vic Perrin (Yasha), Bill Phipps (Trofimov), Jed McKee (a vagrant), Louise Carman (girl), Margaret Field (Dunyasha), Bob Anderson (Lopahin), Richard Lupino (Epihodov), William Cottrell (Firs).

Don Juan in Hell *New York*
Carnegie Hall, one performance, 1951, *writ*. Bernard Shaw, *dir*. LAUGHTON. With:
LAUGHTON (Devil), Charles Boyer (Don Juan), Sir Cedric Hardwicke (Statue), Agnes
Moorehead (Donna Anna).

John Brown's Body *New York*
New Century Theatre, 14 Feb–11 Apr 1953, *writ*. Stephen Vincent Benet, *adapt. and dir*.
LAUGHTON, *mus. and eff*. Walter Schumann, *on stage choral dir*. Richard White. With:
Tyrone Power, Judith Anderson, Raymond Massey *and* Joe Baker, Don Burke, Betty Benson,
Keith Carver, Jack B. Dailey, Barbara Ford, Gillian Grey, Homer W. Hall, Les Helsdon, Bob
Jensen, William Longmire, Donna McDaniel, John McMahon, Roger Miller, Smith Russell
Jr., Lynda Stevens, Jack Vander-Laan, Robert Vaughn, Gordon B. Wood.

The Caine Mutiny Court Martial *New York*
Plymouth, 21 Jan 1954 (opened), *writ*. Herman Wouk, *adapted from his novel*, 'The Caine
Mutiny', *dir*. LAUGHTON. With: John Huffman (Stenographer), Greg Roman (Orderly),
Henry Fonda (Lieut. Greenwald), John Hodiak (Lieut. Stephen Maryk), Ainslie Pryor (Lieut.
Cdr. John Challee), Russell Hicks (Capt. Blakely), Lloyd Nolan (Lieut. Cdr. Philip Francis
Queeg), Robert Gist (Lieut. Thomas Keefer), Eddie Firestone (Signalman Junius Urban),
Charles Nolte (Lieut. [jg] Willis Seward Keith), Paul Birch (Capt. Randolph Southard),
Stephen Chase (Dr Forrest Lundeen), Herbert Anderson (Dr Bird), *and* Larry Barton, Jim
Bumgarner, T.H. Jourdan, Richard Farmer, Richard Norris, Pat Waltz (Members of the
Court).

Major Barbara *New York*
Martin Beck Theatre, 30 Oct 1956, *writ*. Bernard Shaw, *dir*. LAUGHTON, *des*. Donald
Oenslager. With: LAUGHTON (Andrew Undershaft), John Astin (Morrison), Frank Gero
(Footman), Louise Latham (Maid), Cornelia Otis Skinner (Lady Britomart), Frederic
Warriner (Stephen), Glynis Johns (Major Barbara), Myra Carter (Sarah), Burgess Meredith
(Adolphus Cusins), Richard Lupino (Charles Lomax), Sally Gracie (Rummy Mitchems),
Walter Burke (Snobby Price), Nancy Malone (Jenny Hill), Colin Keith-Johnston (Peter
Shirley), Eli Wallach (Bill Walker), Patricia Ripley (Mrs Baines).

The Party *London*
New Theatre, 28 May 1958, *writ*. Jane Arden, *dir*. LAUGHTON. With: Ann Lynn (Henriette
Brough), Joyce Redman (Frances Brough), John Welsh (Harold Lingham), Elsa Lanchester
(Elsie Sharp), Albert Finney (Soya Marshall), LAUGHTON (Richard Brough).

A Midsummer Night's Dream *Stratford-upon-Avon*
Shakespeare Memorial Theatre, 2 June 1959, *writ*. W. Shakespeare, *dir*. Peter Hall. With:
Anthony Nicholls (Theseus), Stephanie Bidmead (Hippolyta), Donald Layne-Smith
(Philostrate), Roy Dotrice (Egeus), Priscilla Morgan (Hermia), Albert Finney (Lysander),
Edward de Souza (Demetrius), Vanessa Redgrave (Helena), Cyril Luckham (Quince),
LAUGHTON (Bottom), Peter Woodthorpe (Flute), Donald Eccles (Starveling), Michael
Blakemore (Snout), Julian Glover (Snug), Ian Holm (Puck), Zoe Caldwell (A Fairy), Robert
Hardy (Oberon), Mary Ure (Titania), *and* Mavis Edwards, Georgine Anderson, Judith
Downes, Margaret O'Keefe, Jean Owen, Malcolm Ranson, Michael Scole (Fairies). (Among
supernumeraries was Diana Rigg.)

King Lear *Stratford-upon-Avon*
Shakespeare Memorial Theatre, 18 Aug 1959, *writ*. W. Shakespeare, *dir*. Glen Byam Shaw,
des. Motley. With: Anthony Nicholls (Earl of Kent), Cyril Luckham (Earl of Gloucester),
LAUGHTON (Lear), Stephanie Bidmead (Goneril), Angela Baddeley (Regan), Zoe Caldwell
(Cordelia), Julian Glover (Albany), Paul Hardwick (Cornwall), Edward de Souza (King of
France), Roy Dotrice (Burgundy), Albert Finney (Edgar), Michael Blakemore (Knight to
Lear), Peter Woodthorpe (Oswald), Ian Holm (Fool), Stephen Thorne (Curan), Michael
Graham Cox (1st Regan Servant), Roger Bizley (2nd Regan Servant), David Buck (3rd Regan
Servant), Donald Eccles (Gloucester's Tenant), Kenneth Gilbert (Doctor), Roy Spencer
(Herald), Peter Mason (Edmund's Captain), Stanley Wheeler (Herald's Trumpeter), Arthur
Allaby (Edgar's Trumpeter), Don Smith (Cordelia Messenger), Richard Rudd (Regan Soldier),
Dave Thomas (Edmund Standard-Bearer).

The Films

Blue Bottles (*silent*)
England, 1928, 20 mins, Angle pictures. *Dir.* Ivor Montagu, *sc. based on a story by* H.G. Wells, *ph.* F.A. Young, *a.d.* Frank Wells. With: LAUGHTON, Elsa Lanchester, Marie Wright, Joe Beckett, Norman Haire.

Day Dreams (*silent*)
England, 1928, 23 mins, Ideal Films. *Dir.* Ivor Montagu, *sc. and a.d.* Frank Wells, *based on a story by* H.G. Wells, *ph.* F.A. Young, *a.d.* Frank Wells. With: LAUGHTON, Elsa Lanchester, Harold Warrender, Dorice Fordred, Marie Wright.

Piccadilly
England, 1929, 89 mins, British International. *Dir.* E. A. Dupont, *sc.* Arnold Bennett. *ph.* Werner Brandes, *a.d.* Alfred Junge. With: LAUGHTON, Gilda Grey, Jameson Thomas, Anna May Wong, King Ho-Chang, Cyril Ritchard, Hannah Jones.

Wolves
USA, 1930, Western Electric on Film. With: LAUGHTON, Dorothy Gish, Malcolm Keen, Arthur Margetson.

Down River
England, 1931, British Acoustics on Film. *Dir.* Peter Godfrey. With: LAUGHTON, Harold Huth, Jane Baxter.

The Old Dark House
USA, 1932, 72 mins, Universal Pictures. *Prod.* Carl Laemmle Jr., *dir.* James Whale, *sc.* Benn W. Levy, *from the novel by* J.B. Priestley, *ph.* Arthur Edeson, *a.d.* Charles D. Hall, *ed.* Clarence Kolster. With: LAUGHTON (Porterhouse), Boris Karloff (Morgan), Gloria Stuart (Margaret), Melvyn Douglas (Penderel), Lillian Bond (Gladys), Ernest Thesiger (Horace), Eva Moore (Rebecca), Raymond Massey (Philip), Brember Wills (Saul), John Dudgeon (Sir Roderick).

Devil and the Deep
USA, 1932, Paramount. *Dir.* Marion Gering, *sc.* Benn Levy, *based on a story by* Harry Hervey, *ph.* Charles Lang, *a.d.* Bernard Herzbrun, *ed.* Otho Lovering. With: LAUGHTON (Commander Charles Sturm), Tallulah Bankhead (Pauline Sturm), Gary Cooper (Lieut. Sempter), Cary Grant (Lieut. Jaeckel), Paul Porcasi (Hassan), Juliette Compton (Mrs Planet), Henry Kolker (Hutton), Dorothy Christy (Mrs Crimp), Arthur Hoyt (Mr Planet), Gordon Westcott (Lieut. Toll), Jimmie Dugan (Condover), Kent Taylor (A Friend), Lucien Littlefield (Shopkeeper), Peter Brocco (Wireless Operator), Wilfred Lucas (Court Martial Judge), Dave O'Brien, Harry Guttman, George Magrill (Submarine Crewmen).

Payment Deferred
USA, 1932, 80 mins, MGM. *Dir.* Lothar Mendes, *sc. from the play by* Jeffrey F. Dell. With: LAUGHTON (William Marble), Maureen O'Sullivan (Winnie Marble), Dorothy Peterson (Annie Marble), Verree Teasdale (Madame Collins), Ray Milland (James Medland).

The Sign of the Cross
USA, 1932, 123 mins, Paramount. *Prod.* Cecil B. De Mille, *dir.* Cecil B. De Mille, *sc.* Waldemar Young and Sidney Buchman, *from the play by* Wilson Barrett, *ph.* Karl Struss, *ed.* Anne Bauchens. With: LAUGHTON (Nero), Fredric March (Marcus Superbus), Elissa Landi (Mercia), Claudette Colbert (Poppaea), Ian Keith (Tigellinus), John Carradine (Leader of Gladiators/Christian).

If I Had A Million
USA, 1932, Paramount. *Prod.* Louis D. Lighton, *dir.* Ernst Lubitsch (Laughton sequence), Norman Taurog (Fields sequence), Stephen Roberts (Ruggles sequence), Norman McLeod

(Raft sequence), James Cruse (Wynne Gibson sequence/May Robson sequence), William A. Seiter (Cooper sequence), H. Bruce Humberstone (Gene Raymond sequence). *Sc.* Claude Binyon, Whitney Bolton, Malcolm Stuart Boyland, Sidney Buchman, Lester Cole, Isable Dawn, Boyce DeGaw, Walter De Leon, Oliver H.P. Garrett, Harvey Gates, Grover Jones, Ernst Lubitsch, Lawton Macakall, Joseph L. Mankiewicz, William Slavens-McNutt, Seton I. Miller, Tiffany Thayes, *based on a story* 'Windfall' by Roberg D. Andrews. *Sound rec.* Frank Grenzbach, Phil S. Wisdom. With: Prologue: Richard Bennett (John Glidden), Fred Kelsey and Willard Robertson (Doctors), Gail Patrick (Secretary). China Salesman: Charlie Ruggles (Henry Peabody), Mary Boland (Mrs Peabody), Irving Bacon (Otto K. Bullwinkle). Harlot's Episode: Wynne Gibson (Violet Smith), Jack Pennick (Sailor). Forger's Episode: George Raft (Eddie Jackson), Kent Taylor (Bank Clerk). Motoring Episode: W.C. Fields (Rollo La Rue), Alison Skipworth (Emily La Rue), Cecil Cunningham (Agnes). Condemned Man: Gene Raymond (John Wallace), Frances Dee (Mary Wallace), Grant Mitchell (Priest), Berton Churchill (Warden). Clerk's Episode: LAUGHTON (Phineas V. Lambert). Marine's Episode: Gary Cooper (Steven Gallagher), Jack Oakie (Mulligan), Roscoe Karns (O'Brien), Joyce Compton (Marie), Lucien Littlefield (Zeb), James Burtis (Jailer). Old Lady's Episode: May Robson (Mary Walker), Blanche Frederici (Head Nurse), Dewey Robinson (Cook).

Island of Lost Souls
USA, 1933, 67 mins, Paramount. *Dir.* Erle C. Kenton, *sc.* Philip Wylie and Waldemar Young, *based on the novel by* H.G. Wells, *makeup* Wally Westmore. With: LAUGHTON, Bela Lugosi, Richard Arlen, Leila Hyams, Kathleen Burke, Arthur Hohl, Stanley Fields, Robert Kortman, Tetsu Komai, Hans Steinke, Harry Ekezian, Rosemary Grimes, Paul Hurst, George Irving and Joe Bonomo.

The Private Life of Henry VIII
UK, 1933, 97 mins, London Films. *Prod.* Alexander Korda, *dir.* Alexander Korda, *sc.* Lajos Biro and Arthur Wimperis, *ph.* Georges Perinal, *a.d.* Vincent Korda, *mus.* Kurt Schroeder. With: LAUGHTON (Henry VIII), Robert Donat (Thomas Culpeper), Lady Tree (Henry's old nurse), Binnie Barnes (Catherine Howard), Elsa Lanchester (Anne of Cleves), Merle Oberon (Anne Boleyn), Franklin Dyall (Thomas Cromwell), Miles Mander (Wriothesly), Wendy Barrie (Jane Seymour), Claude Allister (Cornell), John Loder (Thomas Peynell), Everly Gregg (Catherine Parr), Laurence Hanray (Archbishop Cranmer), William Austin (Duke of Cleves), John Turnbull (Holbein), Frederick Cully (Duke of Norfolk), Gibb McLaughlin (French executioner), Sam Livesey (English executioner).

White Woman
USA, 1933, 60 mins, Paramount. *Dir.* Stuart Walker, *sc.* Samuel Hoffenstein and Gladys Lehman, *based on the story by* Norman Reilly Raine and Frank Butler, *ph.* Harry Fischbeck *a.d.* Hans Drier and Harry Oliver. Carole Lombard's songs by Harry Revel and Mack Gordon. With: LAUGHTON (Horace Prin), Carole Lombard (Judith Denning), Charles Bickford (Ballister), Kent Taylor (David von Eltz), Percy Killbride (Jakey), Charles B. Middleton (Fenton), James Bell (Hambley), Claude King (Chisholm), Ethel Griffies (Mrs Chisholm), Jimmie Dime (Vaegi), Marc Lawrence (Connors), Mabel Johnson (Native chief no. 1), Gregg Whitespear (Native chief no. 2).

The Barretts of Wimpole Street
USA, 1934, 110 mins, MGM. *Prod.* Irving G. Thalberg, *dir.* Sidney Franklin, *sc.* Ernst Vajda, Claudine West, Donald Ogden Stewart *from the novel by* Rudolf Besier, *ph.* William Daniels, *a.d.* Cedric Gibbons, *ed.* Margaret Booth, *mus.* Herbert Stothart, *rec. eng.* Douglas Shearer, *ass. dir.* Hugh Boswell, *cos.* Adrian. With: Norma Shearer (Elizabeth Barrett), Fredric March (Robert Browning), LAUGHTON (Barrett), Maureen O'Sullivan (Henrietta Barrett), Katharine Alexander (Arabel).

Ruggles of Red Gap
USA, 1935, 90 mins, Paramount. *Prod.* Arthur Hornblow, *dir.* Leo McCarey, *sc.* Walter De Leon, Harlan Thomson and Humphrey Pearson, *adapted from the play and novel by* Harry Leon Wilson, *a.d.* Hans Dreier and Robert Odell, *ed.* Edward Dmytryk, *cin.* Alfred Gilks, *rec. eng.* P.G. Wisdom, *ass. dir.* A.F. Erickson, *cos.* Travis Banton, *mus.* Ralph Rainger and Sam Coslow. With: LAUGHTON (Ruggles), Mary Boland (Effie Floud), Charlie Ruggles (Egbert Floud), ZaSu Pitts (Mrs Judson), Roland Young (George Van Bassingwell), Leila Hyams (Nell

Kenner), Maude Eburne (Ma Pettingill), Lucien Littlefield (Charles Belknap-Jackson), Leota Lorraine (Mrs Belknap-Jackson), James Burke (Jeff Tuttle).

Les Misérables

USA, 1935, 108 mins, 20th Century Pictures. *Prod.* Darryl F. Zanuck, *dir.* Richard Boleslawski, *sc.* W.P. Lipscomb, *based on the novel by* Victor Hugo, *cin.* Gregg Toland, *a.d.* Richard Day, *ed.* Barbara McLean, *sound* Frank Maher and Roger Heman, *mus.* Alfred Newman, *ass. dir.* Eric Stacey, *cos.* Omar Kiam. With: Fredric March (Jean Valjean), LAUGHTON (Inspector Javert).

Mutiny on the Bounty

USA, 1935, 132 mins, MGM. *Prod.* Irving Thalberg, *assoc. prod.* Albert Lewin, *dir.* Frank Lloyd, *sc.* Talbot Jennings, Jules Furthman, Carey Wilson, *based on the novel by* Charles Nordhoff and James Norman Hall, *a.d.* Cedric Gibbons, *ed.* Margaret Booth, *mus.* Herbert Stothart, *rec. eng.* Douglas Shearer, song 'Love Song of Tahiti' by Gus Kahn, Bronislau Kuper and Walter Jurmann. With: LAUGHTON (Captain Bligh), Clark Gable (Fletcher Christian), Franchot Tone (Byam), Dudley Digges (Bachus), Henry Stephenson (Sir Joseph Banks), Donald Crisp (Burkitt), Eddie Quillan (Ellison), Francis Lister (Captain Nelson).

Rembrandt

UK, 1936, 85 mins, London Films. *Prod.* Alexander Korda, *dir.* Alexander Korda, *sc.* Carl Zuckmayer, Arthur Wimperis, Lajos Biro and June Head, *ph.* Georges Perinal and Richard Angst, *a.d.* Vincent Korda, *ed.* William Hornbeck, *mus.* Geoffrey Toye. With: LAUGHTON (Rembrandt), Gertrude Lawrence (Geertje), Elsa Lanchester (Hendrickje), Edward Chapman (Fabrizius), Walter Hudd (Banning Cocq), Roger Livesey (beggar), Allan Jeayes (Dr Tulp), John Clements (Gavaert Flink), Raymond Huntley (Ludwick).

I, Claudius

UK, 1936, London Films. *Prod.* Alexander Korda, *dir.* Josef von Sternberg, *sc. based on the book by* Robert Graves, *ph.* George Perinal, *a.d.* Vincent Korda, *cos.* John Armstrong. With: LAUGHTON (Tiberius Claudius), Emlyn Williams (Caligula), Merle Oberon (Messalina), Flora Robson (Olivia, widow of Augustus), Robert Newton (Soldier).

Vessel of Wrath

UK, 1938, Mayflower Pictures. *Prod. and dir.* Erich Pommer, *sc.* Bartlett Cormack *from the novel by* W. Somerset Maugham, *ph.* Jules Kruger, *a.d.* Tom Morahan, *ed.* Robert Hamer, *mus.* Richard Addinsell, *mus. dir.* Muir Mathieson, *tech. adv.* C. M. Morrell, *sound* Jack Rogerson. With: LAUGHTON (Ginger Ted), Elsa Lanchester (Martha Jones), Tyrone Guthrie (Reverend Jones), Robert Newton (The Controleur).

St Martin's Lane

UK, 1938, Mayflower Pictures. *Prod.* Erich Pommer, *dir.* Tim Whelan, *sc.* Clemence Dane, *ph.* Jules Kruger, *ed.* Hugh Stewart and Robert Hamer, *mus.* Arthur Johnson, *lyrics* Eddie Pola, *dance dir.* Philip Buchel. With: LAUGHTON (Charles), Vivien Leigh (Libby), Rex Harrison (Harley), Larry Adler (Constantine), Tyrone Guthrie (Gentry), Gus McNaughton (Arthur).

Jamaica Inn

UK, 1939, 108 mins, Mayflower Pictures. *Prod.* Erich Pommer and Charles Laughton, *dir.* Alfred Hitchcock, *prod. man.* Hugh Perceval, *sc.* Sidney Gilliat, Joan Harrison, *dialogue* Sidney Gilliat and J.B. Priestley, *adapt.* Alma Reville, *from the novel by* Daphne du Maurier, *ph.* Harry Stradling and Bernard Knowles, *a.d.* Thomas N. Morahan, *ed.* Robert Hamer, *mus.* Eric Fenby, *mus. dir.* Frederic Lewis, *sp. eff.* Harry Watt, *cos.* Molly McArthur, *sd.* Jack Rogerson. With: LAUGHTON (Sir Humphrey Pengallan), Horace Hodges (Chadwick, his butler), Hay Petrie (his groom), Frederick Piper (his broker), Leslie Banks (Joss Merlyn), Marie Ney (Patience, his wife), Maureen O'Hara (Mary, his niece).

The Hunchback of Notre Dame

USA, 1939, 117 mins, RKO. *Prod.* Pandro S. Berman, *dir.* William Dieterle, *sc.* Sonya Levien and Bruno Frank *from the novel by* Victor Hugo, *ph.* Joseph H. August, *a.d.* Van Nest Polglase, *ed.* William Hamilton and Robert Wise. With: LAUGHTON (Quasimodo), Maureen

O'Hara (Esmeralda), Cedric Hardwicke (Frollo), Harry Davenport (Louis XI), Thomas Mitchell (Clopin), Edmond O'Brien (Gringoire), Alan Marshal (Phoebus), Walter Hampden (Archbishop), George Zucco (Procurator).

They Knew What They Wanted
USA, 1940, 90 mins, RKO. *Prod.* Érich Pommer, *dir.* Garson Kanin, *sc.* Robert Ardrey, *based on the play by* Sidney Howard, *ass. dir.* Ruby Rosenberg, *ph.* Harry Stradling, *a.d.* Van Nest Polglase, *sp. eff.* Vernon L. Walker, *ed.* John Sturges, *mus.* Alfred Newman. With: LAUGHTON (Tony Patucci), Carole Lombard (Amy Peters), William Gargan (Joe), Harry Carey (the Doctor), Frank Fay (Father McKee), Joe Bernard (the R.F.D.), Janet Fox (Mildred), Lee Tung-Foo (Ah Gee), Karl Malden (Red), Victor Kilian (the Photographer), Paul Lepers (Hired Hand).

It Started With Eve
USA, 1941, New Universal. *Prod.* Joe Pasternak, *dir.* Henry Koster, *sc.* Norman Krasna and Leo Townsend, *based on the original story by* Hans Kraly, *ph.* Rudolph Mate, *a.d.* Jack Otterson, *ed.* Bernard Burton, *mus.* Valverde, Anton Dvorak, Valdesti, Tchaikovsky. With: LAUGHTON (Jonathan Reynolds), Deanna Durbin (Anne Terry), Robert Cummings (J. Reynolds, Jr), Guy Kibbee (Bishop), Margaret Tallichet (Gloria Pennington), Catherine Doucet (Mrs Pennington), Walter Catlett (Dr Harvey), Charles Coleman (Roberts), Leonard Elliott (Revd Stebbins), Irving Bacon and Gus Schilling (Ravens), Wade Boteler (Newspaper Editor), Dorothea Kent (Jackie), Clara Blandick (Nurse).

Tales of Manhattan
USA, 1942, 119–126 mins, 20th Century-Fox. *Prod.* Boris Morros and S.P. Eagle, *dir.* Julien Duvivier, *sc.* Ben Hecht, Ferenc Molnar, Donald Ogden Stewart, Samuel Hoffenstein, Alan Campbell, Ladislas Fedor, L. Vadnai, L. Gorog, Lamar Trotti and Henry Blankford, *ph.* Joseph Walker, *a.d.* Richard Day and Boris Leven, *ed.* Robert Bischoff, *mus.* Sol Kaplan. With *in sequence C:* LAUGHTON (Charles Smith), Elsa Lanchester (Elsa Smith), Victor Francen (Arthuro Bandini).

The Tuttles of Tahiti
USA, 1942, RKO. *Prod.* Sol Lesser, *dir.* Charles Vidor, *sc.* S. Lewis Meltzer and Robert Carson, *adapt.* James Hilton. With: LAUGHTON (Jonas), Jon Hall (Chester), Peggy Drake (Tamara), Victor Francen (Dr Blondin), Gene Reynolds (Ru), Florence Bates (Emily), Curt Bois (Jensen), Adeline de Walt Reynolds (Mama Ruau), Mala (Nat), Leonard Sues (Fana), Jody Gilbert (Effie), Tommy Cook (Riki), Jack Carr (Rapoti), Jimmy Ames (Manu), Ernie Adams (Paki), Jim Spencer (Tupa), Alma Ross (Hio), Teddy Infuhr (Ala).

Forever and a Day
USA, 1943, RKO Radio Pictures Ltd. *Prod/dir.* Rene Clair, Edmund Goulding, Cedric Hardwicke, Frank Lloyd, Victor Saville, Robert Stevenson, Herbert Wilcox. With: LAUGHTON (Butler), Brian Aherne (Jim Trimble), Robert Cummings (Ned Trimble), Ida Lupino (Jennie), Herbert Marshall (Curate), Ray Milland (Bill Trimble), Anna Neagle (Miriam), Merle Oberon (Marjorie), Sir Cedric Hardwicke (Dabb), Gladys Cooper (Mrs Barringer), Claude Rains (Ambrose Pomfret), Jessie Matthews (Mildred Trimble), Ian Hunter (Dexter Pomfret), Ruth Warrick (Leslie Trimble), Kent Smith (Gates Pomfret), Elsa Lanchester (Mamie), Dame May Whitty (Mrs Trimble).

The Man From Down Under
·USA, 1943, 103 mins, MGM. *Prod.* Robert Z. Leonard and Orville O. Dull, *dir.* Robert Z. Leonard, *sc.* Wells Root and Thomas Seller, *based upon the story by* Bogart Rogers and Mark Kelly. With: LAUGHTON (Jacko Wilson), Binnie Barnes (Aggie Dawlins), Richard Carlson ('Nipper' Wilson), Donna Reed (Mary Wilson), Christopher Severn ('Nipper' as a child), Clyde Cook (Ginger Gaffney), Horace McNally ('Dusty' Rhodes), Arthur Shields (Father Polycarp), Evelyn Falke (Mary, as a child), Hobart Cavanaugh ('Boots'), Andre Charlot (Father Antoine).

Stand By For Action
USA, 1943, 109 mins, MGM. *Prod.* Orville O. Dull and Robert Z. Leonard, *dir.* Robert Z. Leonard, *sc.* George Bruce, John L. Balderston, and Herman J. Mankiewicz, *from an original*

by Captain Harvey Haislip USN, and R.C. Sherriff, *suggested by the story* 'A Cargo of Innocence' by Laurence Kirk, *ph.* Charles Rosher. *ed.* George Boemler, *sp. eff.* Arnold Gillespie and Don Jahraus. With: LAUGHTON (Rear Admiral Stephen Thomas), Robert Taylor (Lieut. Gregg Masterson), Brian Donlevy (Lieut.-Commander Martin J. Roberts), Walter Brennan (Chief Yeoman Henry Johnson), Marilyn Maxwell (Audrey Carr), Henry O'Neill (Commander Stone, M.C.), Marta Linden (Mary Collins).

This Land is Mine

USA, 1943, 103 mins, RKO. *Prod.* Jean Renoir, Dudley Nichols, *dir. sc.* Dudley Nichols, Jean Renoir. *ph.* Frank Redman. *a.d. ed.* Frederick Knudtsen. *mus.* Lothar Perl. With: LAUGHTON (Albert Mory), George Sanders (Georges Lambert), Maureen O'Hara (Louise Martin), Kent Smith (Paul Martin), Walter Slezak (Major von Keller), Una O'Connor (Albert Mory's mother), Philip Merivale (Professor Sorel), Thurston Hall (Major Henry Manville), Georges Coulouris (the Prosecutor), Nancy Gates (Julie Grant).

The Canterville Ghost

USA, 1944, 95 mins, MGM. *Prod.* Arthur L. Field, *dir.* Jules Dessin, *sc.* Edwin Harvey Blum, based on 'The Canterville Ghost' by Oscar Wilde, *ph.* Robert Planck, *a.d.* Edward Carfagno, *ed.* Chester W. Schaeffer, *mus.* George Bassman. With: LAUGHTON (Sir Simon de Canterville – the Ghost), Margaret O'Brien (Lady Jessica de Canterville), Robert Young (Cuffy Williams), William Gargan (Sergeant Benson), Reginald Owen (Lord Canterville).

The Suspect

USA, 1945, 85 mins, Universal Productions. *Prod.* Islin Auster, *dir.* Robert Siodmak, *sc.* Bertram Millhauser *adapted by* Arthur T. Hormen *from a novel by* James Ronald, *ph.* Paul Ivano, *mus.* Frank Skinner. With: LAUGHTON (Philip), Ella Raines (Mary), Dean Harens (John), Stanley Ridges (Huxley), Henry Daniell (Mr Simmons), Rosalind Ivan (Cora).

Captain Kidd

USA, 1945, United Artists. *Prod.* Benedict Bogeaus, *dir.* Rowland V. Lee, *sc.* Norman Reilly Raine *from an original story by* Robert N. Lee. With: LAUGHTON (Captain William Kidd), Randolph Scott (Adam Mercy), Barbara Britton (Lady Anne Falconer), Reginald Owen (Cary Shadwell), John Carradine (Orance Povy).

Because of Him

USA, 1946, 88 mins, Universal Productions. *Prod.* Felix Jackson, *dir.* Richard Wallace, *from a story by* Edmund Beloin and Sig Herzig, *ph.* Hal Mohl, *ed.* Ted Kent, *mus.* Miklos Roza. With LAUGHTON (Sheridan), Deanna Durbin (Kim Walker), Franchot Tone (Paul Taylor), Helen Broderick (Nora), Stanley Ridges (Charlie Gilbert), Donald Meek (Martin).

The Big Clock

USA, 1947, 96 mins, Paramount. *Prod.* Richard Maibaum, *dir.* John Farrow, *sc.* Jonathan Latimer *based on a book by* Kenneth Fearing, *ph.* John Seitz, *a.d.* Hans Dreier, Roland Anderson, Albert Mozaki, *ed.* Edna Warren, *mus.* Victor Young. With: LAUGHTON (Earl Janoth), Ray Milland (George Stroud), Maureen O'Sullivan (Georgette Stroud), George Macready (Steve Hagan), Rita Johnson (Pauline York), Elsa Lanchester (Louise Patterson), Harold Vermilyea (Don Klausmeyer), Dan Tobin (Roy Cordette).

Arch of Triumph

USA, 1948, 114 mins, MGM. *Prod.* David Lewis, *dir.* Lewis Milestone, *sc.* Lewis Milestone and Harry Brown, *from the novel by* Erich Maria Remarque. With: LAUGHTON (Haake), Ingrid Bergman (Joan Madon), Charles Boyer (Dr Ravic), Louis Calhern (Morosow), Roman Bohnen (Dr Veber).

The Paradine Case

USA, 1948, 131 mins, Vanguard Films. *Prod.* David O. Selznick, *dir.* Alfred Hitchcock, *sc.* David O. Selznick, *based on the novel by* Robert Hichens, *ph.* Lee Garmes, *a.d.* Thomas Morahan, *ed.* Hal C. Kern, *mus.* Franz Waxman. With: LAUGHTON (Lord Horfield), Gregory Peck (Anthony Keane), Charles Coburn (Sir Simon Flaquer), Ann Todd (Gay Keane), Ethel Barrymore (Lady Horfield), Louis Jourdan (Andre Latour), Alida Valli (Mrs Paradine).

Girl from Manhattan
USA, 1948, United Artists. *Prod*. Benedict Bogeaus, *dir*. Alfred E. Green, *sc*. Howard Estabrook, *a.d*. Jerome Pycha Jr., *ed*. James E. Smith, *mus*. Heinz Roemheld. With: LAUGHTON (The Bishop), Dorothy Lamour (Carol Maynard), George Montgomery (Rev Tom Walker), Ernest Truex (Homer Purdy), Hugh Herbert (Aaron Goss), Constance Collier (Mrs Brooke), William Frawley (Mr Bernouti), Sara Allgood (Mrs Beeler), Frank Orth (Oscar Newsome), Howard Freeman (Sam Griffin), Raymond Largay (Wilbur J. Birch), George Chandler (Monty).

On Our Merry Way
(Also known as **A Miracle Can Happen**. A Charles Laughton sequence was filmed late in 1946 but deleted.)
USA, 1948, 107 mins, Miracle Productions. *Prod*. Benedict Bogeaus, Burgess Meredith, *dir*. King Vidor, Leslie Fenton, (uncredited) John Huston, George Stevens, *sc*. Laurence Stallings, Lou Breslow, John O'Hara *from a story by* Arch Oboler, *ph*. John Seitz, Ernest Laszlo, Joseph Biroc, *a.d*. Duncan Cramer, Ernst Fegte, *ed*. James Smith, *mus*. Heinz Roemheld. With: James Stewart (Slim), Paulette Goddard (Martha Pease), Burgess Meredith (Oliver Pease), Henry Fonda (Lank), Dorothy Lamour (Gloria Manners).

Man on the Eiffel Tower
USA, 1949, RKO. *Ph*. Stanley Cortez, *a.d*. Rene Renoux, *ed*. Louis H. Sackin, *mus*. Michel Michelot. With: LAUGHTON (Inspector Maigret), Franchot Tone (Johann Radek), Burgess Meredith (Joseph Huertin), Robert Hutton (Bill Kirby), Jean Wallace (Edna Wallace), Patricia Roc (Helen Kirby), Belita (Gisello).

The Bribe
USA, 1949, 98 mins, MGM. *Prod*. Pandro S. Berman, *dir*. Robert Z. Leonard, *sc*. Marguerite Roberts, *based on a short story by* Frederick Nebel, *ph*. Joseph Ruttenberg, *ed*. Gene Ruggiero, *mus*. Miklos Rozsa. With: LAUGHTON (J.J. Bealler), Robert Taylor (Rigby), Ava Gardner (Elizabeth Hintten), Vincent Price (Carwood), John Hodiak (Tug Hintten), Samuel S. Hinds (Dr Warren), John Hoyt (Gibbs), Tito Renaldo (Emilio Gomez), Martin Garralaga (Pablo Gomez).

The Blue Veil
USA, 1951, 113 mins, RKO. *Prod*. Raymond Hakim, *dir*. Curtis Bernhardt, *sc*. Norman Corwin, *from a story by* Francois Campaux, *ph*. Frank Planer, *ed*. George J. Amy, *mus*. C. Bakaleinikoff. With: LAUGHTON (Fred Begley), Jane Wyman (Louise Mason), Joan Blondell (Annie Rawlins), Richard Carlson (Gerald Kean), Don Taylor (Doctor Robert Palfrey), Cyril Cusack (Frank Hutchins), Henry Morgan (Charles Hall), Audrey Totter (Helen Williams), Everett Sloane (District Attorney), Natalie Wood (Stephanie Rawlins), Warner Anderson (Bill Ashworth), Alan Napier (Professor George Carter), Henry Morgan (Mr Hull), Vivian Vance (Alicia), Les Tremayne (Joplin), John Ridgely (Doctor), Dan O'Herlihy (Williams), Carleton G. Young (Henry Palfrey), Dan Seymour (Pelt).

The Strange Door
USA, 1951, Universal. *Prod*. Ted Richmond, *dir*. Richard Pevney, *s.c*. Jerry Sackheim, *based on a story by* Robert Louis Stevenson, *ph*. Irving Glassberg, *a.d*. Bernard Herzburn and Eric Obom, *ed*. Edward Curtiss, *mus. dir*. Joseph Gershenson. With: LAUGHTON, Boris Karloff, Sally Forest, Richard Stapley, Michael Pate, Paul Cavanagh, Alan Napier, William Cottrell.

O. Henry's Full House
'The Cop and the Anthem'
USA, 1952, 20th Century Fox. *Prod*. Andre Hakim, *dir*. Henry Koster, *sc*. Lamar Trotti, *based on five stories by* O. Henry, *ph*. Lloyd Ahern, *ed*. Nick De Maggio, *mus*. Alfred Newman. With: LAUGHTON (Soapy), David Wayne (Horace), Marilyn Monroe (streetwalker).

Abbot and Costello Meet Captain Kidd
USA, 1952, Warner Bros. *Prod*. Alex Gottlieb, *dir*. Charles Lamont, *sc*. Howard Dimsdale *and* John Grant, *ph*. Stanley Cortez, *a.d*. Daniel Hall, *ed*. Edward Mann, *mus*. Raoul Kraushaar. With: LAUGHTON (Captain Kidd), Budd Abbot (Rocky Stonebridge), Lou Costello (Oliver Johnson), Fran Warren (Lady Jane), Hillary Brooke (Captain Bonney), Bill Shirley (Bruce Martingale), Leif Erickson (Morgan).

Young Bess
USA, 1953, 112 mins, MGM. *Prod.* Sidney Franklin, *dir.* George Sidney, *sc.* Jan Lustig and Arthur Wimperis, *based on the novel by* Margaret Irwin. With: LAUGHTON (King Henry), Jean Simmons (Young Bess), Stewart Granger (Thomas Seymour), Deborah Kerr (Catherine), Kay Walsh (Mrs Ashley), Guy Rolfe (Ned Seymour), Kathleen Byron (Ann Seymour), Cecil Kellaway (Mr Parry), Rex Thompson (Edward), Robert Arthur (Barnaby), Leo G. Carroll (Mr Mums), Norma Varden (Lady Tyrwhitt), Alan Napier (Robert Tyrwhitt).

Salome
USA, 1953, 105 mins, Columbia Pictures. *Prod.* Buddy Adler, *dir.* William Dieterle, *sc.* Harry Kleiner, *based on an original screen story by* Kleiner and Jesse L. Lasky Jr., *ph.* Charles Lang, *a.d.* John Meehan, *ed.* Viola Lawrence, *mus.* George Dunning. With: LAUGHTON (King Herod), Stewart Granger (Claudius), Judith Anderson (Queen Herodius), Sir Cedric Hardwicke (Caesar Tiberius), Alan Badel (John the Baptist), Basil Sydney (Pontius Pilate), Maurice Schwartz (Ezra), Rex Reason (Marcellus Fabius), Arnold Moss (Micha), Robert Warwick (Courier).

Hobson's Choice
UK, 1954, 110 mins, British Lion. *Prod.* David Lean, *dir.* David Lean, *sc.* David Lean, Norman Spencer and Wynard Brown, *based on an original work by* Harold Brighouse, *ph.* Hack Hildyard, *a.d.* Wilfred Shingleton, *ed.* Peter Taylor. With LAUGHTON (Henry Horatio Hobson), John Mills (Willie Mossop), Brenda de Banzie (Maggie Hobson), Daphne Anderson (Alice Hobson), Prunella Scales (Vicky Hobson), Richard Wattis (Albert Prosser), Derek Blomfield (Freddy Bienstock), Helen Kay (Mrs Hepworth).

Night of the Hunter
USA, 1955, 91 mins, United Artists. *Prod.* Paul Gregory, *dir.* LAUGHTON, *sc.* James Agee, *from the novel by* Davis Grubb, *ph.* Stanley Cortez, *a.d.* Hilyard Brown, *ed.* Robert Golden, *mus.* Walter Schumann. With: Robert Mitchum (Preacher Harry Powell), Shelly Winters (Willa Harper), Lillian Gish (Rachel), Evelyn Varden (Icey), Peter Graves (Ben Harper), Billy Chapin (John), Sally Ann Brice (Pearl), James Gleason (Birdie), Don Beddoe (Walt), Gloria Castillo (Ruby).

Witness for the Prosecution
USA, 1957, 114 mins, United Artists. *Prod.* Arthur Hornblow, *dir.* Billy Wilder, *sc.* Billy Wilder and Harry Kurnitz, *based on the story and play by* Agatha Christie. With: LAUGHTON (Sir Wilfrid Robarts), Tyrone Power (Leonard Vole), Marlene Dietrich (Christine Vole), Elsa Lanchester (Miss Plimsoll), John Williams (Brogan-Moore), Henry Daniell (Mayhew), Ian Wolfe (Carter), Una O'Connor (Janet McKenzie), Torin Thatcher (Mr Myers), Francis Compton (Judge), Norma Varden (Mrs French), Philip Tonge (Inspector Hearne), Ruta Lee (Diana).

Under Ten Flags
USA, 1960, Paramount. *Prod.* Dino de Laurentiis, *dir.* Diulio Coletti, *sc.* Diulio Coletti, Ulrich Mohr. With: LAUGHTON (Admiral Russell), Van Heflin (Commander Reger), Mylene Demongeot (Zizi), John Ericson (Lieut. Kreuger), Liam Redmond (Cpt. Windsor), Cecil Parker (Col. Howard), Alex Nicol (Knocke), John Lee (Aide to Admiral Russell), Gregoire Aslan (Master of the Abdullah), Eleonora Rossi Drago (Sara), Gianmaria Uolonte (Braun), Peter Carsten (Mohr).

Spartacus
USA, 1960, 196 mins. Universal. *Prod.* Edward Lewis, *dir.* Stanley Kubrick, *sc.* Dalton Trumbo, *based on the novel by* Howard Fast, *ph.* Clifford Stine, *a.d.* Eric Orbom, *ed.* Robert Lawrence, *mus.* Alex North. With: LAUGHTON (Gracchus), Kirk Douglas (Spartacus), Laurence Olivier (Marcus Crassus), Tony Curtis (Antoninus), Jean Simmons (Varinia), Peter Ustinov (Batiatus), John Gavin (Julius Caesar), Nina Foch (Helena Glabrus), Herbert Lom (Tigranes), John Ireland (Crixus), John Dall (Glabrus), Charles McGraw (Marcellus), Joanna Barnes (Claudia Marius), Woody Strode (Draba), Harold J. Stone (David).

Advise and Consent
USA, 1962, 139 mins, Columbia Films. *Prod.* Otto Preminger, *dir.* Otto Preminger, *sc.* Wendell Mayes, *based on the novel by* Allen Drury, *ph.* Sam Leavitt, *mus.* Jerry Fielding.

With: LAUGHTON (Seabright Cooley), Henry Fonda (Robert Leffingwell), Don Murray (Brigham Anderson), Walter Pidgeon (Senator Bob Munson), Peter Lawford (Senator Lafe Smith), Gene Tierney (Dolly Harrison), Franchot Tone (The President), Lew Ayres (Vice President), Burgess Meredith (Herbert Gelman), Eddie Hodges (Johnny Leffingwell), Paul Ford (Senator Stanley Dante), George Gizzard (Senator Van Ackerman) Inga Swenson (Ellen Anderson), Paul McGrath (Hardiman Fletcher), Will Geer (Senate Minority Leader), Betty White (Bessie Adams).

The Discs
CHARLES LAUGHTON

78 rpm discs

Regal Zonophone MR 1234 – 'Voice of the Stars', 1934, featuring excerpt from soundtrack of 'The Private Life of Henry VIII'.

VS2 – 'Voice of the Stars – Jubilee Edition' – No. 2, 1935, featuring excerpt from 'The Barratts of Wimpole Street'.

VS3 – 'Voice of the Stars' – No. 3, 1936, featuring excerpt from 'Mutiny on the Bounty'.

VS4 – 'Voice of the Stars – Coronation Edition' – No. 4, 1937, featuring excerpt from 'I Claudius'.

Regal Zonophone MR 2722 – 'Voice of the Stars' – VS5, 1938, featuring excerpt from 'Vessel of Wrath'.

American Columbia S–271–M recorded in Los Angeles, 6 January 1937, Lincoln's Gettysburgh Address.

American Decca Album DA–379, 29M Personality Series. DA 29151/2, recorded in Hollywood in 1944. 'Mr Pickwick's Christmas' by Charles Dickens with original musical accompaniment composed and conducted by Hanns Eisler; subsequently transferred to LP: Decca DL–8010 (USA); 'Ace of Hearts' AH 127 (UK).

American Decca Sets DU–15/16/17/18 'Readings from the Bible'. Issued 1948; subsequently transferred to LP:/ Decca DL-8031; Brunswick LAT 8275.

Australian Decca Y 5917 – 'Oldest Christmas Story' and 'Story of the Three Wise Men' (Reading with Musical Background).

Record No. 45770A – 'The American Way Contests', c. 1950, Radio Commercial.

Long-playing Records

AEI 2121 – 'Greetings from Hollywood' – from radio broadcast c. 1950, 'Baby it's cold outside' with Elsa Lanchester and orchestral accompaniment.

Decca DL–5146. Decca DL–9071. 'Moby Dick'.

Decca DL–8010 (from 78rpm listed above). 'Mr Pickwick's Christmas'.

Decca DL-8031 (USA); Brunswick LAT 8275 (UK); Coral CP 34, 'Readings from the Bible', (from 78rpm listed above).

Columbia OSL–166, 2-disc set recorded 1952, 'Don Juan in Hell' by George Bernard Shaw, with Charles Boyer, Cedric Hardwicke and Agnes Moorehead.

Capitol TBO 1650 (mono)/STBO 1650 (stereo) (2-disc set), 'The Story-Teller: A session with Charles Laughton' – excerpts on Ember LP CEL 907 m/s.

Pelican 114 – Radio Broadcast of 1945, 'The Canterville Ghost' with Margaret O'Brien.

RCA LPM 1136s – 'Night of the Hunter', reading based on the 1955 film and book; with chorus and orchestra.

Star-Tone 203 – 'Calling All Stars' – Radio Shows.

4-Murray Hill 937239 – 'Hollywood's Heroes on the Air' – Radio Shows.

Vogue VA 160126, Hi-Fi Records 405, 1958, 'Songs for a Smoke-Filled Room', Elsa Lanchester, with Ray Henderson (piano) – remarks by Charles Laughton.

Vogue VA 160139, Hi-Fi Records 406, 'Songs for a Shuttered Parlor', Elsa Lanchester, with Ray Henderson (piano) – remarks by Charles Laughton.

ELSA LANCHESTER

78 rpm discs

Columbia 4125 – 'Please sell no more drink to my father' and 'He didn't oughter' ('Riverside Nights'), with Harold Scott, piano. Recorded in London on 26 August 1926.

Columbia DB 81 – 'Don't tell my mother I'm living in sin' and 'The Ladies Bar' with Harold Scott, piano. Recorded in London on 14 February 1930. (Two takes of each song had already been recorded 14 January 1930 but were rejected.)

LP records

CBS SBRG 72063s – Stravinsky's 'The Flood' (as Noah's wife) (conducted by the composer) (recorded 1962).

Decca DL 4833/Brunswick LAT 8678 – Features extract from 'The Bride of Frankenstein'.

Parlophone PMC 7141 – 'All Talking! All Singing! All Dancing' – 'Great Movie Stars of the '30s' – features 'Don't tell my mother I'm living in Sin' from 1930 Columbia 78 above.

Verve MG V-15015/HMV CLP 1417 – 'Cockney London' – Songs with Ray Henderson (piano).

Verve V-15024 – 'Elsa Lanchester – Herself' – An Intimate Musical Review (Censored by Charles Laughton).

Vogue VA 160126 (Hi Fi Records) – 'Songs for a Smoke-Filled Room' with Charles Laughton's introductions.

Vogue VA 160139 (Hi Fi Records) – 'Songs for a Shuttered Parlor' with Charles Laughton's introductions.

Select Bibliography

Arce, Hector. *The Secret Life of Tyrone Power*. New York: William Morrow, 1979.
Bentley, Eric. *The Brecht Memoir*. New York: PAJ Publications.
Dean, Basil. *Mind's Eye*. London: Hutchinson, 1973.
Eels, George. *Robert Mitchum: a biography*. London: Robson Books, 1984.
Guiles, F. Laurence. *Tyrone Power: the Last Idol*. Garden City, New York: Doubleday, 1979.
Halliwell, Leslie. *Halliwell's Filmgoer's Companion*. London: Paladin.
Hardwicke, Sir Cedric. *A Victorian in Orbit*. London: Methuen, 1961.
Kanin, Garson. *Hollywood*. London: Hart-Davis, 1967.
Korda, Michael. *Charmed Lives*. London: Allen Lane, 1980.
Koszarski, Richard. *Hollywood Directors 1914–1940*. London: Oxford University Press.
Kulik, Karol. *Alexander Korda: The Man Who Could Work Miracles*. London: W.H. Allen, 1975.
Leyda, Jay (ed.) *Film Makers Speak*. De Capo Paperback.
Mason, James. *Before I Forget*. London: Hamish Hamilton, 1981.
Massey, Raymond. *One Hundred Different Lives*. London: Robson Books, 1979.
Milland, Ray. *Wide-Eyed in Babylon*. New York: William Morrow, 1974.
Renoir, Jean. *My Life and My Films*. London: Collins, 1974.
Siodmak, Robert. *Zwischen Berlin und Hollywood*. Munchen: Herbig Verlag, 1980.
Taylor, John Russell. *The Life and Work of Alfred Hitchcock*. London: Faber, 1978.
Thomson, David. *A Biographical Dictionary of the Cinema*. London: Secker and Warburg.
Vinson, James (ed.) *International Dictionary of Films and Film makers*. Vols. 1–4. St James Press, Chicago.
Williams, Emlyn. *Emlyn*. London: Bodley Head, 1973.

Arden, Jane. *The Party*. London: Samuel French, 1960.
Bell, Lady. *Angela*. London: Benn.
Bennett, Arnold and Edward Knoblock. *Mr Prohack*. London: Chatto and Windus.
Berkeley, Reginald. *French Leave*. London: Samuel French, 1922.
Christie, Agatha. (*Adaptation*, Michael Morton). *Alibi*, London: Samuel French, 1929.
Dickens, Charles. (*Adaptation*, Cosmo Hamilton and Frank Reilly). *Mr Pickwick*. Unpublished.
Fagan, J.B. *The Greater Love*. Unpublished.
Forester, C.S. (*Adaptation*, Jeffrey Dell). *Payment Deferred*. London: Samuel French, 1934.
Owen, Harrison. *The Happy Husband*. Unpublished.
Merejkovsky, D. (*Adaptation*, Alford and Dale). *Paul I*. Unpublished.
Moore, George. *The Making of an Immortal*. London: Faber and Gwyer, 1927.
Morton, Michael. (*After* Jacques Duval). *Beauty*. Unpublished.
Walpole, Hugh. (*Adaptation*, Benn Levy). *A Man With Red Hair*. London: Macmillan.

Index

www.vintage-books.co.uk